ARAB POLITICAL THOUGHT

GEORGES CORM

Arab Political Thought

Past and Present

Translated by

PATRICIA PHILLIPS-BATOMA AND ATOMA T. BATOMA

THE AGA KHAN UNIVERSITY
(International) in the United Kingdom

Institute for the Study of Muslim Civilisations

Published in Association with the Aga Khan University
Institute for the Study of Muslim Civilisations
(AKU-ISMC)

HURST & COMPANY, LONDON

First published in French as Pensée et politique dans le monde arabe:
Contextes historiques et problématiques, XIXe-XXIe siècle
by Editions La Découverte in 2015

© Editions La Découverte, Paris, France, 2015

First published in the United Kingdom in 2020 by
C. Hurst & Co. (Publishers) Ltd.,
41 Great Russell Street, London, WC1B 3PL

© Georges Corm, 2020

Translation © Patricia Phillips-Batoma and Atoma T. Batoma, 2019

Printed in India

The right of Georges Corm to be
identified as the author of this publication is asserted
by him in accordance with the Copyright, Designs and
Patents Act, 1988.

Published in Association with the Aga Khan University Institute for the Study
of Muslim Civilisations (AKU-ISMC)

A Cataloguing-in-Publication data record for this book
is available from the British Library.

ISBN: 9781849048163

www.hurstpublishers.com

The opinions expressed in this volume are those of the authors
and do not necessarily reflect those of the Aga Khan University
Institute for the Study of Muslim Civilisations.

CONTENTS

CONTENTS

CONTENTS

CONTENTS

CONTENTS

CONTENTS

FOREWORD

Analysing the 'thought' of a national or cultural group comes down to exploring the ways in which the intellectuals within it conceive the world as well as how they understand their place and their role within it. It also involves analysing the influence of the ideas, behaviours, and thought of other nations and cultures on the thought of the group being studied. In addition, it is important to take into account the pressure that geopolitical factors exert on this thought in the interplay of the rivalries, hegemonies, and ambitions of other nations.

In the case of the Arab world, it has often occurred to me that the tête-à-tête between Arab and European thought over the past two centuries has caused them to become trapped by various problematic issues, some of which over time have become somewhat obsessive and unproductive. This is particularly the case concerning the constant comparisons made between the past glories of the Arabs and Europe's contemporary technical, scientific and philosophical achievements from the Renaissance onwards. This is also true of the comparisons between the so-called 'invariants' of a religious Middle East, considered to be the embodiment of an irreducible otherness, and thus a subject of exoticism or mysticism, and a West that appears to be exclusively technical, materialistic, and individualistic.

These comparisons were originally intended to restore confidence in the ability of the Arabs to renew their thought and culture. Instead, they have permeated a large part of the scope of Arab thought itself, as well as the way Arab societies are perceived, especially since the publication of the unsavoury 'Clash of Civilisations' theory some thirty years ago. This theory has been widely used as a point of entry into a completely misleading explanation of the major conflicts that have been tearing the Arab world apart for several decades. In the Arab world, as well as in certain parts of the Muslim world, this has given rise to various forms of a regressive inward turn in the search for identity. Since the 1980s, this has assumed the form of radical Islam, which has now become a completely uncontrollable source of violence.

Within this play of mirrors between 'underdeveloped' Arabs and Europeans emboldened by their colonial and postcolonial superiority, contemporary Arab thought has tried to restore to Arab societies a dignity that was lost. This loss was the result of numerous outside interventions in their affairs that have endured up to the present day, often military and of the most brutal nature. This was also the result of the Arab elite's inability to ensure unity, cohesion, and economic and social development within the different societies they governed.

This book was written during the painful time, which has yet to end, of the disenchantment with the outcome of the great revolutionary waves that spread to almost all Arab societies in early 2011, beginning with the spark that was lit in Tunisia. This is why I have attempted here to show the richness of contemporary Arab thought as well as its cultural landscape. It was also important to draw attention to the constraints that have stemmed from the different political, economic, social, and geopolitical contexts with which Arab thought has had to grapple.

One of the motivations that drove me to undertake this journey into the different ways in which Arab intellectuals think about the destiny of their societies was the importance of highlighting how little credibility and objectivity there is within the different narratives on Arab thought and the Arab mind. These narratives have circulated for the past few decades and have now become 'canonical.' From an anthropological perspective, these narratives have essentially led us to believe that there exists only one rigid, theologico-political structure of thought constituting an invariant Arab 'mind.' However, this approach has and continues to give rise to substantial controversies between Arab intellectuals which I have tried to account for in this book. Some of these intellectuals have even paid with their lives for their opposition to a distorted religious fundamentalism that is impoverishing Arab societies.

When I refer to canonical narratives, I mean books or articles that subscribe to the same line of reasoning, one that simplifies reality, and in so doing, removes from its field of vision everything that does not square with its desired objectives; namely, in the case of Arab thought, its reduction to a thought that is exclusively religious and, by its very substance, resistant to the secular, globalised modernity of the world in which we live. Over the past few decades, this is how the rich thought that I describe in this book has generally been marginalised in academic works and in the media. At the core of this narrative is the Orientalist and exotic romanticism that emerged in the wake of the disenchantment with Third Worldism and with socialist aspirations to build new societies. This disenchantment led many 'progressive' thinkers in Europe and the United States as well as in the Arab world to convert to various forms of rigid neo-conservatism, thereby impoverishing the way of thinking about the world and its evolution.

It is within this framework that the 're-Islamisation' of Arab societies has been seen by some as a legitimate response to a European modernity which for the past two centuries has allegedly violated the Arab-Muslim personality. Once the coloniser was gone, the governing Arab elites that took over continued along the path of depersonalising their people. This was carried out by so-called nationalist and secular dictatorships, considered solely responsible for the current woes in the Arab world and for the violence that is tearing it apart.

Generally speaking, this is the substance of these narratives. They allege that the different forms of Islamism, whether moderate or violent, are much more legitimate in the eyes of the people than the benefits brought by European modernity. The latter is considered incapable of bringing happiness to Arab societies, even though it has long since become a global modernity whose universal qualities have been accepted, on a critical basis, by non-European peoples.

It is obviously not possible to accept such reductionism applied to the complex situations experienced by Arabs in the contemporary world. This reductionism is exclusively ideological and has been dictated by a turbulent geopolitical context, especially since the end of the Second World War. This context is the rivalry between the Soviet Union and the United States; and after the Soviet Union fell apart, that of the policies that aimed to ensure the absolute domination by NATO member states of the strategic geographical crossroads constituted by the Middle East and its exceptional resources of cheap oil and gas. Until now, the Arab world has been the most essential element within this crossroads; but it has also remained the weakest and the most bereft of military power.

This is why between 1947 and 1948, Europeans and Americans succeeded in creating the State of Israel within its centre using the most crude and traditional form of colonial immigration. From its inception, this state was placed above the rules of international law, and it has now become a memorial icon of the vicious genocidal torments inflicted in Europe by Europeans on their fellow citizens of Jewish faith. The Palestinians are the ones who continue to pay an exorbitant price for these actions as no Arab army has succeeded in defending them, and their rights have never been restored.

Some thirty years after the creation of the State of Israel, some Arab governments recruited and trained tens of thousands of young Arab men to fight in Afghanistan against the occupying Soviet troops. In so doing, they paved the way to the current disintegration within the Arab world. Indeed, by bestowing upon these new warriors the noble title of *mujahideen* (or 'jihadists'), a term more appropriately applied to the Algerian resistance fighters who battled to rid themselves of the French occupation, these governments abandoned the cause of their Arab neighbours, the Palestinians, to serve foreign interests, those of the United States and NATO. From that point forward, the unintentionally derisory term 'Islamic revival' would become the focal point of several narratives of ideological justification of the need to prioritise the re-Islamisation of Arab societies.

It was therefore natural for different variants of a canonical narrative to subsequently develop within scholarly research and the media. These served to legitimise the training and deployment of young Arab men to fight in Afghanistan in the name of Islamic solidarity. Meanwhile, the Palestinians were under the yoke of colonisation by settlement in the very heart of the Arab world. According to this narrative, the end of the twentieth century saw the advent of the irrepressible need for Arabs to rediscover their one true identity, that of *Homo islamicus*, an identity which allegedly had not changed since the seventh century, the date when they received the prophecy of the Qur'an.

It is this narrative that would benefit from being deconstructed, something which I have sought to do since the early 1980s through the various books I have written on the Arab world and its turbulent and complex relationship with Europe and the United States. In this respect, I am increasingly struck by the parallels between this narrative and the one created to legitimise the creation of Israel in the face of both international and Arab opinion. Alongside the narrative of *Homo islamicus*, another narrative was established based on the existence of a *Homo hebraicus* with the millenary aspirations of a return to the land where monotheism was born. However, the elements of this canonical narrative that justified the need to create the State of Israel are on the verge of being undermined by the very courageous work of the 'new historians' in Israel. I refer specifically to the late Tanya Reinhart,[1] Ilan Pappé,[2] as well as Shlomo Sand who wrote three successive works deconstructing the myths that legitimise Israel's existence.[3]

The aim of this book is clearly not to present a detailed history of the ways in which these two parallel, canonical narratives have evolved; that is, one focused on Judaism and the seemingly miraculous 'return' of the existence of the Jewish state, and the other on the liberation of the Muslim man from all the slights and snubs he has been made to endure at the hands of modernity. This modernity is allegedly agnostic, materialistic, individualistic, and, therefore, oppressive to this human being whose very essence is collective and derives from his exclusive, eternal, and invariant religious belonging. In some of my earlier works, I have previously criticised the invention of the exclusive martyr narrative of the members of the Muslim Brotherhood at the hands of dictatorial and secular Arab political regimes.

I will continue here in the same vein. My main objective for writing this book is to provide the reader, whether Arab or non-Arab, with an overview of the richness of Arab thought. This is the best way to show the pointlessness of the approach to this thought that focuses on the supposed invariants of a religious nature. In an effort to be objective, I have sought to expose the various constraints and limits that have acted on this thought, as well as the changing geopolitical contexts which could hardly have failed to give shape to the successive modalities of thought in the Arab world, and therefore to how the past has been perceived and the future constructed.

Nonetheless, the reader will find historical and intellectual references here for the emergence of some of these stereotypical narratives, in other words, narratives about the Arab world both within academic discourse as well as in the media. Such narratives revolve around the Arab world's presumed inability to exist except as just one part of the wider Muslim world, a world whose unity it is supposed to be trying its best to restore by way of different politico-religious movements calling for the establishment of a caliphate that would bring together all of the Muslim societies now scattered across several continents. In addition, given the general tendency to politicise and instrumentalise religious identity, much more research needs to be done on the two ideological wars being misleadingly waged in the name of two monotheistic religions, Judaism and Islam, a problem I focused on in an earlier work.[4]

The major difficulty in the formulation of this journey into contemporary Arab thought was not so much the problem of prejudices or stereotypes of an anthropological nature, but rather, the avoidance of a double-edged sword. On the one hand there is the tendency to produce an exhaustive compendium of the works of great thinkers and their schools of thought and those with which they identified. On the other hand, there was the temptation to write a lightweight essay that was easy to read but which would not have done justice to the importance of Arab thought in the complex and shifting cultural and socio-political landscape to which it belongs. I therefore had to choose between a scholarly work of an academic nature that would end up limiting the number of readers, and a work simply intended to inform a broader audience about the numerous intellectual realities of Arab societies within their present-day socio-economic context.

I have therefore tried to stay in the middle of the road between these two options. This may lead to some criticism which, from the outset, I will not contest. Indeed, I am aware that there are several thinkers whose work I wish I could have taken into account, or where I did discuss it, to have further explored all of its different facets. I apologise for this to any Arab intellectuals who are still living but who are not mentioned here. Furthermore, I realise that I would have liked to present a more synthetic approach and a briefer development of certain ideas so as to remain closer to the style of an essay. In this case, however, I would have risked failing to achieve my primary ambition of showing the richness of Arab thought in all its detail. This is the only way to make this thought understood and appreciated. Although I myself belong to it, like many Arab intellectuals I am also steeped in European thought, but in a way that is both critical and detached.

In the future I may try to compare Arab thought to that of Russia, China, Vietnam, Japan, India or Latin America. In fact, in future I think it is imperative for Arab thought to engage more with the thought of other societies. In particular, it should engage with societies that are the heirs to great civilisations which have also experienced the humiliation of their own decline and submission to former European colonial powers, but which were nonetheless able to overcome this and are today moving towards being practically on an equal footing with the technical prowess of so-called Western societies. I therefore think that we cannot judge Arab thought without taking into account the concerns of the thought of other societies that were subjected to one form or another of European domination.

When all is said and done, it seems to me that it would be beneficial to both European-American and Arab thought if we were to work towards shattering the distorting mirrors through which each one views itself and the other. This mutual gaze is actually somewhat perverse and only reinforces the canonical narratives based on countless stereotypes and intellectual simplifications which have contributed so much to the emergence of vicious and warlike ideologies.

INTRODUCTION

Does Arab thought exist?

Since the end of the twentieth century, the Arab world has increasingly been torn apart by terrorist violence. Its economic, social, technical, and scientific development lags far behind relative to its available wealth and in comparison to the progress made in other regions of the world that were also formerly colonised. It is therefore reasonable to ask what role Arab thought might have played in this state of affairs. Is it merely unproductive or does it encourage violence? Has it become completely fossilised within a theologico-political doctrine that leads to or even justifies terrorist violence? A violence which preserves an otherness that is incompatible with modernity and the values it has created, values that are increasingly becoming universals. What then are the frameworks of this thought? That is to say, what are its cultural underpinnings? What are the political and socio-economic contexts that have characterised its long history, starting with the Arab tribes of antiquity as well as those of the numerous Arabised populations in the Mesopotamian Basin and its extensions into the Mediterranean region, Asia, and Africa? Does Islam continue to permeate and obscure all areas and forms of Arab thought 1,300 years after the appearance of the Qur'anic prophecies? These are the major questions that I intend to tackle in this book.

A barely visible cultural richness and complexity

Contrary to the predominant image portrayed in the media and by some academic research since the 1980s, including from several Arab universities, I

1

will try to show here that far from being fossilised within religious conservatism, Arab thought is complex, varied, and vibrant. Indeed, it has vigorously responded over and over again to numerous historical challenges. These are not limited to the challenges posed by the domination of European modernity, but also those that stem from the multifaceted burden of a complex past. In this book I will outline the different frameworks for reading and interpreting this past, which belongs to a very rich cultural context, as I will show in Chapter 1.

With a few exceptions, this cultural richness and complexity are barely visible. In fact, since the 1970s, scholars and specialists of the Arab world, whether Arab, European, or American, have largely abandoned this field of inquiry to focus their attention on what is customarily called 'political Islam'. Over the past few decades, we have witnessed a new 'fascination with Islam', particularly the 'radical' or 'jihadist' version. Maxime Rodinson (1915–2004), the well-known and learned French Orientalist scholar, gave this very pointed title to a work he published in 1980 in which he brought together several studies of the 'Western gaze on the Muslim world'. [1] This fascination has pervaded Arab and non-Arab academia and media, to the detriment of all other forms of analysis of the lived reality of these societies.

As a consequence, Arab thought has the appearance of something purely theologico-political. Moreover, it is seen as a major exception in the world due to its defiance of the criteria of economic, social, and scientific modernity that have nonetheless reached every other region of the planet. At the dawn of the twenty-first century, Arabs and the Muslim world are thus viewed as a major problem for humanity. Their societies are being torn apart by unprecedented violence affecting several major countries such as Iraq, Syria, Libya, and Yemen. In addition, long so-called civil wars took their toll on Lebanon (1975–1990) and Algeria (1992–2000) at the end of the twentieth century. In 2013, Sudan saw the secession of the non-Arab southern part of that country, and who can forget the case of Somalia, located at the periphery of the Arab world but still a member of the Arab League? Furthermore, many Arab youths have been involved in terrorist attacks outside their region of origin. All of this makes it easy to think that the violence in these societies can be explained by their thought and culture, in particular the Islamic religion, which is the faith of a large majority of Arabs.

This book was written in an attempt to tackle this truncated and simplified image. Its aim is thus to respond to legitimate questions that people may have about the relationship between Arab political thought and the failures of these societies to adapt positively to the realities of economic globalisation and to the era of scientific and technical discovery. By situating Arab thought within the complicated political contexts experienced by these societies over the past two centuries, we will better understand the stakes of the great intellectual, philosophico-political, and religious battles that have characterised it. These battles are far from over, but their actors and the very rich works they have often produced are increasingly ignored, despite the fact that they are actually part of the remarkable vitality of Arab culture in all of its artistic, literary, political, and philosophical expressions.

Contrary to what we might believe, critical thinking – including within the religious domain – really does continue to be very active. It is thus remarkable to observe that the authoritarianism of Arab political regimes – in some cases, totalitarianism – as well as the heavy atmosphere of religious conservatism which has set in everywhere over the past few decades, has not quelled the vitality of Arab culture in its various literary and artistic expressions. As we shall see, Arab critical thought flourished in the mid-nineteenth century and still continues to do so today despite the local and international barriers it faces.

It is important to highlight that the origin of the authoritarianism of Arab political regimes, and the historical and geopolitical contexts that fostered and hardened them, have very rarely been the subject of extensive reflection and in-depth analysis within political science or sociology.[2] Likewise, it is interesting to observe just how much Arab nationalist ideology has been attacked in spite of the cultural interpenetration, or in many cases the blending, of Arab societies. Indeed, the products of Arab culture in literature, music, poetry, and political and sociological analysis are well known throughout different Arab societies. This can be seen in their shared artistic sensibilities, and explains why the great poets, singers, and musicians, along with the great novelists from various Arab countries, are read, listened to, honoured, and admired in all Arab societies. However, in spite of this phenomenon, every Arab society subjected to political or socio-economic analysis is usually only presented within the narrow framework of the fragmented countries that emerged as a result of decolonisation. These societies are most often studied by Arab or Western scholars in a manner that isolates them from their broader contexts, both Arab and Middle Eastern, as well as their global context. Moreover, political and sociological studies have made very little use of the wealth of Arab literature, particularly the novel, which provides a very vivid description of the trauma produced by the rapid social changes that are continuously underway in Arab societies.

This book is conceived as a journey through the numerous facets of Arab thought, in particular its political, philosophical, anthropological, and religious aspects. It seeks to demonstrate that, contrary to what is generally perceived, critical thought has not been subdued despite the authoritarianism of Arab political regimes as well as the religious conservatism that has raged for the last few decades. From the nineteenth century to the present day this thought has remained very vibrant. However, it is hardly ever studied and gets even less coverage in the press. Nor has it become a subject of academic research, just as the vitality and unity of Arab culture are more often than not overlooked.

This complex issue can be unpacked by highlighting the fluctuations in the recent evolution of world-views in which the 'return to religion' has figured prominently since the 1970s. Along with this we have seen the collapse of the nineteenth-century style national imaginaries that were responsible for two world wars (1914–1918 and 1939–1945) and the collapse of the various forms of socialism. The latter suffered long-term damage due to the break-up of the Soviet Union, the rise of economic globalisation driven by neoliberal market fundamentalism, and various conservative ideologies fuelled by a 'return' to religion.

The return to religion took on specific characteristics in the Arab world. In the 1980s, some political regimes in the Arabian Peninsula, led by Saudi Arabia, armed and trained young Arab men to fight in Afghanistan in the name of Islam against the 'atheist' Soviet troops who had occupied it. At a time when Israel was not only continuing its occupation of Arab territories gained during the 1967 war, but had also occupied a large strip of Lebanese territory in the spring of 1978, sending young Arab fighters to a non-Arab country such as Afghanistan should have appeared completely incoherent. The Cold War between the Soviet Union and the United States reached its peak during this period, and many Arab states that got caught up in this conflict subsequently encouraged their young men to sign up and fight in this far-flung region. Afghanistan is not part of the Arab cultural sphere, and for several centuries it hardly maintained any business, human, or cultural relationships with the Arab world. The event was nonetheless celebrated in the West as the arrival of the Islamic *mujahideen,* who became known as freedom fighters. In the Arab world, this contributed to a lack of interest in the real problems of its component societies and set off a serious downward spiral in politics and culture. This ushered in the development of armed radical Islamist groups who carried out terrorist acts even within Arab, and other non-Arab Muslim, countries.

During this same period in Iran, a large country neighbouring the Arab world, the 1979 popular revolution was hijacked by religious leaders who set up a new 'Islamic regime'. As we shall see, this also had considerable influence on the destiny of the Arab Levant.

A new 'fascination with Islam'

Starting with these events, a new 'fascination with Islam' dominated the media as well as academic and intellectual circles whenever Muslims were the topic of discussion, especially Arab Muslims. This fascination took hold not only in the West, but it also took over a part of Arab thought, which subsequently became fascinated with its own religion after a century and a half of evolution towards building secular societies. As this part of Arab thought was aligned with the new geopolitical context created by the first Afghan War (1980–1989), it was marked by a huge mobilisation of the Islamic religion. This was encouraged by the United States and its Western allies during the last phase of the Cold War as, during this period, the idea of the demise of the Soviet Union was enough to justify any means necessary.

This aspect of Arab thought therefore enjoyed extensive media coverage as well as academic interest exclusively focused on all of the fundamentalist expressions of Islam. Due to this, the remarkable renaissance of Arab culture and thought, which started in Egypt at the beginning of the nineteenth century during the reign of Mohammed Ali (1805–1849), was quickly erased from memory from the last quarter of the twentieth century onwards. We then saw a spate of studies and analyses of political Islam and its different radical or moderate tendencies. One of the modern 'heroes' of this type of Islamic ideology, Osama bin Laden, was an Arab from a wealthy family of Saudi entrepreneurs. The fact that, against a background of US military involvement, he took over the Arab fighters (*mujahideen*) of the first Afghan War, only added to this new fascination with Islam.

During the second Afghan War, launched in 2001 by the United States in retaliation for the dramatic attacks of September 11, 2001 on New York and Washington, D.C., this fascination was made very apparent by the images of Osama bin Laden that were broadcast on a loop - starting with 9/11 and often played over and over again on every television screen around the world. These were repeat broadcasts of the videotapes that had been sent exclusively to Al-Jazeera television, a media outlet created by the oil-rich Emirate of Qatar in November 1996. These videos showed a figure with a long white beard dressed in biblical garb comprised of a simple robe and sandals, walking in the semi-arid landscape of the Afghan mountains. He thus appeared like a new Moses surrounded by a small group of admirers, leaning on a walking stick, and often carrying a Kalashnikov rifle on his shoulder or in his hand.

As will be shown throughout this book, this development took place within the framework of a 're-Islamisation' of Arab societies, one that was desired by various and contradictory strains of thought, both identitarian and geo-strategic. The ideology of Arab nationalism, with its secular and socialist tendencies, was vigorously countered by these currents. This ideology had dominated the Arab intellectual scene from the end of the nineteenth century to the end of the twentieth century and was the main focus of the academic analyses of European Orientalism. Thus, what would come to be called the anti-national Arab ideology being developed by these new Arab Islamist thinkers spread very quickly and was echoed in an extraordinary and often disproportionate way in the media and academic research. This contributed even more to the difficulty of discerning the continuation within Arab societies of a home-grown, vigorous, rationalist, and critical thought, including thought within the religious domain.

During the mid-twentieth century, the Arab renaissance was the subject of some academic research. However, subsequently it seems to have disappeared from memory in the Arab world and to have vanished from the new Orientalist framework in academia and the newly founded discipline of Islamic Studies in Europe and the United States. This was especially true of the Islamic religious revival that took place in the Arab world between 1820 and 1950, known as the Islamic Enlightenment. This movement was driven by a number of great Arab thinkers, especially the remarkable figures educated at Egypt's great Al-Azhar university. These intellectuals all came from different social strata, both rural and urban, as well as the wealthy and the very poor. The revival became part of a wider movement in Arab thought at a time when it was facing several challenges and was eager to understand the modern world in all its complexity. This was in order to rebuild an Arab society which had stagnated for several centuries in the shadow of the decline of the Ottoman Empire.

This book provides an overview of the foundations and the context of this remarkable renaissance period. In today's analyses of the contemporary Arab world, this renaissance either goes unmentioned, or is described in a negative light and dismissed as being merely the superficial modernisation of Arab societies in imitation of European societies, and for this reason alienating.

Since the Europeans colonised the Arab world and were the successors to the Ottoman Empire with respect to Arab destiny, the religious reform inspired by European ideas is considered in this context to have failed in the Arab world because it was rejected by the devout religious believers of the underclass. Likewise, it is alleged that the reform movement remained the purview of a small group of elites who hardly represented the popular psyche. This identity-based reaction thus appeared to be normal, and Arabs' accession to modernity appeared to require that they undergo a process of re-Islamisation. It is this 'narrative' that will be challenged in this book, a narrative that is now canonical and prevalent in academic research and journalistic articles. This will be done by providing an overview of all of the trends in Arab thought, both those that are overtly political as well as those that are more broadly aligned with the great philosophical and anthropological debates concerning the structures of this thought.

A journey into contemporary Arab thought

Before this essay engages in describing and assessing the different trends of Arab thought, it is necessary to discuss the origins of the Arab culture from which it emerged. This is the focus of Chapter 1, in which the richness and diversity of the modes of cultural expression in Arab civilisation will be demonstrated, a diversity that has endured until today despite the heavy atmosphere of religious intimidation that has reigned in many Arab societies over the past few decades.

Chapter 2 focuses on the complex issue of religious and national identity that has torn Arab thought apart, particularly following the successive failures of governments aligned with nationalist thought. Indeed, understanding this issue is crucial to avoiding the tendency to confuse these two types of thought or to indiscriminately use one or the other term. This approach is indispensable for understanding the general thrust of contemporary Arab thought. Following this clarification, Chapter 3 reviews the epistemological difficulties with understanding contemporary Arab thought. Two other pitfalls that jeopardise the ability to understand this thought will be presented here, particularly the mirror play with European Orientalist traditions. Similarly, the restrictive impact of shifting geopolitical contexts on the issues that Arab thought has had to face will be demonstrated, from Napoleon Bonaparte's expedition to Egypt (1798) to the spread of European colonial domination of the Arab world starting with the occupation of Egypt by Great

Britain (1882). It was during this same period of time that France succeeded in dominating the Arab-Berber societies of North Africa. Finally, the institutional and material conditions of intellectual production in the contemporary Arab world will be briefly analysed.

The fourth chapter looks at the changing political and socio-economic contexts that have affected the Arab world since the early nineteenth century. These include the experimentations in modernising Egypt and Tunisia, the collapse of the Ottoman Empire, and the complete domination of the Arab provinces of this former empire by France and Britain. This was followed by decolonisation, the creation of the State of Israel, and the Cold War. These changes continue to this day and have been accelerated by the invasion and occupation of Iraq by the United States in 2003. This was followed by the wave of popular revolts starting in 2011, which led to new outside military interventions and civil wars (Libya and Syria as well as Bahrain and Yemen). Finally, during the summer of 2014, large portions of Syria and Iraq were invaded by the extremist terrorist movement which calls itself the Islamic State in Iraq and the Levant, and which violently persecuted Christian and Muslim religious minorities. This chapter also reviews the socio-economic and political upheavals brought about in inter-Arab relations by the increase in oil prices from 1973 onwards. These upheavals contributed to the decline in cultural influence of urban societies, particularly in the Arab Levant, in favour of Bedouin societies from the Arabian Peninsula. This major development is largely responsible for the dramatic rise of religious fundamentalism which has affected the entire Arab world to varying degrees.

On the basis of these analyses, Chapter 5 identifies the major sources of disagreement that concerned Arab thought and the political elites. These include the Balkanisation of Arab provinces, the Palestinian question, the Cold War and subsequent American dominance that led to the 2003 invasion of Iraq, as well as the 1979 Iranian Revolution. As these events unfolded, the lack of unity among Arab countries only worsened. This chapter attempts to explain this by seeing the inexperience of the elites as one of its major causes. This inexperience leads us to the problem of the abandonment of power by the Arab elite as early as the ninth century in favour of Turkish and Persian praetorian guards. This explains the catastrophic political management of most Arab countries and the lack of well-established traditions among the elites in power and the intellectuals in their entourage.

Based on this data, Chapter 6 identifies the factors that triggered the Arab renaissance in the mid-nineteenth century. At that time, intellectual inquiry focused on the problem of identity and its relationship to religion as well as the causes of the decline of Arab societies compared to an industrialised and dominant Europe. Following the collapse of the Ottoman Empire, a national Arab consciousness developed. Chapter 7 thus describes this flourishing renaissance, which extended over an entire century (1850–1950), and which was characterised by a burning desire for modernity. Individuals from the religious university of Al-Azhar in Cairo played a key role in this development, and in the early twentieth century an impressive feminist movement also emerged. The issue of the European development model stirred up a back-and-forth debate that turned adversarial in a way that resembled Russia, whose intelligentsia at the time was split between Slavophiles and Occidentalists. The controversies between Arab thinkers nonetheless remained very courteous, such as the one in the early 1900s between the great Egyptian religious reformer Muhammad 'Abduh (1849–1905) and Farah Antun (1874–1922), a Lebanese positivist essayist convinced of the benefits of secularism. Just as courteous were the exchanges between the great Arab intellectuals of the time, such as Jamal al-Din al-Afghani or Muhammad 'Abduh, and some of their famous European counterparts, including Ernest Renan and Gabriel Hanotaux, on the nature of Islam and its ability to adapt to the modern world.[3]

Chapter 8 explores the different forms of Arab nationalism that flourished in the context of the inter-war period and afterwards during the struggle for decolonisation of the Arab world from 1940 until 1980. The work of the main nationalist thinkers will be reviewed first. This was a generation that lived in a different political context from that of the previous generations responsible for the renaissance of language and culture. Secondly, the great political movements that claimed to adhere to nationalist thought will be addressed. Chapter 9 follows on from this by analysing the other forms of nationalism in Arab societies. These include those centred on the Syrian-Iraqi and Palestinian Levant. It also includes those founded on the idea of belonging to the new borders of countries that located their roots in ancient Phoenicia or in Pharaonic or Babylonian civilisation, Maghrebi nationalisms or those founded on community or ethnic sub-identities. The importance of the linguistic and cultural factors that unite all of these societies, despite their rivalries and the divisions that tear apart their various elites, will be integrated into the analysis of the national phenomenon. Finally, two key institutions, the guardians of memory and its cultural identity, are briefly described.

Chapter 10 analyses the effects of successive political failures on Arab political thought. This includes the failure to achieve Arab unity as well as the failure to liberate Palestine. The latter materialised in the dramatic military defeat of three Arab armies (Egypt, Syria, and Jordan) in the face of the Israeli army attack in June 1967. This failure revealed the persistence of a general economic and technological underdevelopment that assured the easy Israeli victory. This is what allowed Israel, the newcomer in the Middle East, to occupy, over a period of six days, all that remained of historical Palestine after Israel's creation in 1948, namely, the West Bank (of the Jordan River) as well as the mountainous Golan Heights of Syria and the vast Sinai Peninsula in Egypt.

This defeat led to the extraordinary appearance of Arab thought that was critical of its intellectual premises. It was also enriched and considerably advanced by a major contribution inspired by Marxism. It became more open to attempts to integrate universals that were beneficial to finding solutions to political oppression and underdevelopment. This new thought also led to serious scrutiny of particular certainties regarding identity, philosophy, and politics that emerged from the 'idealist' thought of the Arab renaissance. From that point onward, Arab political thought was split between two major opposing currents. On the one hand, revolutionary ideologies were becoming more and more radical. This was particularly the case regarding the armed Palestinian movements that sought to question the established order of the Arab world and which would have liberated the potential of the Arab nation and allowed for the liberation of Palestine and the end of imperialist domination of the region. On the other hand, there were Islamic movements that, conversely, saw the salvation of Arab societies in a regressive inward-focused religious identity and a pan-Islamic nationalism capable of creating a 'revival' (sahwa) and leading to a renaissance whose foundations would be completely different from those of the renaissance started in the nineteenth century. From then on, this renaissance was widely considered to be responsible for the successive Arab failures after independence because it had, apparently, fostered the 'Westernisation' of thought and institutions. In so doing, it was considered to have abandoned the glorious theologico-political heritage of the early days of Islam. Ostensibly, this led to the 'depersonalisation' of Arabs, to their 'alienation' from a secular and materialistic culture that was not theirs and which had subsequently weakened their societies. We have here the amplification of an often absurd canonical narrative that is far removed from the reality of the complex socio-economic and geopolitical shifts that Arab societies have experienced.

For this reason, Chapter 11 describes the rise of Arab antinationalist Islamic ideologies that masquerade as substitutes for Arab nationalist thought.

Many consider the latter to be responsible for the failure in relation to Israel, and more importantly, for the invasion of Arab-Islamic civilisation by cultural ideas and products from a West that is considered 'materialistic', secular, and individualistic; and, therefore, incompatible with the spirit of Islam. This virulent ideological thought is at once anti-nationalist and anti-Marxist. Nonetheless, Arab revolutionary ideologies persisted during this period in the armed Lebanese and Palestinian movements until the end of the 1980s. This sharp opposition reflects the heightened struggle for power within Arab societies and among the elites governing the different countries concerned. The new Islamic elites, whose star was just beginning to rise, often expressed radical religious ideas that derived from the same conservatism that had spurred the financial and media power of the oil-rich emirates and monarchies who themselves were just beginning to advance in the regional and international order.

Chapter 12 describes in detail the fierce battle of ideas between modernists attached to a secular concept of the world and religious conservatives who presented secularism as the main instrument for the depersonalisation of Arab Muslim identity. The backdrop to these controversies was the profound repercussions of the 1979 Iranian revolution, which came to be defined as a 'religious' revolution. Indeed, this revolution contributed to the 'Islamisation' of the anti-imperialist and pro-Palestinian ideology and lexicon. Moreover, it cobbled together a curious mix of republican principles of popular sovereignty and Islamic principles of operational control of modern constitutional institutions by religious authorities.

The Shiʻi aspect of the regime change in Iran gave rise to fear and even to anger in Arab circles. Ever since the end of the Nasserist era, a Saudi-driven, Sunni concept of religious revival had dominated. The invasion of Iran by Iraq in 1980, which was supported by Western countries and the allied Arab governments, particularly the oil-rich monarchies, culminated the process of igniting passions and creating confusion in Arab thought.

This chapter therefore describes the development in the Arab world of a conflict of identity between a specific Islamic authenticity declared to be incompatible with modernity and critical thought, including religious thought, open to a changing world and eager to diagnose the causes of Arab 'discontent'. Accordingly, it describes the threats, pressures, and attacks on the reformist thinkers aligned with their great ancestors, whose thought is described in Chapter 7. The rising violence against liberal intellectuals by Islamic movements will thus be discussed, violence that even led to assassinations, such as those of Mahmoud Taha in Sudan and Farag Foda in Egypt.

Chapter 13 looks at the attempts at ideological conciliation between an Islamic identity aligned with the glorious Arab-Islamic past, which has become fossilised and inflexible within political Islamic movements, and the modernist and liberal movements with secular and/or Arab nationalist tendencies. It reviews the different currents of 'accommodators' within political Islam, both those who are capable of accepting democratic processes and those who, on the contrary, think that modernist and secular thought requires radicalisation. In this chapter, the persistence of strong critical thought as a central part of religious reformist thought is therefore described. The thought of some of the great Arab intellectuals who produced major works that have too often been ignored within their own countries or within the Orientalist research community are also analysed. Finally, the last part of this chapter is devoted to the works of eminent clerics and Lebanese laypeople of faith aligned with Arab Christianity who have developed stimulating and productive thought, particularly on Islamic-Christian relationships and on the place of Islam within monotheism and the theology of salvation.

The last chapter offers an overview of Arab thought in the different disciplines of the humanities and social sciences (anthropology, philosophy, history, sociology, economics, etc.). This is done by discussing the works of notable authors who are often not well known in the West. Special attention is paid to economic thought, which seems to be the poor cousin of social sciences in the Arab world. Some of the great thinkers whose works have fallen into oblivion despite their important contributions are highlighted. Most noteworthy are their analyses of the failures of industrialisation and the appropriation of science and technology. These remain burning issues in Arab societies, where such failures have fanned the flames of terrorist violence.

The concluding chapter takes stock of a troubled thought, one which is tending towards becoming circular. It is haunted by the problem of identity and, ostensibly, assaulted by modernity and its universals, both positive and negative. This thought is largely, but not completely, under the heavy influence of European and American academia and media. It is similarly influenced by local media controlled by the oil-rich monarchies that are allies of the United States and European governments. I discuss here the conditions under which Arab thought could be renewed if it were to draw on its roots in the forgotten renaissance. In addition, I look at the numerous thinkers who aspire to philosophical independence as well as the emergence of a new thought capable of bringing an end to the sterile debates that have dominated the Arab intellectual stage for the past fifty years, thus making it possible to address real problems.

In preparation for this journey into contemporary Arab thought, it is important to introduce the reader to the nature and the richness of this culture, whether of pre-Islamic origin or deriving from Arab-Islamic civilisation, which undeniably figures among the great civilisations in the history of humanity.

CHAPTER 1

*The diversity and dynamism of Arab culture**

In a geopolitical and intellectual context in which religion is instrumentalised for political ends, as briefly described in the introduction, the richness of Arab culture is increasingly being ignored. The renewed fascination with Islam as well as the rise of religious fundamentalism over the past fifty years or so has contributed to dissolving Arab culture into a vague concept of Arab-Islamic civilisation. Although this is a prevalent approach today, it does not do justice to either the genius of the Arabic language and Arab cultures, or to the genius of the languages and cultures of the numerous societies that adopted Islam as their religion but which preserved their own languages and cultures. This includes Iranians and Turks, Muslims in the Indian subcontinent, and also those in Indonesia. There is a tendency to forget that Arabs and other linguistic groups who have lived in harmony among them (e.g. Amazighs in the Maghreb, Kurds in the Mashriq) represent only about 320 million of the total 1.6 billion Muslims in the world (in 2011). There is also a tendency to forget the presence of the tens of millions of Arab Christians in the Arab Mashriq, who in the modern period produced many thinkers who actively participated in the nineteenth-century cultural renaissance of Arab societies.

---

* This chapter is a reworked version of the text I wrote for the wonderful catalogue of the Institute of the Arab World's splendid new museum in Paris: *Album du musée*, Paris: Institut du monde arabe/Somogy, 2012.

15

The distinction between Islamic civilisation and Arab culture

Arabs have had their own distinct genius since antiquity. The conflation of Arab identity with Bedouin identity or the Semitic mind, as formulated for example by Ernest Renan, propagates simplistic stereotypes that border on racism. An even more common element of this stereotype is the blending of Arab identity into Islamic identity. Indeed, it is worth noting that if the centre and the north of the vast Arabian Peninsula consists entirely of desert, unlike the southern part that is known as 'Arabia Felix' (present-day Yemen and the Sultanate of Oman), this peninsula has produced great successive waves of migration into Mesopotamia and the Mediterranean beyond. Therefore, even the Arab Bedouin culture had numerous encounters with the great civilisations of the Middle East. Pagan Mecca in the seventh century was a major city of commerce and trade and was one of the most important centres of international trade on what would later become the Silk Road. At that time, the inhabitants of the Arabian Peninsula were Christians and Jews as well as polytheists. The Arabic language was thus enriched by Syriac-Aramean culture from Mesopotamia and the Mediterranean beyond; but also by Graeco-Roman culture, which coexisted with it in this region of the world.

It is this information that explains the surprising diversity of Arab culture, which cannot simply be reduced to Islamic religious thought, as we shall see throughout our journey into Arab thought. In this chapter I attempt to reconstitute the essence of Arab culture, which, far from being closed, was for a very long time open and curious about other civilisations.

At the height of Islamic civilisation, numerous non-Arab thinkers formed part of this culture, particularly Persian and Syriac thinkers who communicated in the Arabic language. Arabic had become a language of high civilisation under the influence of the Qur'anic Revelation, which occurred in an Arab environment and in the Arabic language. This Revelation was, justifiably, a source of pride within Arab and Arabised societies. By Arabised societies, I mean the societies of those populations that lived within the Mesopotamian Basin and their extensions as far as the western and eastern shores of the Mediterranean (Iraq, Syria, Palestine, Lebanon, Egypt, and the countries of North Africa).

The Qur'anic Revelation, the last of the three revelations of monotheism (after Judaism and Christianity), brought vitality, power, and glory to the Arabs. It also served as a basis for the spectacular development of a great multi-ethnic Islamic civilisation at the cutting edge of humanity's progress from the seventh to the fourteenth centuries. This civilisation spread throughout the entire Middle East, Central Asia, the Indian subcontinent, and into parts of Europe, such as the Iberian Peninsula and the southern part of the Italian Peninsula. The first conquests in the name of the new religion were carried out by Arabs, but also, in North Africa and Andalusia, by Islamicised Berbers. The first two great empires were founded by Arabs. These were the two rival dynasties that originated in Mecca, that of the Umayyads who reigned from 661 to 750 AD, then that of the Abbasids (750–905) who brought down the Umayyad empire. Starting in the tenth century, actual power would progressively begin to elude the Arabs, as we shall see in the next chapter, and shifted to the Iranians and the Turks. This is how the Arabs progressively disappeared from the political history of the Middle East after playing a pre-eminent role. In Chapter 3 this important development is examined, one which is not often taken into account in the analyses of the present-day troubles of Arab societies.

However, it would be a mistake to confuse Islamic civilisation with Arab culture. It is true that the Arabic language has been the vehicle for Islamic civilisation, just like Latin was for Christian civilisation in Europe. However, Persian was rejuvenated by borrowing from Arabic and by adopting the Arabic alphabet, becoming once again a language of civilisation. At the same time, the Turkish language went through a major expansion, with first the Seljuk conquests in Asia Minor (1034–1298), followed by the Ottoman conquests (1280–1582). Both the Persian and Turkish languages expanded into central Asia and the Indian subcontinent, where they gave rise to new languages, such as the Urdu language spoken in Pakistan today. Although Arabic progressively ceased to be the exclusive language of classical Islamic civilisation, Arab culture nonetheless continued to be active until the fourteenth century, during which time the rich works of Ibn Khaldun (1332–1406) marked its height. He produced a remarkable synthesis of sociology and historical philosophy drawn from his encyclopaedic knowledge. Following this, Arab culture lay dormant for a few centuries before its rebirth in the early nineteenth century.

This is why it is fitting to distinguish between the great works of classical Islamic civilisation, in which Arabs themselves and the Arabic language played a major but by no means exclusive role, and Arab culture, strictly speaking. The latter existed prior to Islam and during the era of Islamic civilisation, before lying dormant for about 400 years, from the fifteenth to the beginning of the nineteenth century, a time period that saw a dynamic renaissance of contemporary Arab thought, as will be shown in the following chapters. This renaissance was in keeping with the poetic origins of Arab culture, which will be described first. Contemporary Arab poets played a major role in the political mobilisation supporting the nationalist struggle for independence. But as this re-emerging culture found itself face to face with the challenges of the modern world, literature and music became major new modes of its expression, most particularly with the appearance and development of the Arab novel. However, philosophical and reformist thought, both religious and positivist, also held a very important place. Depending on the era, they were either in contest with or mutually supportive of one another.

The poetic and musical mode in Arab culture

Even today, pre-Islamic Arab poetry is revered due to the diversity of its subject matter as well as one of its most celebrated names, Imru' al-Qays (500–540), the great poet famous for his chivalry and love life. His poetry had a lasting influence on later schools, and certain scholars of Arab culture, such as Taha Husayn (1889–1973), have even asserted that some Arab poetry commonly perceived as pre-Islamic was actually written after the Qur'anic Revelation, but attributed to this earlier period in order to escape harsh puritanical religious censorship. The themes of Arab poetry have remained unchanged since the pre-Islamic period. Besides the celebration of the beauty of nature, especially the desert and other places where the poet lived, as well as animals and plants, this poetry has for the most part focused on love and the endless admiration for the beloved whose absence the poet mourns. Since this describes courtly and platonic love, it has led many to speculate that this body of Arab poetry might have inspired the European troubadours and their art of courtly love in the Middle Ages. Poetry also serves to give prominence to the qualities of courage, chivalry, patience, and generosity.

Subsequently, another great poet made his mark on Arab poetry, Abu Nuwas (757–815), whose libertine poetry celebrating love of wine, young boys and women, reflects the sophisticated urban environment of Baghdad in which he lived. His poetry has often been described as racy, sometimes as derisory, but it can take on a tragic dimension when addressing human solitude and the fragile nature of destiny. Poetry was also deployed in the form of a specific genre unique to Arab political society following the arrival of Islam, that is, the praise (*madih*) of an important political leader, his disparagement (*hija*), or his eulogy (*ritha*).

It is obviously not possible to discuss all of the great names of pre-modern Arab poetry here, either before or after the arrival of Islam. However, it is necessary to highlight the importance of poetry in Arab societies today. They continue to fervently honour their poets, both the ancient ones and those who are still living. Indeed, learning how to recite their most beautiful poems, or listening to poetry, is still part of daily life. Among contemporary poets, we can cite Ahmad Shawki (1868–1932), who was nicknamed the 'prince of poets' in his native Egypt. However, in 1914, he was exiled to Spain for his nationalist poetry by the British governor of Egypt, where he remained until 1920. Nizar Qabbani (1923–1998) was a Syrian poet whose work ridiculed Arab regimes, but who also extolled the pain of love. Mahmoud Darwish (1941–2008) was a Palestinian poet who sang of yearning for lost lands but who also called for overcoming this pain to build a common future with the colonising Jewish population of Palestine in a new shared humanity. Ali Ahmad Said (known as Adonis, born 1935), a Syrian poet who lived for many years in Beirut before going into exile in Paris, actively participated in revolutionising poetry in order to break free from its traditional rules. There was also the Lebanese poet, Bechara el-Khoury (1885–1968)[1], known as 'al-Akhtal al-Saghir' (little Akhtal), implying identification with the great poet, al-Akhtal al-Taghlibi (640–710), who lived in Damascus during the time of the Umayyad Empire. Another Lebanese poet, Khalil Mutran (1872–1949), lived in Egypt for large parts of his life and through his poetry participated in the flourishing of Arab nationalism. Equally important is the success of emigrant Arab poets (most of whom are Lebanese), particularly Khalil Gibran (1883–1931), the well-known poet who emigrated to the United States. His collection of prose poetry fables written in English and published under the title *The Prophet* (1923) continues to be one of the best-selling books in the United States.

Famous poems have typically inspired musicians to set their most beautiful verses to music. Along with poets, Arab composers and singers have been honoured all over the world. The great male and female singers, Umm Kulthum, Fairuz, Abdel Halim Hafez, Farid al-Atrash and Warda Al-Jazairia, as well as Mohammed Abdel Wahab and Marcel Khalife, who are both singers and composers, are all names that are more popular than those of any political or religious leaders. This is why song, just like poetry, has always been a major art form among today's Arabs as well as those of the past. It is used to sing about the beloved, but can also express the rejection of injustice, particularly through yearning for the Palestine or Andalusia of former times; likewise it can be used to foster religious devotion and Sufi religious practice. Poetry and song also serve to strengthen religious devotion or nurture Sufi mysticism, which acts as a counterpoint to religious rigourism. The latter most often rejects poetry, music, and the practice of art more generally. Nonetheless, it has never succeeded in imposing a harsh moral order for long periods of time because these rich cultural traditions are a well-established and integral part of Arab identity.

Finally, who could fail to mention the beauty of classical instrumental music, most particularly that of the hammered zither (*qanun*) or the lute (*'oud*)? Moreover, many composers have pursued orchestral music in which they blend Arab melodies with the beauty of European-style orchestral arrangement.

Rhetoric and prose

Anyone who appreciates poetry also appreciates rhetoric and prose. This is why Arab culture has a wealth of literary masterpieces. The beauty and flexibility of the language is based on triliteral roots, from which many ornate words or modern concepts can be derived, eliciting the development of rhetorical rules that provide cadences for strong and sumptuous sentences. These rules can also give rise to sentences that are all the more eloquent because they are short. This was the case of the famous writer al-Jahiz (776–867), particularly in *Avarice and the Avaricious*, and by Ibn al-Muqaffa' (720–757), who wrote *Kalila wa Dimna* (The Book of Kalila and Dimna). Along with *The Thousand and One Nights,* this is one of the best known works in the Arab world. It is a collection of stories whose characters are animals of different species that live together, stories which likely inspired those of the French writer Jean de La Fontaine. They appear to have originated in Indian literature from the first century AD. Ibn Al-Muqaffa' added to these tales a twist of sharp political criticism, for which he was eventually executed by the Caliph al-Mansour in Baghdad.

There is little doubt that the art of rhetoric owes much to the fourth Caliph, 'Ali, the cousin and son-in-law of the Prophet, whose sermons were collected under the title *Nahj al-balagha* (Peak of Eloquence). The strength of thought in this work goes hand in hand with the rhetorical beauty of the language. Indeed, it is the Qur'anic text that paved the way to the rhetorical expression of profound ethical ideas by often bestowing a poetic quality on the numerous descriptions of the cosmic order desired by God. The same can be said of the narratives of the Old Testament that are taken up by many of the suras in the Qur'an and interpreted in a symbolic and moral way rather than in a narrow and literal one.

Contrary to popular belief, although Arab thought is tied to form, this does not preclude the quality of its content, richness, or variety. The great thinkers of classical Islamic civilisation – Arabs, Persians, Turks, and sometimes Christians, Jews or Zoroastrians – were all men whose learning covered several fields of study such as medicine, astronomy, physics, mathematics (particularly algebra, a word that derives from *al-jabr*) and philosophy, which is the focus of the final section of this overview. Their learning was encyclopaedic and prefigured the developments of the European Renaissance and to an even greater extent the eighteenth century in France. What has been largely forgotten today (or in some cases deliberately eclipsed)[2] is just how much the Renaissance and the Enlightenment owe to the great intellectual curiosity that marked the classical period of Arab culture, which in the seventh century became a culture of empire.

First and foremost was the great translation movement of Greek and Syriac texts into Arabic, a language which underwent a huge expansion between the eighth and tenth centuries. Arab culture quickly assimilated this body of knowledge from the Mediterranean basin and from the broader Syro-Mesopotamian region. Subsequently, the close contact with other peoples and civilisations gave rise to a formidable expansion of knowledge, science, and technology that were features of classical Islamic civilisation. Although the Arab conquests were focused on the Mediterranean basin, Persia, and the Caucasus and Asia beyond, there was also intensive cultural contact with India and China. Arab travellers and merchants were curious about everything that pertained to other peoples and civilisations, and Arab culture (as well as culture written in Arabic by non-Arabs) subsequently borrowed extensively from them. The narratives of Arab travellers and geographers, particularly those of the Andalusian Ibn Jubayr (1145–1217), and the African Ibn Battuta (1304–1369), constitute valuable works for understanding the state of affairs of many civilisations at this time.

The Thousand and One Nights is a collection of Arab, Persian, and Indian folk tales, which has many translations into English and French. After *The Iliad* and *The Odyssey*, it can be considered as the ancestor of the great imaginative and romance literature of the Mediterranean world. This is the result of the open-mindedness and curiosity that Arab thought has shown in its interactions with the cultures of neighbouring as well as more distant civilisations. Baghdad and Cairo to the east of the Mediterranean, and Cordoba and Granada to the north were the main centres of an Arab culture that was open to the world, integrating external borrowings into its own cultural fabric. Philosophy was no exception to this.

Arab philosophy

It is fashionable today to deny or to minimise the contribution of Arabs to humanity's common body of knowledge, particularly in the area of philosophy. Many specialists of medieval thought and philosophy in Europe have, nonetheless, described in detail the influence of theological, mystical, and philosophical thought of Arab origin or written in the Arabic language, particularly by Persians, on the development of European thought. The famous Italian Orientalist, Goffredo Quadri, published an authoritative work on this topic in 1939.[3] He claimed that the rich speculative thought that began with the Qur'anic Revelation, and which he called 'Muslim' and not 'Arabic,' had a major influence on the development of reason in Europe.

For Quadri, as well as for other more contemporary scholars such as Alain de Libera, Arab thought did not confine itself to simply commenting on Greek philosophy, but rather, it made use of it to justify the necessity of reconciling faith and reason, and to inscribe the phenomenon of the Revelation within the process of the development of the human spirit.[4] Arab philosophy sought to think rationally about the existence of God, his manifestations, and his immanent justice in spite of the existence of evil, suffering, and injustice. It also tackled the questions of the oneness of God, his anteriority to nature and to the cosmos, his causality as well as predestination and free will. These are all themes that were taken up by Christian scholasticism and later by philosophy, starting with Descartes.

The history of the early centuries of Islam, just like the early centuries of Christianity, was marked by disagreements and polemics, and Arab thinkers at that time were familiar with the Christian disputes as well as with those between Jews and Christians. They sought to go beyond them, as the Qur'anic Revelation itself suggests in its ethical and moral interpretation of the history of the two monotheisms that preceded it, conceiving of itself as the endpoint or the finality; Muhammad is the 'Seal of the Prophets', or the one who finalises and closes the series of divine revelations beginning with Abraham.

In so doing, theologians and philosophers raised new and weighty questions that led to a flourishing of schools for interpreting the Qur'an itself. A book from the early twelfth century by the Persian philosopher and theologian al-Shahrastani (1086–1153), the *Kitab al-milal wa'l-nihal* (Book of Religious and Philosophical Sects), describes the different non-Muslim religions that existed in his time as well as the schools for interpreting the Islamic religion, which were far more numerous than today. It is possible to speculate that this diversity was the result of freedom of thought, and more generally the result of a freedom of opinion that existed at that time with respect to religion, before this great flexibility hardened under the influence of the Turkish sovereigns who came to dominate the Arab and Persian world. This also followed fierce controversies between the proponents of philosophy as a wider framework of belief, giving it a basis in reason, and supporters of the exclusion of reason, which they believed to be capable of endangering faith in God and his all-powerfulness.

The best known names among the proponents are al-Kindi (ninth century), an Arab of noble descent who, in all likelihood, lived in Baghdad and in Aleppo, and is credited with over 200 works in different sciences and disciplines; al-Farabi (872–950), originally from present-day Central Asia, who also lived in Baghdad, Damascus, and Aleppo, and whose best-known work is *al-Madina al-Fadila* (The Virtuous City); Ibn Sina (Avicenna, 980–1037), of Persian origin and also well-known for both his medical and philosophical writings, and who lived in Bukhara and Hamadan; Ibn Rushd (Averroes, 1126–1198), an Andalusian who was also a judge and a physician. Averroes engaged in one of the most interesting controversies of the time with Al-Ghazali (1058–1111), the most illustrious of the refuters of the utility of philosophy. The latter was of Persian origin and also an encyclopaedist. However, he harshly denounced the religious 'errors' of philosophers. In so doing he contributed to the beginning of the decline of Arab thought, in spite of the richness of his work and his inclination towards Sufi mysticism.

Sufism underwent considerable development, not only among Arabs and Persians, but also within the Islam of India and Central Asia. It is a practice of individual moral perfection that leads to greater closeness to God. This form of mysticism was introduced by the 'Letters of the Brethren of Purity' (*Ikhwan al-Safa*), a work that likely dates from the eleventh century and constitutes an encyclopaedia intended for those who aspire to mystical elevation.

Mention must also be made here of the work of jurists who founded the four major schools for the development and implementation of law (Maliki,

Hanafi, Shafi'i, Hanbali). This body of work is just as important as any other for measuring the richness of Arab thought and of thought expressed in the Arabic language. It contains a remarkable variety of opinions issued by the great jurisconsults, some of whom are extremely rigid and literal while others, in contrast, are liberal and reasonable and rely on the notions of public good and the weight of circumstances.

In the classical age, the flowering of rich and varied works contributed by either Arab or Muslim thought, or a combination of both, culminated in the exceptional work of Ibn Khaldun (1332–1406). Born in Tunis, he lived between North Africa, Andalusia, and Egypt, where he spent the last part of his life. Although this extraordinary genius had a turbulent political career, this did not prevent him from composing a monumental work, the famous *Muqaddima* (Introduction), his introduction to a general history of humanity and to the lessons that can be drawn from the study of history.[5] Ibn Khaldun was, therefore, the originator of the philosophy of history as well as sociology, economics (including its monetary aspects), political science, and anthropology. He was the first to develop a theory on the influence of climate on different types of civilisations, which was taken up a few centuries later by Montesquieu. In his *Muqaddima*, he was the first to describe precautions of an epistemological nature that historians of civilisations must take in order to be objective in their judgments. According to Ibn Khaldun, 'it is the nature of information to lend itself to falsehoods,' for which he proposed several reasons. One was the difficult task of remaining neutral and not taking sides, a necessary condition to 'distinguish truth from falsehood'. Additionally, the reliability of the 'transmitters' of historical narratives was not evaluated, and there was a 'lack of attention paid to the true meaning of facts', as well as a tendency to 'seek favours from high-ranking or important people'. But for Ibn Khaldun, the most important reason was the 'ignorance of the nature of the conditions that characterise civilisations'.[6]

This is an astonishing work, not just because of the breadth of its author's knowledge, which was exceptional for Ibn Khaldun's time (geographical, scientific, theological, economic, sociological), but also because of the depth of his reflections on the changes that the passage of time invariably produces in civilisations, peoples, and political regimes. Living in a time of rapid change (the decline of Andalusia, the end of the Crusades, and the Mongolian invasions), Ibn Khaldun endeavoured to theorise about the causes of the expansion and decline of societies. His work was thus a brilliant precursor to the philosophy of history and sociology several centuries before these questions made waves in European cultures. His work alone represents a vast overview of Arab knowledge in the fourteenth century as well as a synthesis of the moral and intellectual state of the world in his time.

The nineteenth-century renaissance of Arabic and Arab thought

Following its dormancy from the early fifteenth century onwards, Arab thought reawakened in the nineteenth century through contact with the rise of European civilisation, particularly with Imperial France, which together with the rest of Europe dominated the Mediterranean Basin. French and other European institutions and customs became subjects of intense study. The translation of the masterpieces of French literature allowed for numerous genres to be better understood. Philosophical and political essays, novels, short stories, and plays were subsequently transposed into Arab culture. This is how the spectacular renaissance of the Arabic language and Arab culture developed after these had remained stagnant during the long period of Ottoman domination, whose decline, however, began early on, around the time of the Battle of Lepanto in 1571.

Once again, Arab culture began to rebuild and enrich itself. The Arabic language was renewed and expanded through the introduction of new concepts imported from French civilisation as well as from within through the pioneering work of poets and scholars. This was the case of Ibrahim al-Yaziji (1847–1906), a Lebanese scholar and writer who was also the son of the poet Nassif al-Yaziji. He lived between Beirut and Cairo and became highly regarded for the large number of modern words and concepts that he helped introduce into Arabic. The work of Butrus al-Bustani (1819–1883) was also remarkable. He authored one of the first great Arab encyclopaedias as well as a dictionary. He played a pioneering role in the creation of 'national' schools, thus contributing to the formation of citizens. He also contributed to the spread of secular ideas by asserting the notion that religion should be rendered to God, but that the nation belonged to everyone. It was also over the course of the nineteenth century that the works of Enlightenment philosophers and liberal British thinkers began to infiltrate. Proof of this cultural renewal is provided by the work of an Egyptian Azhari shaykh, Rifa'a al-Tahtawi (1801–1873). Al-Tahtawi wrote an account of his travels to France when he was named the head of a study mission in 1826 by the pasha of Egypt, Muhammad 'Ali.

This is why it should come as no surprise to see a wave of essays on political, social, and moral philosophy, subjects for which Arab culture became known from the second half of the nineteenth century onwards. As we shall see, these essays were considerably influenced by European doctrines. Positivism, evolutionism, socialism, Marxism, constitutional liberalism, religious conservatism, modernist nationalism, and a regressive inward identitarian turn all fuelled the most diverse currents of thought expressed in an abundant production of essays. The same can be said of the press and the political and social news reviews that were created at that time, an issue that will be examined in more detail in Chapter 7.

In another realm, the abundant production of novels is another feature of contemporary Arab culture. The modern novel flourished in Arabic literature in the twentieth century.[7] Jurji Zaydan (1861–1914) was the author of several novels that narrate the epic Arab conquests, the role of women in these conquests, and the magnanimity of the great leaders of the time. These novels are beneficial to young people because they are written in a simple, yet beautiful, language. Even today, the Arab novel is still highly revered. One of the great contemporary Arab novelists, the Egyptian Naguib Mahfouz (1911–2006), received the Nobel Prize for Literature in 1988. Indeed, the novel is the best reflection of the turbulence and disarray of Arab societies. It provides us with a very detailed portrait of the interplay of social class, the concerns of lower class people living in cities (Naguib Mahfouz), the misery of life in rural areas ('Abd al-Rahman al-Sharqawi, 1920–1987), and disasters that result from rapid changes in lifestyle (Tayeb Salih, 1929–2009). More recently, several women novelists have very successfully described the problems of Arab women (Nawal el-Saadawi, Fatema Mernissi).

Although theatre has not had the same impact as the novel, it is nonetheless an important part of contemporary Arab culture. The popular theatre of social criticism, as seen in the plays and films of the great Syrian comedian Duraid Lahham, has nonetheless been very well received. In reality, theatre has been replaced by cinema, and more recently by television. The cinema is of an uneven quality, and in today's Arab world it is Egyptian cinema that is very popular. Productions vary from being simple entertainment, with a lot of singing and dancing, what we typically imagine cinema to be, to drawing on the great novels or social tragedies to showcase such themes as the generation gap, the status of women, and the fate of Palestinians.

Painting, like sculpture, is an art form that is in the process of being developed and consists of a skillful and beautiful blend of decorative elements from classical Arab culture with the modern canons of figurative art as well as different forms of abstraction.

In spite of a return to religious rigourism starting in the 1970s, not all freedom of thought and creativity in the form of different cultural expressions was stifled. The regressive inward turn of identity that has recently emerged within a rigourist Islam is also inscribed within the general trend of reaction against globalisation and to the standardisation of lifestyles. It is the spread of Wahhabi ideology that has primarily driven this regressive inward turn. This ideology underpins the official state religion of the Kingdom of Saudi Arabia and has become all-powerful within Arab circles. Despite this, the aspiration to freedom and human dignity was expressed during the series of Arab revolts in 2011, while at the same time, the great poetic, musical, and literary arts which are the foundation of Arab culture continue to be active and to express the realities and turbulence of Arab societies.

As we shall see, Arab thought was also influenced by the ideology established in Iran by Ayatollah Khomeini and his supporters in 1979 in order to foster the great popular revolution that broke out there against the monarchy of the Shah. Of course, Iran is not an Arab country, but given its direct proximity and the historical role played by the Persians in the development of classical Islamic civilisation, it inevitably also influenced Arab intellectual production.

Arab thought, however, has been equally influenced by the secular anti-colonialist and anti-imperialist revolutionary movements in the developing world, particularly those in Latin America. Che Guevara remains, to this day, a figure who has marked an entire generation of Arab anti-imperialist thinkers. Mehdi Ben Barka (1920–1965), who was cravenly assassinated in Paris in 1965, was one of the founders and leaders of the Moroccan national movement and the National Union of Popular Forces (UNFP). His story remains symbolic of an entire era during which Arab thought was inscribed in the emancipation movement of the developing world. Frantz Fanon's work *The Wretched of the Earth* (1961) also influenced an entire generation of critical Arab thinkers.

This is the reason why the Arab thought of the past few decades is fraught with major contradictions, particularly as European and American schools of thought continue to exert their influence through various channels that will be discussed in the next chapter. These contradictions have been exacerbated by the major military events affecting the Arab world, such as the great Arab-Israeli wars, the invasion of Iraq by the United States, and the terrorist violence that has shaken these societies for the past thirty years.

It is this turbulence and its impact on Arab thought that will be explored in the chapters that follow, and which are more specifically focused on general political thought. But before undertaking this journey, the next chapter will first identify the ways in which this thought is understood in all its variant forms and constraints, as well as its local, regional, and international environments. Following this, it is appropriate to look at the general geopolitical context which Arab thinkers face.

CHAPTER 2

The complex question of religious and national identity

It is difficult to grasp the turbulent dynamic of contemporary Arab thought. Much confusion surrounds this issue, the most obvious being the conflation of Arab thought with Islamic thought. I have already explained in the previous chapter why it is necessary to historically distinguish between these two perspectives, something which we would do well to maintain with respect to contemporary thought, especially political thought. From the latter we have seen just how much more diverse Arab culture is compared to Islamic culture. But Islamic culture is also very rich, as it was influenced by the prominence of different types of religious studies or the different branches of Islamic theology, which in their heyday were referred to by the pleasant expression 'the science of the word' (*'ilm al-kalam*). Today, the richness of Islamic theology from this golden age has been progressively reduced to doctrines of narrow conservatism, some of which have taken on extreme forms capable of leading to violence. These religious ideologies were influenced by other forms of thought that purport to be of a theological nature but which originate outside of the Arab world, particularly from Indian Muslims seeking to justify their secession from Hindu society. This is why it is necessary to clearly distinguish between Islamic religious thought and Arab political thought.

The need for distinction between Arab and Islamic thought

There are several factors which have led to this blurred distinction. First, within European Orientalism there is a long-standing tradition of confusing these two types of thought, or, at best, of absorbing Arab thought within the wider framework of Islamic thought.[1] Moreover, for scholarly Orientalists, Islamic thought is most often associated with 'classical' Islamic civilisation, that is, its golden age between the eighth and fourteenth centuries. The Arabic language was for centuries the vehicle of this long-gone civilisation. Latin played a similar role for medieval Christian civilisation in Europe, which has since also waned. Whereas Latin is no longer a vector of civilisation and thought today, the Arabic language is still alive and, as we have seen, it has been considerably modernised and revitalised. Therefore, to imagine that an active and vibrant Islamic civilisation still exists, spanning nations and ethnic groups and whose core is contemporary Arab thought, constitutes a major epistemological error in the understanding of this thought. Numerous Orientalists have made this error, as will be demonstrated.

This confusion materialised with the contemporary use of the expression, 'Arab-Islamic civilisation', which creates an artificial historical continuity between Arab culture and classical Islamic civilisation. Only the latter can be characterised as Arab-Islamic due to the major role Arab conquerors played at this time. They were armed with the new Qur'anic Prophecy at a time when intense intellectual activity was emerging and developing in all areas, both religious and non-religious. Along these lines, the famous Lebanese-British Orientalist, Albert Hourani (1915–1993), published a book in 1991 on the history of the Arabs, which actually reads more like a book on Islamic civilisation.[2] In this otherwise excellent and informative work, no information is provided on the history of the Arabs prior to the arrival of the Qur'anic Prophecy; this history only begins with the birth of the Prophet Muhammad. It is entirely conflated with the history of the formation of the new imperial Muslim society, followed by that of the Ottoman Empire. Only in the last two parts of the book, parts four and five, does he focus on the history of the Arabs under the domination of the European powers, followed by the era of independence.

The great Tunisian intellectual, Hichem Djaït, born in 1935, also helped to reinforce the 'Arab-Islamic' concept. In a book published in 1974, he sought to undertake an anthropological analysis of the Arab personality, which he defined as 'Arab-Islamic'.[3] He also published other works focused on Islamic issues, such as La Grande discorde (The Great Discord) (1989), in which the source of contemporary Arab conflict is identified as the disputes surrounding the succession to the Prophet.[4] Likewise, Mohammed Arkoun (1928–2010), an Islamic scholar of Algerian origin well known in French academic circles, published an overview of Arab thought in the popular series 'Que sais-je?' in 1975 which was almost entirely focused on classical Islamic thought. Only the last chapter of this book deals with the 'burst of modernity' within this thought.[5]

It is clearly a source of pride for Arabs that the founding prophet of Islam was an Arab and that this religion, destined to expand to many nations, was born in the heart of the Arabian Peninsula in the seventh century. This pride is still felt today, even among the great secular thinkers, or Syrian and Lebanese Christians who are connected to Arab identity and to the genius of the Arabic language. But this historical fact should not lead to confusion between Arab identity and an adherence to the Islamic religion, which over a long period of time spread to five of the world's continents and to people of diverse customs and ethnic origins.

This identification of ethno-national identity with religious identity constitutes one of the greatest intellectual confusions to plague Arab thought, and the roots of its turmoil can be located within this basic epistemological issue. The regressive inward turn of the last few decades toward religious identity, to the detriment of a richer and broader cultural identity, is a major barrier to the flourishing of Arab societies. This phenomenon has two main root causes: first, the instrumentalisation of religion by those in authority in order to restrain freedom of thought; second, it serves as a form of compensation within the collective psychology of Arab societies for all of the political, military, economic, and scientific failures they have experienced since independence.

Encumbered by a fascination with the past

We should therefore not be surprised by the extent to which fascination with the glorious Islamic past has influenced Arab thought. Many great writers, such as the Egyptians Taha Husayn and Abbas Mahmoud al-Akkad (1889–1964), or Abdullah al-Alayli (1914–1996) of Lebanon, felt the need to write stories inspired by the 'sacred history' of Islam or biographies of the main heroes of this history. They tried to draw out ethical principles or lessons on political morality, or to elevate the heroism of the founding fathers of this new monotheism. Amid the disarray caused by coming to terms with the historical decline of the societies to which they belonged, this return to the past was intended to play a role in encouraging the construction of the future.

However, this type of exercise carries with it a certain number of risks, for how can the future be constructed while looking back at the past? This is what many thinkers denounced, particularly the brilliant Jordanian historian Fahmy Gedaan, along with many others who were influenced by Marxist thought (see *infra*, Chapter 10). In his 1979 book on the concepts of progress and development by contemporary Arab Muslim thinkers, Fahmy Gedaan described the impasse of an Arab thought that sought to return to the past as a means of catching up to its delayed development in relation to modern industrial civilisation.[6] This major but relatively unknown work provides a very useful assessment of the different diagnoses of what caused the decline and the underdevelopment of Arab societies (see *infra*, Chapter 7).

Fascination with the past is pervasive in Arab thought. At a time when Europe was living in the scientifically and economically limited 'Middle Ages', the brilliant achievements of Arab-Muslim civilisation were so extensive that it seems reasonable to seek solutions to this decline by returning to the glories of the past. This was an irresistibly appealing trap into which many thinkers fell. Moreover, modern conservative religious thought became attached, often in a radical way, to the time period of the Prophet himself and of the first four 'rightly guided' Caliphs. This is the period of time preceding the more serious political and religious upheavals that tore apart the early Muslim community, creating passions that seem to be re-emerging today as a result of increased disorder and wars expressed through religious hatred.

As Hichem Djaït wrote in his 1989 book, *La Grande discorde* (The Great Discord), on the subject of these upheavals and the golden age, 'Islamic passion, spanning centuries, has attached itself to this exceptional period in order to draw meaning from it, establishing it as an extension of the prophetic meta-history, enshrouded in spirituality, and as a representation of the true government, that of the true and legitimate Caliphate.'[7] With respect to this Tunisian intellectual who was totally immersed in European modernity, his case seems to provide a good example of a fascination with a long lost past that is intentionally idealised. Even the conflicts and civil wars of this past, which mainly occurred in the context of merciless struggles for power during a time of conquest and accumulation of wealth for the Arab conquerors, are idealised. The following excerpt from the conclusion of his book on the 'great discord' within Islam when it was founded provides evidence of a bombastic aggrandisement that indiscriminately projects the past onto the present and the present onto the past:

Unlike other *fitan*,[8] which were numerous in the first century of Islam but short-lived, this one was the midwife of history. And yet, in its own historicity, it remains a fascinating time to study, one of the most passionate moments in the history of humanity, through its protagonists, its values, its discourses, and because it brought religion into the political universe of struggle. It is a special, weighty, and intense moment, similar to the great revolutions that have rocked humanity, because it was not the expression of pure and needy ambitions, but harboured principles, ideas, and demands. If the founding of Islam was the 'Revolution of the Orient', to quote Hegel, then the *fitna* was a revolution within the revolution; or rather, it enriched Islamic reality through a momentum that has been unequalled in the history of Islam.[9]

It was also Djaït's work on the 'Arab-Muslim' personality that contributed to essentialising this predominance of Islam within Arab psychology, while at the same time seeking to 'liberate society from the stranglehold of religion, or rather, from the institutional content of Islam associated with another age, in order to define a new style of secularism...'[10]

Attempts to create an irreducible Islamic otherness

The result of this modern fascination can be found in the now ubiquitous image of an apparent paralysis of Arab thought within the theological and political realm. It is true that since the 1980s numerous studies (in English, French, and Arabic) have focused on political Islam and its different movements, as if thought in the Arab world had become completely stuck within a theologico-political approach to the world, one that is obsessive and radical, refusing all modernity and any kind of individual liberty which could threaten the cohesion of the 'community of believers'. I have often qualified this approach, whose high visibility in the media and in academia tends to obscure the richness and diversity of Arab thought, as 'millenarian,' because it readily brings to mind the numerous movements in the European Christian world during the Middle Ages that required 'true' believers to return to the supposed purity of the origins of the religion taught by Jesus.

The expansion of this theologico-political Islamic doctrine led to a dangerous atmosphere of intimidation for Arab thought. It also aimed to create a radical otherness between Muslims and non-Muslims by devising the criteria of existence for their *Homo islamicus,* and even more so for an Islamic woman, in a detailed way that focused on physical appearance, clothing, and food.[11] This coincides historically with the development of the financial power of Saudi Arabia, starting with the explosion of oil prices in 1973. This power came about through extensive exports of the abundant energy resources with which this country is endowed. The inexhaustible flow of revenue this created was then used to support the international expansion of the kingdom's official theologico-political doctrine, Wahhabism.[12]

The radical otherness of Muslims advocated by this doctrine concerns the non-Muslim world as much as it does the Muslim world, which is dealing with the tension between those who adhere to this doctrine and those who reject it. However, as we shall see, Wahhabism was originally a movement for the reform and purification of Islam, like many others that have existed in Muslim societies. The alliance between its founder and the Saud family, along with their ambition to dominate the majority of the Arabian Peninsula, is what gave it an aspect of militant extremism, which is a breach of the core message of the Qur'an (see *infra*, Chapter 11). Today, the Wahhabi doctrine mainly aims to make Muslims of the twenty-first century live as the early Muslims supposedly did at the time of the Prophet, in absolute purity. It declares that sovereignty on earth belongs only to God. Therefore, the governing of societies must be completely subject to the law that God gave to Muhammad in accordance with the most rigid, and often the most arbitrary, interpretations of the message of the Qur'an and the practice of the Prophet and his first companions. This explains the duty to combat all 'impious' Muslims who do not follow this law to the letter as well as their governments that will not submit to it.

Hence since the early 1980s we have witnessed a flood of dreary and repetitive literature that seeks to explain the foundations of this doctrine by focusing on three leading Sunni theologians: Ibn Taymiyyah (1263–1328) of Turkey; Sayyid Abul A'la Maududi (1903–1979) of Pakistan; and Sayyid Qutb (1906–1966) of Egypt. Islamic movements have been pored over by academics and examined in all their variations and nuances with an exemplary monotony and repetitiveness. The most audacious examples within this domain are those who identify the famous 'Shaykhs' by their sermons, their radicalism, and even their participation in the formation of so-called 'Islamic' terrorism. A whole area of academic research is thus doing police work and participating in the creation of a new Orientalism that confines the Arab world, and with it the wider Muslim world, in a religious straitjacket. In retrospect, the famous argument made by Edward Said (1935–2003) – the great Palestinian intellectual who enjoyed a brilliant academic career in the United States – on the harmful effects of Orientalism has taken on a renewed relevance.[13] Arabs, just like the entire Muslim world, are today relegated to a primary and invariable anthropological personality similar to those depicted by Islamophobes of the past, with Ernest Renan in the lead. What is worse is that the development of violence in the Arab and Muslim world lends credibility to the 'Clash of Civilisations' theory and to the entrenched hostility between the Muslim Orient and the West, a West which has defined itself over the past few decades as 'Judaeo-Christian'.

Moreover, since the 1980s, many works have reflected a disenchantment with Arab nationalist thought and have sharply criticised it as being responsible for the phenomenon of Arab military dictatorships, a criticism that is part of the general disparagement of developing-world ideologies and the efforts of the Non-Aligned Movement. This is particularly the case with Olivier Carré's book, *Le Nationalisme arabe* (Arab Nationalism), published in 1993.[14] Since this is one of the few books in French on this topic, it is still required reading on this subject for all university students in France specialising in the study of the Arab world. As such, it strongly contributes to the creation of a very negative perception of Arab national thought, which has always sought real independence for Arabs within the international order. Operating within this text is an arbitrary distinction between 'good' and 'bad' Arab intellectuals according to the author's own very subjective criteria. These criteria have been heavily influenced by the alliance of the United States and Western Europe with the Kingdom of Saudi Arabia that emerged in the framework of the struggle to prevent the expansion of communism into the developing world. It is paradoxical that the author has always considered Saudi Arabia to be the regional power capable of moderating the excesses of secular nationalists, that is, as the power that would always accommodate the interests of the great Western powers.

Arab nationalist and unitary thought nonetheless continued to persist with the establishment of the Centre for Arab Unity Studies in Beirut at the end of the 1970s. Although the abundant intellectual outputs of this centre are of very uneven quality, it is nonetheless impressive on several levels (see *infra*, Chapter 9). All of this clearly illustrates the importance of describing the shifting political and geopolitical contexts in which contemporary Arab political culture is embedded, because these contexts are so harrowing and violent.

The need to contextualise the development of thought

The present work is therefore intended to provide a basic understanding of the development of Arab thought since it opened itself up to Europe during the industrial revolution. Specifically, its currents will be connected to the shifting historical and socio-political contexts in which they evolved – something most books on the Arab world fail to do. As we have seen throughout modern history, the starting point of which was the industrial and political, or double, revolution in Europe, the contexts of world history have changed at great speed. This has led to profound socio-economic changes as well as shifts in the very way we think about change itself. The history of thought in the Arab world is no exception to this. It is hardly petrified in an anthropological and cultural invariant. Rather, whether the approach is Islamophile or Islamophobic, in both cases we are faced with a phenomenon of 'fascination/repulsion' with Islam, which has been essentialised as the sole repository for individual and collective Arab identity.

The Islamophiles seek to explain that contemporary collective Arab psychology has been doubly violated, first by European colonialism, then by the 'westernised' Arab elites who were its successors. In their view, this is why radical Islamist movements are simply the expression of a visceral reaction on the part of Arab societies. Having been violated, they are in search of their roots and their heritage, which is alleged to be Islam.[15] The Islamophobes are heirs to the tradition of Ernest Renan. By seizing on terrorist acts committed in the name of Islam or by denouncing the submissive and marginalised role of Muslim women, they view the recent violent developments in the Arab world as the confirmation of an Islamic otherness that is dangerous for civilisation and for the progress of humanity.[16]

This caricature of Arab thought and the context in which it evolved is clearly disproven by the diversity and richness of the works that have been produced by Arab intellectuals since the middle of the nineteenth century. For centuries, Arab societies remained in the shadow of Ottoman power and were imbued with Ottoman worldviews and habits, so much so that they can rightly be qualified as Arab-Ottoman.[17] They faced a succession of surprisingly diverse situations that profoundly changed all socio-economic and political relationships within the Arab world as well as between the Arab world and its geopolitical context. All of these were major challenges for which Arab thought provided rich and diverse responses, albeit responses that were naturally constrained by the environment faced by the intellectual elites.

Firstly, the opening up to Europe during the Industrial Revolution began with Napoleon's short-lived expedition, followed by the gradual colonisation by Great Britain and France, and even Italy, which occupied Libya in 1911.

What came next was the total collapse of the Ottoman Empire, which for Arabs represented the end of the stable and uneventful world in which they lived. This collapse allowed for the consolidation of the military dominance of the two great colonial powers of Europe, France and Great Britain, which at the beginning of the twentieth century, in one way or another, became the occupying powers of the entire Arab world. This led to struggles for national liberation; and at the same time, the discovery of the Bolshevik Revolution and everything it contributed in the way of new political and economic theories as well as revolutionary and anti-imperialist culture.

The independence of the former provinces of the Ottoman Empire took place after the Second World War. This happened in a disorderly fashion in territories of extremely varied sizes. But more important was the extremely unequal distribution of wealth, as some countries had access to energy resources whereas others were completely deprived of them. After independence, the strong winds of the Cold War blew into this strategic region. Even today, the Arab world is still paying the price of the First and Second World Wars, as well as that of the Cold War. It was during this period that many young Arab men received military training and religious indoctrination under the watchful eye of the United States to go to Afghanistan to fight the occupying Soviet Army.

Ever since the collapse of the Soviet Union, Arab countries have lived in a unipolar world dominated by the United States. In the aftermath of the September 11 terrorist attacks, designated as 'Islamic,' the US found a new enemy to pursue in Arab and Muslim countries. Responsibility for the attack was claimed with some delay by the principal movement that participated in the first Afghan War, that of the Saudi Arabian Osama bin Laden. This was a central movement in Islamic terrorism and became one of several pretexts for the invasion of Iraq. Starting in 2011, it was also part of the Arab revolts in Libya and in Syria, but this time they were supported by Western powers, Turkey, and the oil-exporting kingdoms in the Arabian Peninsula. Some years earlier, its presence had also been observed in Bosnia and Chechnya, as well as in the Caucasus and other regions of the world with substantial Muslim communities.

In addition, Arab thought has been exposed to the interpretation of the creation and development of the exceptional power of the State of Israel, which even today continues to occupy all of Palestine in addition to other Arab territories. The regional and international repercussions of the Iranian religious revolution in 1979 and the rise to power of the Saudi-Wahhabi ideology of Islamic radicalism are two phenomena that have considerably influenced the currents of Arab thought. They have contributed to diverting them away from their orientations of the past, those of the period between 1850 and 1930, called the 'liberal age' by Albert Hourani, the British Orientalist historian of Lebanese origin.[18]

The sources of authoritarianism in the Arab world that have been ignored

Arab thought has thus had to evolve in the context of the fragile states that emerged from the dismemberment of the Ottoman Empire and fragile social and political elites who themselves were subjected to divisions, tensions, and fears. The authoritarianism of modern states in this region, which has sometimes bordered on totalitarianism, has several causes. It is important to briefly review these in order to understand the upheavals of Arab thought. The first is the issue of the problematic political legitimacy of the modern states that resulted from the carving up of the Ottoman Empire following its collapse. The second is the entrenchment of a rentier economy in most of these societies, which paralysed industrialisation and created continuous social exclusion and unemployment in spite of government efforts to combat this.

Regarding the question of legitimacy, in 1977 Michael Hudson, a very knowledgeable American expert on the Middle East, aptly described the consequences of the absence of consensus on the foundations of the modern state in Arab societies:

> Arab politics today are not just unstable, although instability remains a prominent feature, they are also unpredictable to participants and observers alike. Fed by rumor, misinformation, and lack of information, the Arab political process is cloaked in obscurity and Arab politicians are beset by insecurity and fear of the unknown. If their behavior appears at times quixotic or even paranoid, the irrationality lies less within themselves than in their situation. Whether in power or in the opposition, Arab politicians must operate in a political environment in which the legitimacy of rulers, regimes, and the institutions of the states themselves is sporadic and, at best, scarce. Under these conditions seemingly irrational behaviour, such as assassinations, coups d'état, and official repression, may in fact derive from rational calculations. The consequences of such behaviour, which stems from the low legitimacy accorded to political processes and institutions, contribute further to the prevailing popular cynicism about politics.[19]

According to Hudson, although Arab culture has its unique qualities, there is no reason to believe that this is what determines political behaviour. He thinks that explanations should be sought 'in terms of implementation of universal categories of analysis'[20] and that the lack of legitimacy of Arab regimes can only be understood if we account for regional interstate relations and not simply limit ourselves to analysing the problems of each state in isolation. Indeed, the origins of this lack can be identified in the profound economic and social transformations that affected all of the societies in this region.[21]

Hudson's brilliant analysis was completed and expanded upon eighteen years later by Nazih Ayubi, a prolific Egyptian intellectual. In 1995 he analysed the phenomenon of authoritarianism of Arab governments, which for him is merely the reflection of the congenital defect of these states or, in 'Hudsonian' terms, their lack of legitimacy. Like Hudson, Ayubi refutes the existence of a 'cultural essence' that explains the failings of Arab states.[22] Authoritarianism and dictatorial behaviour are simply the result of the weakness of the state, of the absence of a hegemonic group, in the Gramscian sense of the term, which grants legitimacy to a state and to its political behaviour. Sharply criticising the conventional Weberian analyses of political science, Ayubi justifiably thinks that there is no clear dichotomy between the state and civil society, but rather, it is often the state that encourages the development of civil society in order to reinforce consensus surrounding its identity and its functions. According to Ayubi, in the case of Arab societies, the modern 'developmental' capabilities of the state have been 'over-stated' in the absence of a homogeneous dominant group. This is what leads to the fragility of the state, which in turn facilitates dictatorial phenomena (or coups d'état) affecting so many Arab societies, as well as the inability to become 'deep' states able to regulate society and ensure its socio-economic development, like the social protection states of industrialised countries.[23]

The permanent state of crisis in Arab states was heightened in the mid-1970s when a rentier economy model resulting from the explosion of oil prices became widespread. On the one hand, this model strengthened states' capacities for repression, as well as the governing elites who controlled the expanding cash flow from the oil windfalls. On the other hand, it exacerbated the frustrations of the excluded masses, especially the younger generation hit hard by the extensive unemployment that resulted from the failure of industrialisation. In reality, the combined progress achieved in Arab societies in the areas of health and education led to a demographic explosion in the

1960s, whose effects were felt on the job market in the 1990s. It was during this time period that the failure of industrialisation and the widespread entrenchment of a rentier economy considerably reduced the opportunities for employment and increased flagrant inequality and social injustice. This phenomenon has hardly been studied, and more importantly, it is rarely taken into consideration as an explanation of the surprising development of so-called radical Islamic movements whose success has been fuelled by extensive youth unemployment that has even affected young people with university degrees.

I have previously described the harmful effects of a rentier economy and its connections to political Islam in my book, *Le Proche-Orient éclaté* (The Shattered Middle East).[24] Ahmed Henni, a keenly observant Algerian economist, has also clearly established the link between what he calls the 'Islamist syndrome' and the oil revenues that many Arab and Muslim states have at their disposal (Algeria, Saudi Arabia, Iran, Indonesia, and Nigeria).[25] Another Algerian economist, Abdelkader Sid-Ahmed, also drew attention to this question as early as 1975.[26] More recently, I have described the different sources of revenue in the Arab world and their socio-economic effects, for there is more to it than just oil revenue. Several types of revenue benefit Arab governments: revenue from the strategic geographical situation (revenues from the Suez Canal, but also from payment for use of oil and gas pipelines), foreign aid that is sometimes immense in order to ensure the loyalty of one political regime or another, the explosion of land revenue resulting from rapid demographic growth, revenue from tourism (low-cost sunny beaches, famous archaeological sites such as the pyramids), increased cash revenues provided by money transfers made by Arab migrants living in oil-producing Arab countries, Europe, or the United States, revenue from exports of raw materials, such as phosphates or cotton, and finally, revenue from those who hold licenses to sell designer brand products for everyday consumption (cars, imported capital goods), and even from the representation of multinational companies bidding within the large markets of these states.[27]

The rentier economy stifled industrialisation and led to an immense concentration of wealth within a few business groups close to the authorities, as well as creating unemployment among young people. It should come as no surprise given these conditions just how easy it is for Islamic movements to recruit the unemployed and the poor who are excluded from an unattainable modernity in the absence of industrialisation, which is the only way to provide enough decent and adequately paid jobs. This became even easier with the arrival of humanitarian Islamic NGOs who have traversed these countries and made their way into zones of exclusion, both urban and rural.[28]

In the analyses of Arab political life and Arab thought, a thought which has attempted to address all of the inconsistencies experienced by these societies, not a single one of the major issues has been adequately taken into account. This has largely contributed to the vapid and repetitive quality of much of what has been written over the last few decades, whether by Arabs or non-Arabs. In these works there is often an attempt to decode the 'Arab mind' using invariants of an anthropological nature, which has primarily contributed to the dissemination of the arguments of Islamic movements, as if these best represented collective Arab psychology. As a result, the rich Arab national thought that is critical and open to the universals of modernity has been completely marginalised. It has even been blamed for the disorder and authoritarian overreach of Arab regimes, thereby setting up so-called political Islam and its different movements as an almost exclusive area of research.

Socio-economic and political contextualisation of Arab thought is thus indispensable to understanding its upheavals, its failings, and even the fact that entire areas within this thought have fallen into oblivion. Geopolitical contexts and the intensity of external political and military interventions in the development of Arab societies constitute another element to be taken into account. However, before doing so, it will help to pause and examine some of the models for understanding Arab thought.

CHAPTER 3

Choosing an epistemological framework and a model for understanding Arab thought

Arab thought cannot be understood, evaluated, or judged in the abstract. We are always consciously or unconsciously guided by a particular analytical framework, often one based on Orientalist or Islamic studies. The latter tends to highlight the otherness of the 'Other's' thought, that which does not derive from the movement of European thought. In the case of Arab thought, it is tempting to confuse it with Islamic thought or to identify within it the uniqueness and constants of an Arab 'mind' that Islamic religion has hardened into invariance. This approach has been heavily influenced by the legacy of European anthropological and ethnological traditions.

In addition, as I have already pointed out, there exists practically no overview in French, or even in Arabic, of recent contemporary Arab thought due to the fact that works on Islam, and especially on political Islam, dominate the entire body of literature on this topic in France. This is not exactly the case in the United States, and to a lesser degree in the United Kingdom, where some Arab and non-Arab scholars continue to study contemporary Arab political and philosophical thought. Academic research in France on the Arab Orient has thus been considerably impoverished over the past few decades. The void created by the deaths of the great Orientalists, such as Louis Massignon (1883–1962), Régis Blachère (1900–1973), Jean Sauvaget (1901–1950), Jacques Berque (1910–1995), Vincent Monteil (1913–2005) and Maxime Rodinson (1915–2004) has been filled by an abundant and unpalatable production on political Islam, the Muslim Brotherhood, and the networks of radical Islamic activists. Not only is this literature distasteful, it is also superficial and repetitive. As we have just seen, it obscures all of the developments that have affected the Arab world, particularly the socio-economic upheavals. It also ignores the numerous connections between the geographical and political sources of Islamic 'radicalism', especially in Saudi Arabia and in Pakistan, and the main Western powers who count these countries among their faithful and respected allies.

In fact, whether it is Arab, European or American scholars who are to blame, academic research on Arab thought has been crippled by two major problems. The first is the legacy of the anthropological approach that seeks to determine the structures and constants of the 'Arab' or 'Muslim' mind in order to better bring to light the otherness of this 'mentality', or its way of seeing the world compared to the European mind. The second problem consists of the endless and often sterile debates on the authenticity of this thought, or on the impact that post-colonialism may have had on it, many of which focus on feminist movements or the progress of secularism, nationalism, and of course political Islam.

The otherness of the Arab mind: Orientalisms and counter-Orientalisms

Various European, Arab, Islamic and Israeli currents of thought have feverishly attempted to identify that which is unique to the way Arabs think. These attempts have several origins and causes. The first, historically speaking, is the racist European anthropology of the nineteenth century. Influenced by the development within linguistics of a division of languages into two categories, Aryan and Semitic, a colonial form of anthropology emerged whose aim was to demonstrate the inferiority of the Semitic mind as embodied by Islam and Judaism. In *Le Proche-Orient éclaté* (The Shattered Middle East), I discussed at length the anti-Muslim and anti-Semitic tradition founded by Ernest Renan, the roots of which however extend back to the ancient theological disputes between Islam and Christianity. Regarding the anti-Semitism aimed at European specialists of Judaism, I presented a detailed analysis of this in *L'Europe et le mythe de l'Occident* (Europe and the Myth of the West).[1] The danger of anthropological approaches, even those developed by anticolonial thinkers, is the petrification of formal differences between peoples or religious and ethnic communities, and the exaggeration of these differences by stripping them of any historical context; the way the evolution of these contexts affected these differences, whether leading to their intensification or, conversely, their reduction and gradual disappearance, is likewise neglected.

The second has been less influenced by the colonial sense of superiority, but rather stems from the development of techniques within a certain area of anthropology whose primary function was to attempt to classify a people or a religious or ethnic community according to a few simple invariants of the character of these human entities. This glosses over the variety of characteristics within one human group as well as all of the changes that this group may experience throughout its history, especially the cultural interactions with other peoples, the variations of their economic activities, the changes in social status within this group, wars, and population movements.

In reality, identity is never stable. This is true of identity that encompasses collective values and behaviours as well as identity as it relates to individuals viewed within their diversity. Anthropological identity, insofar as this actually exists, is nonetheless heavily influenced by the geographical and socio-economic environment in which individuals evolve. The behaviours and thought structures of Arabs are different and depend on whether they belong to a rural or urban setting, live in the desert or on the high-mountain plateaux. They also vary depending on the ideology that is dominant at any given moment, on the nature of the political regime that governs them, on educational programmes in primary and secondary schools as well as universities, and on so many other factors. All of these common sense observations were already made by Ibn Khaldun, as seen in Chapter 1.

Nevertheless, there is a surprising number of works that try to pinpoint the unique and unchanging characteristics of the way Arabs think, in spite of the obvious variety of opinions, behaviours, and aspirations within these societies. A good summary of these controversies can be found in the work of the Palestinian writer, Issa Boullata, who describes the main controversies of Arab political thought. Although the book dates from 1990, most of what he says is still relevant today.[2] Nonetheless, there is a recent controversy that has had significant repercussions within Arab intellectual circles, even if it is already starting to be forgotten. This began in 1980 and pitted Mohammed Abed Al-Jabri, one of the great Moroccan intellectuals, against Georges Tarabichi, a Syrian intellectual, on the issue of the unique workings of the Arab mind and, in particular, the Islamic religious structures that allegedly drive it.

In Chapter 12 I examine in detail the rich and diverse aspects of this controversy concerning both the opposition between a rationality alleged to be a feature of the 'Sunni' mind and what is claimed to be the agnostic mysticism of the 'Shi'i' mind, and the refusal or the acceptance of philosophy by Islam in general. With respect to these two major points, the opposing positions of these two Arab thinkers is sobering. They prove the frivolousness of wanting to understand the essence of the Arab mind through one dominant feature, because they aptly show diverse aspects of this thought, especially in the succession of historical periods throughout time starting with the advent of the Qur'anic Prophecy. This controversy is all the more interesting because it compares the way Arab or Arab-Islamic thought works to the way Western Christian thought works.

All of this is a matter of subtle differences depending on whether the implicit starting point is the requisite uniqueness, and therefore the otherness, of the Arab mind, in particular its Islamic component, or, on the contrary, its similarity to or equivalence with how the thought of other cultural entities works, particularly that of Christianity. Beyond the historical trajectories that are unique to any cultural entity, there are anthropological similarities among the three monotheisms – Judaism, Christianity, and Islam – with respect to the way they function, and while they oppose one another they are nonetheless complementary. This is what I have tried to show in several of my books.[3] Yusuf Zaydan, an Egyptian intellectual who has written about a variety of subjects, described this in a recent book on Arab theology. In this book he sets out to write a history of monotheism, which he calls 'Arab theology', and to identify the roots of the violence that has affected monotheistic societies throughout history.[4]

In this regard, the importance that Arab intellectuals have accorded to Orientalist scholarship by European specialists of the Arab world and/or of Islam is surprising. Ever since the well-known controversy of 1883 between the religious reformer Jamal al-Din al-Afghani (1838–1897, probably of Iranian origin) and Ernest Renan (1823–1892), Arab intellectuals have been fascinated by any European writings in which they feature, whether they are disparaging or celebratory.[5] It is as if the fate of the Arab world ultimately depends on how it is judged by the Western gaze. Numerous controversies among Arab intellectuals have since arisen on this issue. Is it conceivable that the reification of ancient Arab-Muslim heritage resulted from the work of Orientalists through a mirror effect? Or is this regressive inward turn to identity a legitimate response in the face of European domination, followed today by Western domination of the Arab world? Conversely, is this merely a defensive posture on the part of dominant elites who, as has always been the case, seek to prevent progress and liberation of Arab societies from both external and internal oppression? So many questions of this type have dogged Arab thought since the period of European colonialism. Once this colonialism was gone, Edward Said's well-known work on Orientalism and its harmful effects (1978) re-launched these debates with renewed vigour.[6]

The problematic trap of authenticity vs. modernity

To the extent that the principles of European modernity have circulated throughout the entire world and have influenced the destiny of every society, I do not consider that the opening up of Arab culture and thought to this modernity, as well as the way in which this modernity may have influenced this culture and thought, in any way constitutes a flaw that would render them 'inauthentic', as has been suggested by much of the scholarship of European or Arab origin. Nor do I consider that this diminishes the value of the writing produced by modernising thinkers and essayists. This, however, is what has been argued by many contemporary Orientalists and Islamic scholars who consider that just like current radical Islamic thought, many of these writings are 'null and void' because they do not measure up to the 'authenticity' of what Muslim thought is supposed to be; that is, one that has remained exclusively enclosed within the Qur'anic texts and shari'a law. The denunciation of the references or the referential norms of Western thought and of its world view is frequent among certain intellectuals who deem the reformist religious thought of the contemporary Arab revival period inappropriate.[7] Therefore, the literature of Islamist movements, but also that of certain intellectuals who themselves have been Westernised, denounces the 'invasion of the Arab world by Western culture', which has allegedly taken away its soul.

In my view, however, it is important to identify the reverberations of this open-minded modernist thought within the Arab societies in which it has developed as well as its significance and relevance; and not its faithfulness to an ancient cultural heritage which is long gone and impossible to bring back to life. Indeed, the problem is posed in a biased and sterile way by Western Orientalists and Islamic scholars, as well as by Arab and Muslim proponents of a 'return' to an authenticity that has been defined everywhere as an Arab-Islamic one, beginning with the work of the Tunisian scholar Hichem Djaït in the 1970s. It is nothing short of utopian to want to petrify a society based on an imagined cultural heritage long left behind by centuries of progress. A blind faith in this would render a society unfit to enter into 'modernity'. In this case, the 'submission' imposed on this society would also make of it a dim replica of no interest to anyone and would fail to launch a genuine cultural, national and scientific revival movement. As we shall see, it is this that a large number of critical Arab intellectuals have denounced.

We run into a double problem when the analysis of Arab intellectual production remains centred on two contradictory criteria. On the one hand, faithfulness to a cultural heritage, which is the criteria of a prized authenticity within one part of European culture (its conservative aspect), and on the other hand, the adaptation and mastery of what are imagined to be the criteria of modernity. The latter has been completely encapsulated within the European model, which has elevated itself to being the exclusive and absolute criterion for judging intellectual production outside of Europe. When it comes to Arab intellectual production, this tendency becomes even more hegemonic than when it is a matter of analysing and evaluating other productions, such as the literature of Latin America, Japan, and China which is best known in Europe. Very often, Arab critics also allow themselves to be boxed in by this artificial dichotomy through which they attempt to give an account of the forms of Arab thought and how they have evolved: the dichotomy between the authenticity and the modernity of this thought.

We have here a problematic approach that stems from the specificity of European history. When exported to the rest of the world, it often gave rise to an intellectual chaos associated with the social chaos brought on by the intrusion of European influence, which dominated the world during the nineteenth and large parts of the twentieth century. I have sought to analyse this in *L'Europe et le mythe de l'Occident* (Europe and the Myth of the West). I have even called the present chaos in which Arab thought – particularly political thought – is floundering, as a genuine intellectual Guantanamo, referring to the prison in which it has been locked for the past few decades. This will be explained in detail later in an attempt to take stock of the misguided steps and contradictions through which this thought has become entrapped by the web spun by the artificial dispute between 'authenticity', or presumed faithfulness to a cultural heritage that has been completely petrified within an elevated imaginary, on the one hand, and 'modernity', or the successive European modalities and modes of intellectual production, on the other.

Furthermore, traditional Arab cultural heritage, meaning that which is presumed to be 'authentic', has most often been drastically reduced to the religious heritage created by the arrival of Islam. As we have seen, pre-Islamic Arab culture (as well as post-Islamic) was primarily dominated by the practice of a very wide variety of poetic genres, which was supported by a linguistic richness that lent itself to the rhetorical arts. The preaching of the Qur'an only served to enhance this key aspect of the culture through the beauty of the text, its often poetic expression, as well as the breadth of the subject matter.

It is interesting to note that the concept of authenticity (*asala*) has only recently come into use in the Arabic language, and it is not found in the great texts on which Arab cultural heritage is based. The intellectuals of the classical age, or even the last of the great Arab intellectuals of the fifteenth century, Ibn Khaldun, would not have understood the meaning of this term, whose root is *asl*, which mainly means 'origin', particularly tribal and familial. It was in fact the influence of European philosophy, specifically German romanticism and nationalism, that led Arab intellectuals to the issue of authenticity as opposed to modernity. With respect to authenticity, its effects were deemed to be positive as it provided the source of the values and 'soul' of the people. Modernity became synonymous with the loss of meaning and organic social cohesion. Therefore, I will avoid falling into the trap of judging the quality and representativeness of the writings of Arab intellectuals according to the split between authenticity and modernity. Instead, I am more inclined to contrast authoritarian fundamentalist religious thought with open secular modernist thought.

What is important in the analysis of the works of the great novelists, poets and essayists written in Arabic (or sometimes in French or English) is their reception within Arab societies. The critical evaluation of these works by European specialists or Orientalists interested in the Arab world who examine and probe them according to their own highly questionable frames of reference is not important. What is important is how these works have been circulated, evaluated or rejected within the different societies that are connected to one another by the same enthusiasm for Arab music, poetry, and novels. We have seen in Chapter 1 that modern cultural expressions in the Arab world have been and still remain very popular. Knowing whether or not they are authentic (who is the judge of these criteria of authenticity?), or whether post-colonialism, of which some academic research is very fond, succeeded in liberating Arab thought from the influence of the literary and philosophical currents of European and American culture, does not appear to me to be of any interest. On the contrary, this constitutes a waste of intellectual energy, which results in perpetuating a deep intellectual dependency, indeed, a sterility of thought that has turned in upon itself. This applies equally to European and American specialists as well as to Arab critics and intellectuals who study the thought produced by the intelligentsia.

This is the danger of what is referred to as postcolonial studies, which sometimes sees this regressive inward turn by formerly colonised peoples towards their so-called traditional and therefore precolonial culture as a form of resistance to the domination of the rest of the world by the West. This is especially the case at the cultural level and regarding the modes of consumption and organisation of social life of the bourgeois elites. Islam is thus viewed as a reservoir of identity that allows resistance to this globalisation (see *infra* Chapter 7). In this case, the existence of universals that allow for communication between societies is called into question, making the common struggle for a better world more difficult.[8]

We could ask ourselves why this question of authenticity of culture and thought never seems to be asked with regard to Japanese or Chinese literature, whose great contemporary novelists gladly used all of the techniques and resources of the great European literary tradition. Likewise, why is the question not asked with respect to the Latin American novel? It seems to be the case regarding the Arab world that social sciences in America and Europe always feel compelled to measure the authenticity of thought against its faithfulness to a baseline personality, one that is essentialist, inflexible, and inhabited by an Islam that is supposed to permanently serve as the main glue holding these societies together. To some extent this constitutes an Arab or Muslim exception to the laws of evolution and change for all human societies. This obviously does not mean that there is not a problem with the ability of the Arab world to master the elements of the modern world and to account for it on several levels – social, economic, political, and philosophical – without being hostage to an inflexible relationship with its heritage or to a relationship of dependency on the thought of countries that are allegedly more advanced. This is a major issue that will be addressed in the last chapter of this essay.

My intention here is to restore the great richness of Arab thought in all of its different ways of seeing the world. These modes of perception were inevitably influenced by philosophy and by the European doctrines that continue to shape our world, no matter how contested they may be, even by numerous Arabs who have assimilated them. When referring to great authors or political thinkers, I do not consider whether their religious identity is Muslim, Christian, Shi'i, Sunni or Druze, as is done in Orientalist academic circles in Europe or America. This is because it is the content of the works that counts over and above the community or in some cases the ethnic sub-identities (Berber, Kurd or Assyrian, for example) of the authors. Many specialists of the Arab world are content to see in these sub-identities an explanation of the content or the political positions expressed in these works. This approach uses a simplifying and deceptive analytical framework for the political doctrines of the Arab world which some see as being constructed around an imaginary dichotomy between a so-called Sunni majority and Christian or non-Sunni Muslim minorities. I have illustrated the absurdity of this approach from an epistemological point of view in the introductory chapters to *Le Proche-Orient éclaté*.

In spite of this absurdity, the ideology of Arab nationalism has often been seen as the product of theorists who belong to religious minorities and are seeking to escape domination by Sunni Muslims. In the same way, the modernising tendencies in Arab thought have often been attributed to Christian thinkers who are assumed to be closer to European modernity due to their religious affiliation, whereas Muslim thinkers are assumed to have resisted this modernity.[9] As we shall see, this argument has no substance, because for a long time Muslim clerics played a central role in the integration of modernity into Muslim religious culture. To maintain that the effort to integrate European ideas into the cultures of Arab societies was mainly the work of Christian elites thus constitutes a major historical error that makes no sense. This error is the result of an unchallenged axiomatic assumption that categorises Arabs, and Middle Easterners more generally, in an essentialist way based exclusively on sub-identities of an ethnic, community, and religious nature, including those related to the different forms of Islam.

Is Islam really indivisible?

This is the reason why analyses of contemporary Arab thought that portray it as petrified within an irreducible uniqueness, that of an Islam which is allegedly indivisible, as the French historian André Miquel claimed in 1968,[10] contribute to the current sterility of the major currents of European and American Orientalism. Given the power of the academic and media entities of the main Western nations, which attract many Arab students, this also leads to a reinforcement of a theologico-political culture that has been rehashing the same crippling themes for several decades. The glorified words of the leaders of the radical Islamic movements (particularly of Osama bin Laden and the man who inspired him, Sayyid Qutb, of the Muslim Brotherhood), have become hegemonical in the opinion of the West as well as in the Arab world, to the detriment of all other forms of thought and the richness of Arab culture. Since this philosophical and political richness has been ignored by the media and by mediatised academic research, it has become invisible.

Despite the number of reservations one might express with regard to Edward Said's argument about Orientalism, it is still as relevant as ever several decades after it was published in 1978.[11] Even at the time, the book appeared to be a bit excessive, particularly because the great European Orientalists were for the most part learned and sympathetic to the political developments within the Arab world. Today, however, those who have taken the reins from this generation – Maxime Rodinson, Jacques Berque, Régis Blachère, Vincent Monteil, Louis Massignon, and Marcel Colombe – are sharply focused on radical Islamic networks and radical thought. Sometimes they are even involved in police work by identifying and describing the leaders of networks of thinkers associated with an inflexible political theology that refuses to recognise just how much the world has evolved since the early centuries of Islam. At best, some of these scholars focus on trying to elicit sympathy for this type of thought because, presumably, this thought alone is capable of 'liberating' Arab man from a modernity that was imposed on him from the outside and which he supposedly hates.[12] Conversely, others incite Islamophobia by laying out the dangers of radical Islam and its numerous ramifications on a global scale. However, they never raise the role being played by Saudi Arabia and Pakistan, two key allies of the United States, in the ideological formation and support of the most extreme groups of radical Islam.

From this point onwards, a new, more or less radical, political theology within Arab thought has become the only one visible and therefore the only one that is significant. It is opposed to the values of humanism that derive from Enlightenment philosophy and from the French Revolution as well as the universals contributed by globalisation. This evolution is the result of the rise to power of the oil-producing monarchies and emirates of the Arabian Peninsula that felt threatened by the great modernising, nationalist, secular, and anti-imperialist wave that marked the Arab world during most of the last century. It is also, as I have already shown, the product of the Iranian religious revolution which led to the conversion of many modernist intellectuals to reliance on Islamic religion as a comprehensive political, social, and economic system. This reliance is based on its 'indivisibility', thus making it the only system supposedly capable of countering the domination of 'Western' materialism. Narratives which present this materialism as being solely responsible for the decline and underdevelopment of Arabs are becoming more and more prevalent.

In reality, even before Samuel Huntingdon had formalised his 'clash of civilisations' theory in the early 1990s, the intellectual atmosphere of the Arab world was ripe for finding within this theory the affirmation of the ideology shaped by the different forms of Islamic revival, from Saudi Wahhabism to the special blend of the so-called 'religious' revolution in Iran in 1979. Within Western thought, the school of René Guénon (on the positive side) and that of Ernest Renan (negative side) had already sown the seeds of an irreducible opposition between a rational, materialistic, and atheist West, and a religious, mystical Orient.[13]

The conditions of cultural and intellectual production in the Arab world since the end of the twentieth century

An important key to understanding Arab thought can be found in the weakness of the socio-economic and institutional structures in which the intelligentsia has evolved since the opening up to European modernity. During the period of the *Nahda* (the Arab renaissance) so aptly described by Albert Hourani, Arab intellectuals of all geographical origins and religious backgrounds found Egypt to be a great central beacon of culture thanks to the quality of its press, its publishing houses, and the phenomenal development of Cairo University. However, these favourable circumstances changed during the last quarter of the twentieth century. For a short time Lebanon took up the torch (1960–1975) when Beirut partially replaced Egypt as a centre of cultural vibrancy, particularly after Egypt's defeat at the hands of Israel in 1967, followed by the death of Gamal Abdel Nasser in 1970. During this period, the Lebanese capital became an important hub of Arab publishing as well as a refuge for intellectuals and politicians fleeing political changes brought on by coups d'état almost everywhere in the Arab Levant.

Afterwards, while Lebanon was floundering in instability and violence in 1975, individuals who were the producers of thought came to know an increasingly precarious fate. Many of those who could no longer rely on a Lebanese 'refuge', went into exile in London or Paris. Some, however, went to oil-exporting Arab countries whose governments offered them physical and financial security provided they did not criticise any of the local, monarchical, or princely political regimes that were no less authoritarian than the regimes of the republics they had fled.

The social standing and stable income levels that many Arab writers enjoyed during the period of the *Nahda* have been declining since the 1960s. This is due to the crackdown on freedoms following the military coups d'état as well as population growth. This growth overwhelmed the few academic institutions that existed in Egypt, Syria, Algeria, and Iraq. The subsequent increase in the number of universities came with an ensuing drop in the standard of teaching and in the research outputs of these institutions. The research and public teaching services of these countries were overwhelmed at every level by the numbers of students, and their budgets were inadequate. When the press was taken over by the state, this resulted in a decrease in the number of media of expression. Starting in the 1980s, television very quickly led to the further reduction in the number of people reading serious books. The large foreign universities such as the American Universities of Beirut and Cairo became gateways to emigration for brilliant students.

These circumstances explain why no cultural and academic institutions in which a continuous accumulation of thought and knowledge could take place, apart from the purely ideological and circumstantial, were established or developed anywhere. It also explains the exile of a large part of the intellectual elite. The large and prestigious European and especially American universities eagerly welcomed this new intellectual work force in order to develop their own departments within the human sciences dedicated to Islam and the Arab world. Knowledge pertaining to this region was already concentrated in some of these universities where extraordinary collections had been developed containing works and manuscripts produced in the Arab world and dating back several centuries. This knowledge continued to dominate given that academic institutions in the Arab world lacked the financial means necessary to develop the same intellectual firepower.

Under these conditions, it should come as no surprise that locally produced Arab thought dwindled and splintered. Likewise, instead of dedicating their lives to research and to the accumulation of learning registered in the general development of local knowledge, intellectuals were obliged to transform themselves into ideologues whose biting prose was used in service of the major media outlets, especially those run by the governments in the Arabian Peninsula whose wealth derived from oil revenues.[14]

However, the upcoming chapters will show that in spite of this grave situation, important works were produced that reflected major controversies in philosophy, anthropology, and history. Even today these are not well known among the broader 'educated' Arab public. They are also completely unknown in Europe and the United States, whose academic institutions and think tanks are increasingly setting the Arab intellectual agenda to benefit the geopolitics of the West as well as its intellectual and material interests. The Arab brains that emigrated to the major European or American capitals are regularly snatched up by these powerful intellectual and academic institutions. In order to succeed there and find their place in the sun, they have to consciously or unconsciously submit to the requirements of an academia that is increasingly serving the needs of geopolitics and the conflicts it engenders. Such compliance happens often and is made even easier by the fact that whenever someone becomes a star in a European or American university or at a major think tank, this also makes them renowned in the Arab world itself.[15] This leads them to be invited to the Arab world where they are pampered on the basis of a naïve local belief that since they are migrant intellectuals, they are somehow close to Western academic circles and decision-making, which therefore gives them special knowledge that can be exploited locally.

This is why the upcoming chapters will attempt to highlight the trends in Arab thought that are really worth learning about and analysing, in particular, those that are being ignored due to the fact that they do not correspond to the agenda of Arab issues as developed by major European and American institutions. This lack of knowledge seems particularly troubling to me. In fact, due to the media and particular characteristics of academic research, it contributes to confining the visible part of Arab thought to problematics that are narrow and hardly relevant. In particular, these are related to the various Islamic movements or to the progress of formal democracy in the Arab world. This is the reason it is so difficult to construct a system for viewing and analysing our world today that is not completely dependent on the agendas produced to favour the geopolitical interests of the European powers or the United States, as well as the Arab regimes that are the clients of these powers.

In the 2010s, the circumstances that would allow such a system to be constructed are hardly in place at this stage of the history of the Arab world. Nonetheless, it is still necessary to work towards building an awareness of the challenges inherent in achieving a philosophical independence on which a better future could be built for Arabs than the one in which they are presently floundering. A similar call was already made forty years ago by various other Arab thinkers, particularly by Nassif Nassar,[16] a political philosopher born in 1938 (see *infra* Chapter 14). As we shall see, since the collapse of the Ottoman Empire following the First World War, Arabs have faced extremely complex problems which must be taken into account when focusing on the evolution of ways of thinking and philosophising in their societies. They have experienced rapidly changing political, cultural, philosophical, socio-economic, regional, and international contexts. This is why most essays focused on Arab or Islamic thought have been highly influenced by these contexts, something which I will strive to show here.

Albert Hourani's 1962 pioneering overview of Arab thought

Since the 1980s, no overview of ideologies or ways of thinking in the Arab world, or their relation to major political and economic events that have affected this region, has been published in Arabic or French.[17] The last one was by Anouar Abdel-Malek (1924–2012), an Egyptian sociologist and political scientist. Abdel-Malek organised a collection of the best writing by Arab political essayists in 1970, which at that time provided a good overview of the richness and wide variety of Arab thought.[18]

Prior to this, in 1962, the Lebanese-British Orientalist Albert Hourani published one of his first works on 'Arab thought during the liberal age', from the nineteenth century to the first half of the twentieth century, which served as a guide for all those who followed in his footsteps.[19] As this book was translated from its English original into both Arabic and French, it became the most appealing overview of Arab intellectual life during the period of the Arab renaissance (*Nahda*). It had considerable influence on later writers who relied on it to address this subject. Very few of them strayed from the framework he established, which is not without its flaws. This is why it is necessary to provide a brief summary here.

Hourani equates the beginning of the period of the Arab renaissance with the arrival of Napoleon in Egypt in 1798 and its reverberations in Arab intellectual circles. He concludes this period in 1939 on the eve of the Second World War. The first three chapters of his book focus on a brief description of the Islamic state in general, the problems of the Ottoman Empire whose decline began in the seventeenth century, and finally on the first perceptions of Europe by the Ottoman Turkish elites at the height of their Empire's expansion, as well as by the Egyptians who witnessed the French invasion of Egypt in 1798. In this third chapter, he also deals with the emergence and development of Wahhabism in the Arabian Peninsula in the eighteenth century, a doctrine that would provide the basis of the fundamentalist Islamic radicalism that played a major role in the political and cultural life of Arabs from the birth of the Kingdom of Saudi Arabia in the early twentieth century.

The fourth chapter provides an overview of the ideas developed by individuals whom Hourani calls the 'first generation' of thinkers, represented by three major figures in particular, al-Tahtawi in Egypt, Khayr al-Din al-Tunisi in Tunisia, and Boutros al-Boustani in Lebanon. In the two chapters that follow (5 and 6) he successively treats two major figures from the Islamic reformation, Jamal al-Din al-Afghani and Muhammad 'Abduh, while Chapter 7 describes the actions of the followers of 'Abduh in Egypt, who worked to reconcile Islam with European modernity. The eighth chapter discusses the work of the Egyptian nationalists from the time when Cairo became the intellectual capital of the Arab world in the early twentieth century. At this time, the intellectual elites included native-born Egyptians, either Muslim or Coptic Christian, as well as Syrian-Lebanese intellectuals who had emigrated to Egypt after first fleeing the Ottoman autocracy and then the French invasion. Due to this, the development of nationalist ideas in this key country of the Arab world inevitably influenced the development of Pan-Arab nationalism more generally. The nationalist struggle of the Egyptians from the end of the nineteenth century onwards against the powerful protectorate of the British occupier became a model for future generations in other parts of the Arab world.

In the next two chapters, Hourani breaks the thread of the previous chapters in which he discusses Christian and Muslim Arab thinkers indistinctly to suddenly contrast them. Indeed, Chapter 9 is devoted to the figure of Rashid Rida (1865–1935), a Lebanese thinker from Tripoli and a follower of Muhammad 'Abduh. However, after visiting the newly founded Kingdom of Saudi Arabia in the 1920s, Rida abandoned the Islamic liberalism that had predominated until then to devote himself to conservatism and rigourism on the grounds that this was the best way to resist the Westernisation of the Arab world and the depersonalisation that this entailed. Conversely, the topic of Chapter 10 is the work of the 'Christian pioneers' of secularism in the Arab world, particularly Shibli Shumayyil (1860–1917) and Farah Antun (1874–1922).

This way of presenting things is not neutral, especially since, as we shall see, I do not believe that there really are any major differences in this area between Christian and Muslim thinkers. Nor do I think that Christian thinkers have been more radical than their Muslim counterparts in calling for a separation of the secular and the religious. The notion that these thinkers are closer to European secular ideas and more radical than Muslims because they are Christian by birth does not correspond to the reality of the texts in which

Christians and Muslims equally called for the separation of the secular and the religious and for the validation of individuals and their freedom, including the freedom of conscience. Given the prominence that Hourani's book acquired, this dichotomy would unfortunately be reproduced by other authors in spite of its inconsistencies, a subject that I will come back to and discuss at great length.

The eleventh chapter of Hourani's book is dedicated to the emergence of Arab nationalism. He describes in detail the development of Syrian and Lebanese nationalism as well as the two prevailing trends, that of unified and secular Arab nationalism and that of Muslim nationalism with Arab unity at its core. Finally, the last chapter deals with the eminent figure of Taha Husayn and the major impact of his work on contemporary Arab thought. In the epilogue to this work, Hourani claims that on the eve of the Second World War, a chapter of Arab intellectual history had closed. In his view, the outbreak of the war brought an end to Arab nationalism. Indeed, he claimed that nationalism went through three main phases that emerged in the following order: religious nationalism, territorial patriotism, and finally, ethnic and linguistic patriotism.

As I will show in this book, it is difficult to consider the era of direct domination of almost all Arab societies by the colonial powers to be 'liberal.' By doing exactly this, Hourani suggests that the period of independence movements that followed this era is the same as the period of the authoritarian regimes that would ensue. Even more questionable is the idea that considers Arab nationalism to be outdated from 1939 onwards, whereas the period of its greatest expansion is that of the independence movements from 1950 until at least 1975. Given the great impact of Hourani's work, it is important to highlight its implicit ideological limitations. These limitations subsequently provided numerous arguments for Arab thinkers with an Islamic focus to view thought that was qualified as liberal to be 'inauthentic' and completely subjugated to the political and philosophical references of Europe, which dominated the Arab world militarily, economically, and culturally.

More recent overviews

There are other overviews of Arab thought that we need to mention, the most important of which date back to the 1970s. I have already cited the 'Que sais-je?' by Mohammed Arkoun published in 1975 under the title *La Pensée arabe*.[20] Its remarkable conclusion summarises in two pages all of the problematic issues raised by Arkoun's rationalist work. His goal was to revive critical thinking within Arab thought, particularly within religious thought. This was significant because it was religious thought that was used to block the importation of modernity, a topic to which I will return. Alongside this, we should also mention the existence of two other short works on Arab thought. The first was penned by Henri Serouya in 1960 and concentrates on Muslim philosophy and religion.[21] The second, by Vincent Monteil, appeared in 1974 under the title *Clefs pour la pensée arabe* (Keys to Understanding Arab Thought).[22] This is one of the rare books that only devotes one chapter to religious thought and one chapter to mystical thought out of a total of eleven chapters. The remaining chapters cover all forms of legal, moral, social, philosophical, cultural, scientific, historical, socio-economic and political thought. However, it only focuses on the classical period of Arab-Islamic civilisation. We are equally indebted to Jacques Berque for a comprehensive study of Arabs.[23] The work in Arabic by the well-known Jordanian professor, Ali Al-Muhafaza, on the different directions of Arab thought at the time of the renaissance should also be mentioned. However, this work only covers the period from Napoleon's expedition to Egypt up to the beginning of the First World War, a time span which is slightly shorter than the one covered by Hourani.[24]

We cannot overlook the fine work of historian Leyla Dakhli, published in 2009,[25] in which she skilfully provides a context for the work of Syrian and Lebanese thinkers from the 1908–1940 generation. These thinkers discovered political consciousness amidst the renewed atmosphere of hope created by the re-establishment of the Ottoman constitution in 1908, only to face the collapse of the empire and the establishment of separate state entities. Her work gives prominence to women writers, intellectuals, and feminists. In so doing, she has brought recognition to talented individuals who are often overlooked, especially May Ziade (1886–1941), Marie Ajami (1888–1965), and Nazira Zayn al-Din (1908–1976) (see *infra* Chapter 7).

No less important is another ground-breaking work by Caroline Hervé-Montel on the relationship between the literary renaissance and the development of a national consciousness in Egypt and Lebanon during the first three decades of the twentieth century.[26] She writes that '[s]ince any identity is displayed first and foremost within a narrative identity, it is the novelistic genre that is naturally best suited to moving a nation forward.'[27] She aptly discusses the fact that the French language is not necessarily the language of the 'Other' or of the coloniser. It is an alternative language to Arabic, or an 'alterlanguage', 'that can be chosen for various reasons, but mainly because it is a language that allows you to make a name for yourself and to reach an audience on the local political stage as well as on the international one.'[28] Just like Leyla Dakhli, Caroline Hervé-Montel highlights the fine literary production of women in Egypt as well as in Lebanon.

Furthermore, there are two collective works we should mention, *Renaissance du monde arabe* (Renaissance of the Arab World) (1972) and *Renouvellements du monde arabe, 1952–1982* (Renewal of the Arab World, 1952–1982) (1987).[29] The first brings together contributions covering a wide variety of topics by twenty-three specialists of the Arab world (twenty-one of whom were born there) presented during an inter-Arab conference held at the Catholic University of Louvain in 1970. The ten contributions brought together in the second book (four of which written by Arab intellectuals) are focused more on the geopolitical and economic development of the region.

The most important work is undeniably that of the philosopher Paul Khoury who was born in 1921 in a village near the city of Tyre in Lebanon. He devoted his entire life to the description and analysis of Arab and Islamic thought, to Islamic-Christian relations, and to high-level philosophical inquiry (see *infra*, Chapter 14). Between 1981 and 1985 he wrote a series of five works, four of which form part of a tetralogy while the fifth is a stand-alone book. With these he undertook an in-depth study of the landscape of Arab thought of encyclopaedic proportions. His work certainly deserves further attention, or at the very least should be used as a reference by anyone looking closely at the diversity of Arab thought, its different schools and trends, and the issue of its acculturation with European modernity after the Second World War. It is in fact a snapshot of a crucial historical time in the Arab world between 1960 and 1980. While it is very rich in its intellectual content, it is not an overview of all Arab thought since the nineteenth century. The dilemma of tradition versus modernity is a major theme in all four volumes, but the first book in the tetralogy constitutes the first phase of this work. It reviews all of the trends in contemporary Arab thought, the major writers who have contributed to it, and the works they wrote with the greatest influence on their time period.[30] It is here that Khoury analyses the different types of nationalism as well as feminism in the Arab world, and the evolution of both literary criticism and the vision for education. He also describes socialism as viewed by Arab thinkers as well as how these thinkers have diagnosed economic and social problems. He naturally includes the numerous positions and attitudes regarding Islam, particularly the complex issues inherent in the dilemma between tradition and modernity which has caused so much turmoil in Arab thought. It is this dilemma that dominated the author's thinking and which structured his broader philosophical inquiry (see *infra*, Chapter 14).

This first volume is completed by the three that follow. The first comprises 1,287 biographical profiles of contemporary Arab thinkers.[31] The second provides the reader with an analysis of 150 works selected from among the intellectual output of these authors.[32] The third, which was written prior to the others, identifies the main sources for his research, his bibliographic tools, and scholarly works in Arabic or European languages.[33] Khoury also published three preliminary studies of Arab thought in a single volume.[34] What we have here is an analytical review that covers Arab intellectual production on religion, economics, politics, nationalism, socialism, reformism, and philosophy from the beginning of the 1960s to the early 1980s, which is unfortunately difficult to use. It is regrettable that scholars have not made better use of this encyclopaedic work of over 2,800 pages. This is likely due to the fact that it is not well known and that it has not been integrated into academic research.[35]

Apart from these works by Paul Khoury, Francophone and Arabophone readers have not had access to an overview of the evolution of Arab thought in all of its aspects, whereas countless books have focused on the different political and theological trends within Islam. English-language scholarship has not been all that more productive, and many English-language works have favoured the approach that centres on Islam. Nonetheless, we should mention here the ambitious work of the Lebanese political scientist Elizabeth Kassab, published in 2010. It is a survey of contemporary Arab thought from a very interesting comparative perspective, since in this book Arab thought is situated within the broader context of the development of different countries.[36] The value of this work lies in the fact that it reviews articles presented at major conferences held in the Arab world in the 1970s and 1980s, which provides valuable insight into the thought of Arab intellectuals whose work has become well known. Kassab focuses on the turmoil of Arab thought in the period following the 1967 War. During this conflict, three Arab armies suffered a major defeat at the hands of the Israeli army, giving rise to a period of existential questioning of what exactly modernity had achieved within the region.

The same preoccupation was at the heart of an earlier work, already mentioned above, written by the Palestinian author Issa Boullata. He tried to decipher the 'trends and issues in contemporary Arab thought', especially in his analysis of the catastrophe represented by the 1967 Arab defeat by Israel.[37] This is one of the rare works that succeeds in providing a sober and objective analysis of the contradictory trends in Arab thought. It contains a concise and well-presented overview of the ideas and thought of the major Arab intellectuals. However, Boullata carries out his analysis from the unique and specific perspective of the collision between tradition and modernity, which he clearly defines. He writes that 'the forces of modernity, using mostly external ideas and models for change, are oriented towards the future, which they see as opening new horizons for the Arabs. Opposing them, the forces of tradition, using mostly internal ideas and models for change, are oriented towards the past, which they see as an ideal to be repeated because they perceive it as having the promise of certainty and the surety of proven success.'[38] He believes that if this contradiction persists, the intellectual crisis could degenerate into violent conflict 'that may affect not only its cultural heritage but also its nature, its unity, its very existence – depending on the situation.'[39] This was a prophetic prediction in light of the events that followed the Arab revolts in the spring of 2011.

Furthermore, Boullata concludes his fine work by evoking the 'ideological disarticulation that is so pronounced that Arab discourses today are at cross purposes.'[40] It seems unfortunate that this fine overview of the complexities of Arab thought has not been translated into French or Arabic. However, this work can also be criticised for not really addressing the complexities of change in the political, geopolitical, socio-economic, and demographic contexts in the Arab world. It also overlooks the shifts in power relations within these societies that exerted a strong influence on the exacerbation of the contradictions that he denounces within this thought.

In the Arabic language the output has not been any richer in terms of recent books that attempt to provide an overview of contemporary Arab thought. During the twentieth century, especially during the most volatile years of the nationalist period, numerous works presented reviews of Arab thought and its major authors. However, this well seems to have gone dry, as if the accumulation of irreconcilable problems and contradictions within the currents of a thought dominated by a theological and political focus made this task impossible. We should, however, commend the efforts of Khalil Ahmad Khalil, a Lebanese philosopher and political scientist, for publishing a short encyclopaedia of Arab intellectual and literary figures (poets, playwrights, major novelists) of the twentieth century, which provides a biographical profile summarising their works and ideas.[41]

As we shall see in a later chapter, the anxiety surrounding identity reached such heights that any synthesis became impossible. The great ancestors whose thought had been so thoughtfully analysed sank into oblivion. However, other works bravely attempted to surmount these contradictions or to analyse them objectively. Several thinkers have specifically tackled one of the major questions since the end of the 1970s. This is the question of the contradiction between political Islam, which has invaded the entire system of thought, and the indispensable secularisation of thought that would allow it to definitively and successfully enter into the modernity that is overtaking the broader world. In general, these authors are relatively unknown, and their work is rarely discussed. This applies particularly to Mohammed Jaber Al-Ansari, a citizen of Bahrain, to Muhammad Dahir from Lebanon, and to Aziz Al-Azmeh from Syria.[42] Their original thinking will be discussed at length in the following (see *infra* Chapter 13).

Raif Khoury (1912–1967) was a major Lebanese thinker in tune with revolutionary ideals, both those of the French Revolution as well as the Bolshevik Revolution. He wrote in Arabic about modern Arab thought and reviewed all of the Arab authors whose writings were strongly influenced by the French Revolution.[43] His work contains a series of excerpts from the texts of the authors that he reviewed, which allows the reader to get a good sense of the large number of Muslim writers who admired the French Revolution. Raif Khoury belonged to a generation of Arab thinkers concerned with creating a modernist and universalising tradition within Arab thought, but whose works have unfortunately fallen into oblivion. The same goes for another Lebanese thinker and literary figure of the preceding generation, Maroun Abboud (1886–1962), who wrote a book on the vanguards of the Arab renaissance, particularly the major role played by several poets in the renewal of the Arabic language and the variety of the subjects studied.[44]

Since then, except for a few rare and mostly collective works, French- and Arabic-language readers have been deprived of any serious information on the developments in Arab thought. They have also been deprived of the different currents of this thought within the framework of the complex and shifting historical contexts that will be examined in the next chapter. Before describing these changes and their impact on Arab thought, we should dispel the stereotypical narrative that has developed, based on the work of Albert Hourani, on the role of Arab Christian thinkers who are presumed to be different from Arab Muslim thinkers. This is particularly important because this narrative continues to dominate many works on various aspects of Arab thought, particularly with regard to secularism.

Misinterpreting the role of Arab Christian thinkers

We have seen how the essentialist dichotomy between Christian and Muslim thinkers was established by Albert Hourani in his work on Arab thought in the 'liberal' era. This dichotomy is consistent with the anthropological and essentialist approach of Orientalism. This had a significant influence on many Arab intellectuals, including some who denounced it, as well as many first-rate intellectuals who fell into its trap.

The best known of these is Hisham Sharabi (1927–2005), a Palestinian intellectual whose work is widely read and respected in both the Arab world and the West. He received his intellectual training at the University of Chicago where he earned his doctorate before embarking on a long and successful career at Georgetown University in Washington, D.C. Like Edward Said, he was a supporter of Palestinian rights and was sufficiently comfortable in English to use it to write several of his books. He also belonged to the Syrian Social Nationalist Party. In one of his best known works he studies the thought of Arab intellectuals between 1875 and 1914 and its relation to European thought during this period, a time when the French and British colonial powers were completing their takeover of all of the Arab provinces of the Ottoman Empire.[45]

What is surprising about this work is how it presents an irreparable divide between Arab Christian thinkers, especially those in Syria, and Arab Muslim thinkers. Although he creates two categories of Muslim thinkers, the reformist or conservative Salafists on the one hand, and the secularist thinkers on the other, he considers the Arab Christian thinkers as the only true secularists. It is most astonishing that he includes them in one and the same category, which he describes in a rather abstract and decontextualised way, as if to imply the existence of specific Christian mental structures that have been completely unaffected by the Islamic environment in which Arab Christians have lived since the arrival of Islam in the Syro-Mesopotamian basin and Egypt. This category is called 'Westernised Christians', whom he considers to have been totally deracinated and entirely secular. He also holds that the members of this category were only capable of looking to Europe and its value system for their approach to reforming the Ottoman Empire. As proof of this deracination, Sharabi refers to the high levels of migration of Arab Christians to Europe or to North and South America during the time period he studied.

Conversely, he sees reformist Muslim intellectuals, even the secular ones, whose secularising tendencies were superficial in his view, as having been embedded in their natural intellectual environment. In addition, he sees their thought as held in check by the boundaries imposed by this environment and by the Islamic system of thought that set it apart and which could not be challenged at its core.

It is appropriate to feel shocked by the assertion of this dichotomy between an Arab Christian thought, considered to be deracinated and completely turned towards European philosophical and secular thought, and a Muslim thought so deeply rooted in its history that it is only capable of marginal reform. This argument would not fail to appeal to the colonial European approach to the 'Eastern question', which sees Arab Christians as merely 'minorities', leftovers from the history of Christianity which has completely shifted from the 'Semitic' Orient, as Ernest Renan put it, to the 'Aryan' West. Following this line of argument, these Christians allegedly had no other choice but to leave in order to put a stop to the process of being uprooted. The argument is nonetheless completely far-fetched and in no way corresponds to any past or present historical realities. We can only summarise here the historical facts that completely contradict this view of a dichotomy between an Arab Christian thought and an Arab Muslim thought.

I have already talked about the numerous relations established between the Aramaean Christian populations living throughout the entire Syro-Mesopotamian area and the Arab tribes that were either living there or that established themselves there following the conquests of the region after the arrival of Islam. The division between Christian elites and the entire Muslim population came later. This partially resulted from the more modern education provided to these elites by foreign missionaries as well as by some of the local churches that were strongly rooted in the longstanding local cultural contexts of the region, such as the Maronite Church in Mount Lebanon. Although the Catholic missionaries restricted their efforts to local Christians whom they sought to firmly connect to Roman Catholicism, the American Protestant missionaries who founded the Syrian Protestant College in Beirut in 1862 were just as open to Muslim communities as they were to Christian communities.

As for the Syrian Christians that Sharabi mentions, he compares them to Lebanese Christians, and in some ways to Palestinian Christians, even though they were so well established that they were at the forefront of the struggle against the respective French and British mandates of Syria and Palestine after the First World War. The same was the case for Iraqi Christians. Moreover, Arab Christians are comprised, in large part, of rural people with firmly established roots, including Egyptian Coptic Christians. It is therefore absurd to talk about 'uprooting' or 'deracination', especially since this glosses over other inevitable historical factors. These include the great hostility of many completely Arabised Oriental churches (Coptic, Chaldean, Syriac) towards the Byzantine Church. Later, this hostility would be directed toward the Roman Catholic Church and mainly the Melkite Church, which had split from the Byzantine Church.

As I have shown elsewhere, the Ottoman *millet* system preserved the assimilation of Christians, Arabs, Armenians and Greeks. Oriental churches are just as rigid as Islamic communities when it comes to the Westernisation of the thought and habits of their flocks due to the influence of Europe. They claim that their function is to structure the lives of all of the faithful, and their clergy are granted even more power than the Muslim *ulama*. Oriental Christianity is even today pervaded by the confusion of the secular and the religious. In these churches, Sunday morning sermons include more commentary on current political issues than on spiritual, ethical, or moral questions.[46]

With respect to the migration of Christians that Sharabi alludes to in support of his argument, he fails to mention the massacres of the Christians and the Druze at Mount Lebanon in 1840 and in 1860. These resulted from the fierce competition between France and Great Britain for control of the route to India, and thus for the eastern Mediterranean. There were also massacres in Damascus in 1860 related to heavy-handed socio-economic changes. In the same way, he forgets to mention the large number of Muslims who took the migration route, going most often to either North or South America, in the face of the difficult changes that the Arab Orient underwent during the entire period that ranges from 1840 to the First World War. Moreover, he passes over in silence the large numbers of Syro-Lebanese and Palestinian Muslims and Christians who migrated to Egypt in order to remain within a familiar cultural environment and to work together for the Arab renaissance.

Sharabi also does not appear to be aware of the work of three of the greatest Arab Christian literary figures: Khalil Gibran (1883–1931), Mikhail Naimy (1889–1989), and Jurji Zaydan (1861–1914). The first two have loudly and clearly proclaimed their strong attachment to the spirituality of the Arab

Orient and their aversion to the materialism of modern life in the West, which they denounced just as strongly as the numerous Salafist Muslim intellectuals did. The third did a remarkable job of popularising the history of Arab Islam through a series of historical novels, not to mention a scholarly work on the history of Arab culture. By the same token, Sharabi completely overlooks the major political role played by numerous anti-imperialist and nationalist Arab Christians in Egypt, Syria, Lebanon, and Palestine, including the leaders of armed Palestinian movements such as Georges Habash (1926–2008), Wadie Haddad (1927–1978), and Nayef Hawatmeh (1938–).

It is true that from time to time Sharabi tries to soften the extreme nature of his dichotomy between uprooted, Westernised Christians and entrenched Muslims who, even if they have secular tendencies, cannot take their reformist aspirations very far due to their roots. He recognises the contribution of Christian intellectuals to the modernisation of the Arabic language and the added value of their radical reformist aims in their exchanges with their Muslim colleagues, but he does not take this very far. He does not question the validity of his dichotomy or his peremptory assertion about deracination, even though he does recognise the attachment of Christians to the Arabic language, the language of the Qur'an.[47]

Finally, in its failure to acknowledge the courage and the critical thinking of Muslims, and in its concentration on the critical thinking of Christians, Sharabi's work consecrates one of the major stereotypes of certain colonial forms of Orientalism. He does so despite the fact that many great Muslim thinkers, including many women, had proposed reforms that were impressive in their boldness. Figuring among the most eminent of these thinkers were individuals trained at Al-Azhar University in Cairo (see *infra*, Chapter 6). This constitutes an unconscious denial of the possibility that Arab Muslims are able to step outside of a psyche that is allegedly at a standstill and closed in on itself, one that no outside context will ever succeed in changing. This posture of anthropological essentialism is completely paralysing on an intellectual level and denies the possibility of participating in a critical way in the formation of universals that are shared by the world's major cultures.[48]

Given the author's fame, Sharabi's arguments inevitably influenced various Arab intellectuals, more often Christians than Muslims. Since they were only marginally aware of the implications of this dichotomy in the framework of the polemics surrounding Arab identity, these Christian intellectuals found an additional argument in support of their claim that Islam is 'indivisible' and can never assimilate freedom of religion and conscience as practiced in

Europe. These intellectuals sank further into an imaginary belief, a belief that is nonetheless entrenched in their surroundings, according to which Christians are doomed to remain marginalised minorities with an unhappy consciousness incapable of influencing the destiny of their countries of origin. In addition, this false claim provides additional arguments to those who subscribe to the theories of political Islam, particularly the most extreme versions, to assert that Arab Christians cannot be integrated on an equal footing within a 'true' Muslim society because they would constitute an extension of the Christian societies that are fighting against Islam.

Yet it remains true even today that the assimilation of Christians has allowed many of them to hold major positions of political and cultural influence in Egypt, Syria, Iraq, Lebanon, Palestine, and Jordan. Not only have they contributed to creating a national Arab or Pan-Syrian consciousness, they have also produced important scholarship on the religion of Islam itself as well as on the history of the Arabs since the Muslim conquest. Many of them consider that being an Arab Christian means that they are Muslim on the cultural level without necessarily being so at the level of their faith.

In spite of these observations, many solid and learned authors of Christian origin subscribed to Hourani's views, which were subsequently expanded by Sharabi. This is the case of Abdallah Naaman, a first-rate Lebanese scholar, and his book on the secular tendencies in the Arab world, published in 1990.[49] He considers that the pioneers of secularism in the Arab world have 'naturally' been Christians and Jews, who also founded Communist parties, which corresponds to the typical Orientalist argument as well as those of Hourani and Sharabi. However, Naaman's very rich work shows that Muslims as a whole were no less secular than Christians. A very useful index of secular thinkers at the end of the book illustrates the large number of Muslim thinkers who fully integrated the best aspects of the values of political modernity spread by European culture throughout the world into their inquiry.

We encounter the same dichotomy in another first-rate work on secularism (an English term that is not exactly the equivalent of the French term *laïcité*) in the Arab world written by the Lebanese novelist and university professor Nazik Saba Yared.[50] This book, which is very rich in its content, also adopts the position that Arab Christians do not experience the same limits to secularism as imposed on Muslim intellectuals. As usual, it is the same essentialist and rigid view of Islamic religion, although as a background assumption and therefore unlikely to be intentional. It is, however, paradoxical that the texts written by Muslim intellectuals that are cited in this book show not only their broad freedom of thought and how they distance themselves from the sacred text, but also the fact that some of the major Christian thinkers who were so radical with respect to secular thinking were very conservative when it came to any issues regarding the emancipation of women. This starkly contrasts with Muslim authors, both male and female. Finally, this dichotomy was echoed by Hoda Nehme, Dean of the Faculty of Philosophy at a major university in Lebanon, in her work on the progression of secular thought in the Arab world.[51]

Along the same lines, should we also think that there might be a specific thought for Shi'i, Druze or Alawite Arabs, or for the Kurds or for the Amazighs (Berbers) who have been living within Arab societies for centuries? This hardly seems credible to me, and I would only mention in exceptional cases that a specific thinker is Alawite or Christian, or of Kurdish or Berber origin, and only when it is necessary to show just how little influence this specificity has on their thought. Up to this point, my survey of the evolution of Arab thought has explored the themes that polarise it, as well as its contradictions and turmoil. Any approach based on the ethnic or religious origin of thinkers leads to the perpetuation of Orientalism. This is marked by the interplay of ethnic and religious divisions that were substantially exacerbated by colonialism and which even today we have unfortunately been unable to shed.

As we have seen, there exists a versatile and diverse Arab culture that is shared by all Arab societies. An attempt to subdivide this based on the religious or ethnic origin of artists, literary figures, and political thinkers seems to me to be a vain and hollow undertaking. The ups and downs, changes, and contradictions of Arab thought are above all a reflection of the immense socio-economic and geopolitical disruptions this region has experienced time and again. It is hardly the result of the varied ethnic, religious or denominational origins of Arab societies.

CHAPTER 4

The shifting political contexts of Arab societies

In the introduction to this work, I emphasised how important an understanding of the political and socio-economic contexts of Arab thought is to comprehending and assessing its relevance in the contemporary world. Arab societies, like many others that were colonised by an expanding Europe, have experienced many rapid changes since the beginning of the nineteenth century. For a long time they were an integral part of the Ottoman Empire, before falling completely under European hegemony and subsequently fighting for their emancipation. Historical circumstances were such that this was undertaken in a haphazard way during a time when states that had emerged from the Ottoman Empire were fracturing as they were being buffeted by the winds of the Cold War. The ups and downs, contradictions, turmoil, and divisions of this thought can largely be explained by these complex circumstances.

We know from Ibn Khaldun's historical reflections, as well as those of Karl Polanyi[1] in our own time, the extent to which socio-economic and political upheavals can give rise to ideological rigidity and scattered identity-based radicalisms. In the modern world, the upheavals of the industrial revolution in Europe, the end of rural household-based economies, and the establishment of mature capitalism constituted some of the elements that gave rise to fascism and Nazism. In the contemporary Arab world, the succession of abrupt political changes in the first place, followed by rapid socio-economic and demographic shifts, have been contributing factors to the emergence of religious millenarianism at the end of the twentieth century. This process was

71

heavily aided and subsidised within a context where the balance of power had reversed between societies that had built their power and fortune through the development of the global oil industry, which in the Arabian Peninsula largely consisted of Bedouin tribal structures, and older urban Arab societies in the Mashriq and the Maghreb. All of these changes took place against the backdrop of extensive external interventions aimed at gaining control of this strategic region of the world, which will be described in this chapter.

Nothing is more surprising in the eyes of today's modern Arabs than the fragmentation of their societies and the states that emerged from the dismantling of the Ottoman Empire. These societies lack solidarity in the face of challenges from the outside world and are even capable of feeling hostile towards one another. This fragmentation sits in stark contrast to the cultural consciousness of their shared Arab identity, which leads to appreciation of the same thinkers, poets, novelists, singers, and musicians (see *supra* Chapter 1). In addition to this, various differences of opinion across states have become particularly apparent over the past few decades. It has reached the point where it is reasonable to ask what it is that unifies Arabs who are so quick to disagree with each other, and whether, paradoxically, what actually does unify them is their adherence to contradictory currents of thought that span all of their societies. This chapter will therefore attempt to clarify the historical causes for these disagreements.

The dismantling of the Ottoman Empire and the three afflictions of the Arab world

The dismantling of the Ottoman Empire created terrible problems for all Arab societies of the Levant and, to a lesser extent, for societies in North Africa. These problems took many forms.

First, for several centuries, these societies were dominated and directly controlled by non-Arabs, followed by European colonial powers during the inter-war period in the Levant and even earlier in North Africa. Subsequently, it was therefore necessary for them to learn how to be in power and to acquire the ability to manage themselves, both in terms of the internal order of their societies as well as their relationship to the regional and international order. This was no small feat because the fate of the Arab Middle East since early antiquity had been decided by its status as one of the most coveted zones in global geopolitics. Three main reasons explain this 'singular privilege'.

A coveted geographical crossroads. First, this region is situated at a geographical crossroads that is one of the most strategic in the world because it links three of the five continents that make up our planet. During the two world wars of the last century, fierce military battles took place in the eastern Mediterranean, that is, in the Levant, for control of the Dardanelles, the Anatolian plateau, and the Egyptian crossroads. The eastern Mediterranean contains the famous route to India which has always been considered vital to any great conqueror with imperialist ambitions. This has been the case from the time of Alexander the Great, until the era of Napoleon, and up to the period of the British Empire. It was the gateway to Asia, and before that it was a gateway to the vast Russian territories on the borders of Europe and Asia. At the same time, Egypt and the western Mediterranean were the gateway to sub-Saharan Africa. The construction of the Suez Canal in Egypt during the second half of the nineteenth century only increased the strategic geographical value of the Arab world. Whereas the Turks and the Persians were able to fight against large invasions and find within their own imperialist history the energy to resist them, the Arab presence in the Middle East was effaced after the glorious period of conquests by the two short-lived Umayyad and Abbasid Empires.

The birthplace of the three monotheisms. This region of the world is also privileged for having witnessed the birth of the three monotheistic religions. It is home to holy places that have great symbolic and emotional significance for the different monotheistic societies. This is what made the construction of a Jewish state in Palestine appear legitimate in the eyes of many Europeans and Americans, despite the fact that it was undertaken through a settlement policy which hardly differed from other efforts to implant colonial European populations outside of Europe. In other words, by mass eviction of the Palestinian population from its own soil through various violent and intimidatory techniques.

The world's greatest energy reserve. Lastly, the Arab world turned out to be the world's greatest reserve of energy resources vital to the prosperity of the large industrial nations. This wealth led to major damage and upheavals in the societies of this region, whether they possessed these resources or not, and had an impact internally, as well as within the geopolitical order.[2]

On the geopolitical level, European powers feared the loss of control over the Middle Eastern sources of the energy supply. This fear was shared by the United States, as the hegemonic power of the 'free world', in competition with the Soviet Union which dominated the Eastern Bloc countries. It was therefore necessary to keep a close watch to prevent the emergence of Arab governments that might be capable of taking control of these supplies, either alone or with the help of the Soviet Union. It is important to remember that on the doorstep of the Arab world, the Iranian government of Mohammad Mossadegh (1882–1967) was quickly overthrown by a coup d'état orchestrated by the United States when it took control of oil production in 1952. The memory of this event weighed heavily at the start of the 1979 Iranian Revolution and helped fuel its anti-Americanism. It also weighed heavily on the behaviour of oil-producing Arab countries, some of whom defied Western fears by nationalising, either partially or completely, the use of their hydrocarbon resources to produce oil and gas, such as Iraq (starting in 1961), Libya (1969), and Algeria (1971).

Given that this was a coveted strategic crossroads, the birthplace of three monotheistic religions, and the world's greatest reserve of energy resources, was it even possible at the beginning of the twentieth century for the two great colonial powers at this time, France and Great Britain – or later the United States – to allow Arabs to unite as a single state that extended from Morocco and Mauritania to Oman and the Strait of Hormuz? Was it even possible for the new governing elites of these state entities formed in Asia Minor after the First World War under the control of France and Great Britain, and subsequently the Second World War with the decolonisation of the countries of the Maghreb, to abandon their new privileges as state administrators and to take a chance on the creation of a unified Arab state that Western powers would only oppose? Factors of internal weakness and the external effects of foreign domination would in any case coalesce to maintain the fragmentation of the Arab world. This was made even more obvious by the emergence of the State of Israel on Palestinian soil, which shattered the geographical continuity that had existed until that time between the Maghreb and the Mashriq.

The factor of petroleum in the major upheavals of the Arab world

Internally, the first consequence of the energy wealth was the complete upheaval in the socio-economic and political balance between Arab societies. This was most particularly the case between, as well as within, the countries of the Mashriq. This subsequently reinforced the fragmentation of Arabs into different states. As we have seen, the wealth of the monarchies and the small emirates of the Arabian Peninsula exploded from the 1970s onwards, with the quadrupling of oil prices in 1973. Political, economic, and cultural power in the Arab world, which up until then had been concentrated in countries with an established urban civilisation, such as Egypt, Iraq, and Syria, was transferred to countries that were fundamentally Bedouin in nature and which had been newly established in the Arabian Peninsula during the twentieth century. Due to their newly acquired fortunes, they gained considerable political, economic, social, cultural, and religious influence. From that point onwards, material wealth and political careers in the countries of the Mashriq, but also those in the Maghreb, were built on the basis of connections and business relations established with the rulers of these countries who had become all-powerful in every Arab society. The life story of the assassinated former Prime Minister of Lebanon, Rafiq Hariri (1944–2005), came to symbolise this state of affairs in the starkest way possible.

Furthermore, millions of Arabs of all nationalities migrated to the petroleum-exporting countries in the Arabian Peninsula and settled there for decades. They had children who grew up there and who integrated into their culture and ways of thinking, as well as the political and social habits, namely conspicuous austerity and ceremonial religiosity, but also dissolute private lives and fortunes built on corruption. The latter took the form of influence peddling within the inner circles of a princely family, outrageously inflated invoices issued under contracts awarded by the state, negotiation at the behest of the princes with multinational companies who set them up to receive secret sales commissions, sometimes hundreds of millions of dollars, sometimes billions of dollars when it involved the sale of arms. Once they returned to their home countries after being immersed in the habits of petroleum-producing nations and armed with substantial amounts of money, they participated in reproducing what they had experienced during their years of migration. They became the key figures of economic and social life, and widely influenced the moral, ethical, and cultural foundations of their societies of origin to align them with those of the countries where they had lived and prospered for such a long time. Everywhere they returned they were integrated into the dominant political class, became members of parliament, ministers, or people of influence in politics and the media in direct proportion to the excessive fortunes they had amassed in the predatory, oil-producing economies.

More often than not, children born during this temporary migration are sent to Europe or to the United States for their university studies. This is how they integrate into their background both the socio-economic habits of oil-producing societies and neo-liberal American culture that glorifies easy money made through financial speculation and to the detriment of the traditional rules of political economy and business ethics. Together with their parents they have become the successors to the generation of the 1950s and 1960s, who mainly lived in the shadow of republican political regimes with socialist tendencies. This generation benefitted from tens of thousands of scholarships granted by the Soviet Union and the 'popular democracies' of Europe to young Arabs from poor or modest backgrounds who did not have the means to study in Western Europe or the United States. From the 1970s onwards, this explosive mix of consumer society culture and Islamic rigour, a situation aptly described by the Egyptian writer Sonallah Ibrahim in one of his novels entitled *Zaat* (Myself),[3] began to overwhelm Arab political culture, both nationalist and anti-imperialist, but also that stream of it with socialising tendencies or that sought a form of Arab socialism.

This is also the time period during which a puritanical form of Islam, primarily originating in Saudi Arabia, was being exported *en masse*. It overwhelmed and quelled the different tendencies that had emerged from Sunni Muslim reformism during the *Nahda* that lasted from the nineteenth to the first half of the twentieth century. Due to this, the secularism and diverse forms of nationalism that were developing throughout the entire Middle East disappeared to make way for a puritanical Islamic conformism. Within this context, the doctrine of Wahhabism became widespread among many Sunnis.

The early 1970s marked the beginning of an incredible transformation of the social, cultural, and religious landscape of both the Arab and the Muslim world. The 1979 Iranian religious revolution led to competitive displays of puritanism between Sunni Islam, influenced by Saudi Arabia as an ally of the United States, and Shi'i Islam, anti-imperialist in nature and influenced by Iran. It should come as no surprise to see the perception of Middle Eastern geopolitics crystallise exclusively around the notion of Iran as an 'Islamic threat', whereas such a notion is almost never associated with Saudi Arabia.

The impact of the Iranian 'religious' revolution

It is hard to underestimate the influence exerted by the ideology of the Iranian Revolution on Arab intellectual elites. The latter were already in a fully-fledged identity crisis due to the regional failure of their states, in particular regarding the continuous occupation of many Palestinian territories by the

Israeli occupying power. This resulted in a profound disenchantment with respect to modern, nationalist, and socialist ideologies that had done nothing to ensure strength and coherence for Arab societies, still largely dominated by the United States after earlier domination by France and Great Britain. This is why the 1979 Iranian Revolution and all of the symbolism that emerged from it 're-enchanted' a large part of Arab thought, or more precisely, contributed to a re-Islamisation of this thought. This anti-imperialist and pro-Palestinian revolution, in which religion was fully exploited, had a strong impact on many individuals who were trying to remedy the identity concerns and intellectual anguish with which Arab elites were struggling. Since neither liberal, Marxist, nor nationalist thought had achieved unity for the 'nation', they turned to Islam as the cement to hold together their resistance to imperialism and the materialism of the Western capitalist countries that had dismantled Arab and other Muslim societies. This 'national disenchantment' was reflected by the Tunisian essayist Hélé Béji in an excellent book published in 1982.[4]

Many modernising secular intellectuals would repent their past 'blindness' and their adherence to Western doctrines to support the idea that only a return to Islam in all areas of life – economic, social, political, and cultural – could act as a bulwark against Western domination and the extensive dismantling of Muslim societies this had led to under the guise of modernity. Mahdi Amil, a brilliant Lebanese Marxist intellectual, who was assassinated in Beirut in 1987, very effectively showed how 'Islamising' thought came to dominate. This thought perpetuated and spread the notion that the world had been dominated for centuries by the eternal struggle between a 'materialist' and 'atheist' West and an Arab-Muslim Orient that upheld the religious values without which there was no social life worthy of this name (see *infra*, Chapter 10).[5]

It is important to note that at the time, the Iranian Revolution was not especially perceived as a Shi'i revolution. Rather, it was only seen as a manifestation of a return to religion supressed by a Western modernity that had picked apart traditional socio-economic structures and religious legitimacy in Muslim societies. This analysis was shared by some European intellectuals, such as Michel Foucault (1926–1984) and Paul Vieille (1922–2010), which only encouraged Arab intellectuals to follow their lead. During the first months of the Revolution there was a ruthless struggle between the Iranian clerics who had been marginalised and economically disadvantaged under the Pahlavi Monarchy, and the secular parties, especially the Communist Party (Tudeh), and the liberal formations representing the interest of traders whose figurehead was Mehdi Bazargan (1907–1995). Similarly, this struggle was not highlighted at that time. Ayatollah Khomeini was largely co-opted as the emblematic figure of the Revolution, especially after his speeches were widely disseminated by Western media. They expressed complete admiration for this exotic figure of an Iranian cleric who, like any cleric, was looked upon as a future conservative political figure and thus useful to Western interests.

The development of a rentier economy

A third negative effect of oil wealth on the destiny of the region is the development of a rentier economy. The Middle East had just barely entered into the world of modern productivity when it fell back into a new form of rentier economy. This was based on the sale of raw materials in exchange for industrialised products and on drawing high revenues from the production of hydrocarbon exports that were distributed in an unfair and unproductive manner. What followed was major technological laziness made possible by new financial wealth. However, on the other hand, some Arab countries went into major debt. This also contributed to holding up the process of acquiring science and technology since the importation of capital goods financed by loans from developed countries ended up thwarting these efforts.[6] The contrast with the countries of Southeast Asia is striking. With no energy resources or primary raw materials, it was imperative to their survival to join the world of innovation and industrial competitiveness based on the Japanese model, which has been very successful.

This backward evolution was facilitated by the growing number of migrants from different Arab countries who were attracted to the countries of the Arabian Peninsula, from unskilled labourers to bank executives, senior managers to public works contractors. For some countries that were exporting their labour force, as well as experiencing brain drain and a loss of experienced technicians, such as Egypt, Sudan, Jordan, Tunisia, and Algeria, this translated into the disappearance of large parts of the local elite and the middle classes. This led to large economic losses that helped to keep authoritarian powers in place. It is therefore appalling to observe that Arab countries endowed with oil resources, with the exception of those in the Arabian Peninsula with low population density, find themselves in the 2010s to be just as poor, if not poorer, than they were at the beginning of the 1970s. This is the case in Algeria, Libya, and Iraq, but also in Egypt, Sudan, Yemen, and Syria, countries with more modest energy resources. The other major petroleum exporters in the Arabian Peninsula have joined together as part of a 'rich' club, called the Gulf Cooperation Council (GCC), founded in 1980. It prospers in the shadow of an American military presence and inter-Arab divisions and conflicts which have increased ever since petroleum took hold of the economy in this region.

Even worse are the rich princes of the Arabian Peninsula whose immense fortunes come from plundering the petroleum revenues. They have built pan-Arab media empires that oversee the production of daily print newspapers in the major Arab and European capitals, as well as periodicals, and satellite television channels, of which Al-Jazeera is the most typical example. They organise colloquia and seminars and finance pious foundations and research institutes. This is how, since the early 1990s, they have acquired a stranglehold on political and intellectual life in many Arab societies. When the Western liberal media give their traditional lecture to Arabs on the importance of liberalising the press and the media, they only target state media and completely overlook the phenomenon of the various Saudi princes and the Emir of Qatar who have a firm grip on major media organisations. Their ability to put money into their media budgets is unmatched by any other state or political power and completely skews the pluralism of the press and television.

Clearly, petroleum has contributed to the misfortunes of the Arabs – as well as conceivably of the Iranians – by helping to close the door on a future for the societies in the region that would have seen them and their immediate environments, both to the west and the east, move towards peace and normality.

The consequences of the fragmentation of Arab societies in the face of the European challenge

It is customary to locate the moment that Arab elites came to terms with the decline of their society in comparison to Europe as coinciding with Napoleon's expedition to Egypt in 1798. This date looks straightfoward at first glance. This was indeed the first time since the Crusades that a European army had crossed the Mediterranean and occupied a country as important as Egypt. During this period, Egypt was one of the possessions of the Ottoman Sultan. It had been governed for several centuries by the Mamluks, of Turkish origin, who constituted a privileged caste. However, this influential event in the

Levant, taking place at the beginning of European modernity, does not completely fit the bill. First of all, Arabs, like Turks, visited Europe prior to the eighteenth century and were able to observe how advanced it was compared to the different societies that made up the Ottoman Empire at that time (indeed this is an area of research that has been vastly underexplored).[7] Second, there was extensive contact with European merchants, diplomats, curious travellers, and a large number of missionaries throughout the Levant itself. Finally, some of the rare academic research on this issue has shown that intellectual life in Arab societies was not at a complete standstill and that high-quality works were written in the eighteenth century.[8]

Moreover, the Turkish elites were very familiar with Europe during the industrialised era since the Empire was well established in the Balkans and its armies twice went as far as Vienna, although they were never able to conquer it. On the Arab side, particularly in Lebanon and Syria, there was familiarity with Europe as well. This was through the presence of numerous Catholic missionaries, particularly Italians, but also many European merchants who ran large trading posts after prospering in the shadow of the system of capitulations, which had already been in existence for two centuries.

There is one essential difference that has distinguished Arabs from Turks from that time until today. The Ottoman Turks were the governors of a great multi-ethnic and multi-religious empire. They descended from different political entities of a Turkish character that had dominated the Arab world since the end of the Crusades. The Arabs, in contrast, progressively disappeared from the history of the region, starting with the decline of the Abbasid Empire in the tenth century. This was particularly the case in the Levant, but also in North Africa, where the decline was slower and marked by internal wars in Andalusia that accelerated the Spanish Reconquest. The last great Arab empires of the region were those of the Fatimids (909–1171), which extended from the Maghreb to the Near East including Sicily and Egypt, as well as the Almohads (1120–1269) in North Africa. Likewise, a similar contrast can be observed between the weaknesses of the Arab states that emerged from the dismantling of the Ottoman Empire and the ancient civilisation of Iran. Just like modern Turkey, Iran asserted itself in the twentieth century as a regional power, both under the Pahlavi Monarchy that saw itself as the guardian of the Persian Gulf and its spectacular petroleum reserves, and the regime that emerged from the 1979 Revolution which also sought to establish its regional power.

As we shall see, compared to the political and military Turkish and Iranian renaissances, while the Arab renaissance may have been culturally rich, it never produced any positive effects at the political level. As soon as the epic but short-lived tale of Gamal Abdel Nasser had ended in the aftermath of the military disaster resulting from the Arab-Israeli War in June 1967, the Arab world entered a period of successive political upheavals attributable to a complete power vacuum. This resulted from the inability of the political elites to successfully manage the societies they had inherited following the collapse of the Ottoman Empire. This inability is itself related to several historical factors which as a general rule have been overlooked by academic research. This includes both European and American academics as well as Arab scholars living abroad or in their own countries.

In fact, in the former Arab provinces of the Ottoman Empire, what developed was exactly the opposite of what had occurred in Anatolia under Atatürk, who intervened at the behest of France and Great Britain. Despite the fact that Arab populations wished to be unified within one state, at least as far as the Levant was concerned – a fact which was confirmed by a meticulous study of the elites and notables carried out by an American investigation commission, known as the King-Crane Commission[9] – the two dominant European powers fragmented the former provinces of the defunct Ottoman Empire into distinct and more or less viable state entities. There was a striking contrast here with the new and unified Turkey that was being established in Anatolia and along its Mediterranean border. Turkey would very quickly become a respected country in the Eastern Mediterranean.

Consequently, at the end of the First World War, the Arab provinces of the Ottoman Empire were Balkanised into different states. Some of them fell directly under French rule (Syria, Lebanon, in addition to the societies in the Maghreb), and others under British rule (Palestine, Iraq, in addition to Egypt which had been occupied by Great Britain since 1882). Lebanon was separated from Syria and Palestine, the latter of which was destined to become a Jewish state in accordance with the 1917 Balfour Declaration. This document was integrated into the text of the mandate granted to Great Britain by the League of Nations. This was done despite the refusal of the local population, who at that time represented ninety per cent of the total population within Palestinian territory. As noted above, there was a Balkanisation of the territories of the Arab provinces of the Ottoman Empire, which strongly contrasted with the fact that Turkey was able to rebuild itself by preserving the unity of its Anatolian territory. Furthermore, by acting as an element of regional stability it became a respected member of NATO after the Second World War.

Within the provinces inherited by France and Great Britain, no Arab military force was capable of standing up to these two powers. The small Arab military contingent trained in the Hejaz by British soldiers under the command of Colonel Lawrence (who would later become famous for his fictionalised 1926 account of his adventures in Arabia entitled *The Seven Pillars of Wisdom*)[10] never represented anything more than a back-up force for the British army.[11] Moreover, it was crushed with disturbing ease during the battle of Khan Mayssaloun on the border between Syria and Lebanon. This occurred when it tried to prevent the French from reaching Damascus where Faysal, the oldest son of the Sharif of Mecca, had been declared king of Syria that same year by cheering Syrian crowds.

This would incur the wrath of the French army in the Levant, based in Lebanon. The administration of Lebanon belonged to France by virtue of the Sykes-Picot Agreement and Great Britain's support of Faysal's escapade constituted a blatant violation of these agreements. Faysal, for his part, availed himself of promises made to his father by the British to set up a grand unified Arab kingdom. Although they were simultaneously supporting the rise to power of the Saud family in the Hejaz, the British did not completely abandon the Hashemite family. This is because the Hashemites, who continued to exert some influence in the region, were still potentially useful to the British, as they provided a locus for the Arab unity yearned for by the elites of the former Arab provinces of the defunct Ottoman Empire.

Furthermore, Syria turned out to be resistant to occupation by French troops. France (which held a mandate from the League of Nations for Syria) therefore divided it up into different geographical and community entities (Alawites, Druze, Sunni, and the Sandjak of Alexandretta)[12] for a short period of time. Mount Lebanon, after undergoing numerous community transformations as a result of the rivalry between France and Great Britain in the nineteenth century, became a state whose borders were expanded in order to make it more viable.[13] Trans-Jordan was created by Great Britain to accommodate the Hashemite family, the guardians of Mecca who had been chased out of Hejaz by the Saud family, and who were British allies. It was the same for Iraq, a true mosaic on both an ethnic (Arabs, Kurds, Assyrians, and Turkomans) and religious level (Sunnis, Shi'is, Jews, Sabeans, Yazidis, and Christians), where Great Britain installed yet another member of the Hashemite family.

In the Arabian Peninsula, the British had every interest in damaging the prestige of the Hashemite family. This was because they became the champions and voice of the claims to Arab nationalism. This is why, during the 1920s, Great Britain facilitated the emergence of a patrimonial kingdom in the Hejaz, built on the military conquest by the Saud family. The latter adopted the Qur'an as its constitution and the most radical form of Wahhabism as its official theological and political ideology. This constituted a space for refusal of all liberal modernity, a refusal which has endured to the present day.

Added to the geographical Balkanisation of Arab territories was the Balkanisation of their political systems. Iraq and Trans-Jordan became kingdoms as a kind of consolation prize for the descendants of the Hashemite family (Faysal in Iraq after the failure of his short-lived kingdom in Syria, and Abdallah in Trans-Jordan). By contrast, Lebanon and Syria became republics, which added a strong element of political heterogeneity to this territorial Balkanisation. Lastly, one part of the Arab elite was shaped by French modernity while the other by that of the British.

These territorial acquisitions by France and Great Britain placed the entire Arab world under their yoke. Rather than applying the principles of self-determination of peoples advocated by the American president Woodrow Wilson (1856–1924), France and Great Britain colonised the entire Arab world against the wishes of the populations concerned. In Egypt, the British faced a strong nationalist challenge led by Saad Zaghloul (1859–1927), who called for independence and headed a delegation to the Versailles Conference in 1918.[14] This accelerated the development of an Arab national consciousness that wished to rid itself of European colonialism and to unite as a single entity.

The Balkanisation of the Arab Levant that resulted from the colonial agreements between France and Great Britain during the First World War led to instability and chronic violence. It should therefore be no surprise that by the end of the Second World War this region was perceived by the military and diplomatic authorities of the now hegemonic United States to be suffering from a power vacuum. This was particularly dangerous given Soviet ambitions, but it also needed to be filled in order for the United States to succeed the two waning European powers. This was the case during the crisis created by the nationalisation of the Suez Canal in 1956 by Egyptian president Gamal Abdel Nasser. This led to a Franco-British and Israeli military coalition that invaded the Sinai Peninsula and set up camp along the Suez Canal. The United States then forced these three countries to withdraw from Egypt and pushed the two

European powers to quickly abandon what remained of their colonial empires. This was in order to avoid providing the Soviet Union with a pretext to meddle in the affairs of the Middle East by sending aid to national liberation movements.

As we will see in the next chapter, the Balkanisation of the Arab provinces of the Ottoman Empire not only became a source of major disagreements between political and intellectual elites, but it also facilitated the creation of the State of Israel. Contrary to current opinion in Europe and the United States, this seismic event did little to bring Arab elites together. Instead, it gave rise to a great number of inter-Arab conflicts whose deep causes I will try to identify.

CHAPTER 5

The sources of political and intellectual conflict

The proliferation of disputes and disagreement among Arab elites continued to increase following the Balkanised independence process, especially in the Arab Levant. It is therefore important to identify the sources of these disputes and to understand their mechanisms. It is equally important to explain the paradox of how this desire for unity has always led to more conflict instead of success. This is also the case regarding which attitude to adopt towards the creation of Israel and the dispossession of Palestine. Accordingly, after first examining the impact of this pivotal event in the history of the contemporary Arab world, other factors of disunity will be explored, as well as an explanation for the increasing dissonance throughout the long history of the Arabs. After their spectacular emergence in world history following the Qur'anic prophecy, Arabs rapidly disappeared from the historical scene, ceding power to Turkish and Persian elements. Their reestablishment in the history of the region took place at a time when their experience with political and military power, particularly the ability to reunite societies divided by colonialism, had already disappeared.

The creation of the State of Israel and its impact on Arab thought

We will never fully grasp the impact of the creation of the State of Israel, and the continuous expansion of its power in the Middle East, on the evolution of Arab thought. Most of what has been written by European and American Orientalists and Islamic scholars over the past thirty to forty years largely overlooks the impact of this phenomenon on the development of Arab political sensitivities. When they do pay attention to it, it is often in the framework of a simplistic and malicious hypothesis within which the Israeli issue has been artificially inflated by the propaganda of Arab nationalists, politicians, and intellectuals who would do better to focus on the serious problems internal to their own societies.

Nonetheless it would be simply astonishing not to accept that the existence of Israel further complicated the already complex problematics with which Arab thought has grappled since the early nineteenth century. This exemplifies profound bad faith, albeit unconsciously, which can only be explained in terms of the trauma caused by the destruction of Europe's Jews during the Second World War. This trauma is so profound that I have endeavoured to describe in several articles how, for Europeans, Israel is a 'righteous accomplishment' of history, and how anyone who challenges this is seen as a virulent anti-Semite whose gestures are of no importance to the analysis of the realities of the Middle East.

For a long time, the development of the Zionist phenomenon was not analysed by Arab nationalists as emerging from within the complexity of European history. Rather, they considered it to be a simple instrument of European colonialism, especially British colonialism. Arab thought considered that the growing Jewish presence in Palestine would be reduced or brought under control by the time European colonialism was driven out of the Arab world. Seen as a product of British colonial power, they believed it would disappear along with it. This settlement colonisation was considered to be the same type as that in Algeria or in South Africa, and it was thus better to focus on the problems of national construction and on strengthening the solidarity between national liberation movements. This solidarity, embodied by the Non-Aligned Movement whose active members included Egypt and many other Arab countries, is what made it possible to have the United Nations General Assembly approve a resolution condemning Zionism as a form of racism in 1974. The vision that Arab nationalism had at the time of Israel as a purely colonial phenomenon thus seemed to be consistent with the general development of power relations between Western powers and countries formerly under colonial domination.

In fact, until that time there was no 'Jewish question' for the Arab intelligentsia in the Middle East. Arab culture, unlike European culture, accepted the religious pluralism that existed in the societies where it was dominant. The presence of Christians and Jews was part of the social and cultural landscape. The Arab conquests in the name of Islam did not bring about the disappearance of the followers of the two other monotheisms that preceded the prophecy of Muhammad. Even though Christianity disappeared from North Africa, for reasons that have yet to be understood, this was not the case in the Levant where several Christian and Jewish communities, of varying size according to region, played high-level roles in political, economic, and cultural life. The virulent anti-Semitism characteristic of Europe did not exist at this time because the European culture that practiced it was not yet well known. Since the main episodes of the Old Testament were sanctioned and narrated in the Qur'an, many Arabs bore as given names, or surnames, those of the great prophets. It was thus possible to be named Moses or Abraham, Aaron or Isaac, without this indicating that someone was Jewish. Nor did this cause the least bit of antipathy or distrust as it did in European culture.

The draft treaty with the British, initialed by Emir Faysal Al-Hashemi in 1919, according to which the British would assist with the project of a United Arab Kingdom sought by Arabs, while the emir would commit to allowing the envisaged project for a Jewish 'national homeland' in Palestine to materialise,[1] provides proof of this Arab 'innocence' with respect to the Zionist phenomenon. The treaty was never signed, however, since the British never kept the promise they made in 1917 to the emir's father, Sharif Hussein, who at that time was guardian of the holy sites of Mecca and Medina. It was only later that the Arab nationalists of the 1950s considered this act to be wretched behaviour on the part of an emir whom they saw as being completely submissive to British wishes.

The Zionist phenomenon was therefore not of central concern to Arab political culture during the first half of the twentieth century. It was not until 1948, when armed militias sanctioned by the British mandatory power in Palestine scored a resounding victory over the Arab regular armies and a few volunteer Arab militias, that the issue of the spoliation of Palestinian rights was placed at the forefront of Arab national consciousness. The successive Arab-Israeli wars in 1956, 1967, 1973, and 1982 (the invasion of Lebanon and occupation of Beirut) contributed to maintaining the centrality of Palestine within Arab collective consciousness.

The analyses of the Israeli phenomenon and the policies that required implementation in order to free Palestine would soon become the subject of numerous disagreements among Arab leaders and intellectuals involved in politics. These are still ongoing today and have contributed to dividing the

Palestinian movements that made up the Palestinian Liberation Organisation (PLO).

The notion of imperialism as a basis for explanation continued to be prevalent after the United States became the major supporter of Israel from the 1980s onwards. Not only did the Americans take over this role from Great Britain, but they enhanced it. There was an easy tendency at that time to denounce the influence of the Jewish lobby to explain the behaviour of an American government that hardly showed any concern for the legitimacy of the Palestinian cause. In addition, by repeatedly vetoing the proposals of the United Nations Security Council to condemn Israel, the United States placed this country above accepted principles of international law.

Moreover, there is no doubt that the status of 'Jewish state' attributed to Israel has inevitably produced profound repercussions, although possibly at an unconscious level, within Islamist movements. Indeed, they consider that what Jews were allowed to do should also apply to Arabs seeking to establish a new Caliphate to rescue them from modernising and secular governments subjected to the interests of European powers and the United States.

Antoine Zahlan and I, along with a few other Arab writers, have exposed the deep ties that link certain forms of Protestantism to Zionist political ideology. Moreover, generally speaking, little interest has been shown in anti-Zionist Jewish thought.[2] Another current of Arab thought attempted to promote the development of sympathy for the suffering caused by the European genocide of Jewish communities during the Second World War in the hope that this would bring about some concessions by the State of Israel. This was the policy followed by some PLO leaders after the signing of the Oslo Accord of 1993, but it had almost no positive influence on the brutality of the occupation or on the repression of the Palestinian population.

In reality, however, from the 1980s onwards the occurrence of civil war in certain Arab countries, the Iran-Iraq War, the emergence of terrorist movements in the name of Islam, the invasion of Iraq by the United States, the rise of Islamic fundamentalist ideologies, and terrorist movements associated with them, shifted the Palestinian question to the background of the preoccupations of Arab thought. The fact that Iran became the champion of the Palestinian cause and helped the Lebanese Hezbollah, an organisation with Shi'i leanings that was close to the Iranian leadership, to liberate southern Lebanon from twenty-two years of Israeli occupation also became a pretext for 'cooling down' the Palestinian question within a context of rising hostility between Iran and Saudi Arabia.

The complex issue of the lack of unity among Arabs

In a later phase of Arab thought, especially in the twentieth century when the Ottoman Empire collapsed, the lack of unity among the former Arab provinces emerged as a harrowing new issue. Initially, these provinces had fallen under the domination of France and Great Britain and had subsequently achieved independence as fragmented states unable to unify. And yet, there is not a single constitution written for any of these new states that does not indicate that they are Arab states whose official language is Arabic and, most often, Islam their official religion.[3] Why, then, is there rivalry and a lack of unity and effective cooperation, especially economic and military cooperation? This all became apparent during the first confrontation these states had with an external enemy, the State of Israel, created in 1948.

Once again, Arab thought experienced numerous divisions fuelled by the rivalries among the elites of the different former provinces of the Ottoman Empire, which formed the basis on which the new states were built. Each group tried to maximise its influence over the others in a game of making and breaking alliances depending on its current circumstances and the relations maintained with the two great powers, the Soviet Union and the United States. This is how, even within the largest pan-Arab nationalist party, the Baath Party (or the party of Arab resurrection) which came to power from the 1960s onwards, a split occurred between the Syrian branch and the Iraqi branch. From that point foward, the political elites in both countries created two rival states violently opposed to one another. This opposition was so bad that in 1980, rather than support the Iraqi government in its careless pursuit of war with Iran, where the clergy had taken power in 1979, the Syrian government supported the government of Iran.

Nonetheless, the formation of the League of Arab States in 1945 represented an innovative process. It was intended to be a compromise between, on the one hand, supporters of a complete and integrated unity of the former Arab provinces of the Ottoman Empire, a unity which was seen as the only way to restore a meaningful Arab presence in the regional and international order; and on the other, the governing elites of the provinces established as states which had no intention of losing their new-found privileges by blending into a unified Arab state. Moreover, the respective importance of the Arab states that emerged from the Ottoman Empire varied with respect to their population size as well as their available economic resources. Egypt, due to the prestige of its history and the importance of its political and cultural elites, emerged as the engine of the Arab League. This natural leadership role was met with hostility by other Arab leaders with regional ambitions, especially the Hashemite family who reigned in Jordan and Iraq. Moreover, Syria and Saudi Arabia also had their own ambitions. Later, during the early years of independence of the countries of the Maghreb (Libya, Tunisia, Algeria, and Morocco), these rivalries became even more bitter and the game of shifting alliances and hostilities between Arab regimes more complex. This created strong rivalries between political intellectuals orbiting in the spheres of influence of one regime or another.

This lack of unity between states became a permanent theme of Arab political thought in the period following the Second World War. Pan-Arab and anti-imperialist nationalism thrived during the period of Third Worldism driven by the strong figure of Nasser. But it was quickly countered by the development of pan-Islamic nationalism, as we shall see in greater detail in what follows. Thus, the theme of disunity among Arab leaders became tied to that of identity, that is, to the as yet unresolved dilemma between Islamic identity and Arab identity. The disagreements surrounding this issue were also influenced by the rise to power of Saudi Arabia, the champion of pan-Islamism and promoter of a predominately Islamic identity over any other form of ethnic or linguistic identity.

The three basic questions regarding Arab thought are thus closely intertwined regardless of the order or the hierarchy used to present them. Why are we weak and colonised? What is our identity? Why are we not united? In reality this is a single question presented from three different angles. A weak or poorly defined identity leads to a significant weakening of the social body, which allows societies that are more coherent and thus stronger to take over those that are weaker. This makes it harder for the latter to unite or to enter into agreements with other similar societies in an effort to overcome underdevelopment and dependency.

The six contemporary historical factors of Arab conflict

The first factor of Arab conflict that will be described concerns the political inexperience of local leaders during the collapse of the Ottoman Empire. This was due to the fact that these leaders had been absent from the mechanisms of power for several centuries. At best, Arab social elites had been relegated to positions of tax collectors within small communities or to duties of a religious nature, especially within the judicial system. European colonialism only prolonged this state of affairs as its superficial modernisation of institutions was an extension of the modernisation implemented throughout the Ottoman Empire in the nineteenth century, under pressure from the European powers.

The second factor was the Balkanisation of Arab society which followed the collapse of the Ottoman Empire. This Balkanisation created a great deal of bitterness along with a power vacuum in the region at a time when European colonialism was forced to abandon its domination in the 1950s and 1960s. This power vacuum, combined with the strategic nature of the region, enticed both regional and international external powers to intervene in the evolution of different Arab societies.

The third factor was the Cold War, with the Middle East as one of its epicentres. This is what sealed the inability of the newly created Arab states to unite, or at least to unify their foreign policies in order to escape the influence of the United States and the Soviet Union. The relationships among Arab states were characterised by the politics of interstate alignments, each of which was hostile to all the others. In addition to the personal disputes between heads of state, this reproduced the pro-American and pro-Soviet split that divided the Arab elites. However, during the period of Egypt's domination of affairs in the Arab world under Nasser, the countries in this region joined the Non-Aligned Movement created during the Bandung Conference in 1955. Nasser was one of the main supporters of this movement alongside the Yugoslavian head of state, Josip Broz Tito, and the Indian Prime Minister, Jawaharlal Nehru.

The fourth factor was the increasingly heavy-handed dominance of the United States, which took on a military dimension when the Cold War had barely ended and the Soviet Union had ceased to exist. The American leaders were seized with a desire for power that was completely focused on reshaping the Middle East during the 1990s and 2000s. This led them to raise military armadas on an exceptional scale, which subsequently allowed them to establish a presence in the Arabian Peninsula, to punish the Iraqi people beyond all reason, and then to invade Iraq in 2003.

Finally, one of the most important factors was the emergence of the State of Israel and the attitude towards the ongoing development of its military power, the occupation of all Palestinian territories from 1967 onwards along with other Arab territories (the Sinai Peninsula in Egypt, the imposing mountainous massif of the Golan Heights in Syria, a large part of southern Lebanon from 1978 onward, and the Lebanese capital in 1982), and its regional and international standing. Arab countries and their governing elites were unable to find an adequate response to the challenge of this immense development. There were great disagreements, which led to the expulsion of Egypt from the Arab League in 1980 for signing a separate peace agreement with Israel. This lasted until 1989, at which time this pivotal country in the Arab world was reinstated as a member of the League.

These five factors of disagreement therefore prevented any stability in the Arab Levant and are a testament to the havoc wreaked by the Balkanisation of this region of the world.

There is a sixth factor in addition to those above, and it quite plausibly constitutes one of the greatest internal challenges the Arab world has had to face. Generally ignored by both Western and Arab academic research, it consists of the cultural, social, and political upheaval caused by the enormous financial power acquired by the large families of Bedouin descent in the Arabian Peninsula who rule over enormous petroleum resources that the industrial powers long to control.[4] The full extent of this power was revealed after the Arab-Israeli War of October 1973 when the price of a barrel of oil quadrupled. Indeed, the fortune that has been acquired by the presence of 'black gold' in Saudi Arabia, Kuwait, and the United Arab Emirates has granted these three quasi-patrimonial states an inordinate amount of influence over the older, learned, urban societies of the Levant and North Africa. Through various forms of financial influence, this impact has been just as substantial within financial, political, media, and academic circles in Europe and the West.[5] This change, along with its drastic consequences, will be described later in more detail.

We can date the Islamisation of Arab thought and the numerous efforts to 're-Islamise' the societies in the region to the beginning of the 1960s. This period saw the emergence of the idea of a global Islamic league capable of acting as a counterweight to the Arab League, which was strongly influenced by the Arab nationalism promoted by the Baath Party. This project was supported by the great Lebanese journalist Kamel Mroueh, owner and editor of the daily newspaper *Al-Hayat*, who was very close to the Saudi government (and who was assassinated in 1966).[6] The idea took shape in 1969 during a meeting of the heads of Muslim states in Rabat (Morocco) following an arson attack on the Al-Aqsa mosque in Jerusalem. In 1970, a meeting of the ministers of foreign affairs of Muslim states was held in Jeddah in Saudi Arabia, during which it was decided that this city would be the home of the permanent secretariat of a new international organisation called the Organisation of Islamic Cooperation (counting thirty member states at its founding),[7] whose pivotal member and major financier was Saudi Arabia. It was intended to compete with both the League of Arab States, which was dominated by the so-called 'progressive' and anti-imperialist states, and the Non-Aligned Movement. In 1974, the Islamic Development Bank was created in Jeddah. Sometime later, in the 1980s, tens of thousands of young Arab fighters were trained in Saudi Arabia and Pakistan to fight the Soviet occupation of Afghanistan. At a time when Israel's occupation of all of Palestine had been ongoing since 1967, Arab states behaved as if Afghanistan were a major ally.

These six points are strong explanatory factors for the conflict and violence that have affected the Arab world since its independence. Through a process of Balkanisation, it was fragmented into a plurality of states with questionable borders as well as highly variable geographical sizes and population densities. As has been demonstrated, this fragmentation contrasts with the reconstitution in the 1920s of the modern Turkish state that was buttressed by the vast territory of Anatolia as well as its maritime fronts on the Mediterranean and the Black Sea. It also contrasts with the continuity of the Iranian state. Despite dynastic changes and a political regime change in 1979, Iran is an immense entity and heir to one of the oldest civilisations in the Middle East. These two bodies were thus able to form coherent states founded on an active nationalism that kept the major powers at bay, especially in Turkey. This was less the case in Iran under the Pahlavi Dynasty during which time Russia and Great Britain as well as the United States interfered in its internal affairs. The reaction to this was felt during the Iranian Revolution of 1979.[8]

In the Arab world, external interference as well as interference from powerful Arab states in the affairs of other states in the region has become the rule since independence. Hence, starting in 2011, even the Principality of Qatar, a miniscule and decidedly undemocratic state, has sought to be a major player on the Arab revolutionary scene by supporting various Islamic movements, the Muslim Brotherhood, and armed groups aligned with Osama bin Laden. On the intellectual level, a political and geopolitical culture of dependency on international powers has developed. Since the attention of political scientists, sociologists, and major media analysts is monopolised on a daily basis by the politics of the major powers, or regional powers, it has not focused on the reasons for the innate weaknesses of Arab states and the ways to remedy them. Arab intellectuals coping with political and geopolitical issues are thus intensely focused on the analysis of foreign powers, which they end up knowing better than their own countries.

This explains why so much of what has been written about Arabs in the contemporary world has over the past few decades been affected by an appalling 'presentism.' Indeed, the situations of the moment are described exclusively within their geopolitical context without taking into account the chaotic historical developments and internal social upheavals that Arab societies have experienced.[9] The historical understanding of these dramatic historical contexts is rarely raised, which leaves the field open to debilitating interpretations of an anthropological and essentialist nature. These interpretations fossilise the Arab individual into a few facile stereotypes such as tribalism, patriarchal family structures, negative aspects of Islam (the religion of a great majority of Arabs), the inferior status of women, the rejection of the other that borders on fanaticism, authoritarianism, and other flaws; all of which explain violence as something that is allegedly inherent to Arab societies. In contrast, the detailed knowledge of the workings of European powers and the United States is very sophisticated, with every utterance by an expert or minister scrutinised in minute detail.

These contemporary factors have created a rocky geopolitical environment and a complicated general context for the harmonious political development of Arab societies, and thus for their political thinkers. These factors also came as a surprise to Arab societies and their elites who had not exercised sovereign political power for centuries. The Arab renaissance, which began in the nineteenth century, gave rise to aspirations for change and for overcoming the decline of Arab societies in comparison to Europe. The shifting political contexts progressively led to the conflicts that I have identified and increasingly divided Arab thought. But these no doubt also had deeper roots, not just within the 'great discord' described by Hichem Djaït. They were also rooted in the fact that for a long time, Arab elites had lost the experience of unified power and now found themselves struggling for power and influence due to the fragmentation of the former provinces of the Ottoman Empire into separate states. This is a useful hypothesis to examine, as it will allow us to better understand the difficulties encountered by the Arab renaissance in search of its identity, which I will take up in the next chapter.

An enigma of history: the Arab abandonment of power in the ninth century

How is it that the Arabs entered history with so much panache in the seventh century, buoyed by the Qur'anic prophecy, only to make a complete exit a few centuries later when they ceded the management of their societies to other peoples? This major historical development does not appear to have given rise to very much intellectual curiosity and research in order to understand it.[10] However, if we ignore its importance, we will be unable to interpret the major political events of the contemporary Arab world and its failure to build modern states. Due to their complete exit from the political history of the Levant, the Arabs lost the very memory of their experience of political power which the Abbasid Caliphs ceded to their Turkish or Persian praetorian guards.

Many factors explain this historical enigma, but pending more in-depth research and historical inquiry, only certain assumptions can be made. From a demographical point of view, the Arabs were a minority within the vast territories they conquered and they largely blended with the populations of their new empire. Some populations were Arabised but not Islamicised, which was especially the case concerning Christians in the Levant. Others were Islamicised but not Arabised, which was the case concerning the Amazighs in North Africa and the Kurds in the Mesopotamian Levant. If we take into consideration the rivalries that tore apart the dominant Arab group following the death of the Prophet, especially the splits surrounding his succession that gave rise to different readings of the Qur'anic prophecy, it is possible to understand how Arab domination was unable to endure.

It should be added that this governing class of Arab notables widely practiced intermarriage with the women of other peoples – Turkish, Iranian, Circassian, and Byzantine. Thus, the dominant group did not remain closed. With the great wealth it had acquired, it ended up losing the momentum of the early conquests. Moreover, when no rules for succession to the head of the empire were adopted, this only exacerbated the internal rivalries between brothers who were candidates for succession. Theoretically, every new caliph was supposed to receive approval from the club of great notables, the *bay 'a,* but this tradition quickly disappeared. Political life, particularly under the Abbasid Empire, consisted of one assassination after another of caliphs or sons of caliphs designated for succession. Three of the four caliphs known as the 'righteous,' who inherited the political role of the Prophet, had already been assassinated. In the Ottoman Empire, the assassination of contenders for succession, or of the children of the sultan designated for succession, also became commonplace. This is why dynasties did not last very long. This is also why, from the outset, state structures were frail. In Europe, in contrast, these structures were bolstered by the strengthening of the dynastic monarchical regime by divine right which emphasised primogeniture.

Another element that explains this major development can be found in the broad political and military decentralisation of the two Arab empires, made necessary by the extent of their conquests. The provincial governors appointed by the caliph were given far-reaching powers, and as a result they developed strong personal ambitions. Therefore, although the Abbasid Empire theoretically remained an entity until the Mongolian invasions in the thirteenth century, it had actually split into several independent sultanates, a fact that renders meaningless the theory of the caliphate and the necessary political unity of the believers.

Indeed, as early as 945, a Persian family who had converted to Shi'ism and whose members were involved in different armies of the caliph, effectively gained power in Baghdad and founded a dynasty of 'great emirs,' the Buyids or the Buwayhids (945–1055). The caliph's power was only nominal at that point. Numerous rebellions driven by socialist-like principles had broken out in the empire as early as the ninth century, particularly a revolt by slaves (*zanj*) with Shi'i leanings that took place in the southern part of present-day Iraq (869–883). The slaves tried to organise into a state before the central power ordered a massive armed intervention to crush them. Another famous rebellion in the history of this period is that of the Qarmatians. This group also had Shi'i tendencies (Ismaili), including a form of socialism that prefigured the birth of a Qarmatian state on the island of Bahrain in 899, and which had a profound influence on the entire region. Also of note is the important Kharijite Rebellion in North Africa between 943 and 947.

At the same time, in Egypt, the Turkish governors appointed by the caliphs seized power and became completely autonomous, successively founding the Tulunid Dynasty (878–905) and the Ikshidid Dynasty (935–969). The arrival of the Fatimids from North Africa in 969 led to the establishment of a Fatimid Caliphate in Cairo that practiced Ismailism and which lasted until 1071, the year the Seljuq Turks conquered the Arabised Levant.

In the meantime, a dynasty of Arab emirs, the Hamdanids, established a powerful and brilliant kingship (936–967) in Aleppo and Mosul that was heavily influenced by Shi'ism. The marginalisation of Shi'ism only began with the domination by the Seljuq Turks (1055–1094), who became the protectors of the caliphs in Baghdad because the latter were now more powerless than ever.

Following the Abbasid Empire, no other political entity was ever able to reunite all Muslims again. Even the Ottoman Empire only reigned over a small part of Islamised societies. Political and cultural vitality had shifted to the Indian continent where the Moghul Empire had created a brilliant synthesis between Hindu and Muslim civilisation. Moreover, starting in the sixteenth century, the Ottoman Empire was weakened by endless wars with the Persian Empire that mostly revolved around domination of the Mesopotamian Basin and the Caucasus.

Finally, we must not forget the muted struggle in the early centuries of Islam between the Arab and non-Arab elements of both the Umayyad and Abbasid Caliphates. Although Islam does not recognise any distinction between believers of different ethnic origins, except on the basis of their piety, the fact remains that the Arab element considered itself to be favoured by God. This was because God had sent a revelation to humanity through the Arab people and in the Arabic language. Having spread this revelation far and wide through military conquests, or by more peaceful means through Arab merchants in the Far East, the Arab elites who were the bearers of this new religion saw themselves as an aristocratic class in comparison to the conquered peoples. Any insurgency movements among the conquered peoples were considered to be a grave danger to their cohesion. A special term was used to designate national awakenings on the part of people who had been conquered and Islamised, but who had kept their culture and heritage, such as the Persians. This was the concept of the *shu'ubiyya*, which can be translated as the notion of ethnic 'populism.' It is analogous to cosmopolitanism as opposed to nationalism since the term *shu'ubiyya* designates those peoples who did not recognise that they were under absolute Arab domination. Moreover, during the early centuries of Islam, the non-Arabs were called *mawali* ('clients') who were now under the protection of new Arab masters.

In the end, the question is whether the Arabs were outdone by the indigenous elements, Persians and Turks, with whom they had maintained close relations as they expanded the brilliant Islamic civilisation that they had initiated and in which they played a key role. An answer to this question would require socio-economic research of a historical nature in the wider framework of the issues laid out here. In particular, it would require a departure from the perpetual conflation of Islamic and Arab identity in order to properly distinguish between the profane history of the peoples of the Middle East and their religious history; that is, the history of the Islamic religion and its complexity, which is much like the history of Christianity.

This notion of populism took centre stage again when Arab nationalism was revived in the twentieth century after so many centuries of dormancy. It was disproportionately used in the context of the war that Iraq started with Iran in 1980. Saddam Hussein, followed by many Arab nationalist intellectuals, evoked time and again the 'Persian danger' to Arab national identity. They also evoked the great victories of the Arab armies during the conquest of Persian territory, particularly the one known as al-Qadisiyyah in 636, during which the Persian armies were definitively defeated. Nowadays, with the intensification of the rivalry between Saudi Arabia and Iran, Arab polemicists have abandoned the field of the clash of national identities and have returned to religious sub-identities; or in other words, to the 'great discord' between Sunnis and Shi'is that Hichem Djaït highlighted in his work.

All of these explanations are subject to further evaluation and confirmation by historical research. If nothing else, they shed light on questions surrounding the ephemeral character of Arab empires and the disappearing influence of the Abbasid Empire from the second half of the tenth century onwards. They also explain the ephemeral quality of the Arab-Berber political entities in Africa and their irrecoverable decline starting in the fifteenth century.

It is also interesting to note that the last Arab empires and kingdoms in the Levant often had Shi'i leanings. Thus, the Fatimid Empire (909–1171), which originated with a North African dynasty, developed in Egypt where the great religious university of Al-Azhar was founded. The same was true of the Hamdanid Emirate (947–1002), whose capital was Aleppo. But the arrival of large Turkic tribes from Central Asia, and the establishment of political entities exclusively managed by them, such as the Seljuq Empire, followed by the Mamluk governments that resulted from this, led to the exclusion of the Persians from the region. This also eradicated Shi'ism, or at least significantly pushed it back, in order to impose the Sunni dogma which was more straightforward and flexible to govern. From that point onward, Shi'i communities were marginalised and sometimes persecuted, which largely explains their disadvantaged social standing as well as their inward turn. This distanced them from any aspirations to actively participate in the social life of an environment that otherwise remained multi-religious. This situation did not change until the twentieth century when the states that resulted from the dismantling of the Arab provinces of the Ottoman Empire were created.

As has been demonstrated, any approach to political life and to the worldview of the intellectual elites in Arab societies that does not account for this difficult and tempestuous context will only fall prey to anthropological and ethnic stereotypes. This distortion has been made even easier by the various forms of Islamic radicalism that are actually quite alien to what is known as the religion of the 'right balance', a hallmark of Islam (see *infra* Chapter 13); a radicalism that has caused a phenomenon that almost anyone would find appalling: increasing numbers of women wearing full body veils, construction of mosques that are often gigantic, a rush to Friday-night prayers, meticulous adherence to dietary restrictions, and the month of fasting (Ramadan) practiced in an increasingly strict manner. Lastly, in Saudi Arabia and Pakistan, imams are being trained in larger numbers; and fighters who have returned from Afghanistan after battling the Soviet occupation have formed an international network of 'jihadists' – which is an inappropriate term – willing to go anywhere where guns are being fired (Bosnia, Chechnya, Caucasus, Libya, Syria, etc.).

The Arab revolts of 2011 on the one hand no doubt shook up the political stagnation of an Arab world divided into monarchies that were more or less corrupt and more or less legitimate, and on the other, military dictatorships whose presidents were self-perpetuating or attempting to install one of their children as their successor. But these revolts have also fanned the flames of the most burning existential questions that have remained unresolved for more than fifty years. This is why it is important to study in more detail the diverse aspects of Arab political thought since its opening up to European modernity.

CHAPTER 6

The factors that led to a renaissance of thought

From the expedition of Napoleon Bonaparte to the present day, many questions have haunted successive generations of Arab thinkers. As will be demonstrated, the answers have differed from one generation to another. Nonetheless, the same nagging and painful questions continue to be the subject of strong ideological disagreements between different ways of thinking about and grasping the evolution of the world and the challenges facing Arab societies.

Once the European presence along the southern shores of the Mediterranean became multi-faceted, it was no longer possible to avoid an in-depth reflection on the causes of the civilisational decline experienced by Arabs as well as Ottoman Turks, their rulers and protectors, whose almighty power had been challenged. As we shall see, the basis for this reflection was established by Rifa'a al-Tahtawi in his account of the time he spent in Paris in 1826. There are three specific issues he addresses in this text: education and science, the status of women, and the modern form of dynamic social cohesion embodied by the liberty and equality of individuals in their status as citizens. This indicates that the issues that even today continue to occupy Arab thought were actually already formulated almost two hundred years ago.

Identities and historical decline?

Given that this is the case, there is a broader question that must be examined. At what level of identity should the issue of historical decline be addressed?

Should it be asked at the level of Muslim consciousness in general? This consciousness has largely structured social and family mores shared by Turks and Arabs, and even by Iranians; in other words, by all three major ethnic groups that make up the entire region known as the Middle East. Or should it instead be asked more specifically with respect to the Egyptian society from which al-Tahtawi originated? Or even more broadly with respect to Arab society, to which Egypt belongs through its language and its culture? The problem of identity thus became a major issue given the ambivalent nature of collective Arab consciousness, which was vascillating between a consciousness with an Islamic dimension presumed to completely encompass Arab consciousness, on the one hand, and on the other that of an Arab identity whose Islamic dimension was only one component among others. Finally, once independence from European colonisers had been accomplished, a third and momentous question arose, that of unobtainable Arab unity and the growing lack of unity among Arab states.

Three major questions have thus challenged Arab thought, but until today no satisfactory answers have been found. In addition, no sweeping reforms have established a better future in spite of all the revolutionary circumstances that the Arab world has experienced over the past 60 years, the most recent of which being the revolts of 2011.

In this chapter the thought of the generations that have succeeded one another from the beginning of the nineteenth century to the era of independence will be studied. Understanding contemporary Arab thought involves taking into account not just the local, regional, and international contexts in which it is evolving, but also the intellectual training of the elites, whose systems of perception and worldview are forged by these contexts. I have already discussed the context of the Arab world's coming into contact with Europe, one which saw the Arab world come under European control after the collapse of the Ottoman Empire in 1918. Despite the colonial behaviour of France and Great Britain from 1830 (the beginning of the conquest of Algeria) until the occupation of Egypt in 1882, the first generations that emerged from these contacts with Europe continued to be in tune with the progress of the industrial civilisation broadly embodied by the European powers, and to a lesser extent by the United States starting with the role it played in the First World War.

Firstly, it is useful to focus on the complex question of identity and the feeling of collective belonging before approaching the question of the nature of the decline in relation to Europe and the ways to remedy it. As will be shown, the answer almost unanimously favoured calling for in-depth religious reform, since the decline of the Arabs and other Muslim peoples was primarily attributed to a decline in the practice of religion.

The problem of identity and its complexities

When the Arabs opened themselves to European civilisation, the issue of identity became front and centre. Should they react to Europe's lead and the superiority of its institutions and science as Muslims, subjects of the Ottoman Sultan who was the commander of the faithful? Or should they instead react as Egyptians, subjects of the Albanian Dynasty that had gained power there, while at the same time paying lip service to the pre-eminence of the Ottoman Sultan? Or should they perhaps react as Arabs with a language and culture different from the Turks? This was a complex problem of multiple identities and of prioritising the different elements of identity, a question that Arab societies are nowhere near resolving, even today. The problem was further complicated by the creation of separate Arab states at the end of the First and Second World Wars, the dynamic of which could not but also create specific identities that would ensure the loyalty of their inhabitants.

It was al-Tahtawi who introduced into Arabic vocabulary the notion of citizenship, which he brought back from his trip to France. In the Egyptian context, which was his homeland, he asserted that all Egyptians were equal in belonging to a homeland (citizenship) and that there should be no distinction between Muslims and Christians (Copts), who were an important component of society. Al-Tahtawi also stressed the importance of education and the necessity of building academic and scientific institutions like those in Europe. Furthermore, he promoted women's access to education. The Egyptian sovereign, Muhammad 'Ali, declared equality between Muslims and non-Muslims. A few years later, in 1839, the Ottoman sovereign did the same for the entire Empire, a principle that was reiterated in 1856.[1] However, the practical application of this was not easy, due to the strength of historical tradition.

In any case, major intellectual battles centred on the components of Arab identity and on the primacy of one component or another over the others. Were Arabs primarily Muslims, members of the *umma* (community of the faithful), before being members of the narrower community of Arabs? Or, on the contrary, were they first and foremost members of the state that governed the society in which they lived and to whom they owed complete and total allegiance? Indeed, the importance of identity comes from the fact that it forges political and social allegiances, and no power can be indifferent to this. The Arab elites, up until the time they became aware of European superiority and the decline of the Ottoman Empire, had considered themselves to be faithful subjects of this Empire in terms of identity and allegiance.

From the beginning of the nineteenth century until 1918, the date of the Empire's collapse, the question of identity came into sharp focus because it was this that determined an individual's allegiance in the face of numerous Arab political movements. In other words, it was a question of knowing what type of identity and consequently what type of nationalism should be pursued. This question became even more acute as the European national model became better understood and emerged as a major element of Europe's strength and superiority.

How and in what geographical space should a nation be built? But more importantly, which nationalism should be championed? Should it have been a Muslim or pan-Islamic nationalism which did not recognise any specificity of an ethnic or cultural nature and whose major institution was embodied by the caliphate, which as far as the Arabs were concerned, had been retained by the Ottomans since the sixteenth century? Or rather, should it have been an Arab nationalism intended to re-establish the forgotten glories of the great ancestors who built the Abbasid and Umayyad Empires following the Arab Prophet? Or perhaps it should have been a 'provincial' nationalism because it was associated with geographical specificities, such as the Nile Valley, Mesopotamia or the 'land of two rivers'(Bilad al-Rafidayn). It could even have been associated with the 'land of Damascus' (Bilad al-Sham), the Arabic word for the region that encompasses Palestine, Lebanon, Jordan, and Syria; or perhaps even the lands of the West (al-Maghrib), those along the south-western shores of the Mediterranean known collectively as the Maghreb (Algeria, Tunisia, Morocco and Libya)?

Ever since these questions first emerged, Arab thought has remained imprisoned within this formidable labyrinth. Over the past few decades, numerous Arab intellectuals have attempted in vain to reconcile these three types of nationalisms, which are all very different, indeed contradictory, and thus in reality not reconcilable. We will need to return to this question as it is far from being settled today, as demonstrated by the unrest and violence that led up to some of the 2011 Arab revolts. Indeed, this question is a preliminary step towards the reconstitution of free and peaceful societies.

The first generations of intellectuals and their relationship to Europe

At the beginning of the nineteenth century, Arab intellectuals did not conceive of the Arab world turning inward because the waning Ottoman world in which they lived was clearly no longer a centre of progress that could ensure the wellbeing of its populations. Nonetheless, this was still an era during which the legitimacy of the Ottoman Empire remained intact. Belonging to the Empire was experienced as being faithful to a Muslim political entity whose leader often bore the title of caliph. This title is in fact inappropriate, since this leader did not bring together all Muslims, indeed, not even the majority of them. In Egypt, which had become the intellectual centre of the Arab world since the beginning of Muhammad 'Ali's reign in 1805, the trend was towards greater autonomy for the Pasha of Egypt with respect to the Sublime Porte (the central government of the Ottoman Empire). Muhammad 'Ali set out to unify all Arabs by conquering Libya, Syria, and Palestine in 1830, eventually seeking to replace the Ottoman Sultan by attempting to conquer Istanbul, which led to a serious crisis with the European powers as well as among the European powers themselves. Nonetheless, in 1840, the Egyptian expansion was halted by their joint military intervention. In return for abandoning his 'expansionist' dream and his attempt to build a European-style modern economy, these powers confirmed him as 'Viceroy' of Egypt, that is, a monarchist regime that would last until the Egyptian Revolution of 1952. His successors would subsequently pursue his modernising dream in the area of customs and culture.

In the nineteenth century, Europeans were welcome in Egypt, especially Saint-Simonians, because they were able to accelerate the country's development. Lebanese and Syrians were also welcome because of their active role in the cultural renaissance of the Arab world, especially since they founded newspapers, periodicals and publishing houses. Cairo became a major publishing and press hub and subsequently spread its influence across the entire Arab world. The city absorbed a large concentration of thinkers, essayists, philosophers, religious reformers, and linguists. These different generations of intellectuals had been nurtured by European thought, which they transmitted in their works. This helped Arab readers to become familiar with Darwin's theories on the evolution of humanity, which directly contradicted the creation narrative of the Old Testament and the Qur'an. They read the Encyclopaedists, John Locke, Hume, Voltaire, Montesquieu and Rousseau; and of course Karl Marx as well as British social thinkers. They were interested in all aspects of the history of Europe and in the development of civic, political, and religious institutions. For them, the Protestant Reformation was a model to follow in order to rid Islam of its mummified aspects.

They also read the literature of the great French novelists such as Balzac, Flaubert, and many others whose works were widely translated into Arabic. At the end of the nineteenth and the beginning of the twentieth century, the first great Arab novelists appeared, particularly Jurji Zaydan and Muhammad Husayn Haykal. In short, this was a period of exceptional openness to European literary and political culture, without any loss of Arab collective consciousness that centred around a love for their language and acceleration of its modernisation, especially its simplification aimed at making it much more accessible to the new middle classes that were rapidly developing at that time. This major push towards openness did not give rise to protests, nor were the prominent members of these generations of intellectuals, who were completely open to the European model, subjected to attacks by conservative and reactionary forces. It was a time when the most brilliant minds were Al-Azhar shaykhs whose flexible and critical thinking often made them intellectual powerhouses. There is no evidence that they were hostile to European culture even as colonial expansion had become brutally apparent in Algeria and Egypt. Some of these prominent religious men, such as al-Tahtawi and Taha Husayn, have already been discussed. Their role and the contribution of their works will be discussed in more detail in the following chapter.

Arab thought in the face of colonial expansion: the failure of Ottoman patriotism

At the time, the concerns of Arab thought, in fact, lay elsewhere. This has already been noted, but it is important to raise it again. Indeed, European colonial expansion gave rise to an 'Ottoman patriotism' that was expressed in two main ways. One consisted of the emergence of a political pan-Islamism that aimed to protect the Ottoman Empire, which was being subjected to various forms of pressure from Europe. Since this pressure was collective, it was fitting to have a collective response. It thus became necessary to strengthen the legitimacy of the Empire by emphasising its Islamic dimension, even though it was a multinational empire including Greeks, Armenians, Slavs, and Arabs. On top of this, it was multi-confessional and encompassed various religious beliefs – Jewish, Greek Orthodox, Catholic – but also Muslim communities of different denominations. Since Europe was Christian, which was made particularly apparent by its export of numerous Catholic and Protestant missionaries, the Orient was seen as Muslim by its own progeny. Its last line of defence thus consisted of the Ottomans as well as the consolidation of the role of Islam in collective identity as a bonding agent between Arabs and Turks.

It is important to emphasise that this late nineteenth and early twentieth century pan-Islamism bears no resemblance to the one that drove transnational Islamist movements from the end of the twentieth century. The former was open to Europe, to its civilisation and its scientific, industrial, economic, and social achievements. There was engaged dialogue with Europe's intellectuals as evidenced by, for example, the exchange of letters between Jamal al-Din al-Afghani and Ernest Renan in 1883. The later pan-Islamism has walled itself off from anything that concerns the Western environment, its mores, public freedoms, and its ways of being. All of this has been completely devalued and given the name 'secularism'. It is seen as the destroyer of social ties and established hierarchies in addition to being considered, in essence, as dangerous atheism. This has become the basic argument of intellectuals who reject all conceptions of Arab nationalism in order to argue in favour of a return to a single Islamic identity. This is in order to save Arab societies from the corrosive effect of European ideas and the cultural alienation that these ideas allegedly produce.

The other reaction to colonial expansion that involved an attachment to the Ottoman Empire consisted of consolidating its political structures by persuading the Sultan to decentralise the Empire and grant his non-Turkish subjects representation in an elected chamber in which all voices could be heard. This is how the Ottoman Administrative Decentralisation Party was created in the Arab Levant in 1912, which included many Lebanese and Syrian Christians. The reestablishment in 1908 of the 1876 Ottoman Constitution, which had been suspended in 1878, created high hopes in the Arab provinces of the Empire since it was believed that Arab claims for autonomy would finally be heard in Istanbul. Subsequently, it was also believed that the stronger solidarity between Arabs and Turks would improve their ability to confront the destabilising European pressure on the Empire, which had lost sovereignty over the Balkans and the Caucasus. The Ottoman Administrative Decentralisation Party hoped that the Arabs, who were in the midst of a cultural and linguistic renaissance, would be recognised as a major component of the Empire, an Empire they wanted to defend against European colonialism.

This aim, however, collided with the development of the nationalist and Jacobin ideology of young Turkish officers. These officers wanted, conversely, to speed up the process of making the Empire more Turkish in order to bring an end to the aspirations of non-Turkish communities for autonomy and even independence (e.g. Armenians and Kurds). When the constitution that had been re-established in 1908 by Sultan Abdulhamid II was suspended one year later, there was great disappointment among Arab elites. After showing loyalty to the Sultan, this development made them distraught. Since the middle of the nineteenth century, these elites had included many remarkable men, particularly Jamal al-Din al-Afghani (1838–1897), but later also two great Lebanese intellectuals from the Druze aristocracy, the brothers Shakib and Adel Arslan (1869–1946 and 1887–1954 respectively), as well as another Lebanese scholar who became famous, Ahmad Faris al-Shidyaq (1804–1887), who was a Christian convert to Islam. In North Africa, this also included Khayr al-Din al-Tunisi (1822–1890) in addition to Amir ʿAbd al-Qadir (1808–1883), one of the first members of the resistance to the French invasion of Algeria, who was subsequently exiled from his country.

The first steps of modern Arab nationalism

It was, in fact, the modernisers and reformers who considered that strengthening the religious ties between Turks and Arabs was the best way to slow down European colonial expansion. Their main enemy consisted of the radical nationalist and Jacobin ideas supported by the movement of the Young Turks. As the influence of the latter in the management of the declining Empire increased, this current of Arab thought lost its relevance in favour of anti-Turkish and anti-Ottoman nationalist tendencies. In the eyes of the first Arab nationalists, the Turks were responsible for both the decline of Islam and of the Arabs. They were accused of closing the doors to the exegesis of the Qurʾanic text and for limiting the application of Shariʿa to four Sunni schools of law (Maliki, Hanafi, Shafiʿi, Hanbali), which put an end to the richness and vitality of thought in the Muslim world. They were also accused of being incapable of modernising and of encouraging science and technology, whereas Europe was undergoing a cultural, scientific, and philosophical boom, thereby practically coming to dominate it.

The most distinguished thinker within this school of thought was ʿAbd al-Rahman Al-Kawakibi (1855–1902), an inhabitant of the great Syrian city of Aleppo, whose two books caused major reverberations among Arab elites.[2]

Indeed, in the context of this era these works very courageously denounced the absolutism and arbitrariness of Ottoman power and called for the caliphal institution to be returned to the Arabs who had developed and maintained it during the early centuries of Islam. He argued that this was how they had built the most brilliant of civilisations, which the Turks had caused to regress and come to a standstill, leading to its lack of development. Al-Kawakibi's line of argument was taken up repeatedly by Arab nationalist thought, especially since he considered that the caliphate should be restricted to spiritual matters, with temporal matters being managed in a modern way, that is, by respecting the liberties of citizens and their equality before the law. Nationalist thought thus began to flourish at the same time as the Empire was growing weaker, as demands for autonomy were not being met, and as European powers were extending their domination of the Arab provinces in the Empire.

However, from this point onwards the entrenched rivalry between pan-Islamism and pan-Arabism came to dominate Arab thought. It was eclipsed only during the short-lived triumph of Nasser's Arab nationalism in the 1950s and 1960s. Even today, the issue is still being debated on several levels. Some Arab historians consider that responsibility for the collapse of the Empire lies with the Arabs. This was because they put an end to Islamic solidarity through their alliance with the British during the First World War in order to participate in the war effort against the Ottoman army in the Levant. This is the argument developed by Zayn al-Zayn in a book published in 1968, in which he tried to demonstrate the artificiality of Arab nationalism compared to the strong, age-old ties of a religious and political nature that existed between Arabs and Turks since the arrival of the latter in the Levant.[3] Even worse, this alliance with British colonialism, far from leading to independence for the Arabs in the Levant, placed them under the control of the dual colonialism of France and Great Britain who between them divided up the Arab provinces of the Empire. Thus, betrayal of the Ottoman Sultan did not lead to Arab emancipation or to independence for the former Ottoman possessions.

This argument is relevant on a formal level. Nonetheless, the weakness of the contingent of Arab soldiers mobilised during the latter part of the First World War when the Empire allied with Germany was such that its presence on the ground did not change very much regarding the balance of military power between the Ottoman and British armies in the Levant. It was more on the political level that the actions of the Hashemite family, guardians of Mecca and of Medina, who agreed to rebel and join the European coalition, were significant. But this sensational act did not come to fruition since the British never kept their promise to help build a unified Arab kingdom in the Levant. The birth of the Arab nationalist movement in the midst of British imperialism, which produced no results, would fuel the polemic between Muslim nationalism and Arab nationalism with secular tendencies. It continues to weigh heavily and fuel controversy even today. Were the Hashemites merely agents of British imperialism as many Arab nationalists of later generations thought? This is the view of Anis Sayigh (1931–2009), a Palestinian activist and Director of the PLO Palestine Research Center, in a book that constitutes an uncompromising indictment against all the members of this family.[4] Or, rather, was it courageous of the Hashemites to take upon themselves the responsibility of igniting the first spark of Arab nationalism and to rise up against the Ottomans, paying no mind to the religion-based legitimacy that for so long had made the Arabs accept Turkish domination? The question is still open, although it is possible to consider that the Hashemites did well to side with the future victors of the war, and that by doing so they instituted the Arab demand for independence, even if this demand was not met.[5]

Nonetheless, the development of Arab nationalist ideology continued to gain traction throughout the twentieth century, until the crushing defeat by Israel in 1967. But this ideology took many new directions, which will be described later in my discussion of the thought of the independence generations after the Second World War.

Awareness of historical decline and underdevelopment

The second question that concerned Arab thought following its increased contact with Europe was that of historical decline and underdevelopment. A wide variety of thought was dedicated to identifying the causes of this decline and to providing solutions. Here again, complex issues were at play. Most Muslim Arab thinkers from the generations prior to independence identified the main cause of underdevelopment as the decline of Islam. For them, it was almost exclusively the rigid religious conservatism that had taken hold of Islamic civilisation for several centuries that was the source of the decline of Arab and Muslim societies.

The issues of ossification of socio-economic structures, the lag in the appropriation of modern science and technology, the completely inadequate tax system, and the concentration of wealth in the hands of feudal landlords were not discussed as such. When they were raised within the framework of European progress, Arab and Turkish decline was seen as a simple product of religious conservatism.

This is why a key part of this generation's thought was dedicated to supporting a broad movement of reform in the area of reading and interpreting Arab religious heritage, a way of reading that had become so conservative that it prevented the adoption of institutional reforms aimed at modernising society. For these reformers, the social and cultural practice of Islam had descended too far into various superstitions and rigid behaviours that were contrary to an in-depth understanding of religious precepts. Only towards the end of the nineteenth century, with the influence of Marxist and socialist ideas, did economic issues emerge in Arab thought. As will be shown, this influence manifested itself more in the area of philosophy than in the area of research on the specific scientific and technical causes of the industrial revolution. Unfortunately, this research did not extend to the influence of the Saint-Simonians, which was significant in Egypt.[6]

The dominant theme in Arab thought up to the present day has thus been the religious debate and the conflicting philosophical dimensions this entails, as demonstrated by the fierce battles surrounding the meaning of secularism that will be described in Chapter 12. This polarisation around religious thought nonetheless produced an Islam of Enlightenment that flourished throughout the nineteenth and early part of the twentieth century before sinking under the effect of a variety of factors into a rigid and ultra-conservative Islam, capable at its core of engendering violence and terrorism. It also produced a feminist movement at the end of the nineteenth century that has lasted until today, something which will be explored in the next chapter.

CHAPTER 7

The flourishing of the Arab renaissance, 1850–1950: the desire for modernity

The period of the Arab renaissance began with al-Tahtawi's mission to France and extended well into the twentieth century. It attests to the strong desire of Arab intellectuals to make up for lost time over previous centuries, and to absorb and acculturate locally the arts, thought, and sciences of European modernity. In the overview of this renaissance provided here, I begin with the extraordinary religious reform whose main thinkers spent time at Al-Azhar University in Egypt. This is why it is strange to hear people today calling for a 'reform' of Islam in both the Euro-American context as well as in the Arab press and political arena, because it illustrates just how much this renaissance has been completely erased from memory.

This also shows the extent to which, since the latter part of the twentieth century, there has been a break from the remarkable *aggiornamento* of the ancient practices and jurisprudence of Islam. This is nothing short of a 'memory lapse' that has affected Arab political culture, profoundly transformed, as has been shown, by the dominance of petroleum-producing monarchies that export Islamic fundamentalism. The discussions that follow will show the richness of Arab religious reformist thought from the start of the renaissance movement as well as that of the Arab feminist movement that appeared at the end of the nineteenth century. They will also reveal the profound questions that were raised regarding the model of European development, which will be compared to the questions raised by the Russian intelligentsia at the end of the nineteenth century. In the conclusion to this chapter, the complex issue of Shi'i religious reform will be discussed in comparison to Sunni reform.

The pivotal role of the Azharis in an Islam of Enlightenment

The pioneers of the renaissance considered the 'religious question' to be fundamental. It is this concern that gave rise to what could be called an 'Islam of Enlightenment' or a 'reformed Islam,' that is, one that sought to be in unison with modern times. It was not so much the secular as the religious intellectuals, particularly the shaykhs who had trained at Al-Azhar, who were the most radical when it came to reforming social mores through the reform of religious practices. They sought to update and modernise legal prescriptions (*shari'a*) that came from the interpretation of the Qur'an and the sayings of the Prophet (*hadith*) that had been recounted by his various companions and compiled much later by prominent jurists. The reformers therefore addressed the problem of the authenticity of many of these reported narratives.

It was the incorrect usage of a concept that led some contemporary Arab Orientalists and intellectuals to refer to this reform movement as 'fundamentalist,' implying that it was a 'return to the sources' of Islam that would allow the religion to rid itself of the practices of subsequent centuries, particularly those of decline. Some have even gone so far as to include within this movement the Wahhabi doctrine that emerged at the end of the eighteenth century among the Bedouin in the heart of the Arabian Peninsula, a desert society. This was a time when European ideas were far removed from this very isolated world. To my mind, this constitutes a major error because these religious reformers, even when they claimed that they were returning to the purity of the original ideas for obvious ideological reasons, were often radical modernists whose positions were exactly the opposite of the closed and rigid ideas of Wahhabi fundamentalism. This was also the case regarding the status of women, educational reforms, and even the question of power and its relationship to religion and how this related to the different modern forms of nationalism that were broadly integrated into Arab political culture.

For all of the reformist authors, the waning practice of Islam was considered to be one of the main causes of decline in relation to Europe. The issue of the status of women, the absence of modern educational institutions, and the lack of interest in the practice of science were all attributed to a poor understanding of the spirit of Islam. The latter, in former times, had been a spur to the development of culture, philosophy, and science; but with time it had become a hindrance to progress and development. Many writers, following al-Kawakibi, blamed the centuries of Turkish rule for bringing thought in the Arab world to a standstill in order to more easily dominate the area.

Moreover, the updating and adaptation of Qur'anic exegesis was undertaken by prominent religious men who, curiously enough, had trained at Al-Azhar, a bastion of Islamic conservatism. Five of these scholars left their mark on the intellectual life of the Arab world through their work and personalities from the second quarter of the nineteenth century until the middle of the twentieth. In chronological order, these are Rifa'a al-Tahtawi (1801–1873), Muhammad 'Abduh (1849–1905), Ahmad Amin (1886–1954), 'Ali 'Abd al-Raziq (1888–1966) and Taha Husayn (1889–1973).

I cannot emphasise enough just how much Egypt, along with the rest of Arab political and literary culture, is indebted to the exceptional figure of al-Tahtawi. As discussed earlier, he was delegated to lead a mission to Paris by Muhammad 'Ali, the governor of Egypt and one of its great reformers. They departed on their mission in 1826 and returned to Cairo in 1830. While there, al-Tahtawi demonstrated an exceptional ability to master the French language and to adapt to French culture. He wrote an account of his journey in a well-known work that was filled with insightful observations about France at that time as well as al-Tahtawi's perception of the French state and its institutions from his religious and Arab cultural viewpoint.[1]

The scope of al-Tahtawi's work is enormous, primarily because he was mainly concerned with setting in motion a vast translation movement into Arabic of the major works of French political literature. After being named as head of an institute of languages and translation that he created upon his return from Paris, it is alleged that he translated or oversaw the translation of over 2,000 works.[2] This activity alone is what made it possible for Arab culture to open itself to European modernity at that time. In spite of his exclusively religious training at Al-Azhar, al-Tahtawi understood the essence of this modernity. He also understood the vanity of trying to escape from it for anyone who had any concern for the progress and prosperity of the society in which they lived. For him, the degeneration of Arab-Islamic civilisation was obvious, while European institutions were an indisputable source of material and moral progress. This included the status of women, the educational system, and the notions of citizenship and patriotism. He is the one who introduced these key concepts into Arabic vocabulary, concepts which constituted the focus of his work and activities. For him, it was not a matter of leaving behind Muslim religious heritage, but rather, to regenerate it and to give it a second wind. This would allow it to catch up with the evolution of arts and sciences as they were expanding in Europe where they were a source of strength and prosperity.

Similar issues drove Shaykh Muhammad 'Abduh, who was born half a century after al-Tahtawi in 1849, at a time when Egypt had already been considerably modernised thanks to the concerted efforts of Muhammad 'Ali. 'Abduh himself was a follower of another great Muslim reformer at the time, Jamal al-Din al-Afghani. The origins of al-Afghani are difficult to determine, and he led a very unstable life. Nonetheless, he founded an actively reformist and enlightened pan-Islamism in an effort to assist with the reform of the waning Ottoman Empire. Muhammad 'Abduh, just like al-Tahtawi, had trained at Al-Azhar, and like his illustrious predecessor is remembered for his modernised re-reading of the Qur'anic text and the spirit of shari'a, which he argued should not constitute a barrier to economic and social progress. It took courage to successfully re-open the gates of exegesis of the sacred text in order to prevent it from remaining imprisoned by older readings. Just like al-Tahtawi, he was a rationalist and a modernist, and was attacked by conservatives for collaborating with the British who occupied Egypt. He also eventually became the Grand Mufti of Egypt in 1889. Together with his student Rashid Rida, he wrote an extensive commentary on the Qur'an.[3] However, Rida subsequently turned towards conservatism, most particularly following a trip to the Kingdom of Saudi Arabia, newly constituted in the 1920s in close alliance with the proponents of the puritanical doctrine of Wahhabism.

These rationalist tendencies that paradoxically emerged from Al-Azhar reached their peak at the beginning of the twentieth century with the prolific and magisterial work of the three other Azhari Shaykhs mentioned above, Ahmad Amin, 'Ali 'Abd al-Raziq, and Taha Husayn. All three of these intellectuals came of age in the late nineteenth century and were living in Cairo at a time when it was the great intellectual centre of the Arab world. This explains the exceptional influence of their thought and written works. All three were trained at Al-Azhar, and their acute critique was clearly a reaction to the narrow and rigid conservatism inherent in the teachings they received there. This becomes very clear from the memoirs of Taha Husayn as well as those of Ahmad Amin.

Husayn clearly expresses his frustration with the rigid and poor quality teaching at Al-Azhar and his joy at the opportunity to take courses at the newly created Cairo University. Here, the teachers included foreign professors, often well-known Orientalists, as well as Egyptian professors. He describes how he learned French, a language which opened the gates of Enlightenment literature for him. Moreover, he came into contact with the vibrant world of the Egyptian press and began to write as a journalist. He also attended the literary salon of the poet and essayist May Ziade (1886–1941).[4]

Amin provides an autobiographical narrative that is filled with insights into the mind-set of the Arab intelligentsia that was just beginning to form at that time. It is a remarkable testimony to the open-mindedness of these major reformers.[5] In one particularly moving passage, Amin tells the story of how, when he was first named imam of a mosque in Alexandria, he decided to spend his free time learning English. For him, the acquisition of this language was a great discovery because, as he said, it was an opening that made him realise he had been living like someone who was blind in one eye. From that point forward, he claimed he was able to view the world through the fullness of both eyes. What a wonderful image! In this autobiography he also described the time he spent in Turkey in the 1930s and praised the reformist work of Kemal Atatürk who, according to Amin, was already causing the Europeans to worry. This testimony from a devout Muslim who trained at Al-Azhar incidentally invalidates all the later narratives that present the founder of modern Turkey as a persecutor and violator of the Muslim character of his fellow citizens.

Ahmad Amin also wrote a monumental history of Islamic civilisation in eight volumes (1928–1953) in which he produced an elegant synthesis between the state of traditional Arab knowledge and that of European Orientalist scholarship. The work is divided into three parts, each of which marks different stages beginning with the dawn of Islam (one volume), followed by its flourishing (three volumes), and its maturity (four volumes). As a devoted rationalist and modernist, he lamented in his description of the Mutazilite doctrine (see *infra*, Chapter 12) that it did not succeed in prevailing in the Abbasid Empire. Had this happened, the 'destiny of the Arab and Muslim world could have been changed,' most likely, in his view, by avoiding its spiral into decline. He also wrote another thought-provoking and well-documented work on the reformers who preceded him, particularly Jamal al-Din al-Afghani, Khayr al-Din al-Tunisi, 'Abd al-Rahman al-Kawakibi and Muhammad 'Abduh.[6] In the conclusion to this extremely valuable but relatively unknown work, Amin claimed that the reformers could be classified into two groups, the political thinkers and activists who refused any level of compromise with the colonial occupiers, and those who thought that maintaining contact with the coloniser was necessary in order to speed up modernisation and progress to peacefully achieve independence. It is clear that he had a preference for the latter group. Moreover, Amin founded the Egyptian Popular University, and in 1914 he became the head of the Committee for Literary Production, Translation and Editing. He was also a judge in the religious courts and a professor at Cairo University.[7] Two of his sons became very well known in the world of political thought. His son Galal was a brilliant economist who will be discussed in Chapter 14, and Hussein became famous for his book *The Sorrowful Muslim's Guide*.[8]

'Ali 'Abd al-Raziq is the fourth of the great Azharis and left his mark with a pivotal work *Islam and the Foundations of Political Power*,[9] published in 1925. Today, this work is more relevant than ever as it addresses a number of controversial issues. Its author challenged the idea of a caliphate inspired by the Qur'an. This is because the latter says nothing about systems of power except for a few Sibylline verses whose use to legitimise this institution on religious grounds is seriously questionable. 'Abd al-Raziq's work angered the Egyptian king who at the time was a contender for the caliphal succession following Atatürk's abrogation of this institution in Turkey in 1924. For this reason, the book was banned and copies of it were burned. The author also lost his position as professor at Al-Azhar University. Nonetheless, the book was so successful that several editions of it were subsequently published, and it continued this way until the time that political Islam began to monopolise everyone's attention, thus marginalising the works of the great thinkers of the *Nahda* renaissance.

'Abd al-Raziq used the same methods as those of *fiqh* (jurisprudential scholarship) to demonstrate that prescriptive Qur'anic verses only make up a miniscule part of the Holy Book; and that most of the time these end with a reminder of God's mercy, or a reminder that God alone is the judge of human behaviour and thought. The publication of this work makes it clear that critical thinking was no longer taboo and that it had become well established in the Arab world despite the short-lived and ineffective attempts to block it.

Taha Husayn, an exceptional individual

Taha Husayn, who also trained at Al-Azhar, is the last of this group of religious reformist thinkers. Born into poverty in rural Egypt, he was struck by blindness at the age of two. Nonetheless, he was able to overcome this major handicap in an extraordinary manner at a time when modern methods for helping the visually impaired to read did not exist. The education he received early in his life was entirely religious since he attended Qur'anic school in the village where he was born. He then enrolled at Al-Azhar, and it was during these years that his rebellion against the way they taught religion and non-religious subjects began to grow. His talent as a great writer became apparent very quickly. His first articles drew the attention of Ahmad Lutfi al-Sayyid (see below), one of the most prominent intellectuals in Egypt at the end of the nineteenth century. Al-Sayyid introduced him to cultured society and gave him column space in a major newspaper of which he was head. He also advised him to enrol at the newly opened Cairo University.

In his memoirs, Taha Husayn describes his growing outrage at the institution of Al-Azhar and his delight when he enrolled at Cairo University, where he discovered the intellectual richness of a new world that was now available to him through its teachings.[10] He also started to learn French, a language he came to love. Thanks to a scholarship provided by the Egyptian government, he went to France to continue his studies during the First World War. He first lived in Montpellier, followed by Paris where he obtained his doctorate for a thesis on Ibn Khaldun. He married Suzanne Bressau, a French woman he had met in Montpellier and who later wrote a biography of her husband.[11]

His work quickly established him as one of the most prominent critical thinkers of the twentieth century due to the scope and audacity of his thought, which shattered taboos. His work is of an astonishing variety because it covers such a broad range of topics. These include the early years of Islam as an institution and the depiction of the genius of its founding Prophet, the story of the first caliphs and the trauma that ensued when three of them were assassinated, and the lives of some of the great Arab poets. He wrote novels and numerous essays, including one entitled, 'Those who are subjected to suffering' (*Al-Mu'azzabun*).[12] He also translated several works and published his collected memoirs in two volumes. The first of these (*Al-Ayyam*) focused on his childhood. It was translated into French and English, with the English-language version becoming widely acclaimed.[13] The second volume covered his adult years beginning in his adolescence (*Mudhakkirat*).[14] Lastly, he published two very famous works, one on pre-Islamic poetry and the other on the future of culture in Egypt.

The book on poetry scandalised conservative religious circles. He was put on trial for apostasy and attempts were made to have the book confiscated, but Taha Husayn was cleared of all charges of crimes against religion. The book on the future of culture in Egypt was also the subject of numerous controversies because Husayn considered that Egypt, due to its unique history, belonged to the European Mediterranean rather than the Arab-Islamic world. In it, he demonstrated the profound reciprocal influences between Pharaonic Egypt, Greece and Rome. He also recalled how Christian Egypt had resisted Byzantium. Certainly, for him, it was the Arabic language that had contributed to the genius of Egyptian culture, but he felt that the latter should continue to remain open to Europe because together they shared several centuries of exchange. To this end, he proposed a curriculum that would maintain this connection to European culture, particularly through the teaching of Greek and Latin in schools, alongside English, French, and other major European languages such as Italian and German. Obviously, such an opinion was bound to incur the wrath of both Arab nationalists and conservative religious circles who believed that the genius of Islam was enough, entirely specific, and a world completely sufficient unto itself.

In any case, Taha Husayn's life was largely devoted to developing free education in Egypt in order to accelerate its development. Like many reformers of his time, he saw education as key to all progress and development. In 1993, the United Nations Educational, Scientific and Cultural Organization (UNESCO) published an excellent article paying tribute to the major influence he had in Egypt by making free education available to the working class and for making a convincing case in favour of universal education in order to form a nation that was both coherent and open to the world.[15] The article points out that for Husayn, 'education was just as necessary to people as water and food,' because 'education alone is what differentiates humans from other animals.' Taha Husayn's career culminated in being named Egypt's Minister of Education in 1950. He worked to open other universities, particularly the University of Alexandria, where he held the position of rector. He also paved the way for teaching new subjects in universities, particularly in the medical and agricultural sciences.

It is clear that the reformers who studied at Al-Azhar, from Al-Tahtawi to Taha Husayn, had exceptional career paths, and that their works contributed greatly to the changes that took place in Arab societies during the inter-war period and in the early years of independence. Given the courageous and revolutionary aspects of their subject matter, and their bridging of traditional and modern culture, these works would have had much more lasting impact had it not been for the major geopolitical changes and profound upheavals in the relations between urbanised and Bedouin societies in the region, as will be shown in more detail in the upcoming chapters. In any case, it is unfortunate that such an important body of work produced by successive generations of reformers, and which is still relevant in today's world, is now being ignored by generations of young Arabs. It has been marginalised by cultural evolutions brought about by changes in context. The same can be said for the Arab feminist movement. After playing such an important role in the *Nahda*, it has long since been forgotten. So much so that it has been succeeded by an infatuation with a so-called 'Islamic' feminist movement which has fought for women to be recognised as full-fledged members of society from within the framework of an Islamic worldview.

The emergence of a rich Arab feminist movement

I have already pointed out that the status of women was of central concern to the religious reformers. The need for women to have access to the modern system of education that was emerging in the Arab-Ottoman world was a consistent component of their work and very quickly allowed for the formation of a major feminist movement in Egypt. This was fuelled at once by a sense of nationalism in opposition to the British stranglehold on the country. It was also fuelled by demands for women to be free to come and go, to practice a profession, and to choose their spouse. There was also strong resistance to polygamy and the ease with which husbands were permitted to repudiate a wife. Numerous critical works were published on the condition of women which served as the basis for doctoral theses produced at the Sorbonne. One particularly remarkable aspect of this feminist movement is that among the intellectuals who participated in it there were as many men as there were women.

The extraordinary figure of Qasim Amin (1863–1908) is a case in point. In 1899 he wrote a book entitled *The Liberation of Women,* in which he challenged the notion that the veil is prescribed by the Qur'an; and in 1901, he wrote another book entitled *The New Women,*[16] thereby paving the way for other courageous texts to be written on this subject. One of these was a thesis on the condition of women in the Islamic tradition by Mansour Fahmy of Egypt (1886–1959). The doctoral thesis he defended in Paris in 1913 was supervised by the great sociologist and anthropologist Lucien Lévy-Bruhl.[17] Another doctoral thesis on this subject was by Abdallah el-Yafi (1901–1986), the future prime minister of Lebanon, which he defended in Paris in 1926.[18]

It was in Egypt that a very broad-based feminist movement developed early on in this period. This was spearheaded by the energetic efforts of Huda Sharawi (1879–1947), who launched the movement for the unveiling of women and called for equality with men. During this same time she founded *L'Egyptienne*, a feminist review. She was followed by Doria Shafik (1908–1975), who fought for the right for Egyptian women to vote, which was granted in 1956. Another Egyptian woman worth mentioning is Malak Hifni Nasif (1886–1918). She considered the issue of the veil to be less important compared to the decline of Arab-Islamic civilisation versus the development of Europe. She did not directly oppose those who claimed it was necessary for women to unveil, but rather, emphasised the necessity of education for women in order to put them on an equal footing with men.[19] Another great feminist was Nazira Zayn al-Din (1908–1976) of Lebanon. Over the course of several controversies surrounding the wearing of the veil that rattled the early twentieth century, she never stopped calling for an end to this practice, which she considered to be a leftover from the past and a tradition that had become rigid and stifling.[20]

The endearing and heart-breaking figure of May Ziade (1886–1941) must also be mentioned here. Born in Nazareth in Palestine, she was the first accomplished Arab woman writer and scholar of Lebanese-Palestinian descent. She lived most of her life in Egypt where she held a literary salon that attracted many important figures from academia, the art world, and the political realm. She also wrote an analysis of the work of Malak Hifni Nasif. For ten years, she corresponded with the great Lebanese poet Khalil Gibran, who had emigrated to the United States. However, they never had the chance to meet in person. Carmen Boustani has written that:

> May Ziade fought during her lifetime and through her work to liberate the Arab woman from slavery and ignorance. She sought to eliminate the flaws that have devalued and denatured women by making them subservient to the masculine yoke. She compared the worlds of men and women in order to better highlight the inequality of sex-based roles. Ziade was both a writer and a feminist who preceded Simone de Beauvoir in the early twentieth century to take up the cause of the poor, the oppressed, the downtrodden, and of course women. In this regard, it is fitting to note her talk given during the centennial celebration of Butrus al-Bustani and one of her works entitled 'Equality', in which she raised the issue of inequality in society, between the sexes, and between peoples.'[21] She was an unmarried woman whose fate is heart-breaking. After her parents passed away, the other members of her family seized the opportunity on her return to Lebanon to have her committed

to a psychiatric hospital for several years before friends and admirers were able to release her. She died young, at age fifty-five, and left behind a significant body of work that despite her fame, has ultimately not been studied very thoroughly.

The tradition of Arab feminism continues with two prolific writers, the Egyptian scholar, activist, and writer Nawal el-Saadawi as well as Fatema Mernissi of Morocco. Their works and published books are well known, especially in the English-speaking world.

The life and works of Nawal El Saadawi deserve to be given full attention here. Born in Egypt in 1931, she is an exceptional person who became a physician as well as a social and political activist. Not only did she possess a broad range of talent as a writer (brilliant novelist and essayist, philosopher of political and social revolution), but she also implemented her ideas by participating in Egyptian political life. This led to her imprisonment in 1981 under President Anwar Sadat, whose regime she opposed. She even went so far as to run for president during the regime of Hosni Mubarak. Her career in Egypt became turbulent when she began denouncing the various forms of oppression of women, especially female genital mutilation. Prior to this, she had held the position of Director General of the Department of Health Education in the Ministry of Health from 1958 to 1972. During this period, political Islam had not yet acquired the dominant influence it would later have on cultural life in Egypt, and El Saadawi was therefore able to remain in Egypt for a few more years in a role at Cairo University. The condemnation of her work by religious fundamentalists and their threats against her forced her to leave Egypt to teach in the United States. She did not return to Egypt until February 2011. Her many works constitute as much a defence of women's rights as a call to liberate societies from the weight of authoritarian traditions. She considers, in fact, that human beings are perfectly capable of governing themselves and have no need for a few individuals to claim the right to control them, including in democratic regimes.[22]

Born in Morocco in 1940, the life of Fatema Mernissi was much calmer. She had a traditional university career in Morocco, and her research and publications became very well known in the United States where she often travelled. Her work mainly focused on a double deconstruction of relations between the sexes in general,[23] and dealt more specifically with this issue within the context of Islam.[24] She also wrote other books on the role of female sultans in the Muslim world,[25] on Moroccan women,[26] and on love in Muslim countries.[27]

It should be added that Arab women are increasingly becoming renowned novelists whose work has broad appeal. Over the course of the past few decades, they have become very courageous in their often raw descriptions of the struggles many young women face within their families and society in general as they seek sexual emancipation from traditional moral values that subjugate women.

Other major figures of the Arab renaissance

Many other eminent figures deserve to be discussed in more detail, but this is not possible in the framework of this book. It is important nonetheless to mention some of them, especially those who have been forgotten despite the major role they played in opening up Arab culture to European modernity and its major schools of philosophy, sociology, and anthropology.

Firstly, the figure of Ahmad Lutfi al-Sayyid of Egypt (1872–1963), who was born into a family of rural notables. He was the first rector of Cairo University, which was founded in 1925. A fervent nationalist and anti-colonialist, he founded the Al-Umma party and created the *Al-Jarida* daily newspaper. While serving as director of the National Library, he held two government positions, one at the Ministry of Education and the other at the Ministry of Interior. He had a major influence on his entire generation through the large number of didactic articles he wrote that were often published in newspapers. He expressed a rationalist and positivist thought that was a far cry from any kind of romanticism, especially religious romanticism. He was instrumental in spreading awareness of the thought of John Stuart Mill, Jean-Jacques Rousseau, Auguste Comte, and Herbert Spencer, and he translated Aristotle's *Nicomachean Ethics* into Arabic.

Another major figure from the same generation is Ismail Mazhar (1891–1962). He helped to make Darwin known to the Arab world by translating his major works into Arabic. He established a scientific review, and for a few years (between 1945 and 1948) he directed the famous *Al-Muktataf* science review. His works were varied, but they all centred on liberty and its advantages, democracy, the liberation of women, and the tension between science and religion. He also wrote a book on the life and personality of Gandhi.

It would be unthinkable not to bring Jurji Zaydan back into this discussion. Not only did he author twenty-three historical novels that relate the history of the Arabs and the Arab conquests following the Qur'anic Revelations, but he was also a person with encyclopaedic knowledge who left his mark on his time. Zaydan was of Lebanese origin but settled in Egypt in 1862. In 1892 he founded the famous review *Al-Hilal*. He also wrote a history of the Freemasons, a general history of the world, and a history of the Greeks and Romans, in addition to a five-volume history of Islamic civilisation and a five-volume history of Arab literature. He was put forward to teach the history of Islamic civilisation at Cairo University, but was unable to assume the position due to objections from conservative Muslim circles. They disapproved of his openly secular leanings, and his positivist reading of Islam, but claimed their objections were based on the fact that he was a Christian.[28] What is certain, however, is that Zaydan's work laid the broad foundations for the emergence of Arab nationalist ideas that arose following the First World War, as will be discussed in the next chapter.

There are many other people who contributed to the Arab renaissance in Lebanon, Syria, and Egypt. These few examples are however sufficient to illustrate the extent of the knowledge acquired during this period, which subsequently spread throughout society. This can be attributed to the creation of numerous news organisations and the publication of many important books. It testifies to the deep intellectual curiosity and to the fervent desire to see Arab society develop and prosper through education and acquisition of the knowledge required to meet the challenges that arose from the unequal development of the Arab world in comparison to Europe.

The same focus can be found in the works of the major reformers in the Maghreb who were the contemporaries of their counterparts from Al-Azhar. First and foremost is Emir Abdelkader of Algeria (1808–1883), who was exiled by colonial France in 1847 for resistance to the occupation of his country. He was one of the most refined Algerian intellectuals of his time, very well read, and committed to an open and mystical concept of Islam. This is highlighted by his *Lettre aux Français* (Letter to the French People), written in 1885, which shows both his high-mindedness and the extent of his knowledge.[29] The emir earned the respect of the French people through his ability to preserve his dignity. In the early stages of the Algerian state, which he established in order to better resist the French invasion, he regularly enlisted the help of Christian and Jewish scholars. During his years of exile in Damascus, he actively participated in the protection of the Christian citizens of this city who were threatened by uprisings that devolved into anti-Christian violence.[30] The emir's descendants include other important political figures, such as his grandson, Amir Khaled. Born in Damascus in 1875, he studied with the Lazarists in Damascus and completed his education at the St. Cyr Military School in France, where he served for a short time in the French army. Upon returning to Algeria in 1913, he played an important role in an attempt to move the colonial system in the direction of equality between the Arabs and the French. Faced with the futility of his efforts, he returned to Damascus in 1925 where he died in 1936.[31]

Khayr al-Din al-Tunisi (1822–1890) is another major figure. Born in the Caucasus region, he was brought to Tunisia when he was seventeen years old. With his exceptional intellectual abilities, he was able to build a remarkable career within the Tunisian government. He became minister of the Navy, then President of the Council of State, whose statutes he had authored, and finally, Prime Minister. He is credited with the first wave of modernisation in Tunisia. But he was manoeuvred out of power by the local bey and in 1878 went into exile in Istanbul, where he spent the rest of his days. In Istanbul, Sultan Abdulhamid II put his abilities to good use because he became prime minister after overseeing a commission on the financial reform of the Ottoman Empire. Faced with a number of obstacles, he resigned from his position in 1879 and became a member of the Council of Notables. He left behind a large body of written work, in particular a very informative book on the causes of the prosperity of nations, which bears the eloquent title of *Aqwam al-masalik li ma 'rifat ahwal al-mamalik* (The Surest Path to Knowledge concerning the Condition of Countries). His memoirs *À mes enfants: ma vie privée et politique* (To My Children: My Private and Political Life) were written in French and describe his struggles to reform Tunisia as well as Ottoman institutions and his fight against corruption.

As a member of a later generation, 'Abd al-Hamid Ibn Badis (1889–1940) played a major role in the formation of a nationalist movement in his country Algeria. He studied at Al-Zaytuna, a religious university in Tunisia, which, similar to Al-Azhar in the Mashriq, had widespread influence on the societies of the Maghreb. After travelling to Mecca and Damascus, where he became familiar with the reformist thinking of the Mashriq, he disseminated his reformist ideas through reviews and the Association of Ulama, which he created in 1931. In addition, he opened schools which adopted modernised curricula with updated teaching methods. Aside from his numerous articles and his commentaries on the Qur'an, Ibn Badis was a refined poet, similar to Emir Abdelkader.

Questioning the European development model

In the background of the reformist agenda were two other prominent questions that were just as significant to Arab thought. The first revolved around the circumstances that gave rise to Europe's domination and which subjugated the Arab world. The second concerned the negative circumstances that brought about the decline of Arab society. As will be shown, these questions were for the most part rhetorical as Arab intellectuals were unable to reach any consensus among themselves. Moreover, Arab and European thought were locked in a tête-à-tête. This resulted in an absence of alternative perspectives since no other reference points were available except those provided by European culture. Europe was seen as both something to admire and to fear, but rarely as something to disregard. Its culture, philosophy, and model of development were the only references available and the only mirror in which Arab political culture could view itself and measure the extent of its underdevelopment.

Along these lines, Fahmy Gedaan, who was discussed earlier, wrote a book that took stock of Islamic reformist thought.[32] The author correctly believed that the sense of decline among Arabs did not start with Napoleon's expedition to Egypt in 1798. Instead, it began with the work of Ibn Khaldun, a historian and sociologist of the cycles of history, that is, the phases of civilisational development and decline of kingdoms and empires. Indeed, Ibn Khaldun was one of the most knowledgeable historians and acute witnesses to the decline of classical Islamic civilisation and the beginning of Europe's rise to power.

Gedaan nonetheless recognised that after Ibn Khaldun, Arab thought did not get back on track until the nineteenth century, at which time it resumed its reflection on the causes of power and decline. He aptly illustrated the impact of the European model of progress on Muslim reformists, but he was careful to point out their misgivings about the European model and its underlying industrial and materialistic civilisation. Gedaan correctly explained that for them, in order for Muslim society to remain true to itself, it had to preserve its primary ideals of a just and mutually supportive society, in which material concerns were subordinate to the spiritual and humanist imperatives of Islam. They could not conceive of a society without religion, and all of them sought to bring back the spirit of Islam in its original form, one which had built a great civilisation in which philosophy and science flourished.

In his exhaustive work, Gedaan first revealed the great difference between the lived reality of ancient Arab societies after the arrival of Islam and the idealised historical narratives. He then expanded on the thought of the various generations of Muslim Arab thinkers. By including lengthy direct quotations to accompany his commentaries, he provided the reader with direct access to the thought of the authors being studied. These ranged from the Azharist Shaykh Hasan al-'Attar (1766–1835) of Egypt to Sayyid Qutb (1906–1966) and Mustafa Husni al-Sibai (1915–1964). The latter two were figures from the Muslim Brotherhood movement in Egypt who emphasised the idea that a 'true' Muslim society must be built on the concept of solidarity, which cannot solely rely on social justice. Gedaan's work contained a summary of the lives of the forty-one Arab thinkers who claimed allegiance to Islam and who supported its reform. The author summarised all of their positions in terms of the direction they thought human progress should take.

There is no disputing Gedaan's conclusion. He considered this school of thought on progress to be completely idealistic and removed from the reality of Arab societies. The author, who himself was an adherent of Mutazilism, faulted modern reformist thought for its failure to resolve the debate surrounding the extent of the domain of divine as opposed to human will, a question that tore Islamic society apart in the early centuries. He argued that this inability made it easier for Arab political regimes to exploit religion in order to consolidate their authoritarianism. In his view, modernist Muslims today need above all to decide for themselves where they stand in relation to these two contradictory schools of thought. One school considers that everything is divine will, and the other, in contrast, thinks that God granted a certain amount of autonomy to humans. These reformers should, in his opinion, 'first consider without any hesitation or doubt that, in the first case, the result can only be the immobility and stagnation of the present conservative situation, whereas the second position is, indeed, the only one that can lead to a change in this state of affairs and situation of degeneration in order to move towards something better, that is, towards progress.'[33]

The author adds that Arab thinkers should adopt two main guiding principles for their reflections on the conditions of progress. The first concerns the need for an appropriate methodology for understanding sociocultural and economic reality in all of its aspects in order to draw out appropriate and sustainable solutions for Arab societies. The second is the firm belief in the virtue of liberty as an axiom that is indispensable for achieving progress and change in the Arab world. He adds that the latest generation of reformists who adhered to Islam did not pay much attention to these two main principles. As a result, reformist thought became for the most part purely ideological instead of achieving a balance between philosophical and religious thought.[34]

The message here is very clear. However, Gedaan focuses more on the movements of political Islam from the past half a century and less on the works of the great pioneers of the early generations. In my view, his generalisation of an entire body of work by disparate authors cannot be justified. This is due to the simple fact that its historical contexts changed over the long period of time extending from al-Tahtawi to Sayyid Qutb. It is important to keep in mind that the European model was at first very well received and understood on several levels by the generations from 1830 to 1950. But the model began to tarnish as colonial authority became more heavy-handed. In 1978, when Edward Said's famous book on Orientalism was published, it expressed the pent-up exasperation that had been growing over the course of the twentieth century. Said gave vent to this by accusing European culture of devaluing Arabs, and more generally Muslims, by relegating them to clichés and degrading ethnic stereotypes.[35] This made it easy for proponents of an Islamic social order to deride European civilisation. They did so by drawing on the works of all the disenchanted Europeans who believed that material progress had weakened the foundations of their traditional societies, a tactic that was used extensively by several writers.

Arab and Russian thought: the same contradictions

arabs were not the only ones to compare themselves to developments in Europe. The case of the Russians tells a similar story. Rather like Arab elites, the Russian intelligentsia was fascinated by the model for development provided by nineteenth-century Europe. However, it either took the form of admiration or various combinations of hatred and regressive inward identitarian turns. Battles were waged between 'Slavophiles' who were in favour of an inward turn of the Russian soul towards its religious and mystical component embodied by the Orthodox Church, and 'Westerners' who admired Enlightenment philosophy, the French Revolution, and European political institutions. On the one hand, there were the 'reactionaries' attached to the institutions of the past, including serfdom, absolute monarchy by divine right, and the central role of the Orthodox church as guardian of the identity of the Russian people. On the other hand, there were the modernising 'progressives' with goals of radical, and in some cases revolutionary, reform.

They wished to change Russian identity in order to liberate it from the weight of the authoritarian traditions of the absolute monarchy, and the Orthodox Church that endorsed them, in order to allow Russia access to intellectual and industrial modernity.

In Russia at the end of the nineteenth century, the major clash between these two irreconcilable intellectual standpoints engendered a climate conducive to terrorist activities targeting symbols of the existing political order. From this ensued a context favourable to the long, cruel civil war that followed the 1917 October Revolution. Europeans intervened forcefully in this war to support the counterinsurgency forces that refused to allow the Tsarist monarchy to be abolished.

No-one has described this situation better than Nina Berberova (1901–1993), the famous Russian exile who lived in Paris and whose work was discovered in France late in her life. Her writings bring to mind the situation experienced by Arabs, particularly since the 2011 revolts:

> It was not the split between the intelligentsia and the people, but the split between the two parts of the intelligentsia that always seemed to me fatal to Russian culture. The separation between intelligentsia and people was much less pronounced than in many other countries. It exists everywhere – in Sweden, in the U.S.A., in Kenya. One person watches television, another at the same time reads books, a third writes them, a fourth tumbles into bed early because tomorrow he must rise with the sun. X will not go to see a musical, Y will not go to see a play by Strindberg, Z will go neither to one nor the other but will stay home to write his own play. And a fourth has not even heard that there is a theatre in town. All this is in the order of things. But when the intelligentsia is severed in two at its foundation, then the very hope disappears for something like a strong, spiritual civilization uninterrupted in its flow, as well as national progress, because there are no values that might be respected by everyone.[36]

Similar forms of division took root in Arab thought as it came to terms with European dominance, and this produced similar effects. The same concepts were used to describe the major currents of thought that gave rise to clashes between members of the Arab intelligentsia. The 'progressives' of the twentieth century were those in favour of radical revolution along the lines of the Russian or French model. They enthusiastically supported the development of anti-imperialist Arab nationalism and the creation of mass movements in the form of one-party systems or dominant parties. The 'reactionaries' were the partisans of the established order and were hostile to all modern nationalist ideas and any radical reform challenging rural property structures that bordered on feudalism. They were just as hostile to any aspect of modernity that would marginalise the social and political role of religion. At the centre of this conservative intellectual constellation was the Muslim Brotherhood, which vigorously defended the central role of religion as the guardian of identity and the protector of traditional values.

However, it is especially in the relationship of Arab thought to the West where differences can be observed. The Arab progressives were anti-imperialist, but they were also very much in favour of radical Western-style socio-economic reforms along the lines of the French and Russian revolutions. The conservatives were very hostile to such reforms and denounced the Western life style as being contrary to conservative Islamic values. However, they were not particularly opposed to Western powers whose protection was indispensable to their ability to survive the pan-Arab revolutionary wave.

The concerns of the Arabs in the face of European military, economic, and scientific predominance did not only resemble those of the Russians, but also those of the Chinese. Starting with the Boxer Rebellion (1900–1901) and its subsequent atrocities,[37] and up to the Cultural Revolution and the death of Mao Zedong in 1976, Chinese intellectuals experienced the same internal divisions between progressive and conservative thought. There are dozens of similar examples to note, even in the Middle East. Turkey experienced radical reforms under the energetic leadership of Mustafa Kemal Atatürk, as did Iran under the impetus of the Pahlavi monarchy. Nonetheless, although the 1979 revolution in Iran occurred outside the Arab world, it still had a major impact on it, as has been shown. Shi'i thought, which until that time had been sidelined in favour of the study of Islamic reform in the Arab and Muslim worlds, once again became a topic of study.

Does Arab Shi'i reformist thought exist?

During the great age of the Arab renaissance, between 1825 and 1950, nobody worried about whether or not an Arab Muslim belonged to the Sunni majority, to Shi'ism or its various derivatives, to Kharijism or even to other 'minority' groups that were offshoots of Islam such as the Druze or the Alawites. This question only became important at the end of the twentieth century at a time when sectarian religious feelings were erupting in the Arab world. When the 1979 Iranian Revolution was appropriated by religious clerics, they established an unusual political regime that simultaneously drew on modern principles of popular sovereignty and the historical heritage of the

Shi'i community. Obviously, within the heavy atmosphere of a return to religion in the Middle East, this brought the specific characteristics of Shi'ism to the forefront.

Is there an Arab Shi'i reformism that is vitally different from the Muslim reformism described in this chapter? This brings us back to the question raised in Chapter 3, and the absence of any characteristics specific to religious communities that allegedly dictate how Arab intellectuals think. The research that single-mindedly focuses on these characteristics based on the ethnic or religious origins of the thinkers falls into the realm of ethno-religious essentialism. Jamal al-Din al-Afghani was arguably a Shi'i. The Arslan brothers, Shakib and Adel, pioneers of the first pan-Islamic reformism, were Druze. Later, one of the founders of the Baath party was an Alawite (Zaki al-Arsuzi, 1899–1968), while another was Christian (Michel Aflaq, 1910–1989). Moreover, Sati al-Husri, one of the figureheads of Arab nationalism, was of Kurdish origin and a Sunni Muslim, an issue that will be discussed in more detail later.

The historian Sabrina Mervin has published an academic work on Shi'i reformism in southern Lebanon, an area where a large part of the Lebanese Shi'i community is concentrated.[38] One valuable aspect of this book is that it highlights the major role played by the Shi'i ulama in the modern history of the region. In the sixteenth century, the Safavid Empire called on them to help convert Persians to Shi'ism. Until that time, most Persians had been Sunnis, but they converted in order to better resist the power of the Ottoman Empire, which defined itself as the collective representative of the Sunnis. Mervin has aptly contextualised the reformist Muslim thought that emerged in the nineteenth century from the Ottoman, Arab, and Persian secular elites and their calls for the modernisation of institutions and for movement in the direction of a constitutional monarchy. Moreover, the recommendations of the Shi'i ulama were hardly different from those of their Sunni counterparts in Tunisia and Egypt: '*Instruire, Éduquer, Former*'(Instruct, Educate, Train) is the title of Chapter 5 of her book, which contains a wealth of information on this issue. Similarly, the ulama sought to reform the rites surrounding the commemoration of the death of Imam Husayn, the son of Caliph 'Ali. These rites were performed during the celebration known as 'Ashura and involved self-flagellation by participants. The ulama also worked to reduce the differences that set Sunnis against Shi'is during the era that Hichem Djaït called the 'great discord' (see *supra* Chapter 2).

The region of Jabal 'Amil that Sabrina Mervin aptly describes is a major locus of memory for Lebanese Shi'i religious thought. However, this did not prevent this region, home to a large number of erudite religious scholars, from becoming an important site of communist and Arab nationalist revolutions one generation later, in the 1960s and 1970s. Indeed, at the time, young people from this Lebanese community threw themselves wholeheartedly into communist or Arab nationalist revolutions by becoming involved in various anti-imperialist or Arab nationalist movements to resist Israel alongside armed Palestinian movements. This demonstrates that group identity or affiliation is hardly stable, contrary to what many political scientists and anthropologists believe about identity structures in the Arab world.

It was during this period, in the framework of the struggle against communism, that the Lebanese government reached out to the pro-Western monarchy of the Shah of Iran. They asked Iran to send the charismatic cleric of Lebanese origin, Imam Musa al-Sadr, to Lebanon, where he founded the Movement of the Deprived (Amal). Its aim was to expand the rights of the Shi'i community within Lebanon's system of power sharing and distribution of public office.

Until that time, awareness of a collective identity among Shi'is was neither a visible nor an active driver of Arab thought. It was clearly subjected to the influence of the 1979 Iranian Revolution, which ended with religious clerics seizing power. From that point onward, there was no way to avoid the impact that Khomeini's ideology would have on the development of Arab thought. It had the appearance of finally being able to reconcile traditional 'authenticity' with 'modernity' by sanctioning the religious establishment's strong influence on the functioning of new public institutions, and at the same time adopting modern constitutional principles (a republican constitutional structure and a parliamentary assembly and president of the republic both elected by universal suffrage). Moreover, the ideology of the new regime was decidedly anti-imperialist and anti-Zionist. The liberation of Palestine and Jerusalem, Islam's third holiest site, was a centrepiece of this new political discourse, and thus had common ground with one of the main preoccupations of Arab nationalist thought. Iranian influence on the Arab world materialised following Israel's 1982 invasion of Lebanon, which led to the formation of Hezbollah, modelled after Iran's Revolutionary Guards. Hezbollah was defined in Lebanon as 'Islamic resistance' to the Israeli occupation following the 1982 invasion. This decimated the secular parties and led to the departure of the armed Palestinian movements that had been established in Lebanon after the Israeli defeat of the Arab armies in 1967.

This new 'Shi'i reformism' was revolutionary in nature and very specific to Iran. Since it mainly originated from Iranian Shi'i religious spheres and not from Arab ones, Iran achieved a much greater regional influence than it had ever been able to do under the Shah. This gave rise to strong Arab opposition. Both the oil-producing principalities and monarchies of the Arabian Peninsula in the vicinity of Iran had a very negative view of this new regime, as well as the secular and Baathist Republic of Iraq, led by Saddam Hussein, who also feared a destabilising effect, especially since the Shi'i community in Iraq was a demographic majority. Large Shi'i communities were also present in Saudi Arabia, Kuwait, and Bahrain. This conjunction of interests between Iraq and its neighbouring monarchies led to the launch of a disastrous war with Iran in 1980, one which profoundly altered the course of events in the Arab world (see *infra* Chapter 11).

From that point onward, Shi'i reformism from Iran preached a theory of 'religious democracy'. This theory reconciled modern principles of popular sovereignty with the principle of granting power to experts in religious law to oversee the proper Islamic running of the new institutions.[39] In contrast, in Sunni Islam, power belongs to a caliph or, in some cases, to a prince or king who is independent from the caliphal power but who still applies the principles of Islamic law. The introduction of the concept of an Islamic republic within Shi'i revolutionary reformism thus represented something completely new. It should also be noted that traditional Arab Shi'ism did not follow the Iranian path. Even in Iran, several high-ranking clerics within the religious hierarchy refuted Ayatollah Khomeini's theory of a government controlled by jurisconsults.

The relatively recent development of the specific characteristics of Shi'i reformism driven by the Iranian revolution represented a major change from the Shi'i reformism that appeared during the period of the Arab renaissance and which was very similar to the dominant Sunni reformism of the time. Prior to the revolution and the rise to power in Tehran, many Shi'is in Lebanon, Syria, Iraq, and Bahrain had started to join the ranks of nationalist and secular parties (see the next chapter). This zigzag pattern of evolution clearly shows that political identity in the Arab and Muslim world is far from being stable and fixed within anthropological and religious invariants. The description that follows of secular Arab nationalism, open to socialism and modernisation, and the theologico-political counter-reaction that came after its inception in the 1980s, will aptly illustrate the instability of a collective Arab consciousness torn between contradictory intellectual currents which were themselves part of the broader contexts of regional and international politics.[40]

CHAPTER 8

The theories and political parties of Arab nationalism (1940–1980)

After the end of the Ottoman Empire, the various forms of patriotism that stemmed from the lengthy inclusion of the Arabs within this empire no longer made sense. Henceforth, Arab nationalism in all its different forms began to blossom. However, it still had to co-exist with the emerging 'provincial' patriotisms that were officially sanctioned following the consolidation of the new states that occurred after the dismantling of the empire. At this time, a new generation of thinkers emerged who took over from the liberal, secular, and religious reformists who had left their mark on Arab thought following the innovative work of al-Tahtawi.

However, in the realm of political reality, the contrast was particularly stark between the aspirations of the revolutionary Arab nationalists stemming from the generations that had fought for independence and speedy economic development, and their successive failures in realising these aspirations. The latter included Arab unity, restoration of the rights of Palestinians with respect to new Israeli power, ending the vicious cycle of underdevelopment, and entry into industrial modernity. This is why even today the congenital weakness of Arab nationalism remains an enigma. It was never able to produce a military power capable of confronting either the colonial or neo-colonial ambitions of the European powers, who were then succeeded by the United States at the end of the 1950s.

Revisiting Arab military weakness and its impact

The first military battle that was lost occurred in Khan Maysalun in 1920, an area on the present-day border between Lebanon and Syria, after the collapse of the Ottoman Empire. The battle was waged against the French army who had invaded Syria against the will of the population. It resulted in a catastrophe for the small contingent of nationalists who were loyal to Emir Faysal, who had just been crowned King of Syria. Led by a courageous notable from Damascus, the miniscule Syrian army was defeated after a short two-hour battle during which its leader, Yusuf al-Azma, was killed. The reign of Faysal thus came to an end just a few months after his triumphal entry into Damascus.

This first defeat was a harbinger of all those to follow after the Second World War. It was followed by a defeat by Israel, after which the Iraqi army was defeated in the war against Iran begun in 1980. Subsequently came the defeat of this very same army in 1991 by the coalition of Western allies under US command; then, in 2003, its collapse in the face of the invasions of Iraq by a similar coalition. The same applied to the armed Palestinian movements believed to be firmly entrenched and well armed in the Lebanese mountains, until their defeat during the Israeli invasion of Lebanon in 1982.

The surprising weakness of the Arab military had the appearance of being something akin to a 'congenital' issue. It was a far cry from the major military successes of the seventh and eighth centuries during the great conquests carried out under the banner of Islam. This weakness sharply contrasted with the successes of the Young Turks in their quest to, first, drive out the allied European armies that were carving up Anatolia, and, second, to lay the foundations for a secular, modern nation state endowed with a strong and well-respected army. The Arab weakness also contrasted with the military successes of other societies in the developing world that had struggled against all-powerful colonial armies and those of the United States. This was the case concerning Vietnam for example, and, prior to this, China, at the time of the Korean War in 1950. Ultimately, this brings us back to the explanation put forth in Chapter 5 and which attempts to understand this innate weakness. In other words, the effacement of Arab elites from the political and military management of the political entities that emerged from the progressive dismemberment of the Abbasid Empire starting in the ninth century. This explains their complete lack of military and political experience.

Shortly after the 1967 military defeat at the hands of the Israeli Army, one of the most original Arab thinkers, Yasin al-Hafiz (1930–1978), wrote a book denouncing this spectacular defeat. However, even more importantly, he pointed out that from it a defeatist ideology had developed among the elites that had devastating effects on Arab collective psychology (see *infra*, Chapter 10). I have also described in *Le Proche-Orient éclaté* (The Shattered Middle-East) how a dynamic of failure took hold, which Arabs to this day have not been able to overcome.

What matters most is to observe the extent to which the entrenchment of this defeatist ideology and dynamic of failure caused increasingly profound damage to the credibility of Arab nationalism. As will be shown, after a romantic and revolutionary surge of a part of Arab thought that believed in the redemptive virtues of the armed Palestinian movements that developed following the 1967 defeat, the decline of Arab nationalist thought would follow in its course.

The blossoming of secular and anti-imperialist Arab nationalism (1919–1967)

As the First World War came to a close, Arab elites were on the move. At the beginning of the twentieth century, many intellectuals from the Levant had sought refuge in Paris, to such an extent that the French capital at one point was referred to as the *capitale arabe*. Here they created journals and held congresses, especially during the First World War. For the Arabs from the Levant, the most dangerous colonial power at the time was Great Britain, whose global imperialist power extended to the four corners of the world. For them, France remained the country of human rights and generous republican principles, in spite of its conquest of Algeria. Paris was a large European capital and warmly welcomed political refugees, students and anyone aspiring to rebuild a country left behind by the industrial revolution and lacking the modern political principles established by the French Revolution.

Many Lebanese and Syrian names shone in this context. Some directed scholarly journals on the Orient, such as Georges Samné (1877–1938) and Nagib Azuri (1870–1916), both well-known writers, as well as Shukri Ghanem (1861–1929), author of the opera libretto *Antar*. The project to create a unified Arab kingdom as a French protectorate at that time troubled Levantine elites and Arab political and diplomatic officials. There is some irony in observing that this immense modernist nationalist movement that took hold of a broad spectrum of Arab elites has not been the subject of academic research in France in recent decades. In contrast, several works have been published in the English-language literature that provide a very detailed overview of these elites, of the different personalities involved, and the ideas they developed. As one of these works clearly illustrates, the ideas of Arab nationalism at this time fitted within the general framework of the nationalist movements of nineteenth-century Europe. They all highlighted the relationship between democracy and the emancipation of the nation from autocratic regimes that stifle the aspirations of the people and their desire for progress and change.[1]

Another event that considerably expanded the horizon of the thought of Arab elites was the Bolshevik Revolution of 1917. This was because it revealed the secret negotiations that took place between the colonial powers behind the backs of their Arab allies (particularly those that led to the 1916 Sykes-Picot Agreement that laid the foundations for the Arab provinces of the Ottoman Empire to be distributed between the French and the British). Henceforth, the French Revolution was no longer the only revolutionary model. Marxist thought attracted just as much interest, particularly after the new Russian power organised a 'Congress of the Peoples of the East' in Baku (Azerbaijan) in 1920 that aimed to encourage the desire of Muslim peoples to free themselves from European imperialism. The Soviet Union presented itself as an anti-imperialist power ready to come to the assistance of oppressed peoples. In this way it encouraged and enriched Arab nationalist thought. From that point onwards, a large part of the Arab intelligentsia took an interest in everything Russian. Some members even converted to socialist ideas, and socialism became the formula for the Arab world to overcome its underdevelopment. After the Second World War, the Soviet Union's prestige increased even further as it openly helped the national liberation movements by providing them with economic and military aid. Subsequently, it also provided aid to the governments of the newly independent nations and opened its universities to tens of thousands of young Arabs. This led to a flourishing school of Arab thought that subscribed to Marxism as a method of analysing reality. It offered the possibility of finding a path to liberation from colonial, neo-colonial, political, cultural, and economic oppression as well as from underdevelopment. Arab thought progressively distanced itself from its exclusive fascination with the European liberal economic and political model which had largely dominated the previous century, that of the generations of reformers.

Arab critical thought became more acute and bore some of its finest fruits, as will be described later. Lenin's opuscule, *Imperialism, the Highest*

Stage of Capitalism, was widely read in the Arab world and caused the previous admiration for the Western liberal model to reduce. It thereby paved the way for military revolutions that would change the face of the Arab world from the 1950s onwards. At the same time, the partial turn of Arab thought to Marxism caused the ideology of Islamic fundamentalism to become even more rigid at a time when it was in steep decline. Fundamentalists viewed the extreme form of secularism that characterises Marxist thought, its denouncing of religion as the 'opium of the people,' as the most dangerous precursor to the dissolution of traditional morals and the grip of religion on social life. Saudi Wahhabists and the Egyptian Muslim Brotherhood movement took to using any means necessary against their common enemy, atheism masquerading as secularism and Marxist materialism. It is this anti-Marxist phobia that later led to the deployment of young Arab fighters in Afghanistan in 1980 to combat the atheist Soviet occupier. It also marked the beginning of the decline of the concentration of Arab consciousness on the liberation of Palestine. This was because its attention was increasingly being 'Islamised' in favour of 'Muslim' causes in places other than Palestine (Bosnia, followed by Chechnya and the Caucasus after the collapse of the Soviet Union).

Following this, a rigid vocabulary took hold of an entire area of Arab political literature from this period. Along with the military revolutions in Egypt, Syria, and Iraq, a relentless struggle emerged between, on the one hand, nationalists claiming to be progressive, socialist, and anti-imperialist, and, on the other hand, religious fundamentalists who decried secularism. The latter saw Marxism as corrosive of social ties and likened it to one of the worst diseases that could infect the Arab and Muslim world (see *infra*, Chapter 11). In reality, the Arab intelligentsia had been broadly secularised since the mid-nineteenth century, even if, as we have seen, some of these intellectuals had argued in favour of maintaining religious ties among Muslims in order to better resist the European colonial advance. Thinkers such as al-Afghani, the Arslan brothers, and al-Shidyaq were very positivist and open in their thought. Many even considered al-Afghani to be a member of the Freemasons, which had many followers among the Arab intelligentsia. Their use of religion was mostly circumstantial and opportunistic within the context of the anticolonial struggle. Once the Ottoman Empire had ended, the use of scholarly and open-minded pan-Islamism became obsolete. This paved the way to the construction of a much more formidable pan-Islamism, one which vehemently opposed any modernising reform of Islam.

This was the type of thought that pushed fundamentalism to extremes that Islam had never encountered in practice. The declared enemies of this new pan-Islamism were first and foremost the positivist Arab nationalists whose basic principle asserted that the boundaries of the nation went no further than Arabic-speaking societies, because religious ties alone were insufficient to build a nation. These nationalists sought to transform underdeveloped Arab societies through accelerated development policies. This involved importing European institutions, in most cases either inspired by a liberal or socialist approach. Nonetheless, some argued for the necessity of finding a 'third way' between socialism and capitalism. This led to the development of 'cooperative socialism' in Egypt under Nasser. Similarly, in Libya, Muammar Gaddafi published his *Green Book* in 1975 in which he laid out his specific ideas on economic and political organisation. These attempts to find a 'third way' show up in later works on Islamic economics. They begin with an analysis of the flaws of socialism and capitalism and then extoll the principles of a so-called Islamic economics that blends the advantages of both systems, dressing them up in the finery of religious language.

This rivalry between the nationalists and the Islamists increased with the rising winds of the Cold War that were moving into the Arab world. The struggle for domination of the societies of this region pitted the Soviet Union, aided by the new, so-called 'progressive' military republics, against the United States, aided by Saudi Arabia and the pan-Arab expansion of the Muslim Brotherhood. The issue was even further complicated by the creation of the State of Israel and its impact on Arab intellectual life; but also, as has been shown, by the 1979 Iranian Revolution and the 'Islamic Awakening' (*al-sahwa al-islamiyya*) led by Saudi Arabia.

The post-Second World War generation of Arab nationalist thinkers

What can be said about the cultural heritage of the young generation of intellectuals who galvanised the struggle for independence after the Second World War? In summary, it comes down to two main points: religion and the urgent need to close the socio-economic gap with the industrialised countries of Europe.

Regarding religious heritage, so-called enlightened or reformist Islam appeared to have become permanently established throughout the Arab world, with the notable exception of Saudi Arabia. The success of Shaykh Khalid Muhammad Khalid's (1920–1996) work in Nasser's Egypt is evidence of how widespread it had become. Khalid was another Egyptian thinker who had studied at Al-Azhar.[2] As modern education developed and universities were created following the European model, fewer and fewer Arab Muslims attended Qur'anic schools. Private schools established by missionaries (Catholics and Protestants) or by European countries also flourished. The movement towards modernisation and extension of the educational system to include the previously excluded lower classes gained considerable traction, since Nasser's Egypt was the model to follow at the time. However, the regimes that emerged from military coups d'état and which were subjected to the hostilities of the Western bloc became radicalised. Subsequently, schooling was used for the purpose of mass mobilisation and indoctrination. Private foreign schools were affected, as missionary schools and American universities were progressively brought under state control, or even nationalised, except in Lebanon and Egypt.

This did not mean that the rigid and fundamentalist version of Islam disappeared from the political and cultural landscape. The emergence in 1928 of the Muslim Brotherhood in Egypt occurred shortly after the creation of the Kingdom of Saudi Arabia, which very quickly became the centre for dissemination of radical Islam as the exclusive factor for social and political organisation. Is this purely a coincidence, or a case of cause and effect? It would require extensive historical research to establish this with any certainty. The ideological evolution of Rashid Rida, a Lebanese cleric from Tripoli and a follower of Muhammad 'Abduh (see *supra*, Chapter 3), nonetheless provides evidence of the early influence of Saudi Arabia and its dissemination of the Wahhabi doctrine (see *infra*, Chapter 11).

There was thus a simultaneous ebb and flow within Islamic thought, where reformists and fundamentalists challenged each other both openly and behind the scenes. The reformists were generally either pan-Arab nationalists or, more often than not, what I have called 'provincial' nationalists. They considered the provinces of the Ottoman Empire where they were born as the main homeland to be defended, but saw this within the framework of pan-Arab solidarity centred on the Arab League. The fundamentalists, however, were hostile to any form of modern state nationalism. As they were pan-Islamists, they considered the only valid struggle to be the one that took place across the Muslim world in general. Their aspirations can be best summarised as the goal to re-establish a caliphate that would bring together all of the Muslims in the world and allow them to live together according to God's law. In 1950s Egypt, Sayyid Qutb (1906–1966), who became an emblematic figure of the Muslim Brotherhood, developed his a-temporal and a-historical theory of the sovereignty of God that must be fulfilled on earth. In order to prop up their theologico-political model, the fundamentalists vehemently criticised the European model of progress, which they perceived to be exclusively materialistic and, consequently, unable to satisfy the spiritual aspirations of human beings. They considered the modern nation state to be an abomination and, by extension, they saw Arab nationalism as a diabolical invention, a servile imitation of colonialist Europe. This explains why it was so important to them to denounce Arab nationalism as contrary to the teachings of Islam.

This generation of pan-Arab nationalist thinkers was thus subjected to the constant and uncompromising hostility of the fundamentalists; but almost always received the support of religious reformers. However, the cultural and political dominance that they managed to establish for a few years within the Arab arena was very quickly undermined by disputes between the rival nationalist political movements, military defeats at the hands of Israel, and failure to unite those Arab states whose ideology was Arab nationalism. Moreover, as I have already mentioned, starting in 1973, the quadrupling of the price of oil provided the oil-exporting monarchies and emirates with unprecedented financial means. They invested this in the promotion of the religious book and the works of fundamentalist thinkers; but also in the development of pan-Arab media outlets with Islamist leanings.

As far as their relationship with Europe, especially France and Great Britain, and its history of colonisation and imperialism was concerned, the new generation of Arab nationalists were heirs to the culture of the *Nahda* that had lasted from 1825 to 1950. As has been shown, this cultural heritage was open to Europe and its institutions because they provided a pathway to ending underdevelopment. Although by the end of the nineteenth century colonisation had tarnished the positive image of Europe, admiration for European ideas and institutions remained very strong among the intelligentsia. They saw anti-colonialist Europeans as proof that all was not rotten in Europe.

At the beginning of the 1950s, the Arab intelligentsia was very well versed in all of the philosophical and political movements of European thought. Many thinkers of this generation had studied in Paris or London, and they had mastered European culture just as much as their own. The existentialism of Jean-Paul Sartre and the personalism of Emmanuel Mounier were well known to Francophone Arab intellectuals, and even an Anglophone like Edward Said was considerably influenced by the thought of Michel Foucault.

The rich canvas of European political movements did however create many divisions among Arab intellectuals, particularly among those who had studied in Europe or Soviet Russia and who had sometimes adopted, in full, one or the other ideology. These divisions prevented the formulation of a nationalist thought capable of bringing people together. The criticism of this thought by the nationalists with Marxist and socialist leanings, notwithstanding the thought-provoking nature of this criticism, exacerbated the rift between 'progressive' (often Third-Worldist) nationalists and liberal nationalists who were fascinated by American democracy and the economic and scientific achievements of the United States.

Factors that led to the radicalisation of nationalist thought

The generation of thinkers and political activists that came of age in the years that followed the Second World War had witnessed, as young people, the techniques of mass mobilisation of people in Europe, especially by communists and fascists. These techniques seemed useful for implementation in the Arab world in order to more quickly overcome underdevelopment and to put an end to colonisation. The idea that it was necessary to create a single party, or one dominant 'avant-garde' (*tali 'i*) party, that could lead the nation to liberation and to accelerated economic progress began to dominate. Liberalism and liberal individualism soon lost their influence in favour of a highly secular progressive radicalism.

This movement was accelerated by the radicalisation of the anti-colonial struggle, especially following the 1956 joint attack on Egypt by three armies – French, British, and Israeli— in response to the nationalisation of the Suez Canal by the Egyptian President, Gamal Abdel Nasser. Another accelerating factor was the high profile of the Soviet Union in the region after this date and through the tens of thousands of scholarships it granted to students from Arab countries to attend universities in Moscow and other major cities of Eastern Europe. Most of these students returned as proponents of Marxist-Leninist theories. Henceforth, major currents of Arab culture, in particular political thought, became attracted to a certain progressive radicalism that sought more fervently than ever to remedy the historical decline of Arab societies. They no longer referred to the French Revolution and to the Enlightenment as their only models. Instead, they referred to the Soviet revolution, Marxist-Leninism, and Chinese Maoism. They also referred to the struggle of the Vietnamese people against French and, later, American imperialism, as well as to the guerrilla model of the Cuban Revolution embodied by the two central figures of Fidel Castro and Che Guevara.

Within this radical anti-imperialist movement, one fundamental idea came to dominate, that of achieving the unity of Arab peoples that British and French colonialism had prevented following the collapse of the Ottoman Empire. With regard to the progress made at the international level since the end of the First World War in favour of the right of peoples to self-determination, it should be emphasised that only the Arabs have not been able to enjoy this right despite everything that they have in common, including their language, culture, history, and religion. This statement may appear provocative today, because over the past few decades anti-nationalist theories have flourished in the Arab world and both Western and Arab intellectuals have attributed many of the region's problems to the Arab nationalist period of the 1950s and 1960s. Moreover, many religious and ethnic sub-identities have developed in the Arab world (see Chapter 9) just as they have elsewhere. In the same way, there has been a growing attachment to, in a sense the reverse, something which I have called mega-identities of a mythical nature, such as the Orient and the West, or the Arab-Islamic and Judaeo-Christian worlds.[3]

We have seen how Arab nationalism took shape as a result of several successive evolutions. The first was the collapse of the Ottoman Empire and the expansion of secular Turkish nationalism. The notion of brotherhood and the bonds of religion lost their value as a rallying cry. This was in contrast to the end of the nineteenth and the beginning of the twentieth century when the religious legitimacy of Ottoman power was used to unify people around the nationalist cause in order to better resist European colonialism. It also paved the way for various forms of Arab nationalism to emerge that were disconnected from religion and, as it turns out, strongly influenced by European theories and ideas of nationhood.

Subsequently, however, the former provinces of the Empire achieved independence. This occurred in scattered fashion after the European powers took control of what remained of the unoccupied Arab territories (Tunisia and Morocco became French protectorates in 1881 and 1912 respectively; Libya was occupied by Italy in 1911; in 1920, Syria and Lebanon became French mandates while the mandate for Iraq and Palestine went to the British). The League of Arab States was created in 1945 in recognition of the reality that these states were now independent and separate within the regional and international order. At the same time, this served to acknowledge and institutionalise their solidarity. However, their desire for unity quickly collided with the interests of the various elites within each state. This was despite the fact that they subscribed to the idea of Arab unity within their own discourses and had inscribed the Arab character of their new countries into their constitutions. The anti-colonial struggle that had lasted for decades also had a pan-Islamic character and continued to exert a strong influence. These same elites incorporated the importance of Islam (to a greater or lesser extent) as the source of law and state institutions into the constitutions of their newly independent countries.[4]

The idea of Arab nationalism was thus borne equally by intellectuals who were not directly involved in politics and by activists who founded political movements, many of whom were also learned and scholarly. This was the case concerning the Baath party (the party of the 'Arab resurrection') created in Damascus in 1947, which quickly became a pan-Arab party by developing branches in several other countries in the region (Iraq, Lebanon, Jordan, etc.). These parties also had leaders who were men of action and combat, such as in the Arab Nationalist Movement. Undeniably, however, it was the strong and charismatic personality of Gamal Abdel Nasser, who became president of Egypt following the coup d'état in July 1952, that towered over the evolution of the Arab world between 1956, the date of the Suez expedition, and 1970, the date of his untimely death. These political currents were strongly influenced by a few great intellectuals whose writings exerted a powerful moral influence from the 1940s onwards.

The main nationalist thinkers

Ever since the beginning of the *Nahda*, many Arab intellectuals have reflected on the future of the Arab world, its emancipation, and the means to overcoming its economic, scientific, and technical decline using a global rather than a provincial approach (in reference to the different sub-identities constituted by the Arab provinces of the Ottoman Empire). Several major intellectuals such as Taha Husayn and Ahmad Lutfi al-Sayyid framed their reflections within an Egyptian rather than an Arab context, but the impact of their work was a major factor in the development of Arab culture in general. Husayn's work raised issues that were common to all societies in the region, specifically those regarding the organisation of education and the place it should assign to European culture alongside Arab culture.

Other thinkers were more concerned with emphasising all of the factors that naturally united the Arabs, despite those that could potentially divide the cultures of the Arabian Peninsula from those along the Mediterranean rim. The former were more attached to the Asian continent and were marked by strong tribal structures, while the latter were more attached to Europe. This was the case of Lebanese writer Amin al-Rihani (1876–1940), a proponent of a modernist approach to Arab nationalism whose collected articles were published in 1956.[5] He also undertook an exciting journey throughout the Arabian Peninsula in the early 1920s which produced a wonderful narrative in Arabic entitled *Muluk al-'Arab,* later translated into English as *The Kings of Arabia.*[6]

I have already mentioned the volume edited by Anouar Abdel-Malek in 1970, a work which gathers together several texts by Arab thinkers who came from different provinces. Abdel-Malek re-inserted the nationalist movement of the time within the broader framework of the anti-colonialist emancipation efforts of developing countries.[7] When he proposed that the term 'nationalitarian' be substituted for 'nationalist,' he did so for a very valid reason. In his view, developing world societies were in search of the realisation of the nation, whereas in Europe, nations had established themselves from the eighteenth century onwards and had blossomed in the nineteenth century by opposing one another in the pursuit of power. He therefore suggested that the term 'nationalist' should be reserved for European movements seeking to maximise their national power and extension beyond their borders. In contrast, the term 'nationalitarian' would better express the effort to construct a nation after a long period of oppression by a foreign power.

Abdel-Malek also wrote about Arabs as a 'two-tier' nation, with one tier formed of all Arab societies together and the other of its various different societies (Egypt, Syria, Iraq, Morocco, etc.). In reality, Arab identity is much more complex and includes many more 'tiers' of identity: identities of provincial states created by colonial divisions, which gained strength over time and which significantly overlapped with the provincial geographical sub-identities; identities of lineage in which the structures of the genealogical family (tribes) have remained strong; and finally, identities of religious community (Christians of different churches and Muslims of different theological denominations – Sunnis, Shi'is, Druze, Alawites, Ismailis, etc.). To these should be added the sub-identities of ethnic communities such as Berbers, Kurds, Assyrians, Turkmens, Armenians, etc. For centuries they have lived peacefully alongside Arabs or Arabised populations and have often blended with them through intermarriage. As a general rule, elites from these ethnic communities have always been bilingual (in their own language and

Arabic) and this is still the case today. Nonetheless, the demands for autonomy by these ethnic communities have been growing, at least with respect to their claim to a cultural identity, which has been encouraged by the general worldwide movement towards affirmation of 'minorities.' The two extremes of this situation are noteworthy. On the one hand, there are the recurrent conflicts between the Kurds and the successive Iraqi governments (which are part of a broader set of geopolitical rivalries within the region); and, on the other hand, the remarkable integration of the Armenians into the Arab Levant where they were welcomed with open arms, especially those who survived the genocide that occurred during the First World War in the waning Ottoman Empire. The identity structure of contemporary Arab societies is therefore extremely complex, something which did not go unnoticed by nationalist thinkers.

This is how four other great thinkers made major contributions to Arab nationalist ideology. The first of these is Sati al-Husri (1880–1967), who was of Kurdish origin and a follower of King Faysal. In 1920 he followed Faysal to Iraq where the latter was crowned king of this province, which had been inherited by the British Mandate. Following this, al-Husri was named Director of the Ministry of Education, a position he held until 1927. He produced an extensive body of didactic works. In his view, Arabs possessed all the elements required of a nation in the modern sense of the term, in particular a shared language, a key element in nation building. Al-Husri was obviously influenced by the thought of the German philosopher Johann Gottlieb Fichte (1762–1814), who saw language as one of the most important elements of national cohesion. Indeed, how is it even possible to build a nation without a means of communication that is shared by all of its members? This does not exclude the use of other languages that may co-exist alongside the main national language, but for al-Husri, use of Arabic was the primary criterion for belonging to an Arab nation on its way to reconstruction after centuries of effacement. He also described the dangers of provincial nationalism in the smaller territories whose borders had been established by European colonisers at the end of the First World War. Al-Husri produced an extensive body of work, because he engaged with many different subjects related to the barriers facing the Arabs as they sought to unite as a single entity. He strongly criticised provincial nationalism which, in his view, sought to thwart the emergence of a unified Arab state.

Another great thinker was Constantine Zurayk (1909–2000), a prominent Syrian intellectual whose complete works were published by the Centre for

Arab Unity Studies (the role of this organisation will be discussed in Chapter 9). The story of his life was told by another great Arab thinker, Aziz al-Azmeh, in an excellent book published in 2003.[8] Born into a well-respected family of the Syrian bourgeoisie, Zurayk had a stellar academic career; first as President of the University of Damascus, then as a well-respected professor at the American University of Beirut, and finally, as President of the Institute for Palestine Studies (see *infra* Chapter 9). For him, Arab nationalism was a necessity imposed by the political and economic organisation of the modern world into nation states that possess a territory and sufficient resources. Since the Arabs possessed all of the elements necessary for a nation, to abstain from the pursuit of Arab unity was a grave abdication of duty and a rejection of modern statehood that would leave the fragmented states inherited from the colonial period in a situation of dependency on the large European nation states. As for the indispensable acquisition of science and technology needed to overcome the underdevelopment affecting all Arab societies, he argued for unity and joint efforts rather than remaining isolated within faltering state entities that were heterogeneous due to their different population and geographical size. His work had considerable impact throughout the entire Arab world and influenced the Arab Nationalist Movement in particular (see below).

A third great Arab thinker who has also passed away is 'Abdallah 'Abd al-Daim (1924–2008). He was a high-calibre academic of Syrian origin, just like Constantine Zurayk, whose stellar professional and academic career was devoted to education. In addition to serving as Minister of Education in Syria, he spent most of his career working as an experienced specialist of educational planning and development in Arab countries, as well as being a longterm expert at the United Nations Educational, Scientific and Cultural Organization (UNESCO). Alongside his work on the problems of education in Arab countries, he authored several remarkable works on issues such as nationalism and humanism, socialism and democracy, and the routes to achieving the creation of an independent Arab nation.

His realistic and penetrating analyses of Arab nationalism were summarised in a book published in 1994. In it, he examined this issue within the framework of the new world order that resulted from the collapse of the Soviet Union and the development of economic globalisation.[9] 'Abd al-Daim responded to all the criticism directed at Arab nationalism by accepting some of it as valid and by demonstrating the lack of consistency in others. He believed that in order to work efficiently towards building a nation it would require two 'sparks' to unite: the spark of a mind that is pure, critical, and analytical; and the spark of emotion and a religious conscience. Any preference given to one of these sparks to the detriment of the other would paralyse the national struggle. This explains the necessity of combining enlightened minds with a dose of strong emotion in order to give rise to Arab action that is both serious and deeply rooted.[10] For him, abstract reasoning, especially over-subtle reasoning lacking in emotion and religious belief, and which is devoid of conscience, can lead to endless hesitation, fear, and ultimately, acceptance of the existing order. At the opposite end of the spectrum, if left alone, the passions operating at the deepest level of consciousness are capable of becoming a destructive fire if they are not channelled and flanked by the enlightened mind and the power of thought.

Two major features characterise his nationalist thought. The first is the conviction that Arab nationalism can only succeed if it relies on socio-economic data from Arab societies and on 'building a form of socialism with an Arab face, written in the Arabic language, that benefits from the experiences of other countries without copying them, and which relies on existing realities such as Arab history and cultural heritage.'[11] The second consists of showing that without an efficient nationalism, there can be no sustainable renaissance; and that given the choice between an anti-humanist globalisation and a humanist nationalism, humanist nationalism is the obvious choice. The end of this work includes two important and noteworthy chapters. One of these is an analysis of the period of union between Egypt and Syria (1958–1961) and the causes of its failure. The other is an analysis of the efforts made by imperialist Great Britain, Zionism, and the State of Israel to prevent the emergence of a unified Arab nation.

Finally, among the thinkers who left a mark on their generation we cannot fail to mention Nadim al-Bitar of Lebanon, who passed away in 2014. His work is no less important than that of the three theorists of Arab nationalism discussed above. Al-Bitar authored over fifteen books that focus entirely on rereading the history of the Arabs and the Arab world in terms of a history of revolutionary changes that affected these various societies. The vision he developed, which was present in the very first book he wrote, *L'Idéologie du bouleversement* (The Ideology of Upheaval), calls on Arabs to become revolutionaries and to change the course of their history. The works that followed were all further developments of this first book. In these, he analysed the underdevelopment of Arab societies, the rationale for nationalism, the barrier formed by the emergence of fragmented Arab states, and the failure of the Arab intelligentsia to achieve unity.

He devoted two of his works to the study of European historical experiences in which the formation of the major nations, in particular France and Germany, was constructed around a central core that progressively conquered the peripheries through brute military force, matrimonial alliances, or, more often than not, a combination of both. Accordingly, Bitar argues that it is not sufficient for theorists of Arab nationalism to draw on the factors that should naturally unite Arabs into a single state or to preach about various federal structures. On the contrary, they need to become aware that the military force of a central core, such as Egypt, can be utilised to build unity on the ground, unity which will not happen on its own through mere reliance on nationalist beliefs.

Nadim al-Bitar's works were a rich source of history and culture and were very successful in the Arab world. But since the author had spent most of his life teaching in the United States, his absence from the Arab political and cultural scene undoubtedly limited the extent of his influence. When he died, numerous articles were written about him in the newspapers of many Arab countries and on Arab nationalist websites.

The main political currents adhering to Arab nationalism

Three major political currents that adhered to Arab nationalist thought left a mark on their era. These were the nationalist ideology of Gamal Abdel Nasser, the Baath party of the Arab resurrection, and the Arab Nationalist Movement. The Nasserist movement underwent exceptional expansion throughout the entire Arab world because it took place during the phase of decolonisation: the Algerian War, the joint Israeli-Franco-British expedition against Egypt in 1956, and the mounting tensions followed by war with the State of Israel. Nasser's charismatic personality combined with the development of the technology of long-distance audio-visual communication provided broad coverage to the anti-colonialist nationalism promoted by Nasser and to the socialist ideas that he helped to disseminate through his speeches. This led to the adulation of Nasser in the Arab Levant as well as in the Maghreb, particularly since he had provided support to the Algerian National Liberation Front (FLN). During this period, Cairo became a hub for all of the liberation movements on the African continent.

The Baath movement and the Arab Nationalist Movement were primarily focused on the Mashriq. The former relied on a vast body of doctrinal literature that had been produced by the Syrian intelligentsia in the early days of the movement. Later, this literature was expanded by other thinkers from Jordan, Iraq, Palestine, and Lebanon, and it influenced many Arab thinkers of the 1950s and 1960s. The Arab Nationalist Movement represented a radical revolutionary period in the Arab Mashriq that promoted armed struggle as a means of liberating the region from reactionary and anti-progressive forces. It also promoted the elimination of the remains of foreign occupations, especially in Palestine and certain areas of the Arabian Peninsula that were still controlled by Great Britain in the early 1970s (specifically Dhofar and Yemen). This period was one heavily influenced by Marxism, and Marxist concepts were an integral part of its revolutionary discourses.

These three movements all advocated political union and pan-Arabism, but they also represented different political leanings. Nasserism was a type of movement with a charismatic and authoritarian figurehead, a hero who fascinated the Arab public with his strong personality as well as the realist and positivist content of his discourse, which also included self-criticism. Baathism, by contrast, was a movement of intellectuals and political figures. For a long time, they sought to keep parliamentary life and pluralistic political parties in place, until the movement spiralled into various forms of military dictatorship. Its doctrine was marked by a strong romantic penchant for metaphysics and an exaltation of the inherent qualities of the Arabs and their past glories.

The Arab Nationalist Movement was the last to emerge in the political arena. It therefore sought to overcome the failures of the two previous movements through an all-out radicalisation that promoted armed struggle against the remaining forms of imperialism in the Arab world. This of course included Palestine due to the occupation of its territories by the State of Israel, first in 1948 and then again in 1967. But it also included the British colonial presence that persisted in the southern part of the Arabian Peninsula. The political and intellectual history of the Arab Mashriq has been characterised by the disputes and polemics among these three doctrines, as well as the nuances that are integral to each of them, nuances that are rarely negligible.

In what follows, a chronological approach will be adopted and the ideologies of Baathism, Nasserism, and the Arab Nationalist Movement will be successively examined.

The Arab nationalist doctrine of the Baath Party

Baathist doctrine is today considered to be responsible for the downfall of the Arab world. The tragic events in Iraq and Syria, two countries that, ironically, are adversaries, and where the Baath Party established complete hegemonic control over society, along with the authoritarian nature of their regimes, have led to a complete lack of awareness of the actual content of this doctrine. Moreover, nobody has tried to analyse the deep dichotomy between this reality and the political practice that claims to adhere to it.

This party's doctrine, which took shape during the 1940s, attracted many members of the political, cultural, social, and economic elite in the Arab world, particularly in the Levant. The Baath Party is considered to be the heir to a party called the Organ of Nationalist Action ('Isbat al-'Amal al-Qawmi), which was founded in 1933. Even at that time, it brought together many anti-colonialist intellectuals from Syria and Lebanon. The party had a progressive socio-economic platform that was far ahead of its time.[12] It was initially developed by two Syrian intellectuals, Michel Aflaq (1910–1989) and Zaki al-Arsuzi (1899–1968), both of whom belonged to the modernist middle class that was open to European culture, particularly French culture. Al-Arsuzi is generally considered as the philosopher who contributed most to the creation of Baathist doctrine. This is due to the large body of work he produced that was founded on an encyclopaedic knowledge of Arab civilisation and his familiarity with the exceptional richness of the Arabic language.[13] Aflaq also wrote many texts, but these were dictated more by political circumstances. They focused more on action and were inspired by his intellectual training in Paris where he had studied history, as had al-Arsuzi.

Existentialism and personalism were pervasive in Baath party doctrine. Just as influential was a strong nationalist romanticism that was heavily influenced by European nationalist theory that exalted the past glories of a nation in order to produce a patriotic and creative momentum intended to launch the rebirth of that nation. French nationalism can be found in the idea of equality and fraternity among all Arabs regardless of their geographical origins or even their religious, ethnic or tribal affiliations. German and Italian nationalisms are also very prevalent in Baathist texts, to the extent that both responded to the need to create unity among various separate political entities whose subjects nonetheless spoke the same language and shared the same history and culture. Garibaldi and Bismarck were clearly models for the Baathists. Garibaldi was seen as a resister of foreign occupation and a proponent of partisan warfare, while Bismarck was a politician who succeeded in solidifying German unity with respect to Prussia. The Baath doctrine was thus very influenced by the romanticism, or even the mysticism, of these two European nationalisms that exalted the German or Italian soul and which glorified their past. For German nationalism, this meant the story of the Germanic tribes that had conquered Europe, and for Italian nationalism it was the story of the Roman Empire. The influence of Fichte and his glorification of the German language is clearly reflected in the conception of Arab nationalism, which is also centred on the unity and beauty of the Arabic language.

This is why, unlike the doctrine of Nasserism,[14] the writings of some Baathist thinkers include the idea that Arab unity can only be achieved through the use of force, either to remove the occupier or to reunite the Arab provinces of the Ottoman Empire into a single state for the purpose of achieving national unity. This also explains why many of the military coups that took place in the Levant appealed to this desire to realise unitary Arab nationalism, because it was a way for them to establish their legitimacy. The ruthless struggle between the two Baathist states of Syria and Iraq for the leadership of the party started in 1969, the year Saddam Hussein came to power in Baghdad. It led to a deep fissure that compromised the credibility of the party and the popularity it had enjoyed up to that point in countries like Yemen, Jordan, Lebanon, Tunisia, and Kuwait.

Even worse, in 1980 when Iraq started a war with Iran, a country that had just undergone a popular revolution resulting in the establishment of an Islamic republic led by Ayatollah Khomeini, Syria condemned the attack and became the only Arab ally of the Islamic Republic of Iran. This situation was preposterous, because the Iraqi president presented himself as the new Arab hero, an adversary of the Persians who were once dominated by the Arabs at the beginning of the conquests of the eighth century. He was also seen as the standard bearer of the secular values of Arab nationalism, specifically the Baathist version. At the same time, the Syrian regime appealed to the anti-imperialist character of the new Iranian regime that had replaced the Shah of Iran. This was because the new regime was a valuable ally in the struggle against US and Israeli intentions in the Middle East. However, already in 1961, the breakup of the union between Egypt and Syria (implemented in 1958) under intense pressure from all the political parties in Syria, led by the Baath Party, had dealt a serious blow to the widespread aspiration to achieve Arab unity. At the time, it seemed easier to lecture about unity than to actually achieve it. The wide gap between the legitimate and unanimous aspiration for unity and its concrete realisation became glaringly obvious. Henceforth, the reality of the states that resulted from the breakup of the Ottoman Empire, no matter how artificial these were at the outset, constituted an almost insurmountable obstacle.

All of this proved fatal for the ideology of the Baath Party and the idea of unitary nationalism that it had always promoted. The party's economic ideas suffered the same fate. These ideas were nonetheless attractive as they called for the creation of a specific form of Arab socialism that rejected Marxist ideas deemed too materialistic and therefore incompatible with traditional Arab values. Although this concept of Arab socialism was never very clear, it nonetheless included the goal of an economy that worked for the fulfilment of all citizens and for creating equal opportunities. This was in fact the idea of a welfare state, to fight underdevelopment and to provide education and healthcare to the poor in urban and rural areas. This was intended to increase the chances for equal opportunity and represented almost the same economic vision as the one advocated by Nasserism.

In practice, the breakup of the union between Egypt and Syria in 1961, the failure of the tripartite union between Egypt, Syria, and Iraq dominated by the Baath Party in 1963, and another military coup d'état in Damascus in 1966, unfortunately led to an economic radicalisation in Syria that resulted in wide-scale nationalisation of small and medium-sized businesses. This resulted in the flight of a large part of the country's economic elite and contributed to discrediting the party and its doctrine. However, in Iraq, Saddam Hussein took over the party and the state apparatus and imposed a harsh dictatorship that was nonetheless able to quickly bring about the economic, social, and military development of the country. This important accomplishment was wasted by Hussein's major mistake of becoming involved in a war against Iran in 1980 and the invasion of Kuwait in 1990.

Finally, the party did not deny that religion had contributed to the formation of the Arab nation. On occasion, they even celebrated it, because they considered that the prophecy of Muhammad had solidified Arab collective consciousness.[15] Over the course of the same period of time, this contribution would nonetheless acquire an increasingly audacious secular aspect. In order to achieve this, there was an attempt to remove references to religious identity in the constitution and to stop emphasizing that legislation drew on the Qur'an (or shari'a) as a source of law. They also nationalised private schools (including Christian schools) and stepped up efforts to fight against the Muslim Brotherhood. Furthermore, the essentialisation of Arab 'greatness,' defined in one of the party's major slogans as a nation 'with an eternal mission,' is a regrettable example of excessive Arabocentrism.

The final negative aspect of this party's practice, in both Iraq and Syria, was the exercise of authoritarian power, placed solely in the hands of the two heads of state, Saddam Hussein and Hafez al-Assad. Both leaders exercised very strict control over a security apparatus with excessive reach that tracked the daily lives of citizens, their thoughts, and their social and political networks. Furthermore, the immediate family members of these heads of state were given important roles in the management of their respective country's political, economic, and security affairs.

Just as for the doctrine of Nasserism, it would be helpful if the Baathist doctrine were to be better understood and more extensively analysed, especially since both are an integral part of the history of the contemporary Arab world. Many intellectuals joined the Baath Party at one point or another in their political careers, including Munif al-Razzaz (1919–1984), who published a very rich and relevant critique of the party's missteps in 1967. Al-Razzaz was one of the party's leaders and his critique focused specifically on the party's behaviour during its union with Egypt and the period following its breakup.[16]

The Nasserist mode of Arab Nationalism

Nasserism very quickly became a dominant school of thought in the Arab world. I have written elsewhere about the charismatic personality of Egypt's head of state and the educational value of the many speeches he gave.[17] Although Nasser (1918–1970) only wrote a small body of work entitled *The Philosophy of the Revolution,* which summarises his vision of Egypt's geopolitical insertion into the world of the Cold War, his collected speeches comprise several volumes. Nasser's speeches were followed religiously, and his writings became required reading for anyone involved in politics in Egypt and the wider Arab world. His work therefore had an unprecedented impact on the political life of the region.

The 'Nasserist vision' is the title of a collected volume of articles edited by French journalists Paul Balta and Claudine Rulleau.[18] The phrase applies to the vision that unfolds in the pages of Nasser's *Philosophy of the Revolution.* In this work, he asserts Egypt's central role in the national liberation movement, which at that time extended to all of the former European colonies in Africa and Asia. Nasser believed that it was Egypt's calling to mobilise these emancipatory energies because the country was situated at the centre of three realms: the Arab world, Africa, and the Muslim world. This explains the central role Nasser played in the formation of the Non-Aligned Movement alongside Tito, Nehru, and Sukarno. Under his leadership, Cairo became the centre of gravity for many national liberation movements, especially from North and sub-Saharan Africa. This subsequently conferred upon Egypt a political, cultural, and intellectual radiance that it has never been able to recapture.

Egypt's importance within the Arab world strengthened its central position in global geopolitics. Since the time of Muhammad 'Ali, Egypt had already become very influential in the Levant. In 1945, Cairo was chosen as the headquarters for the League of Arab Nations, and its successive general secretaries were all Egyptian (except from 1980 to 1989 when Egypt was excluded from the Arab League for signing a separate peace agreement with Israel). Egypt naturally became the unifying element of the Arab world. The call for political union among the Arab entities that resulted from the dismantling of the Ottoman Empire did not, however, come from Nasser. Rather, it came from a Syrian leader who from the 1950s onwards loudly called for a union with Egypt. Poorly prepared and ill-conceived during the precipitous events of 1958, this union gave rise to an ephemeral United Arab Republic that was dissolved three years later in 1961. This was in the midst of a military coup led by Syrian officers with the backing of the most important unionist party in Syria, the Baath Party. Nasser did not attempt to maintain this union by the use of force. It was considered a defeat for his regime and a failure of the entire unionist ideology. It is possible that the fate of the Arab world might have been different if the Egyptian army, which was much more powerful than the Syrian army, had re-asserted the irreversibility of the union.

In any case, this was a traumatic event for the Arab nationalists and for the unionist thought that drove them. The subsequent attempts to recreate unions between Arab states were all doomed to failure. This was due to sterile power plays in which the leaders of rival states would increase efforts to establish the dominance of the states they governed over all the others.[19]

Nasser's thought has unfortunately been insufficiently studied, as has the failure of this first attempt to create a union. In reality, the richness of his thought can be found in the numerous didactic speeches he gave for the benefit of both the Egyptian people and other Arab societies. The issue of underdevelopment and the means to overcome it, understanding the interplay of social classes in Egypt within the struggle to emerge from this underdevelopment, dependency on the major powers, and the policies implemented by some conservative Arab states who allied with them and were labelled 'reactionaries,' were all recurring themes in Nasser's lively and astute thought.

There is one book in which the content and structure of Nasser's language has been thoughtfully analysed. However, to some extent it has remained marginalised within the sparse literature on this subject in French, English, and even Arabic.[20] Its author, Marlène Nasr, shows the extent to which the thought of the Egyptian leader was in tune with the secular and material realities of Egypt's population at this time. Reference to religious identity and appeals to the competing values of the Orient and the West almost never appear. Nasser was, in fact, a militant anti-imperialist, but completely open to industrial modernity. His thought was thus secular and realist.

Obviously, the detractors of Arab nationalist ideology judged this thought harshly. They claimed it was demagogic and that it had led Nasser to commit fatal errors in his fight against the major powers and the State of Israel. They claimed that these errors led to the crushing defeat in 1967, from which the Arab world has yet to recover even half a century later. In addition, Nasser established one-party rule in Egypt along with the secret services, a model subsequently followed by other 'revolutionary' leaders. This development led to the suppression of public freedoms as well as the indiscriminate nationalisation of local and foreign businesses. This accusation is not without merit, but the trial that ensued failed to account for nuances and 'attenuating' circumstances, that is, the political and cultural context of the time. This context includes the eradication of colonialism and widespread anti-imperialism in developing countries, but also the strong influence of different forms of Marxism in Europe as well as among the intelligentsia of colonised societies.

It was interesting to observe the 'return to grace' of Nasserist thought during the revolutionary events that began in Egypt in 2011. The main reform party that was founded in 2012, the United Nasserist Party of Habdeen Sabbahi, openly adheres to Nasser's thought, and portraits of Nasser reappeared during several popular protests.

The 'Nasserist' period has been given insufficient attention as a research topic. It is high time for Arab thought to focus attention on it with a view to improving knowledge of the history of the contemporary Arab world. Furthermore, it is high time to move beyond this deep partisan divide. On one side are Arab intellectuals who are hostile to any form of Arab nationalism. They point out, with no lack of arguments to back them up, that nationalism gave rise to dictatorial systems responsible for the region's woes. On the other side are those who remain convinced that without a modern ideology of identity, and without the development of shared political values that could form the basis for solidarity among Arab states, Arab societies will continue to be troubled and will progressively disintegrate due to numerous divisive factors that exist both within and among individual societies. This has been illustrated by the serious and violent events that have shaken the Arab world since the outbreak of revolts in January 2011, and which provide new pretexts for intervention by European powers, the United States, and Turkey. Nasser's thought remains largely unknown to younger generations, and there has been no detailed academic study of the hundreds of speeches he gave during his short life that strongly influenced the thought of an entire generation in the 1950s.[21]

The Arab Nationalist Movement

The core of this movement was founded by the student body of the American University of Beirut. In contrast to Saint Joseph's University in Beirut, which was founded by Jesuits and whose student body was mostly derived from Lebanon's upper class Christian families, the American University was a crossroads for Arab students of all nationalities, Muslims and Christians alike, and was fertile ground for the emergence of Arab revolutionary aspirations. This is the place where many future intellectuals first met, thinkers who shared the goal of liberating the great Arab nation from all forms of colonialism and alienation. They were driven by two major concerns, the liberation of Palestine from the clutches of the State of Israel, and the departure of the British, who still occupied large parts of the southern Arabian Peninsula in the early 1960s.

This is what gave rise to the formation of the Arab Nationalist Movement. It was founded by Georges Habash, a Palestinian medical student at the American University of Beirut. Similarly, the extension of the Arab Nationalist Movement into the Arabian Peninsula, the Front for the Liberation of Occupied South Yemen (FLOSY), was also formed in this context.[22]

The man who inspired the Arab Nationalist Movement was Constantine Zurayk, a high-calibre intellectual and academic whose extensive work has already been discussed. Despite climbing the academic ladder to become Rector of the University of Damascus and then President of the American University in Beirut, he nonetheless never had an official role in the Arab Nationalist Movement, or in any nationalist party. His main influence stemmed from his rich intellectual output. He focused exclusively on the need for Arab unity according to the prevailing nationalist mode. This mode had provided the framework for modernity and for the system of international relations that the Arabs were subjected to and could not escape. Therefore, in order for Arabs to be successful and well respected, they had to accept the constraints of modernity, that is, the creation of a strong nation supported by a 'developmental' state that guarantees education and healthcare and oversees the appropriation of science and technology. For Zurayk, the defeat of the Arabs at the hands of Israel could be explained by their inability to organise themselves within the framework of a modern nation and to appropriate science and technology to their own advantage.

Arab nationalism thus appears to be more specific to the societies of the Levant (Mashriq) than to those of the western part of the Arab world (Maghreb). Moreover, as will be discussed in the following chapters, it competed with other forms of nationalism that espoused the borders drawn by colonisation or were based on different forms of sub-identity.

CHAPTER 9

Other forms of nationalism in the Arab world

Any study of the main theories of Arab nationalism must not exclude other expressions of identity. These include the theories of Antoun Saadeh (1904—1949), the founder of the Syrian People's Party, in addition to specific forms of Maghrebi nationalism. However, as will be discussed, cultural and linguistic consciousness remain common denominators for different types of societies. This chapter will therefore end with a discussion of two major nationalist and pan-Arab cultural institutions: the Centre for Arab Unity Studies, and the Institute for Palestine Studies. Both of these constitute privileged spaces for maintaining Arab political consciousness.

The Syrian People's Party: A distinct nationalist movement

In the Mashriq, another major transnational party was the Syrian People's Party which played a very active political role in the Levant from 1940 to 1975. This party did not make any claims to Arab nationalism, but rather to a form of nationalism built on the idea of cultural and civilizational unity across the entire Syro-Mesopotamian area. The Maghreb and the countries of the Arabian Peninsula were therefore not integrated into this vision. The inspiration for this came from the party's founder, Antoun Saadeh. Originally from Mount Lebanon, he was the son of a physician who had emigrated to Latin America and who had become an important intellectual figure within the small circle of Arab immigrants there.[1] Antoun had a fascinating political and intellectual career that nevertheless came to a tragic end.

He returned to Lebanon in 1932 and in the same year founded the Syrian People's Party, a bold secular party that cast its net widely across the various religious communities of the Levant. The party's doctrine, created by its founder, was at once nationalist and anti-imperialist. However, the nation it dreamed of assembling was not an Arab nation, but a Syrian nation broadly conceived; that is, extending across the geographical regions in which the Aramaic-Syriac civilisation had flourished and which directly preceded Arab-Muslim civilisation. These regions are known as the 'Lands of Damascus' (Bilad al-Sham), and include provinces such as Palestine, Jordan, the Eastern Mediterranean coast, ancient Cilicia, and the entire southern slope of the Mesopotamian Basin that also formed part of Aramaic civilisation. These areas had always basked in the glow of the great city of Damascus whose prestigious history extends back to antiquity.

For Saadeh, this entire region was characterised by strong sociological and cultural homogeneity. The spoken Arabic was practically the same everywhere, as was the rural and urban architecture. The region shared a common history. It had experienced the same invasions and cultural influences (Greek, Roman, Byzantine, and Arab). It had been unified under the Seleucids, and also by the Umayyad and Abbasid caliphates. Damascus had always constituted the largest and most influential urban centre as it was the seat of powerful rulers during the long reign of the Turks. While he recognised its affinities with other Arab societies in the Arabian Peninsula and in the Maghreb, Saadeh felt that the most urgent priority was to build a Syrian nation (according to his broad definition of the term).

A man of great culture, Saadeh never stopped warning the 'Syrians' of their shortcomings as a nation, which he regarded as inherited from centuries of external domination, of which the French and British were the last representatives. Having artificially established state borders where they should not have existed, the latter fanned the flames for developing the specificities of religious and ethnic communities. The party that he founded was thus intended to shatter the artificial borders created between Palestine, Lebanon, and Syria. For several years, France had even tried to divide Syria into community-based states (Alawi, Druze, and Sunni). For Saadeh, it was important to fight against the artificial development of community sub-identities that colonial France had encouraged in Syria and Lebanon. This created what he called the 'isolationist identity' (al-in 'izaliyya) that sought to close itself off from its wider context and to establish itself as a separate society.[2]

These are the reasons why this man of strong character and clear ideas only lived a short turbulent life. It ended tragically in July 1949 after he was extradited from Syria to Lebanon, subjected to summary judgment, and executed by a firing squad. This was carried out on the very questionable grounds that earlier that year he had been behind a failed assassination attempt in Jordan of Riad El-Solh, the very popular prime minister of Lebanon.[3]

Saadeh was also accused of being a fascist sympathiser because he modelled his party's organisation on that of European fascist parties and allowed himself to be addressed as *za'im*, an Arabic term that designates a charismatic leader able to galvanise the members of his movement.[4] His written work, which was substantial, was republished in 2001 in a twelve volume collection of his books, articles, and letters by the cultural foundation that bears his name. Some of his main works include 'The Birth of Nations' (*Nushu' al-umam*), a broad fresco of historical anthropology (1938); 'Christianity, Islam and Nationalism' (*al-Masihiyya wa'l-Islam wa'l-qawmiyya*), a scholarly study of the relationships between these two great monotheisms and the development of nationalism (1940); and 'The Intellectual Struggle in Syrian Literature' (*al-Sira' al-fikri fi'l-adab al-suri*), published in 1942.[5]

Even though the party gradually declined following Saadeh's demise due to disagreements surrounding his succession and the repression that targeted it, both in Syria and elsewhere, it nonetheless remained an important crucible of secular nationalism. For several decades, the party attracted many young intellectuals searching for a form of nationalism that was better centred geographically and culturally and which in no uncertain terms denounced community sectarianism, particularly prevalent in Lebanon.

The nationalisms of the Maghreb

Unlike in the Mashriq, where Arab nationalism played a central role in the political life of the various states that resulted from the break-up of the Ottoman Empire, the parties created in the Maghreb were particularly focused on the struggle for independence within the state borders established by colonial France. Their claims for independence thus centred on the liberation of the state and not on building Arab unity, or more simply, Maghrebi unity.

The Maghreb is composed of three core entities. These include the ancient monarchy of Morocco which succeeded in preserving its independence from the Ottoman Empire, only to lose it in 1908 when it became a French protectorate. Just next door, to the east, Algeria and Tunisia were both Ottoman provinces for several centuries before coming under French sovereignty at different times and with a different status (Algeria was integrated into French territory, while Tunisia became a protectorate). In addition, the Libyan provinces (Cyrenaica, Tripolitania, etc.) were also under Ottoman rule until the 1911 Italian occupation. And lastly, Mauritania, which is partially Arab, also forms part of the Maghreb.

The colonisers succeeded in exploiting the heterogeneity of the various tribal entities such as the Amazigh and the Berbers, as well as that of Arab identity. In addition, the heterogeneity of the local Jewish identity was exploited. Indeed, the 1870 Crémieux Decree gave French nationality to all Algerians of Jewish faith. Similarly, there were also large tribes living in the Sahara desert, such as the Tuareg.

The challenge for the elites leading the anti-colonial struggle was to maintain cohesion between nationalist movements that were enclosed within the 'modern' state framework imposed by France. Islam was emphasised more than Arab identity because it united Berbers and Arabs. In Morocco, the Alawite dynasty combined religious and national identity, just like the Sanussi Monarchy in Libya, which had established a frail national unity. Furthermore, the workers' unions, which followed the French model and which counted many local communists among their members, were also an important force of anti-colonialism.

Four national movements that were firmly entrenched in the local reality of each state were thus formed. The first was the Algerian National Liberation Front (FLN), created in 1954 to launch a 'war of liberation' that lasted for seven years. It went on to become a mass party whose ideology, at once Arab and Islamic, was infused with a strong dose of socialism. The Algerian state maintained this strong nationalism, which became radicalised after independence in 1962. This took on a socialist dimension up until the reforms of the 1980s, in addition to being Third-Worldist and anti-imperialist. The strong personality of Colonel Houari Boumediene, who led a coup d'état against President Ahmed Ben Bella in June 1965, turned Algeria into a major centre of support for anti-colonial emancipation movements. Following Nasser's death in 1970, Algeria partially assumed the role formerly played by Egypt under Nasser, prior to Egypt's pro-Western turn initiated by President Anwar Sadat.

The second was Bourguibism, which refers to the name of Habib Bourguiba (1903–2000), who in 1956 became the first president of newly independent Tunisia. Under Bourguibism, Tunisia became the vanguard of secularism and women's liberation in the Arab world. Lastly, in Morocco, there was an alliance between the monarchy and the Socialist Union of Popular Forces (USFP), the people's movement led by socialists. Mehdi Ben Barka (1920–1965), an anti-imperialist political leader, became the unfortunate hero of this Moroccan nationalism when he was kidnapped in Paris, most likely on the order of King Hassan II, his body never being found. Ben Barka was an influential figure during the post-war period as he fought not only for the independence of his own country, but also for that of all Arabs and the entire developing world. He was a major player in bringing together the countries of the developing world into a tri-continental organisation whose first conference was held in Havana in January 1966. This was the crowning achievement of the Non-Aligned Movement. A book that recounts Ben Barka's key role in the success of this initiative also confirms its pan-Arab and international dimension.[6] The powerful personality of this Moroccan leader strongly influenced this era of revolutionary hopes. His political writings constitute an exceptional record of both the nationalist and internationalist revolutionary thought that was widespread in the Arab world during the 1960s.[7]

The issue of the former Spanish Sahara, which Spain evacuated in 1975, gave rise to a bitter dispute between Algeria and the Kingdom of Morocco. Algeria supported the local liberation movement, the Polisario Front, while Morocco asserted its sovereignty over this territory by claiming it had always belonged to the kingdom. Even today, this situation continues to poison the relationship between the two countries, whose shared borders have been closed since 1994. It has also paralysed the efficient functioning of the Arab Maghreb Union that was created in 1989 during a brief period of detente between Morocco and Algeria. Indeed, the excessive local nationalism of both of these countries hindered the development of an Arab, as well as a Maghrebi, nationalism[8]. It also prevented the main nationalist doctrines of the Mashriq from being broadly adopted (with the exception of a strong infatuation with Nasserist ideology and some degree of sympathy for the Baathist doctrine).

In 1969, the coup d'état in Libya, led by Colonel Gaddafi, abolished the monarchy and loudly proclaimed Gaddafi's alignment with Nasserist ideology, whose legacy he sought to continue. This new head of state was therefore a 'unionist' who claimed he would work towards Arab unity. He made successive attempts at uniting Libya and Egypt, followed by Libya and Tunisia, although none of these ever succeeded. Disappointed, and not very well liked by his peers due to his antics, Gaddafi set his sights on sub-Saharan Africa. Using the financial means provided by Libya's oil revenues, he was able to exert a strong influence over several countries. Situated between the Maghreb and the Mashriq, Libya was never able to settle on its identity despite the fact that, like the other countries of the Maghreb, it defined itself as both Arab and Islamic. Gaddafi's fall in 2011 following a popular uprising and a NATO intervention exposed the Libyan state structure as extremely fragile, whereas those of other countries were better able to resist the winds of destabilisation.

Even though the societies of the Maghreb never adopted the forms of Arab nationalism of the Mashriq, some of their thinkers attained pan-Arab stature due to their high-quality work concerning Arab thought overall. The Tunisian intellectual Hichem Djaït is one example, along with the Moroccans Abdallah Laroui and Mohammed Abed al-Jabri, whose works will be discussed in Chapter 12. While Maghrebi nationalisms remained enclosed within their 'modern' state frameworks, the philosophical, historical, and anthropological thought of this region engaged with all the major subjects and issues that were relevant to wider Arab society. In this sense, despite the fragmented nature of their different states, the Maghreb and the Mashriq remain until today closely entwined within a common culture that is shared by the entire Arab entity that extends from the Atlantic Ocean to the Sea of Oman and the Indian Ocean.

Other forms of identity-based nationalisms in the Arab world

To complete this chapter on the history of Arab thought, it is important to discuss the development of other types of nationalism that I will call identity-based nationalisms. These still exist today and stem from a diverse set of factors. The first consists of the consolidation of state entities created in the aftermath of the First World War. Their leaders needed to devise a state identity that could consolidate their power, especially in the face of the mounting wave of Arab nationalism. To do this, they turned to the European model that laid claim to prestigious ancestors of the distant past in order to create a national identity for the present. Some intellectuals therefore appealed to the glories of the past, such as the civilisations of the Pharaohs in Egypt, the Phoenicians in Lebanon and Tunisia, and even the Babylonians in Iraq.

The second factor is the politicisation of religious and ethnic identity, which gave rise to a communitarianism that easily devolved into sectarianism.

What made this all the more likely to occur was the fact that governments were not able to ensure a socio-economic development that facilitated the creation of a notion of citizenship that was relevant for all regional, religious, and ethnic identities. This resulted in a Kabyle – or more broadly Amazigh – nationalism, a Maronite nationalism in Lebanon, a Coptic nationalism in Egypt, and a Kurdish nationalism in Iraq, to give just a few examples.

The third factor is the division of states into kingdoms and republics. The monarchies succeeded in creating a national identity based on allegiance to a royal family, including the Hashemites in Jordan, the Alawites in Morocco, and the Sauds in Saudi Arabia. The same is true of the Sultanate of Oman where allegiance is pledged to the family of the sultan. It was more difficult for the republics to find a shared identity, because the effects of the revolutionary years (1950-70) and the consequent social gains were quick to fade. It should therefore come as no surprise that these states drifted into a pattern of building dynastic republics. The heads of state put their family members in positions of power and prepared their children to succeed them. This was the case with Hafez al-Assad in Syria, Hosni Mubarak in Egypt, Ali Abdallah Saleh in Yemen, and Muammar Gaddafi in Libya. These republics tried to create more allegiance to the reigning family and its policies than to the state entity, which it governed with an iron fist. This is the reason why the republics turned out to be much more fragile than the royal governments during the wave of Arab revolts that extended from Oman to Mauritania in 2011.

The last factor in the development of these particular nationalisms was the oil wealth of the kingdoms and emirates of the Arabian Peninsula, which forged some very specific nationalist movements driven by the billionaires involved in looting their countries' oil and gas revenues. This was the case in Qatar, Saudi Arabia, Bahrain, and the United Arab Emirates. It is no coincidence that allegiance to the royal and princely families is very strong in these countries, and that they have managed to form unions with one another that the republics have been unable to achieve. This is the case, for example, with the Federation of the United Arab Emirates created in 1971 by Abu Dhabi's leader, Shaykh Zayed bin Sultan al-Nahyan (1918–2004). He federated several small emirates whose budgets at the time were supplemented by the substantial federal budget originating in the enormous oil revenues of Abu Dhabi. The success of this is surprising on two levels. Firstly, the fact that the federation is still going strong forty years later. And secondly, the fact that the Emirate of Dubai, also a member, was able to develop itself into one of the region's most important business hubs under the strong leadership of the

Maktoum family. The thoroughly liberal atmosphere that reigns in Dubai attracts countless companies along with their multi-national upper management. This achievement starkly contrasts with the atmosphere of Islamic austerity that Saudi Arabia has imposed throughout the rest of the Arabian Peninsula.

Moreover, in 1980, this wealth-based nationalist club succeeded in creating the Gulf Cooperation Council (GCC). This organisation brought together all the kingdoms and emirates of the region with the exception of Yemen, one of the poorest countries in the Arab world and, incidentally, a republic. In addition to military coordination among its members, the GCC established an economic union. This included common external trade tariffs and the freedom for anyone from the member states of the Council to invest and set up businesses in any of the other member states. Iraq requested membership in the GCC but was denied participation. It is easy to imagine that if Iraq had been included, the Iraqi invasion of Kuwait in 1990 could have been avoided along with a whole series of other misfortunes. Naturally, this wealth-based nationalism was placed under strong U.S. military protection, and the United States has maintained several military bases in Bahrain and on the Arabian Peninsula ever since the failed Iraqi invasion of Kuwait.

It should also be noted that since the beginning of the 1970s, millions of Arabs of all nationalities have emigrated to find work in these 'paradises of wealth' in the Arabian Peninsula and have been able to enjoy the material comforts that the privileged few are able to acquire for themselves. At the same time, with the exception of the city-state of Kuwait, public freedoms are non-existent. In Saudi Arabia, which receives the largest number of immigrant workers, the religious police strictly enforce the most rigid Islamic moral code in accordance with the teachings of the Wahhabi doctrine, which serves as the kingdom's official ideology of identity.

The accumulated effects of the aforementioned factors, along with the failures of the various republican Arab regimes that adopted Arab nationalism as their ideology of identity, led to the development of an acute national selfishness within each state. This translated into slogans based on sub-identities that were often aggressive in tone, such as Lebanon, Syria, or Iraq 'before all else' (*awwalan*). In other words, these slogans were the expression of a narrow and sometimes chauvinistic state nationalism. Their appearance also signalled the end of an Arab nationalism that had ensured the kind of cooperation among states that had allowed them to better cope with the pressure from the major powers exploiting their perpetual disunity. This is what prevented a serious collective effort to achieve Israel's evacuation of the occupied Palestinian territories. As of 2015, collective Arab identity based on nationalist principles has crumbled. However, it is not yet clear whether the sub-identities of each state, the sectarian identities, or those based on ethnic and religious communities are robust enough to ensure the wellbeing of the populations concerned.

The Arabic language: a reservoir of collective culture

Despite all of these often contradictory national aspirations, there is one constant that can be found at all levels of expression of Arab nationalism, apart from those based on community or ethnic sub-identities. This is the linguistic nationalism that has made Arabic into the 'national' language of all the states in the region, even those inhabited by large groups that speak their own language (e.g. Berbers and Kurds). This language is also a source of pride for all the provincial nationalisms, even in Lebanon, which for a long time was hesitant to identify itself as Arab. Nonetheless, the appeal by the 'Lebanese' nationalists to their Phoenician past, in an effort to distance themselves from an Arab identity they feared would consume them, did not prevent the persistence of something akin to national pride for having preserved and modernised the Arabic language.

This was demonstrated by the Palestinian linguist, Yasir Suleiman, in a book published in 2003.[9] In this work, he brings to the fore an ancient distinction between 'Arabs' and Persians that dates back to the early years of the first conquest. Persians were called *'Ajam,* a word that has become synonymous with foreigner or the 'other'; someone whose language is not the same as the one spoken by Arabs. Suleiman also looks back at the struggle to resist Turkification from the time of the Seljuq conquests in the thirteenth century, but in particular during the Ottoman Empire and the period of the Young Turks when the empire was declining. By studying the works of three Egyptian nationalists (Salama Musa, Taha Husayn, and Louis Awad), he shows how the Arabic language played a central role in their nationalisms. Suleiman concludes his work by underscoring the inherent contradiction in the assessment of the role of language between secular nationalists (both pan-Arabic and provincial) and Islamic nationalists. For the latter, the importance of the Arabic language stems from the fact that it was the language of the Qur'anic prophecy. For the former, it constitutes a rich universe and a source of pride that unites all Arabic speakers.

Two privileged spaces of Arab nationalist thought

This chapter would not be complete without mentioning two key institutions in the Arab world that have played an important role since the 1980s regarding the questions of identity and memory.

The Centre for Arab Unity Studies

In 1975, a meeting took place of several Arab intellectuals who were convinced that their societies were in the midst of a serious crisis. They were further convinced that they were powerless to unite in order to face the challenge of Israeli expansionism and the external hegemonies that were affecting the Arab world. They first considered the idea of establishing a research centre in Kuwait, which after Lebanon was the freest society in the region. However, the suspension of Kuwait's parliament by the princely family, under pressure from Saudi Arabia – which had already succeeded in suspending the Parliament of Bahrain, another place of relative intellectual freedom – and the temporary restoration of calm in Lebanon after two years of violent unrest between 1975 and 1977, led to the decision to establish the Centre in the Lebanese capital. The founders subsequently elected its first director, Khair El-Din Haseeb, an Iraqi, former director of the Central Bank of Iraq and a political refugee in Lebanon. Haseeb was indomitable and in the space of a few years built a major institution that produced a variety of content. Moreover, it helped keep alive the notion that Arab nationalist thought was the only way out of the continuous divisions, ordeals, and weakening of the Arab 'nation' due to external dominance. Haseeb was also responsible for the creation of sister institutions of the Centre for Arab Unity Studies, most particularly the Arab Organisation for Translation and, more recently, the Arab Anti-Corruption Organisation. He was also a driving force behind the creation of the Arab Organisation for Human Rights in Cairo in 1983. This followed a conference in Cyprus initiated by the Centre in the previous year on the theme of 'Arab Democracy and Human Rights'. This conference marked an important turning point in Arab thought because it put the issues of democracy and human rights on the table decades before George W. Bush decided to remake the Middle East by imposing democratic regimes – by force if necessary.

The Centre undertakes two main types of activity. The first is its publishing house, which, between 1978 and 2010, published over 637 titles. It also publishes a widely distributed monthly journal, *al-Mustaqbal al-'Arabi* (The Arab Future). Everything of import in the intellectual realm, from the Mashriq to the Maghreb, is discussed in this publication. The Centre also organises academic conferences that allow intellectuals from different Arab countries to meet on a regular basis. The director also initiated the creation of an association of Arab unity activists called the Arab National Congress (al-Mu'tamar al-Qawmi al-'Arabi). The Congress meets annually in an Arab capital that hosts it to discuss a report on the 'state of the nation' (*hal al-umma al-'Arabiyya*) using direct and uncomplicated language. It does so in order to unambiguously denounce the drifting apart of Arab society and the submissive policies of most Arab regimes towards American and Israeli dictates. The first Congress was held in Tunisia in 1990.

Some years later, in 1994, Khair El-Din Haseeb was once again the driving force behind the establishment of the Islamic National Congress, a parallel entity to the Arab National Congress that meets every two years. The idea for this emerged during a conference organised in Cairo by the Centre for Arab Unity Studies in 1991 on the theme of 'National-Religious dialogue.' Haseeb's main objective was to reconcile Islamic religious nationalism with secular Arab nationalism. This was a noble intention, but instead it contributed to focusing more attention on anti-nationalist thought and to providing it with an additional platform. This explains why the Centre's publications broadened in scope to include the writings, books, and articles published in the *al-Mustaqbal* journal by adherents of a regressive inward turn towards Islamic identity as a means to better respond to external challenges. As discussed previously, the number of these adherents increased following the religious revolution in Iran and under the influence of the 'Islamic Revival' promoted by Saudi Arabia.

The Institute for Palestine Studies, a place for preservation of memory

This institute was created in Beirut in 1963 in order to increase awareness of the importance of the Palestinian question and to study its historical, cultural, and socio-economic aspects. From the outset, two individuals have been key to its development. The first is the historian Walid Khalidi, who has served as the Institute's General Secretary since it was founded. Born in Jerusalem in 1925, Khalidi was a member of a prominent Palestinian family steeped in both Arabic and English-language culture. He pursued an academic career that led him to teach at Oxford, the American University of Beirut, and in the

United States. He authored several books and articles on the history of Palestine as well as its future, and was the first in 1978 to conceptualise the idea of an independent Palestinian state that would co-exist with the state of Israel along the June 1967 borders.[10] He also edited a remarkable collection of articles on Palestine from the birth of the Zionist movement, very eloquently entitled 'From Haven to Conquest.'[11] The second individual is Constantine Zurayk, whose career I have already described. He was the first president of the Institute's Board of Trustees, which has always included distinguished figures from various Arab countries among its members. The Institute was mainly financed by Palestinian businessmen who were compelled to emigrate to other Arab countries. It also received government funding, gifts from other Arab institutions, and revenues from the sale of its publications.

Over time, this institution has become the true guardian of Palestinian memory. Thanks to its periodicals, it has also become an astute observer of developments in the plight of the Palestinians. These periodicals include the *Journal of Palestine Studies,* published in Washington, D.C. where the institute has a satellite office; the *Revue d'études palestiniennes*, published in Paris from 1982 to 2008, but discontinued due to insufficient financial resources; and its sister publication in Arabic, *Majallat al-Dirasat al-Filastiniyya*, published in Beirut, London, and Ramallah. Special attention has been paid to tracking the development of settlements and to the question of Jerusalem, which is the focus of two other periodicals, one in English (*Jerusalem Quarterly*) and one in Arabic (*Hawliyyat al-Quds*). Similarly, the Institute's annual publication on the Palestinian question in Arabic, which was published from 1964 to 1972, provides an extremely precise account of Israeli-Palestinian negotiations.

The Institute has also published many first-rate books on the numerous aspects of the Palestinian question, including a major reference work on the evolution of France's attitude towards the issue.[12] In addition, the Institute has published a large number of essays on the regional and international dimensions of the Israeli-Palestinian conflict.[13]

The quality of the Institute's publications, its capacity to archive thousands of documents on Palestinian existence prior to and after 1948 (the year Israel was created), and the prominent and highly respected members of its Board of Trustees, Executive Committee, and Study Committee, make this a pivotal institution for the survival of Palestinian existence within the consciousness of the Arab world and the wider global academic community. In comparison to Israel's resources and the numerous Western countries that support it, the Institute's resources appear trifling. Nonetheless, within the sinking ship that is the Arab world today, the Institute constitutes a privileged space of knowledge and memory, and continues to be well run with very limited resources. The Palestinian catastrophe, combined with other resounding Arab failures, has become a more widespread topic of critical self-reflection within Arab thought. This first became apparent at an intellectual level in the mid-1960s, and will be the subject of the next chapter.

CHAPTER 10

Arab thought in the face of successive political and military failures since 1961

The dynamic of Arab revolutionary successes that had inspired many anti-imperialist thinkers and Arab unity activists did not continue long after the period of independence, which lasted for about a quarter century, from 1952 to 1970. This period was marked by spectacular defeats that led to self-doubt within unionist and revolutionary Arab thought. The period of positive events, as conceived of by this thought, was ushered in with the 1952 military coup d'état in Egypt. The leaders of the coup first suspended and then abolished the monarchy, a symbol of corruption and submission to British colonialism, which was still all-powerful at that time. The coup pushed Egypt in a new direction, towards increased social justice and national independence, and thus appeared as the dawn of a new era.

In 1956, in the aftermath of the nationalisation of the Suez Canal by the Egyptian government, Egypt was the target of a military assault by a coalition of two major powers, France and Great Britain, along with the new State of Israel, spoliator of Palestinian rights. This resulted in complete political failure and inflamed pan-Arab and anti-imperialist sentiments in every Arab society. Finally, in 1958, several major events seemed to vindicate pan-Arab nationalist thinkers and movements. First, at the request of Syrian leaders, a union was formed between Syria and Egypt in the fervour of a popular movement whose hero was Gamal Abdel Nasser, the Egyptian president worshipped by many throughout the Arab world. At the same time, a military coup d'état in Iraq led to the abolition of the monarchy. It also ended the Hashemite axis (between Jordan and Iraq), which had had close ties to Great Britain. In Jordan and Libya, popular movements seemed to be on the verge of tipping the two countries into the fold of the United Arab Republic that had just been formed between Syria and Egypt. In any case, these protests were very hostile towards U.S. policies in the region that aimed to assemble the Arab countries, Turkey, and Israel along an anti-Soviet axis.

The growing complexity of the Arab political landscape

This 'people's spring' did not last very long. In 1961, there was a military coup in Syria backed by Syrian political parties, including the Baath Party that had spearheaded Arab unity. This brought an end to the unity with Egypt, whose president avoided bloodshed by refraining from using his army to maintain it by force. The United Arab Republic, the dream of millions of Arabs, ended up lasting only a few months. Six years later, in 1967, the Egyptian, Syrian, and Jordanian armies were thoroughly defeated by the Israeli Army. In six days, Israel conquered and occupied the Egyptian Sinai, the mountainous region of the Syrian Golan, the entire west bank of the Jordan River, and the Arab part of Jerusalem where the holy places of the three monotheistic religions are located.

This catastrophe was all the more bitter because it magnified the political, ideological, and military failures that had dogged Arab unitary and anti-imperialist aspirations. Nasser, the unlucky hero of this epic pan-Arab tale, died in its midst from exhaustion in 1970, leading to a fierce struggle among Arab political and intellectual elites to claim his legacy. Chief among these were the Baath Party and the Arab Nationalist Movement, the latter of which was increasingly focused on the liberation of Palestine. The Popular Front for the Liberation of Palestine emerged from within this movement along with Fatah, the main component of the armed Palestinian movements.

In the Maghreb, the Algerian president, Houari Boumediene – responsible for the June 1965 coup against Ahmed Ben Bella – and the elites gathered around him, also presented themselves as the successors and continuators of Nasserist policies. These policies aimed at bringing Arabs together against imperialism and in solidarity with other formerly colonised countries in the framework of the Non-Aligned Movement and the Tricontinental Conference led by the strong figure of Fidel Castro. Iraqi and Syrian leaders did not remain on the sidelines of this increasingly acute inter-Arab rivalry; meanwhile the pan-Islamic ambitions of Saudi Arabia were becoming more and more apparent.

This explains the growing complexity of the Arab political landscape from the end of the 1960s onwards. It was characterised by a double contradiction: on the one hand, an increasingly acute anti-Israeli and anti-imperialist radicalism that not only supported the armed struggle of the Palestinian people but also the anti-colonial struggle in South Africa and sub-Saharan Africa; and on the other, a realist and subdued school of thought that accepted the failure of anti-imperialist nationalist policies and that felt the time had come to put an end to the Nasserist cycle by reaching out to Western powers as sources of scientific and technical progress required by Arab societies in order to overcome their underdevelopment. This school was launched in Egypt under President Anwar Sadat (1918–1981), Nasser's successor. Firstly, Sadat disposed of Soviet influence. Then, in 1973, he won a partial victory against the Israeli army when Egyptian forces were able to cross over to the east bank of the Suez Canal, which had been occupied by Israel since the 1967 victory over the Sinai Peninsula. After going to Israel in 1977, a major event at that time, Sadat signed the Camp David Accords with Israel in a two-step process (1978 and 1979).

Within these two opposing political and intellectual contexts, Arab thought evolved in an increasingly contradictory manner, between revolutionary radicalism and the subdued realism of acceptance of defeat. The dream of building an Arab nation was in tatters, and the socialist-style gains had been repudiated. This sterile confrontation facilitated the rise of conservative and antinational political Islam as the only ideological escape route. Their proposals took on a whole new intellectual register, that of religious authoritarianism based on a theologico-political vision that relied on a literalist reading of the sacred text and its most restrictive and constrained interpretations. This ideological escape route is summed up by the slogan 'Islam is the solution' (see *infra*, Chapter 11).

Furthermore, the 1967 military defeat at the hands of the Israeli army led a number of major intellectuals who did not subscribe to either one of the political trends that emerged from this context to engage in in-depth reflection on the causes of the disaster, the persistence of underdevelopment, and the inability to build institutions appropriate for the modern world.

Reflexive thought on the failure experienced by the Arab world

Starting with the failed union between Syria and Egypt in 1961, but in particular following the 1967 defeat, many Arab intellectuals from diverse backgrounds began to critically revise their way of thinking in response to the magnitude of the failures experienced by the Arab world. The nationalist and anti-imperialist revolutionary certainties of the generation that had come of age during the period of independence gave way to a revision of thought and of political, social, and cultural practices. More often than not, as we shall see, this revision promoted ideological radicalisation, either against imperialism and all of the local social forces aligned with it (Yasin al-Hafiz), or against religious obscurantism (Adonis, Sadiq Jalal al-Azm).

This was also the period during which Arab Marxist thought delivered a critical analysis of the regimes in place, judging them to be *petit bourgeois* and too timid regarding the imperial powers with whom these regimes were trying to negotiate. There were increased calls for popular revolutions, sometimes along the lines of the Chinese example under Mao Zedong. Two other Palestinian resistance movements promoted popular armed struggle against Israel: the Popular Front for the Liberation of Palestine (FPLP) led by Georges Habash, the leader of the Arab Nationalists Movement; and the popular bases of Yasser Arafat's Fatah movement. In 1969, Nasser was sharply criticised by these movements for accepting the 'Rogers Plan,' named for the American secretary of state at that time and which provided for indirect negotiations with Israel as a first step.

Conversely, other intellectuals, some of whom were Marxist, started to settle down and openly promote improved relations with the United States, which in their view was the only power capable of influencing the arrogant behaviour of Israel. This new school of thought flourished particularly in Egypt, where it was encouraged by President Anwar Sadat. He involved Marxist intellectuals in the running of the country, while at the same time holding the door wide open for the return of the Muslim Brotherhood to national politics. This was also the beginning of the period during which some radical and secular intellectuals began to evolve towards a regressive inward turn to Islamic identity as a substitute for Arab nationalist identity (see *infra* Chapter 11). Similarly, the liberals of the former *grande bourgeoisie* began to receive better treatment. The nationalisation initiatives started by Nasser were brought to a halt and assets that had previously been seized were re-privatised. In short, Sadat prepared Egypt's major turn in favour of peace with Israel, which was accomplished in the aftermath of the new Arab-Israeli war in October 1973.

Yasin al-Hafiz and radical revolutionary thought of a secular nature

Starting in the 1970s, Arab thought was influenced by several thinkers who sought to identify the deep causes of the spectacular defeat of 1967. They also rejected the defeatist conclusions of other intellectuals who argued for acceptance of defeat and abandonment of the nationalist and revolutionary ambitions of the Nasserist period. What differentiated this school from others was its call for secularism and for containment in the area of religious faith, which was strongly criticised as a perpetual source of decline. I will discuss here only the best known thinkers, on the understanding that there are many others.

One of the most productive thinkers of this school of thought was Yasin al-Hafiz, born in Syria in 1930 and who died prematurely in Beirut in 1978. He was an influential member of the Baath party in Syria before breaking with it in 1967 to form the Arab Revolutionary Workers Party. This led to his imprisonment for a year in Syria and his emigration to Lebanon in 1968 where he went on to found a publishing house. He subsequently became a highly respected intellectual, particularly for his direct manner of posing pertinent questions about the Arab defeat and internal Arab divisions. One of his most important works was a book he wrote in Arabic shortly before his death entitled 'The Defeat and Defeatist Ideology' which was reprinted many times.[1] He began by painting a broad picture of successive Arab defeats, starting with the 1917 Balfour Declaration and ending with the June 1967 war, before severely critiquing the superficial ideologies that both the Arab nationalists and Arab Marxists had been willing to adopt.

This work was a prime example of one of the rare instances where Arab thought had looked to something other than Europe as its exclusive historical frame of reference. As such, it was a strong criticism of the rationality of Arab thought, which had not sufficiently expanded its horizons. Another work, 'Irrationality in Arab Politics', published in 1975 as a collection of articles and other writings, asked several crucial questions.[2] These included how to determine whether the Arab defeat was simply the result of accumulated errors or whether it stemmed from a more fundamental issue of irrationality; and whether the lag in Arab development was related to technical issues or stemmed from political and ideological backwardness. These two major questions are still relevant today. Al-Hafiz also published a very enlightening book in 1976, 'The Vietnamese Historical Experience: A Comparative Critical Evaluation with Arab Historical

Experience,' in which he compared Vietnam's historical experience of struggle against colonialism to that of the Arabs.[3]

His early works were collected and published in 1965 in a volume entitled 'On Some of the Problems of the Arab Revolution.'[4] In it, he first raised many of the questions that would become the focus of his later works, especially the need to Arabise Marxism, that is, to use it in a way that accounts for the specificities of the socio-economic structures of Arab social classes; but also the need to avoid verbal revolutionary demagoguery. The articles in this collection were written prior to the shock of the 1967 defeat. This is especially interesting because in these articles the author seeks to identify the lessons learned from the failure of the Syro-Egyptian union between 1958 and 1961, which he saw at that time as a foreboding of the failure of the Arab nationalist and progressive advance.

Al-Hafiz's interesting diagnoses were heavily influenced by the thought of Frantz Fanon, whom he cited extensively.[5] He made broad use of the concept of '*petite bourgeoisie*,' a social group that emerged from the popular masses but which tended to disconnect from them to align with the *grande bourgeoisie*. The latter emerged from the wealthy land-owning class, and from the intellectual elites close to those in power. For al-Hafiz, the nationalist convictions of the *grande bourgeoisie* were only verbal, because they always sought to accommodate the former colonial power. He criticised the chauvinism and narcissism that characterised their expression of nationalist ideas by continuously bringing up the glorious past of the Arab nation, its unique genius, and the grandeur of its heritage. This, for al-Hafiz, is what caused Arab nationalist ideology to slide towards fascism and to adopt a reactionary stance.[6]

Clearly alluding to the way the Baath party had sacralised the Arab nation by using a slogan to convey the existence of an 'Arab nation bearing an eternal mission' (*risala khalida*), al-Hafiz launched a sharp critique of the metaphysical and ahistorical concept of the Arab nation. He perfectly summarised the dilemma surrounding '*petit bourgeois*' Arab thought that had abandoned the democratic and progressive elements of the idea of a nation. 'The national movement,' he claimed, 'has only two paths, either it gets transformed into a popular movement, or it simply becomes a pretext for making a fuss about the glorious past and a sterile movement that spins in place.'[7] Further on, he explained how the metaphysical concept of a nation as an entity that has always existed leads to a denial of the impact of history, evolution, and change: 'The eternal presence of a nation in the past can only have repercussions for the future, which is also stable and eternal.'[8] Conceived of in this way, history is repetitive instead of being characterised by assimilation and change.

In this invaluable collection of reflections, al-Hafiz also stated that there are no immutable specificities in a nation's character. Its features are neither absolute nor devoid of change, nor do they derive from some supposed eternal spirit. Rather, they are the result of difficulties that a nation has been subjected to over the course of a given historical period. To support his point of view, al-Hafiz showed that Arab thought is not unique, but rather, that it has taken different forms within different frameworks. In one era, it was religious, metaphysical and magical; in another, it was religious but revived by the scientific mind; and, in yet another, it was pragmatic. 'The overriding truth of Arab thought and the Arab mind', says al-Hafiz, 'is not embodied in a predetermined, isolated, and abstract intellectual mould that is detached from the path of the historical evolution of Arab society. On the contrary, [...] [it] is inscribed in the framework of different stages of the historical evolution of society, [...] in the torments of social reality and, because of this, [...] [it] advances and goes beyond itself through its search for the truth.'[9]

In this volume, Yasin al-Hafiz also provided a very relevant description of how nationalist ideology slipped into metaphysical ideology focused on the past, since it ignored social issues and, consequently, abandoned the revolutionary potential of the people who wished to free themselves from foreign tutelage as well as the tutelage of the *grande bourgeoisie*. He denounced the use of 'religious' McCarthyism that caused nationalism to drift towards a fascist ideology that completely ignored the interests of the dominated and impoverished classes. In short, for al-Hafiz, a nationalist ideology that does not account for the interplay of the conflicting socio-economic interests within society becomes a reactionary ideology that paralyses the progress of a nation and its economic and political independence.

In 1981, other important works by al-Hafiz were published posthumously in a collected volume entitled 'The National Democratic Question' by his Lebanese publisher Dar al-Talia. This publishing house was founded by the remarkable Lebanese intellectual Bashir al-Daouk (1931–2007), who directed it until his death. Al-Daouk was an Arab nationalist, a socialist, as well as a member of the Baath party, and the catalogue of his publishing house is one of the richest in terms of the number of works written by Arab nationalist and progressive thinkers. The themes in this last work by al-Hafiz are varied and include new Arab unionist perspectives, the causes of the failure of the union between Syria and Egypt, the evolution of the unionist thought of Gamal Abdel Nasser, minority and communitarian problems, especially in Lebanon and Egypt, and the need for secularism, Marxism, and Arab religious thought. It clearly shows the critical and deconstructive approach used by Yasin al-Hafiz to free Arab thought from its constraints. The work produced by this activist intellectual is more relevant than ever today and deserves wider attention from contemporary younger generations of Arabs. This is because it contains key means for understanding why Arabs have been powerless to build one nation, or ultimately to build different, coherent and well-respected, Arab states.

Sadiq Jalal al-Azm and Adonis: their fight against religious obscurantism

Born into an upper class family in Damascus in 1934, Sadiq Jalal al-Azm wrote brilliant prose and was gifted with a critical mind and a sarcastic wit. With his vast knowledge of the Western philosophical tradition, he first became known in the Arab world following the 1967 military defeat when he published a vitriolic pamphlet against Islam and its practices. In 'Critique of Religious Thought,' which appeared in Arabic in 1967 in Beirut, he blamed this defeat on the obscurantist religious mind which he accused of being responsible for Arab weakness.[10] He even denounced certain verses of the Qur'an for creating an imaginary that was mythical and harmful, especially those verses that dealt with the existence of the devil (*iblis*).

Under pressure from the Muslim religious authorities of Lebanon, this pamphlet caused al-Azm to be relieved of his teaching duties at the American University of Beirut. He was then denounced within Arab Muslim religious circles as a dangerous atheist influenced by Marxist materialism. However, this was a time when Islamic movements had not yet started to call for the deaths of atheists and Muslim thinkers who criticised the rigid and excessive positions found in the theologico-political theories along the lines of those formulated by Sayyid Qutb, one of the central thinkers in the Muslim Brotherhood movement.

Al-Azm was therefore not the target of assassination attempts and was able to continue his intellectual career as a free thinker. He was invited to teach in various European and American universities before returning to Damascus in 1977 to become the Director of Western Philosophical Studies at the National Syrian University in Damascus, which was controlled by the Baath party. This decision surprised Arab democratic circles since this move might have appeared to be an endorsement of the Syrian dictatorial regime. Twenty-two years later, in 1999, he left Damascus once again to move between Beirut and various European capitals where he was invited to give lectures.

Al-Azm's work is varied and often focuses on denouncing 'taboos.' In 1989, Imam Khomeini, who had become the Supreme Leader of the new Iranian state following the 1979 revolution, issued an edict (*fatwa*) calling for the death of Salman Rushdie, the Indian Muslim author of *The Satanic Verses*, an event that became known as the Rushdie affair. Al-Azm courageously defended Rushdie and denounced all those who blindly participated in the condemnation of his work without even reading it or understanding its literary and philosophical symbolism.[11] He also authored brilliant critical analyses, including in particular a lengthy study of Edward Said's *Orientalism*. Al-Azm found that in his approach to the work of Western Orientalists, Said had employed the holistic method – modelled on the approach of Michel Foucault – which was the very method Said had denounced the Orientalists for using. In so doing, according to al-Azm, Said had petrified and essentialised this community of scholars as promoters of a set of anthropological stereotypes and invariants that allegedly made Islam ill-suited to modernity. Thus, in al-Azm's view, Said had created an 'Orientalism in reverse.'[12]

Despite being a great critical intellectual, Al-Azm also took much-criticised positions on the tragic events in Syria since 2011. Indeed, when speaking about this topic at conferences in Europe, al-Azm unfortunately lapsed into an oversimplified communitarian analysis by condensing the conflict into a clash between the harshness of the Alawite minority in Syria, who allegedly held all the power, and the majority Sunni population, who were therefore oppressed by the Alawites.[13] He also expressed confidence in the moderate Islamist movements on the grounds that they were open to the West and therefore capable of governing Syria.

I turn now to Ali Ahmad Said, known as Adonis, who is also from Syria. Born in 1930, he is a major intellectual and literary figure in the Arab world and the recipient of numerous awards for his poetry. After joining the Syrian People's Party, he was imprisoned in Syria while doing his military service in 1954. In 1956, he left Syria for Lebanon, where he established himself and founded an avant-garde journal entitled *Shi'r* (Poetry) with another major Lebanese poet, Youssef al-Khal. In 1969, he founded a second journal, *Mawaqif* (Positions), which promoted secularism as a solution to the problems of the Arab world.

Beyond the world of poetry, his major work comprised his doctoral thesis, which he defended in 1973 at the University of Saint Joseph in Beirut. In it, he developed an excessively critical approach to Islam, which he blamed for derailing any attempt to bring about change and progress due to the restrictive constants it imposes on culture and thought. Published in Arabic as 'The Constant and the Changing',[14] this work constituted a strong manifesto against the central tenets of Islam and its supposedly rigid founding principles that thwart every attempt at in-depth reform of Arab society and culture. It was a direct and open call, within the tradition of Muslim reformers, to shake off the yoke of religion and its clerics (the *ulama*). This work is very representative of secular and revolutionary Arab thought, even though the author does not make any claims to the Marxist ideology that contributed to radicalising the national aspirations for change. Unlike Sadiq al-Azm, Adonis was able to maintain a certain distance from the warring factions of the bloody Syrian crisis.

The original and enlightening work of Abdallah Laroui

In order to conclude this brief overview, it is necessary to discuss the work of Abdallah Laroui. Born in Morocco in 1933, he is one of the most original critical thinkers in the Marxist tradition who attempted to explain the permanent crisis of Arab intellectuals. However, his work cannot be characterised as that of a fully Marxist Arab thinker because, unlike the authors previously discussed, or those to come, the concept of class struggle does not dominate his analysis. Although he adheres to Marxism, the main concepts of Marxism do not form the underpinnings of Laroui's thought. To be sure, Laroui's thought is primarily dialectical, but this analytical technique is applied generally to the relationships between the Arab world and Europe. He provided a relevant framework of analysis for many points used to explain the evolution of ideas in Arab society regarding the relationship of dependence on European thought. In this sense, his reflection is more nuanced than that of Edward Said, and for this reason more useful. Laroui is more interested in analysing the relationship of dependence than in an overall denunciation of Europe's dominant position with respect to the Arab Orient.

His major work, *L'Idéologie arabe contemporaine* (Contemporary Arab Ideology), is a highly stimulating essay that attributes this crisis to the fact that Arab intellectuals were late to integrate the different stages of European modernity into their vision. 'Every time an Arab writer provides a diagnosis of their society that sheds light on its flaws and deficiencies, there is a specific image of the West that is implicated within it', he explained in this book in

1967. 'For the past seventy-five years, many definitions of Arab society have been put forth. To what extent were these definitions determined, or not determined, by the very idea of the West that was prevalent?'[15] For Laroui, there are three major figures of the Arab intellectual. The first is the cleric, entrenched within the binary oppositions of Orient versus West and Islam versus Christianity. Next is the politician who replaced the cleric and now occupies centre stage. Being the 'new man,' he has declared that the despotism of various Islamic regimes is not really Arab, nor is it even Islamic. Lastly, there is the technophile, who succeeded the two previous figures. He believes that Western power comes primarily from its scientific and technological successes, and not necessarily from liberty and democracy. In Laroui's critical description of this technophile, he is presented as someone who believes that he has moved beyond both the cleric and the politician. He has abandoned the major inquiry into the causes of the decline of Arab societies and believes he has finally unlocked the secret of the West's success: 'he believes he has moved beyond the cleric and the liberal politician; in fact, he has quickly and effortlessly appropriated the West, having cut himself off a bit too readily from his past; this has not made the West any clearer to him, rather, it is his own history that has now become more opaque.'[16]

'These three men,' adds Laroui, 'actually represent three moments in Arab consciousness, which has attempted since the end of the last century [nineteenth] to understand itself and to understand the West. They have been described here in an abstract way because they can be found in different literary expressions – essays, newspaper articles, plays – and are not embodied in the same man for all Arab countries.'[17] This major work of Arab thought thus concentrates on the critical deconstruction of the dialectical interplay between the consciousness of the West and the consciousness of the self, as well as the search for authenticity. This is where Laroui's expression 'the future anterior' comes from, and in this respect he shares some of the conclusions reached by the Jordanian historian Fahmy Gedaan (see *supra*, Chapter 7).

Continuing his tripartite analysis along the same lines, he identified three types of historical consciousness in contemporary Arab thought. The first is reflective history, or that which accepts decline as part of the order of things and therefore accepts that there are discontinuities in history. Next is hypostatised history, which refers to seeking refuge in the Arabic language and in the cultivation of classical heritage. The last of these is positivist history, which allegedly continues to be imprisoned by the writings of Western Orientalists and by the trials and errors of contemporary Arab historians. For

Laroui, positivist history can only emerge once a modern state has been established within Arab society; but also once the sacred history of Islam and the various narratives from the classical period are marginalised in a manner that reveals how the evolution of socio-economic structures determined the disruptions and continuities.

In this same work Laroui argued in favour of an objective Marxism that could replace positivism. He presented Marxism as the tool of the future for achieving unity within Arab society, a unity that would not be cut off from the universal because this mode of thought by definition aspires to the universal. 'In truth,' Laroui states, '[Marxism] is the complete and satisfying model that everyone is unconsciously seeking without being able to grasp it due to the unfinished structuring of our society and its incomplete interpenetration with the West.'[18] For him, Marxism is the best 'truth system' because it is the 'system of systems,' 'the methodical summary of Western history in which the accuracy of details hardly matters.' He later adds: 'the West can be either Bergsonian or phenomenological, the Arab Orient can only give a positivist reading to that which has been integrated into the Hegelian register.'[19] In fact, Laroui's main preoccupation is the integration of Arab society into the global evolution of humanity led by the West and the values forged by its modernity. This is what leads him to state that it is a matter of 'gradually unifying the "self" (tradition) and the "non-self" (the West)', but that it is necessary to abandon the 'imaginary mode' in order to stop experiencing the dialectic as an ideology and to 'use it as a method.'[20]

A few years later, in 1974, Laroui wrote a follow-up to this work entitled *The Crisis of the Arab Intellectual*, in which he extended his previous analyses and reiterated his belief that Marxism was the only intellectual method through which the Arab world could overcome its backwardness with respect to European modernity.[21] In it, he claimed that there was a need for a 'historicist' view of the evolution of societies as opposed to that of 'traditionalism', and argued that there were two types of nationalisms in the Arab world, one that is focused on preserving the past and the other on change and progress. Likewise, he analysed the disenchantment of European positivist thought, now in search of new metaphysical horizons, which resulted in lending more credibility to mysticism and transcendency, and therefore to certain aspects of Islam. This trend influenced Arab positivist thought and led some Arab intellectuals to see their traditional religious heritage differently. As in the work of other thinkers who were more clearly nationalist and Marxist than Laroui, and who will be discussed later, there is an attempt in his book to analyse the social make-up of Arab intellectuals and their classification as '*petite bourgeoisie*'.

Finally, in 1987, perhaps because he was giving in to the trend towards a return to religion, Laroui wrote *Islam et modernité* (Islam and Modernity). In this book he returned to the idea of a crisis in Arab society in a chapter entitled 'Islam arabe et crise de culture' (Arab Islam and Crisis of Culture),[22] in which he referred to this crisis within the Arab intelligentsia as 'historic, social, and psychological.' He also identified the various parameters that constitute this intelligentsia and described how they affect its lack of coherence. These parameters include a loss of fascination with ideologies, the multi-faceted crisis of the developing world to which this intelligentsia belongs, the fragmentation of the Arab homeland into uneven and heterogeneous entities, the heterogeneity of local elites, and the diversity of educational methods. For Laroui, neo-Islam along the lines of the Muslim Brotherhood 'is a reflection of the historical crisis that Arab society is experiencing without ever being its solution.'[23] He concluded the chapter in a rather crude way that is nonetheless somewhat justified. For him, the Arab intellectual 'is exhausted by the very contradiction he has set up for himself, and which he has made into the theme of a melodrama that he continually performs, analyses, and describes.' He added that 'he flails about without helping society to change; and society, for its part, is not changing fast enough to present him with a *fait accompli* that would invalidate his private melodrama, his antinomies, and even his problematics.'[24] In short, Laroui seems to express a strong yearning for an Arab version of Lenin, someone who is at once a revolutionary thinker and both actor in and producer of a profound revolution.

This work does not really encompass Islamist thought, which he referred to as neo-Islamic, except in the second to last chapter of the book entitled, 'Islam and Enlightenment Philosophy.' In it, the author shows how the 'Salafism' of the Muslim Brotherhood started with the same premises as those of al-Afghani and Muhammad 'Abduh; then turned against them, accusing them of secularism, gradualism, and even of belonging to the Freemasons. This led to the discrediting of the Enlightenment philosophy that had so strongly influenced the first Muslim Arab reformers.

I have chosen to delve a bit further into Laroui's work because his originality is indisputable and his critical analysis of the successive stages of Arab thought (clerical, political, technical) still seems valid today. Laroui published not only in French (with Arabic translations for each one of his works), he also wrote several works directly in Arabic. Among these, one addressed the concept of the state, another the concepts of ideology and ideologisation, and yet another the concept of liberty.[25] Another work he wrote in Arabic was on Arabs and historical thought.[26]

National thought through the prism of Marxist critical reflection

Several other important thinkers who drew on registers of Marxism other than those of interest to Laroui (those relating to the interplay of social groups), have left their mark on Arab culture and thought. Ironically, as will be shown, this opening to the Marxist view of the world did more to enrich national and critical thought within Islam than it did for economic thought about the underdevelopment of Arab societies. Several of the key concepts that became widely used at that time in various developing world Marxisms, especially those stemming from South America, will no doubt be useful here for understanding the Western capitalist domination within which Arab societies have evolved. This is the case with the concept of 'comprador-bourgeoisie', a social class that prospers only from the crumbs left over by large international corporations. This concept contrasts with the concept of a 'national bourgeoisie' that is trying to develop an industrial capitalism capable of breaking the bonds of dependence between the global capitalist centre and the societies on the periphery who are either colonised or under the influence of neo-colonialism. The distrust in this case is just as deep with respect to the *'petite bourgeoisie'* who have distanced themselves from the poor and working class masses to follow their dream of a Western-style consumer society. In reality, it was the search for coherent nation building that gave Marxist-inspired Arab thought its strong aspiration for states to be truly independent and thus the ability to put an end to the humiliating situation of economic and military dependence on former colonial powers. To this end, the desire for Arab unity became a logical necessity in order to expand the different markets that resulted from the fragmentation of Arab states by colonialism and to build a socialist form of industrialisation.

Samir Amin's Marxist internationalist humanism

One of the best known representatives of Marxist Arab thought is Samir Amin, an Egyptian economist (born in 1931) who has become known internationally for the numerous works he has written on capitalism in the countries of the global South and the relationships between the developed capitalist centres and the underdeveloped peripheries, as well as between Egypt and the Arab world. He is also known for his involvement in founding the World Social Forum in 2001, alongside his fellow countryman Anwar Abdel-Malek, another scholar whose importance has already been discussed (see *supra*, Chapter 8),[27] Samir Amin expressed in his work an openness to Marxist internationalist humanism, which was a far cry from other types of entrenched dogmatic thought. He strongly criticised Nasserist Egypt for not being revolutionary enough with respect to changing socio-economic structures and relations of production within Egypt as well as its relationship to the capitalist developed world. This, he argued, is what prevented Egypt, a key country within the Arab world, from ending its socio-economic underdevelopment once and for all.[28] He also wrote a very interesting book on the 'crisis of Arab society,' which was published in 1985. In it, he undertook a systematic critique of radical Islamic fundamentalism, such as that formulated, for example, in Sayyid Qutb's work on social justice in Islam, along with a broader critique of what he somewhat inaccurately called 'Salafism', which was on the rise at the time this work was published.[29]

In criticising Qutb's work, he focused on his division of humanity into Muslim and non-Muslim societies. According to Qutb, only Muslim societies have any value and, therefore, they have no need to draw inspiration from any other model of society. Amin readily shows that there is no single Islamic model of society, but rather, that Muslim societies have evolved for centuries as a result of socio-economic changes. This explains the development of a wide variety of Islamic jurisprudence up until the twelfth century. At this time, the doors to Qur'anic exegesis were closed under the influence of al-Ghazali, who denounced philosophy for its potential to alienate people from religion. Furthermore, Amin clearly demonstrates the similarities with the evolution of Christianity. He discusses at length the sterility of the opposition between tradition, which alone is seen as authentic, and modernity, which is viewed as having disfigured and alienated Muslim society. For him, the rise of religious fundamentalism is the result of the widespread socio-economic crisis in the Arab world, although he provides no solution to it.[30] He correctly believes that arguments that pit the notion of 'heritage' (or of 'tradition', *turath*) against that of modernity are highly abstract and stymie the development of reform programmes and changes necessary for Arab society to address contemporary life. This, as he explains, is because there is not one single Islamic model, but rather, many different ways to be Islamic, as the history of different periods of time have shown.[31] In his conclusion to this work, he argues that two main factors have contributed to the crisis in Arab society. 'On the one hand, failure and disappointment, on the other, an inability to meet people's needs. It is the failure of the Arab bourgeoisie and its national hopes.' Furthermore, he adds, it was 'the ideology of the Arab left that did not see that failure was inevitable,' and that this failure would lead to the return of 'domination by comprador capitalism and the strategic aims of the dominant imperialism.' The rise of Islamic fundamentalism is therefore due to this failure, and it is merely a desperate response to a crisis that 'justifies all compromises in the national and social field.'[32]

Mahdi Amil's critical deconstruction

In line with Samir Amin, whose intellectual career flourished internationally in terms of his reflection on the problems of the developing world, the Marxist thinkers who remained in their own countries focused their intellectual efforts on deconstructing the conservative and reactionary use of the notion of Arab Islamic heritage and its instrumentalisation by the Arab 'bourgeoisie' in order to maintain the underdevelopment of Arab societies. This was done brilliantly by the Lebanese intellectual, Hassan Hamdan (1936–1987), who was assassinated in Beirut in 1987. Better known under his nom de plume Mahdi Amil, he used his caustic pen and boundless wit to demonstrate the drifts and contradictions within the thought of many Arab intellectuals who 'reified' and idealised this heritage, thereby rendering it a barrier to change and modernity. Very few Arab intellectuals were spared the criticism of Amil, an intellectual who called for the constitution of an elite to represent workers and exploited groups in the Arab world. He did so, with a view to bringing an end to the reign of the intellectuals in the dominant strata of society and to overcome dependence and underdevelopment.

One of his books, written in 1974, provided a remarkable deconstruction of the presentations given by several Arab intellectuals during a conference held in Kuwait in the same year on the 'crisis of Arab civilisation'.[33] In it, Hamdan demonstrated the essentialism that pervaded most of these presentations with regard to Arab civilisation and deconstructed the ideology of modernity. He also deconstructed the discourse on heritage (*turath*) that is so often imported from Hegelian discourse and from the discourse of European Orientalists. This discourse itself created the concept of heritage that justified the concept of modernity. For Hamdan, 'powerlessness is not to be found in the Arab mind, which is not underdeveloped, but it is to be found in the colonial-style Arab bourgeoisie who aspire, in vain, within their class-based imaginary, to assimilate into the imperialist bourgeoisie.'[34] This is because, as he had previously explained with his inimitable caustic logic, 'the Arab mind cannot restart its development unless it ceases to develop in relation to everything related to the Arab mind. What then is to be done? Either the Arab mind restarts its development and thus becomes a non-Arab mind, or it remains an Arab mind and continues to halt its development.'[35] It would be hard to find a better way to frame the crisis of Arab thought in the grip of a serious identity-based psychosis, that of either losing or sublating its heritage, or remaining imprisoned by the essentialisation of this heritage.

In his last work, which he had not finished writing when he was assassinated, Mahdi Amil continued his caustic criticism of contemporary Arab thought, which he denounced as day-to-day thought (what the French historian François Hartog might have called 'presentism'), which allows itself to be influenced by both major and minor events on a daily basis.[36] Amil also provided a forceful criticism of Adonis, the most famous living poet of the Arab world, as this form of thought is expressed in his book, 'The Constant and the Changing.'[37] He also criticised the enthusiasm Adonis expressed for the 1979 Iranian Revolution, which contradicted all of the secular positions he had taken in the past. Amil strongly objected to the conceptual language that Adonis used, which omitted any analysis of opposing structures and social forces, language that he argued was essentialist and culturalist. Other Marxist thinkers such as Tayyeb Tizini (born in Syria in 1934) and Husayn Mroué (1908–1987) directed similar criticism towards thinkers who focused on the issue of Arab heritage and the almost immutable mental system it allegedly creates. I will come back to this issue.

When it comes to his criticism of Adonis, Amil also faults him for confining himself to the conceptual universe of European idealist thought, thereby refusing a social dialectical approach and its relation to the world of ideas. To support this criticism, Amil cites a sentence written by Adonis which clearly demonstrates the problem. In his description of religious heritage, Adonis states that he 'settled for the study of cultural phenomena in and of themselves by excluding their material basis.'[38] Being a thoroughly conscientious reader of the writers he critiqued, Amil demonstrated all of the contradictions that run through Adonis' work concerning the impossibility of escape from the constraints of religious heritage and the epistemological fluctuations inherent in his method of analysis. One sentence summarises the relevance of his criticism particularly well. In it, he shows how the poet's thought is confined within a completely unrestrained essentialism due to which the author sees in Arab culture only an 'essentialist struggle between essence and essence', the essence of the Arab individual 'torn between himself in his being and himself in his non-being, that is, between himself and the other to the extent that this other is the reification of being.'[39] Amil also explained how God is also reified within this conception of Arab culture maintained by many thinkers, even those with secular and rationalist tendencies. He argued that it represents an exclusively metaphysical thought (*ghaybiyya*) with no connection to reality.

In this same work, Amil used his sharp and caustic mind to denounce the way in which many intellectuals fluctuate between being dyed-in-the-wool modernists, sometimes even Marxists, and marvelling at the revolutionary potential of religion following the events in Iran in 1979. He cited, deconstructed, and ridiculed numerous newspaper articles written by secular thinkers who lauded the Iranian religious revolution without even realising that in so doing they were renouncing everything they had believed in up until that time. For many thinkers of this period, the Iranian revolution substantiated the claim that an essentialist difference existed between the Orient and the West. Amil mocked this dichotomy and denounced the entire ideology of the specificity of the Orient with respect to the West as a 'deceptive' (*muzayyafa*) ideology, one embedded within thought that in and of itself embodies deceit.[40]

At the same time, Amil considered that this thought produced by an alterity that was closed in on itself was reinforced in many Arab thinkers through their reading of Jacques Berque (*Les Arabes d'hier à demain*,[41] [The Arabs from Yesterday to Tomorrow]) or Frantz Fanon's *The Wretched of the Earth*,[42] and of Sartre's preface to this work. In reality, he put on trial the binary problematics of an anthropological and ontological nature, still fashionable today, that divide the world into the self and the other, winners and losers, and the developing world and the West.[43] Nonetheless, Amil recognised that the thought of Frantz Fanon, who experienced the Algerian revolution from the inside, could not be equated with that of the thinkers he referred to as 'Islamists' (*muta'aslimun*), as Fanon's thought was truly revolutionary and warned against the temptation on the part of the national bourgeoisie to join the imperial bourgeoisie.[44] Indeed, he referred to members of the intellectual elite as 'Islamists who have rediscovered the potential for political instrumentalisation of religious heritage.'[45]

Amil was one of the most forceful and rigorous thinkers of the Arab world, with an exceptional capacity for critical analysis. While it is certainly possible to find fault with his Marxist approach, his conceptual apparatus was nonetheless still very clear. His frequent use of the term '*bourgeoisie*' in his work can, in my view, be seen as the equivalent of dominant class or group, a reality that is difficult to deny.

The important works of Tayyeb Tizini and Elias Morcos

Another great thinker from Lebanon who was also assassinated in 1987 is Husayn Mroué. Mroué became famous for his materialist reading of heritage in a three volume work entitled *Materialist Conflicts in Arab and Islamic Philosophy*.[46] In an excellent analysis of his thought, Mroué was referred to as the 'shaykh of materialist thought,' and the richness of his approach, which can be described as consisting of a comparison of ancient ideological disputes with those of the present, as well as an analysis of the interaction between local and foreign philosophies and thought.[47] Mroué showed that the impact of external thought on internal thought was connected to the nature of existing relationships between different currents of internal thought and the social forces and relationships of production that drove them.

There are other Marxist-inspired thinkers who should be mentioned here, although it is not possible to expand on their rich and abundant body of work that is, nonetheless, worthy of careful study. This is the case regarding Tayyeb Tizini, who devoted his life to teaching philosophy at the University of Damascus after earning his doctorate in Germany. Tizini produced a considerable body of work focused on the analysis of Arab thought in the classical period at the dawn of Arab-Islamic civilisation and compared it with the evolution of socio-economic structures of the time. He showed that this thought was inscribed within the general evolution of human thought while still maintaining its specificity and its originality. He thus warned against jumping on the bandwagon and using new schools of European thought, such as structuralism and functionalism, schools that he claimed were ahistorical.[48]

Lastly, another name worthy of mention here is that of Elias Morcos (1927–1991), a Syrian who devoted his life to teaching in his country and who was very close to Yasin al-Hafiz. He left behind a large body of work characterised by a systematic Marxist critique of both the 'rationality' of the Arab mind and contemporary nationalist thought as well as the practice of armed Palestinian movements. Nor should we omit to mention an important ancestor of Arab Marxist and humanist thought already described in a previous chapter, Raif Khoury (see *supra*, Chapter 3). In 1937, he wrote a remarkable essay on human rights and on the need for the Arab world to adopt their socialist version, that is, a version that contains the complete set of social rights, all at a time when the concept of social rights was still unknown to many European liberal democracies.[49]

Many of the thinkers discussed in this chapter have now either passed away or have reached an advanced age. They introduced incredibly rich critical methods into Arab thought and often had encyclopaedic knowledge of the history of the East as well as that of the West. However, their thought was marginalised by circumstances that encouraged an Islamist thought that was anthropological and essentialist in nature. This played a major role in negating the contribution of critical thought, and even demonised it by claiming it was Marxist or secular and, therefore, anti-Muslim. It is this thought that will be examined next.

CHAPTER 11

Islamic nationalisms as anti-nationalist Arab thought

It is tempting here to qualify the Islamist thought that structures its worldview exclusively according to the narrow concepts of Islam as anti-national, rather than anti-nationalist. This is for reasons that will be clarified by describing the context in which this thought emerged. In its early period, Islamist thought maintained a strictly defensive stance of protest against the catastrophes caused by Arab revolutionary leaders. This was prior to it going onto the attack, starting with the war to liberate Afghanistan, which at the time was occupied by the Soviets. Its virulence intensified following the attacks on New York and Washington, D.C. on 11 September 2001, which put the spotlight on Osama bin Laden, the man to whom the attacks were attributed. Bin Laden did not immediately take credit for them, but when he did so a few weeks later, he was suddenly broadcast on television screens around the world.

The different forms of radical Islamic thought have been broadly outlined and disseminated within academic literature and the media over the past few decades, as I have already indicated. This chapter will therefore only briefly summarise this school of thought, since there are countless general interest works on this topic that readers can consult. It is more important to return to a detailed examination of the internal Arab and the external geopolitical contexts that marked the period during which anti-national Arab thought developed. This is the only way to truly understand its workings and its logic.

A return to the context in which 'anti-national' Islamist thought emerged

Chapter 4 contains a brief description of the general evolution of the political and geopolitical contexts that constrained and oriented the various different currents of Arab thought. The impact of the Cold War on the rivalries and contradictions of Arab regimes were discussed, as well as the policies of instrumentalisation of religion by the United States, particularly through its strategic alliance with Saudi Arabia and Pakistan. This instrumentalisation was reinforced by providing military and religious training to many young Arab 'jihadists' who were sent to fight Soviet troops in Afghanistan throughout the 1980s. This major effort contributed to deflecting attention away from problems that were specific to Arab societies. These included problems related to social and economic development as well as the unacceptable fate of the victimised Palestinians; but also the ongoing Israeli occupation of parts of Syrian and Lebanese territories.

Henceforth, people thought less within an Arab framework and more within the framework of the Muslim world, which was considerably larger. This gave a strong boost to the Islamist school of Arab thought, embodied by movements such as the Muslim Brotherhood, which had been active since the 1930s. At the same time, the radical Wahhabi doctrine spread by Saudi Arabia, now a major international player within the framework of the Cold War due to its petroleum resources, increasingly became the major current of thought within the 'orthodox' Islam aligned with Sunnism in the Arab world and in non-Arab Muslim societies more generally.

This is the context that fostered the emergence of anti-national thought in the name of achieving a transnational Islamic society, a context that differed greatly from the one that had stimulated pan-Islamic thought in the nineteenth century. Bear in mind that the pan-Islamic school of thought considered that in order to face the challenge of the vigorous expansion of European colonialism, all Muslim peoples needed to rally around the Ottoman Sultan. Islam needed to be modernised and reformed in order to adapt to the modern world. European colonialism was seen as a global phenomenon that required a global response from colonised peoples. These first generations of thinkers, whose work was described in Chapter 6, nonetheless continued to view Europe as a source of inspiration for reform.

However, this school of thought had not adequately accounted for the widespread nationalist sentiments fuelled by the circulation of European political ideas outside Europe. This circulation weakened traditional imperial structures that grouped people of different languages and cultures together, which was the case in the Ottoman and Austro-Hungarian Empires.[1] Similarly, the pan-Islamism of the nineteenth and early twentieth century, while open to certain aspects of European modernity, did not realise that religion alone could not serve as the glue to hold together a multi-communitarian imperial structure. Nor did it realise that the nationalist claims of the different peoples within the empire would soon deeply undermine its historical legitimacy.

As has been demonstrated, those who promoted reformist pan-Islamism were often referred to as 'Salafists', that is, 'religious conservatives.' The use of this term is misleading because while it claims to reflect the original spirit of Islam and the genius of the 'founding fathers' of this new religion, the proposed reforms themselves reflect a modernist spirit. The content of many Qur'anic verses was reinterpreted as having been the source of modern ideas such as the improvement of the status of women, the establishment of a form of political power that requires leaders to solicit a broad number of opinions, and institutions that support social justice; especially the care of ageing parents, widows and orphans, as well as payment of a tax on wealth (*zakat*) along with a requirement that the revenues collected be dedicated to improving the lives of the very poor.

This was quite different from the Arab anti-nationalism of an Islamic nature that began to develop in the second half of the twentieth century in a context that was no longer that of European colonialism in rapid decline. Rather, it was the context of the Cold War and the Arab nationalist and socialist-style dictatorships that dominated the Arab scene at that time. In the midst of these circumstances, an alliance was formed, which has endured to the present day. This was between the United States and the so-called conservative Arab monarchies whose existence was severely threatened following the end of the Second World War and during the period of decolonisation by the rising revolutionary and unionist tides in the Arab world.

It is no small task to try to understand this unnatural alliance between developed industrial democracies and patrimonial-type monarchies, one of which, namely Saudi Arabia, had established an extremely authoritarian political and religious regime. This regime relies on a religious police force that exercises perpetual daily control over the life of all of the king's subjects and forbids all freedom of worship within the kingdom, except for the Wahhabist version of Islam. In reality, at the time of the Cold War, the idea was to revive the old pan-Islamism of the Ottoman era, which had completely disappeared from the Arab intellectual landscape. Pan-Islamism had been intended to act as a dam against European colonial expansion and to prevent the dismantling of the Ottoman Empire. The new form of pan-Islamism relied on the old identity-based theory of the unity and solidarity of Muslim societies whose purpose was not so much that of acting as a dam against European colonialism, but rather, to fight the expansion of communism within the ranks of young people in the Arab world and elsewhere in Muslim contexts. Consequently, it was fitting to 're-Islamise' Arab and Muslim societies to make them less susceptible to anti-imperialist Marxist doctrine.

A pocket guide to the thought of modern Islamic movements: Wahhabism and the Muslim Brotherhood

This new Islamic thought drew its inspiration from two main sources, that of the Wahhabi doctrine that emerged in the eighteenth century in the heart of the Arabian Peninsula, and that of the Muslim Brotherhood organisation formed in Egypt in 1928, whose most important thinker was Sayyid Qutb.

Wahhabism is a puritanical religious doctrine developed by Muhammad ibn 'Abd al-Wahhab, a preacher born in Najd in 1703, roughly one hundred years before Napoleon's expedition to Egypt. This doctrine did not therefore result from a clash with European ideas, but from the ambition of a preacher who formed an alliance with a local tribal chief, 'Abd al-'Aziz ibn Sa'ud, to conquer the Arabian Peninsula. The emergence of this doctrine had nothing to do with the major Islamic reform movement and with the renaissance of a consciousness of collective Arab identity previously described.[2] This, however, is the error made by most analyses of the Islamic reform movements that incorporate Wahhabism within the manifestations of Islamic reform inscribed in the Arab cultural renaissance that began in the nineteenth century.[3] The birth date of the founder of Wahhabism, 1703, in and of itself should have prevented any confusion about the origins of this movement. This clear historical reference, however, was of no use to some who have analysed the 'Islamic awakening of the past decades.' We are treading here in the terrain of a romantic and exotic historical fiction that has established a narrative on Islamic reform that is completely disconnected from the complexities of the real world.[4]

It is true that the alliance of Wahhabism's founder with the Saud family, an alliance continued by their respective successors, constituted the major foundation of an expansion within the entire Arab world that aimed to re-establish the unity of Muslims and to set up an Islamic regime in every country where they could seize power. Wahhabism rejects any worship of saints within Islam, which it equates with paganism. It holds that the tombs and monuments erected in their memory must be systematically destroyed, something we still see today with the Taliban, and with followers of the 'Islamic State' (known as 'Daesh' according to its Arabic acronym) and al-Qaida in the Islamic Maghrib (AQIM) in the Sahel. This doctrine also rejects any innovation or change regarding a completely literal reading of the Qur'anic text.

Wahhabism actually established itself in two stages. The first, exemplified by the ephemeral conquest of the early nineteenth century, was marked by the rejection of state borders on the pretence that the conquests needed to continue until Islam had succeeded in establishing its puritanical and radical formula in every Muslim society and by converting other peoples. The second, more modern stage resulted from the establishment of Saudi Arabia within state borders, something the followers of the doctrine were obliged to accept, through the Saud family's use of force in 1921, assisted by the British army. At this point the Wahhabi warriors had wanted to continue the movement of conquest and extend it to other Arab and Muslim countries.[5]

Today, the Wahhabi doctrine rejects two features of modernity. Western secularism, as it is equated with atheism, and the plurality of opinions and religions within Muslim societies, in virtue of the monopoly that Wahhabism claims to exercise over the interpretation of Islam with all of its prescriptions of the most extreme form. Excommunication (*takfir*), or the act of denying Islamic identity to someone who does not follow religious precepts to the letter, is the standard practice implemented by this radical school of thought. It is also what makes Wahhabism one of the most rigid Islamic doctrines, with its origination of a movement for the purification of practices. Although worship of saints (*al-awliya*) developed almost everywhere in the Muslim world, the Wahhabi doctrine alleges that these practices strayed from the monotheistic prescriptions of the Prophet. Takfirism thus promotes the killing of any Muslim considered to be 'unfaithful' to their religion or who has abandoned its rigorous practice under the influence of Western morals. Of course it also allows for the killing of non-Muslim infidels who oppress Muslim peoples or who impose 'non-Islamic' morals.

These elements of the Wahhabi doctrine can also be found to varying degrees in the literature of the Muslim Brotherhood. The birth of this organisation is contemporaneous with that of the Kingdom of Saudi Arabia, which is unlikely to be a mere coincidence. In a book published in 2009, the Egyptian political scientist Amr el-Shobaki correctly analysed the double face of this organisation. The language of one face seeks to accommodate Islam within modern democracy and has members of the Brotherhood participate in parliamentary life whenever possible. Its other face is more secret and radical and relies on a covert armed militia.[6]

The radicalness of the Muslim Brotherhood's ideological stance, notwithstanding all of its efforts to soften it, relies on the work of Sayyid Qutb, a member of the Brotherhood and indisputably the most gifted thinker of the modern Islamic movement. Condemned to death and executed in 1966 by Nasser's regime after being accused of plotting to kill the Egyptian president, Qutb is venerated as a martyr. He was a particularly gifted writer with a flamboyant style, and in his abundant body of work he created an enchanted world based on the idea that Islam could represent a type of perfection if only its principles and its institutions were implemented in every area of social and political life. This idealised 'Qutbian' vision is what gave rise to the very appealing slogan, 'Islam is the solution', claiming that society could be cured of its woes (poverty, corruption, inequality, immorality, weakness and underdevelopment, etc.) through the complete application of the principles of religion.

Qutb's work draws on elements from both the doctrine of Muhammad ibn 'Abd al-Wahhab and that of Sayyid Abul A'la Maududi (1903–1979), a Muslim Indian thinker who actively worked towards the creation of a state that would gather together all of India's Muslims so that they could live separately from Hindus. This was achieved through a bloodbath in 1947 with the creation of Pakistan ('country of the pure' in Urdu),[7] the constitution of which was apparently inspired by Maududi. In addition, in 1941 he formed the Jamaat-e-Islami party, which is still active as of 2015 in several Asian countries and engaged in armed struggle for the incorporation of the Muslims of Kashmir into Pakistan.

The main elements of Qutb's doctrine can be summarised as follows: realisation of the sovereignty of God and of his law over all men, which explains why every Muslim is obliged to fight for this goal through continual combat against Arab political regimes declared to be 'impious' because they have returned to the *jahiliyya,* the pagan period that preceded the Qur'anic Revelation. Qutb reproaches the new Arab states that resulted from the collapse of the Ottoman Empire and the anti-colonial struggle for secularising and modernising institutions according to a Western model. In his view, only the Qur'an and shari'a law, which is simply the implementation of the prescriptions in the Holy Book according to the numerous subsequent legal draftings, can be used as the sources of an Islamic government, one which alone is capable of making justice reign among all believers.

The work by Qutb that probably most contributed to the prestige that his school of thought still enjoys today is his book on social justice in Islam. A very good French translation of this work was published in Beirut in 2003[8] and an English translation in 2002.[9] Citing numerous verses from the Qur'an, Qutb explains in this book how God is allegedly eager for men to achieve justice on earth. This constitutes a major difference to Christianity, which believes that the oppressed, the poor, and the excluded will receive their reward in the kingdom of heaven. 'Why is it', Qutb asks, 'that people in what is called the "Muslim world" don't take stock of their own spiritual and intellectual capital before thinking about importing principles and ways of being, modes of government and of laws, that are borrowed from countries located far beyond the vast plains, on the other side of the sea?'[10] The logic of this approach is obviously that of a complete 'disconnection' of Muslim societies from the rest of the world, and a religious revolutionary elite that seizes power and attempts to apply Muslim principles and institutions through the use of force.[11] This explains the double face of Islamic movements: movements motivated by the ideal of attaining perfect justice on earth, which is particularly the way it is presented to the international press; and movements motivated by the subversive aim of seizing power at the polls or through the use of arms.

'Islam is the solution': the triumph of a slogan in the 1980s

Starting with the period of the Cold War, and thanks to financing from Saudi Arabia and other petroleum-producing states in the Arabian Peninsula, the works of Ibn Taymiyyah and Maududi, and later the works of Qutb, were widely distributed and promoted everywhere in the Middle East. At the same time, the works of the Muslim reformist thinkers that were discussed earlier began to slowly disappear from bookshops, and were banned in Saudi Arabia. Following this, in the 1980s, the failures of Arab nationalism as well as of industrialisation and economic development capable of providing employment and social dignity facilitated a rapid spread of the anti-national school of thought of Islamic radicalism. Henceforth, the slogan of the Islamic movements, 'Islam is the solution' was seen and heard everywhere.

This imaginary return to the time of the Prophet and the first Caliphs, known as the 'righteous', helped to give credibility to the idea that the wrongs that Muslims were being subjected to in the modern world at the hands of Western imperialism could only be made right by a hard-line Islamic regime capable of restoring justice and human dignity. From that point onward, Islam became the only visible magnet that attracted Arab thought. This is illustrated by the fact that numerous intellectuals, even some of the most secular ones, felt the need to keep up with the times and write works on Islam and politics, Islam and law, Islam and social change, and so forth. Suddenly, Arab societies were perceived and studied through the lens of Islamic 'religious fact'.

This was also a time when major progressive intellectuals converted to various forms of Islamic thought. This was the case concerning Hassan Hanafi, Adel Hussein, and Tariq al-Bishri in Egypt, all of whom increased their renown and influence by doing so.[12] It was a means of staying intellectually relevant, not just in the Arab intellectual scene but also in Europe and America. Adel Hussein, a hard-line Marxist as well as an Arab nationalist in the Nasserist vein, apparently described the reasons for his conversion to this ideology to François Burgat, a specialist of Islamism, in the following way:

> Nasser emphasised economic integration and independence. There is no doubt that economic integration is important, economic independence as well, but prior to this, cultural independence is even more important and that is where we must begin. This is how everything started for me. The more I studied, the more I discovered the sources of Islamic culture and the more I discovered that this was true and that this was a real force [...] For Islam is the very identity of this nation.[13]

It is odd that this former Marxist even refused to account for the most basic common-sense evidence that the evolution of a culture is strongly influenced by the development of a society's socio-economic structures.

As for Lebanon, this conversion of intellectuals was very well presented in a work published in 2013. This volume contains the collected narratives of nine well-known intellectuals who have completely changed their ideological position over the past few decades and who were extensively interviewed by the author of the book.[14] Almost all of them justified their conversion by claiming that they were not the ones who had changed their position, but rather, that it was the world that had completely changed. This change apparently opened their eyes to the error of their past ways; it was their blindness, they alleged, that had led them to endorse the dictatorships of progressive regimes inspired by the Soviet experience and an inefficient and demagogical Arab nationalism. They all expressed feeling at 'peace' with their conscience through their conversion from a Marxist or nationalist ideology to an apology for political Islam, both Sunni and Shi'i, and to communitarianism, or allegiance to very wealthy Arab rentiers.

It was therefore not surprising that new Islamic studies in Europe and the United States took delight in the way Arab national identity was collapsing into this 'petrified' and 'intractable' form of Islam (see *supra*, Chapter 3). This is exactly the version of Islam it had preached when promoting the 're-Islamisation' of Arab societies in order to address the communist threat, but also to deal with the unitary and secular Arab nationalism that had posed such a threat to Western economic and strategic interests in the Middle East during the era of Gamal Abdel Nasser and the predominance of major Arab nationalist mass parties at that time (see *supra*, Chapter 8).

Intensification of the struggle for power in Arab societies

The collapse of Arab power starting in the middle of the tenth century has already been discussed (see *supra*, Chapter 5). Arab elites returned to the political scene in the twentieth century in a haphazard manner and in the midst of a major fragmentation of the various states. They subsequently engaged in struggles for power that played out both between Arab states and within each state entity, struggles that immediately turned merciless. They used any means necessary to rise to the top of the socio-political hierarchy in societies where the successive collapse of the Ottoman and colonial orders, followed by successive failures in the face of Israel, paved the way for ambitions of every sort. The accelerated pace of successive socio-economic changes prevented any stability of institutions and of social status. Military coups d'état only prolonged this state of affairs and accelerated the instability of social and political positions. When the revolutionary republics based on the model of Nasserist Egypt put socialist-style policies into practice, this only heightened these ambitions. This was because these policies opened new doors to rapid socio-political advancement: nationalisation; universal education; and educating large numbers of students abroad, particularly in the Soviet Union, which accepted those who were less wealthy, but also in Europe for those who had the means to live in a host country with a high cost of living compared to their home country or to the Soviet Union.

At the same time, the ambitions of the political elites were served by two competing ideologies that dominated Arab societies, that of the unifying nationalist aspiration of the nation fragmented by European colonialism, and that of a return to a radical Islamic regime capable of purifying Arab society of all of its ills. The success of Nasser's personality made the new elites of the states that emerged in the aftermath of the First World War fear that he would dominate political life and diminish their newly-acquired power in these countries. They therefore broadcast the fact that they were Arab nationalists while at the same time working underhandedly to strengthen the sovereignty of their own fragmented state in order to prevent other more powerful or popular Arab leaders from gaining power. This, as we have seen, was one of the factors that led to the rapid break-up of the union between Syria and Egypt, since the heads of the major political parties in Syria could not tolerate the idea of merely playing second fiddle in a United Arab Republic dominated by Nasser and Egyptian bureaucracy. This factor also explains the entrenched rivalry within the Baath party between the Syrian and Iraqi branches, with the leaders of each country fearing they would be absorbed by or relegated to the background of the political scene. The jealousy among these elites is still very much alive today.

In the second case, regarding the triumph of Islamic ideology, there was a competition among leaders within states to show that they were more pious than anyone else and therefore capable of getting close, at least in appearance, to the ideal of an Islamic state in its pure form. Here again, the plurality of states only increased the competition between these leaders that began very early in the twentieth century as soon as the Ottoman Empire disappeared and the 'caliphate' (in reality a sultanate) was abolished by Mustafa Kemal Atatürk. This was the caliphate that had been institutionalised in history and which had bestowed so much glory on their predecessors. Can anything other be seen in this than the ancient Arab dream of this caliphate finally being returned to them? This is what 'Abd al-Rahman al-Kawakibi courageously called for at a time when the Ottoman Sultanate was still in existence (see *supra*, Chapter 6).

With the creation of the Kingdom of Saudi Arabia, followed by its consolidation under British stewardship during the 1920s, were these new conquerors who shook up the secular status quo in the Arabian Peninsula not deserving of this prestigious title? Or should it have been given to the Hashemites who reigned over two kingdoms created for them by the British in Transjordan and Iraq, and who could take pride in the fact that they were the direct descendants of the Prophet? Or should it have been the king of Egypt, who was the head of the largest Arab country, whose society was likely the most pious? As for Morocco, located further away from the epicentre of the Arab world, was the Alawite Dynasty not also directly descended from the Prophet and therefore in a position to claim a historical continuity that no other Arab contender could match?

Such questions might appear paltry and unrealistic today, but following the abolition of the Ottoman 'caliphate', the British and French powers, when not openly hostile to the idea of grouping Muslims together under a single religious authority, stoked Arab fantasies, as long as that authority remained devoted to their cause. As early as the 1860s, France already foresaw the creation of a great, unified 'Arab kingdom' under French control, which would be based specifically on its occupation of Algeria since 1830.[15] Parallel to this, in the Indian subcontinent, Great Britain later sought a form of Islamic unity that led Indian Muslims to secede, thus weakening the growing nationalism of the Hindus, who were a demographic majority.

This project to re-establish a caliphate resurfaced in Islamist literature from the early 1990s onwards. The danger represented by such a return became one of the predominant themes in the speeches given by US President George W. Bush after September 11, 2001, in which he repeatedly referred to the desire of Osama bin Laden to re-establish an Islamic caliphate and, more broadly, the danger represented by his 'Islamo-fascism'. For a long time, the caliphate project appeared as something beyond utopian, but subsequent developments in Iraq gave it credibility, with the proclamation in June 2014 by an armed radical Islamist movement, the 'Islamic State' (also known as 'Daesh'), of a caliphate in Mosul, a large city in northern Iraq. Its combatants seized on this by hunting down Christians and Yazidis and by preparing themselves to fight against Shi'ism and Hezbollah in Lebanon. President Obama, in a move that bore a strong resemblance to post-9/11 events, announced at that time the formation of an international coalition to fight the Islamic State (IS), whose leader, unlike bin Laden, had proclaimed himself caliph. In some ways, this was reminiscent of what had happened with bin Laden and his organisation: the overreaction of the West inflated the image of this organisation and inflamed the imaginaries of the most radical politico-theological Islamic movements.

It should be borne in mind that since 1969 there has been a semblance of a worldwide Islamic government organised under the leadership of Saudi Arabia, due to its exceptional financial resources. I refer here to the Organisation of Islamic Cooperation (OIC), headquartered in Jeddah, which has given rise to numerous Islamic cultural, economic, and banking institutions. Alongside numerous Islamic NGOs, it guarantees the perpetual and far-reaching influence of the Saudi kingdom and its religious doctrine over all Muslim societies as well as those with large Muslim communities. This includes Europe as well as the Philippines, Thailand, and China, in addition to sub-Saharan Africa.

This is how in many fragmented states, Arab anti-nationalism of Islamic origin led to a major rivalry between Arab elites looking for their place in the sun, as well as being in competition with secular elites, either Arab nationalists or practitioners of a somewhat artificial nationalism.

The role of foreign influence on the elites

The external factors were no less important than the internal ones in the interplay of Arab elites that stemmed from state fragmentation. Indeed, the colonial powers had succeeded in keeping their clienteles, who in many Arab countries remained devoted to them after achieving independence, either from a direct interest as information agents, or from admiration that was either naïve or more circumspect, for the technical, scientific, or cultural achievements of these powers as well as their democratic, economic, and social institutions. Lebanon provides a caricature of a political elite that is unable to think beyond the desires of regional and international powers because to varying degrees it has remained their client.

Once French and British influence was drastically reduced following the unfortunate Suez expedition to Egypt in 1956, the influence of the United States became predominant. Many books reveal the names of political figures in the countries of the Mashriq who received monthly subsidies from the CIA allowing them to finance the purchase of a local clientele.[16] The influence of the Soviet Union was also significant, but more limited, for two main reasons. The first concerned the paranoia of the new political regimes regarding the expansion of communism in their state. The crackdowns that took place were often brutal, especially in Egypt, but also in Iraq, Libya, and Sudan (which boasted the largest communist party in the Arab world). However, they did not receive a lot of coverage. The reason for this is simple: in their desire to vigorously promote Islamic identity as an antidote to communist-inspired and anti-imperialist Arab nationalism, the Western media for the most part ignored these crackdowns and only denounced those that were carried out against the Muslim Brotherhood or other radical Islamic movements. Furthermore, many members of the Muslim Brotherhood sought refuge in major European capitals (particularly London and Frankfurt) or in the United

States. As for Egyptian communists, some of them sought refuge in Paris, including two major intellectuals, Anwar Abdel-Malek and Lotfallah Soliman.

The Soviet Union did not always attach great importance to the local communist parties, which they abandoned to their fate in order to maintain its strategic relations with its Arab state allies. These states often encouraged, either directly or indirectly, the rise of radical Islamic ideology as a weapon against the spread of local communist parties. Indeed, these parties provided spaces of warm-hearted companionship for people from various social classes and different communities, and ethnic, or religious origins. Had it not been for their involvement in the communist party, they would not have had the opportunity to get to know each other and cooperate politically. The communist parties were thus always looked upon with distrust by local leaders who saw them as meeting points where their population might intermingle, something they would not be able to control and which could pose a threat to their power if brakes, checks, and even crackdowns were not applied.

It should therefore not be surprising that the communist parties were subjected to persecution and slander. Western media, academic research, and the local propaganda of these regimes all participated equally in denouncing them for their atheism and their secularism, as well as accusing them of being a fifth column in the service of the Soviet Union and the subversion it spread throughout the world. In books published in Europe and the United States, Arab communist parties were often described as not being representative of the collective identity and as having been created by members of ethnic or religious minorities who were the only ones they attracted. This is why in the 1960s and 1970s when it became clear that these parties were gaining strength and were capable of bringing together large numbers of dyed-in-the-wool Muslim members, encouragement of efforts to re-Islamise Arab societies only increased. The financial power of Saudi Arabia, a key ally of the United States since the Second World War, helped out with this re-Islamisation. At the same time, the financial ties between the Saudi royal family and prominent members of the American establishment, particularly the Bush family and the family of Dick Cheney, became increasingly stronger. Such business relationships that were hardly compatible with American national interests were denounced in various works written in the United States. Nevertheless, these had no influence whatsoever on the type of relationship that Saudi Arabia, and today Qatar, have crafted with Western leaders.[17]

Starting in the 1990s, when the United States established itself as the sole imperial power, it sought to remake the Middle East, especially the Arab world. The United States encouraged all of the opposition movements in the region to open satellite offices in Washington, D.C. in order to be mentored by the American government. This led to bloody military expeditions against Iraq (1991 and 2003), the establishment of permanent US military installations in the Arabian Peninsula, and to a watertight alliance with Saudi Arabia. Henceforth, the Arab world was governed solely by the United States in concert with this new ally who provided valuable financial support for this involvement. Thus, in order to continue to remain relevant in the political and cultural realm in the Arab world, many intellectuals adjusted their thought to this new state of affairs.

Thinkers were therefore either labelled 'Islamicists' or 'liberal' democrats, despite the rich ideological mix that existed between these two opposing tendencies. US-Saudi policy embodied this opposition quite well in its mixture of support for both the Islamic and liberal democratic movements, even though the latter were banned in Saudi Arabia. Arab thought became more and more engulfed in the dilemma of Islam versus Arab identity, to which was added the question of radical versus moderate Islam. In a strange twist of events that followed the Iranian religious revolution, radical Islam or, more simply put, fundamentalist Islam, was suddenly embodied, in the eyes of many observers, including Arabs, by the 'regime of Mullahs' who were highly anti-imperialist and therefore opposed to this US-Saudi axis.

The Iranian religious revolution was held in high regard by a large part of the nationalist and socialist Arab elite. They saw in Ayatollah Khomeini's theologico-political ideology a substitute for Arab national ideology, which had been in crisis since the end of Nasserism and the Baath party's split into two separate branches. It was also seen as a substitute for the Marxism inspired by the Soviet experiment, which had lost its credibility following the military invasion of Afghanistan by Russian troops. In search of a new revolutionary romanticism, they viewed the Iranian revolution from afar and did not fully grasp the internal violence and the exclusion of non-religious elements within it. In fact, the ideology of the revolution was conflated with Khomeinism and the progressive role that Iranian clerics had allegedly played.[18] In addition to anti-imperialism, Iranian revolutionary discourse promoted the idea of the need for a state to care for the 'disinherited', that is, the poorest and most marginalised segments of society. The Marxist idea of the proletariat was thus replaced by that of a social justice to benefit the poorest strata of a population. A substitution occurred of one concept that was very alien to Arab and Muslim culture, that of the proletariat, with two other concepts that strongly resonated in the Arabic language, *mahrumin,* or classes of people who have been disinherited, and *mustada 'fin,* those who are exploited as a result of their weakness.[19]

As a result, Iranian revolutionary discourse immediately created a major challenge for Arab elites, especially those in the emirates and kingdoms of the Arabian Peninsula, as well as in Egypt where President Sadat was engaged in a peace process with Israel. For the former, the emergence of another type of Islamic religious legitimacy in the Middle East that was characterised by flamboyant anti-Americanism and anti-Israeli rhetoric calling for the liberation of Palestine could only be threatening to their regimes, which were closely tied to the United States. For the new Egyptian elite that emerged with Sadat's help in the interest of eliminating the influence of Nasserist ideology, and who theorised about the need to maintain excellent relations with the United States in order to achieve peace with Israel and ensure the return of the occupied Sinai Peninsula, the Iranian politico-religious rhetoric was also very destabilising. Furthermore, this rhetoric was also hostile to secularism within the political order, which was embodied by the Baathist regime in Iraq. This regime feared becoming the target of attempts to destabilise it through the use of propaganda by the new Iranian regime, which was attacking the Baath party's secular Arab nationalist doctrine.

The ideological fallout of the Iranian revolution was thus far-reaching and complex for the elites of different Arab states. Within Saudi Arabia, which felt increasingly threatened in its position as leader of a puritan Sunni Islam, a major thesis was developed to counter the Islamic slogans of the Iranian revolution, that of a need for an 'Islamic awakening' (*al-sahwat al-islamiyya*). This thesis was taken up by most Arab intellectuals, who at that time had repurposed themselves to accommodate this increasingly high-profile ideology preached by the almighty financial power of the Saudi kingdom. It claimed that only a powerful Islamic awakening could repair the catastrophes engendered by secular-style Arab nationalism. This nationalism was in fact described as being responsible for the irreparable defeats suffered by the Arabs at the hands of nationalist, secular, and socialist political parties, in addition to the defeats by Israel and by external hegemonies over the region. Secularism and atheist socialism were alleged to have brought about a depersonalisation of the Arabs and the abandonment of their religious traditions and beliefs, seen as the primary cause of their weakness. A return to religion and a re-Islamisation of society's values thus constituted one and the same urgent over-arching imperative. Starting with this historic moment, the identity-based quarrel among Arabs re-emerged with renewed vigour, giving rise to numerous ineffectual polemics.

The harmful effects of confining thought within the dilemma between Islam and Arab identity

Nothing has caused more ink to flow from Arab intellectuals over the past few decades than their feverish attempts to conciliate Arab national thought with antinational thought inspired by an intransigent Islamic doctrine. Thousands of pages have been written and innumerable redundant conferences continue to take place focused on this or related topics, such as Islam and the state, power in Islam, modernity and authority in Islam, and so forth.

The starting point for this unsolvable set of issues is the confusion surrounding the term *umma* (nation of believers), which refers to the bond that unites people based on their faith, but which has nothing to do with the modern use of 'nation' to refer to an organic society strongly unified through its state institutions. The Qur'an itself clearly states in one of its verses that if God had wished to do so, He would have made humanity as one single nation. Similarly, another verse of the Qur'an claims that God created diverse peoples in order that they get to know each other. Thus, when the Qur'anic text uses the term *umma*, it only refers to the spiritual bond that might unite believers or respect for the prescriptions promulgated by the sacred text as a guide for proper conduct in temporal affairs, specifically regarding family and social relationships.

There is no Qur'anic verse that prescribes an established form of power or society, except that of cooperation among believers. Therefore, any body of law developed regarding the institution of power within Islam would be the work of human beings: jurists constructed the body of shari'a law, which has hardly any relationship to the original holy text, much like the canonical law of the Catholic Church has little to do with the New Testament. As such, shari'a law is completely open to being critiqued and amended in order to adapt to historical change. This is precisely what was done from the middle of the tenth century onwards, when the power of the caliphs began to fade and jurists were gradually forced to recognise the existence and legitimacy of other forms of political regime beyond that of the caliphate. Legitimacy was subsequently granted to the sultanates and kingdoms that were being created and which acquired complete independence from the caliphate, which was only evoked in prayers as a spiritual symbol of the unity of believers. In the political history of Islam, the caliphate ceased very early on to be the only legitimate institution that could meet the requirements for assembling and governing the Muslims of the world. It is therefore not irrelevant to observe that the last two great Muslim empires that ruled over large parts of Asia and Africa (and even some parts of Europe, in the Balkans), the Mughal Empire in India and the Ottoman Empire in the Middle East, were not called caliphates, but rather, sultanates. Ever since the weakening and subsequent decline of the Abbasid Caliphate in 1258 following the Mongol invasions, Muslims have never been reunited within a single political entity. The community of believers continued to be fragmented from Andalusia, which was split into miniature states, to central Asia, and to the Indian subcontinent. In this way, it remained a kind of spiritual community and no longer a temporal one.

No one can therefore fail to be surprised by what constitutes a modern paradox, that is, a radical Islamic doctrine promoting the assembly of all Muslims throughout the world under the sovereignty of God's law, embodied by a unified political and social regime led by a caliph, or 'commander of the faithful'. This perspective starkly contradicts centuries of fragmented temporal practice of power, whose only religious obligation was to enforce the moral values and social practices inspired by the Qur'anic prescriptions and their sometimes divergent interpretations by different legal schools. The alleged 'intractability' of Islam and its supposed congenital inability to separate the temporal from the spiritual is thus in many respects a myth. By virtue of being repeated over and over again, this myth has become an axiom that is nonetheless completely inconsistent with the historical reality of Muslim societies. This problematic generalisation of a complex set of issues seems to derive from the specificity of the history of Europe during the unification of the continent under the influence of Christianity and the papacy. It makes no sense to apply this to Muslim societies, nor to Buddhist, Hindu or animist ones. At best, it is appropriate for monotheistic societies, but it has been applied very differently to Christian in comparison to Muslim ones, which include Arab societies.[20]

This belief in the impossibility of separating the temporal from the spiritual, a claim that has been made for the past fifty years or so, is paradoxically a belief that is shared by the followers of radical Islam and by those who despise a supposed Islamic otherness in the modern world. It is largely responsible for the radical anti-national Islamic thought that seeks to group all Muslims together into a single political entity; and, apart from this, to impose this axiomatic concept of a political regime on Muslim societies. It is therefore important to understand why such a passionate intellectual investment was able to develop, one that paralysed Arab thought and which led to serial impasses. These have prevented any national cohesion among Arabs, including at the level of the fragmented state structures that emerged from colonial divisions and of building a unified Arab nation, even of a federalist type.

Never has such a simple question led to so much useless flow of ink. Since the terms of this disagreement have not been properly established, it is imperative to expose the impasses to which they have led. If Islam constitutes the exclusive flesh and blood of the identity of Arabs, how is it possible to build a nation that would not also encompass all of the Muslims of the world regardless of the diversity of their languages, the course of their histories, their values, and their artistic and cultural sensibilities? In addition, if political Islam were to constitute the foundation of the state, sovereignty, and society, there would be a great risk of excluding or forming minorities of non-Muslims or followers of non-orthodox Muslim doctrines rejected by Wahhabised Sunnism. It is already clear just how much tension has existed since the Iranian revolution between the followers of each of the two different Islamic political systems. One is a system based on the direct sovereignty of God according to the creed of Sayyid Qutb (a follower of Sunnism). The other is the Iranian-style system of a constitutional civilian government controlled by religious leaders who claim allegiance to a Shi'i heritage as revised and corrected by Ayatollah Khomeini without ever reaching consensus.

The obviously impossible task of ever achieving an Islamic political regime confirms that it is nothing other than a dangerous utopia in which one form or another of radical Islam can only be imposed by a government that is fatal to freedom and completely controlled by the *ulama* in its service. This utopia is much more dangerous and naïve than that of the Arab nationalist aspiration, which is open-minded and liberal in the area of religion, in addition to being much more realistic. The latter nonetheless continues to be denounced and criticised with exceptional virulence by Arab intellectuals who have repurposed themselves within different forms of American-style neo-conservatism or authoritarian Islamo-centrism. The same is true of some of the works produced by recent Western Orientalism, which are exclusively 'Islamocentric' and continue to consider nationalist aspirations as a source of the Arab world's present woes.

Moreover, this is a completely sterile discussion, for it is clear that Qur'anic prophecy represents the biggest event in the history of the Arabs and the foundation for classical Arab culture, including both religious and secular culture. It is equally clear that Arab identity existed prior to the appearance of Islam, and that Arabs have always played an important role in the Levant by creating kingdoms in the area. This pre-Islamic history is not just a tribal history, it is also a history of the symbiosis established with other cultures in the region. This comprises mainly Syro-Aramaic culture, which laid the foundation for the blossoming of the Arabic language and the development of Arab-Islamic civilisation proper, following the prophetic arrival of the third monotheism. To reduce Arab identity to Islam and its religious rituals and precepts would thus constitute an unacceptable impoverishment of the ancient history of the Arabs.

The criteria that separates modern Arab national consciousness from an exclusively anti-national Islamic identity is therefore an awareness of the totality of Arab heritage, both its pre-Islamic as well as its Islamic heritage, in addition to the legacy of the modern renaissance of Arab consciousness that occurred in the nineteenth century under the impact of ideas that came from Europe. Any other approach to Arab identity would seriously take away from the richness of its heritage. It would reduce the idea of a rich and complex Arab identity to the robotic model of an alleged *Homo islamicus* exclusively confined to practicing religious rituals and adhering to dietary restrictions (see *supra*, Introduction). Furthermore, there is no possibility of conciliation between an identity that is reduced to its religious aspect alone and a complex identity that is the result of numerous interactions and amalgamations that Arabs have experienced throughout their long history. Notable among these is the extraordinary adventure of the Arab conquerors who left the Arabian Peninsula at the end of the seventh century and who intermingled with so many peoples, some of whom converted to Islam, while others continued to practice their own religions. Still others retained their language and traditions whilst merging with the Arabs by virtue of having converted to Islam.

The absorption of these multiple identities into a personality forged exclusively from religious prescriptions constitutes an impoverishment whose tragic effects can be seen in the violent terrorism of some followers of the theologico-political movements that resulted from this rigid view of identity. Since the 1990s, these movements have spiralled into violent and sectarian behaviour that is entirely forgetful of and oblivious to the richness of Muslim history and heritage. This is why the idea of an absolute primacy of religion over every other aspect of identity is an impasse that cannot lead to a blossoming of modern Arab culture or to making up for the lag in their economic situation. What is at stake is the potential of Arab society for a future, its collective knowledge of the world, and its own heritage. My analysis of the long-term controversy that opposed two of the finest Arab intellectuals regarding the structure of Arab thought at the end of the last century, which constitutes a major part of the following chapter, will clearly show what is most at stake. This chapter will also demonstrate the fierce disagreements between Arab intellectuals who are proponents of secularism as the gateway to modernity and their adversaries who virulently denounce modernity. These disputes have led to assassinations and attempted assassinations as well as the banishment from Egypt of a professor from Cairo University. Subsequently, Chapter 13 will show how some Arab thinkers have assessed and judged these contradictions in order to propose solutions to overcome them.

CHAPTER 12

The major controversies generated by Islamic nationalism

The rise of Islamic movements and currents of thought led to major intellectual controversies that sometimes turned violent. Some intellectuals were attacked or even assassinated, while others had to leave their countries to go into exile. The circumstances were such that some of these movements took up arms: assassination of President Anwar Sadat in Egypt, attacks on tourists in Luxor in Upper Egypt as well as on active government ministers, as well as the assassination, again in Egypt, of Farag Foda. My choice here is to describe two major controversies that pitted Islamist intellectuals against modernists. Firstly, the controversy around the nature of Islamic religious heritage and its constants, and secondly that surrounding the benefits and drawbacks of secularism for Arab and Muslim societies. This will also allow me to give an overview of the itineraries of some of these intellectuals whose physical wellbeing was threatened by radical Islamic movements.

Islamic heritage: the controversy over an open or closed universe

Between 1980 and 2000, a major dispute took place over the issue of the constitution of the Arab mind and its specificity. This was between Mohammed Abed al-Jabri (1935–2010), Professor at the University of Rabat, and Georges Tarabichi, born in Aleppo, Syria in 1939, who was the Arabic translator of several works from the European philosophical tradition, as well as being a literary critic with a sharp mind, and a learned historian of Arab-Islamic culture. This dispute unfolded in the major works of Tarabachi, who critiqued and commented on the various works by al-Jabri on the structures of the Arab mind.[1] This dispute teaches many valuable lessons worthy of a major academic study to bring them to light.

Yet, except for a few rare newspaper articles, this controversy has practically gone unnoticed in today's world despite revealing some of the crucial problems of Arab identity. Until now, there has also been complete silence in the academic world, both in contemporary Orientalism, which is exclusively focused on theologico-political Islam and its movements, and in the Arab world. Yet again, it seems that only American academia has taken any interest, although in a completely marginal way. A very substantive, clear, and well-written Master's thesis defended at the University of Texas at Austin presents a critical analysis of Georges Tarabachi's critique of al-Jabri, explaining why it is important, and how it corresponds to a historical reality that should not be ignored.[2] In addition, an Arab scholar in Canada, Alexander Abdennur, discussed their dispute in a chapter of a very dense book focused on the structures of the Arab mind.[3]

Al-Jabri's three modes of operation of Arab thought

Al-Jabri's work is spread over three successive books which he wrote on the formation (*takwin*) and the structures (*buniya*) of the Arab mind. His main argument is that the structures and modes of operation of the Arab mind were forged during a single unique period, what he calls the period of codification and formalisation of Islam ('*asr al-tadwin*). This era shaped all of the concepts and religious sciences subsequently borne without change by Muslim culture. Al-Jabri identified three major frameworks of knowledge.

The first framework is that of 'declarative' or 'enunciative' (*bayani*) Islam, which appears to have only started during the Abbassid Caliphate in 143 of the Hegira. This is the period during which the language was refined and the universe of conceptual references was created for the purpose of grasping and understanding the reality of the physical world. It was within this framework that the method of theological discussion, or 'science of the word' ('*ilm al-kalam*), was developed, which aimed to demonstrate the existence of God, without whom the physical world could not be understood. Indeed, for al-Jabri, this was the universe of Sunni religious orthodoxy. The second framework is that of mystical Islam ('*irfani*), in which the Shi'i tradition played a major role. It called for seeking the profound truth of God and the universe beyond the literal reading of the sacred text, which required a gnostic-style vision reserved for those who had been initiated. The third, according to al-Jabri, supposedly represents the rationalising tendency, that of Islam 'establishing proofs' or a 'demonstrative Islam' (*burhani*), which kept only one element of Greek philosophy, the rationality of Aristotelianism. This framework developed in Andalusia, especially through the work of Averroes (Ibn Rushd), the spirit of which can still be found today in the Islam of the Maghreb.

For al-Jabri, demonstrative Islam, which appeared rather late in Muslim history, came to the rescue of enunciative Islam, which was subjected to the corrupting influence of mystical Islam. According to al-Jabri, this mystical Islam came from Iran and from the Arab Orient and was only incorporated by Shi'ism, unlike Sunnism, which did not incorporate it and was geographically located in the Arabian Peninsula, Egypt, North Africa and Andalusia, or what he called the 'Arab West'. Only this Sunni Islam, he claimed, preserved the original heritage of rationalising religious sciences, whereas the Islam of the Orient (the Syro-Mesopotamian Basin and its extensions into Iran and more broadly into Asia) apparently exerted a corrupting influence that led to the 'resignation of the mind' in all of Islam, thus paralysing its capacity for rationality.

Tarabichi's deconstruction of al-Jabri's work

Al-Jabri's thesis is attractive, but it is permeated by a fundamental hostility to Shi'ism and to various forms of mysticism and gnosticism. In addition, as Tarabichi shows very clearly, it relies on an artificial geographical dichotomy between the Arab Orient and Occident. In fact, as I see it, when al-Jabri called his research project a 'critique' of the Arab mind, he meant first and foremost an exclusively Islamic mind, without accounting for all of the very rich cultural expressions of this 'Arab mind', in particular poetry, philosophy, architecture, and music. Furthermore, his entire approach is that of stylised history, that is, a narrative organisation that excludes all of the facts and subtleties from the analysis that might affect the purity of the narrator's historicist hypothesis.[4]

Georges Tarabachi's objections to al-Jabri's approach to what he claimed to be the structures of the Arab mind fall into several categories. First, al-Jabri describes these frameworks as a coherent and closed whole removed from any historical context and from any study of Arab culture during the second century of the Hegira era (the eighth century of the Christian era). At that time, the Arabs had entered into a period of tremendous cultural intermingling with the other cultures in the region – Persian, Byzantine, and Aramaic-Syriac. Except for the single reference to Aristotle's influence on the third and last type of mental framework, which he called 'demonstrative', his demonstration is a closed construction in which the Arab mind appears to have emerged *ex nihilo* based solely on the text of the Qur'anic prophecy, and subsequently on the orally transmitted narratives of the sayings and the deeds of the Prophet during his lifetime (*hadith*). What al-Jabri proposes here is completely impossible and implausible. In my doctoral thesis on religious pluralism, I demonstrated the influence of Byzantine legislation (concerning the treatment of pagans and heretics) on Islamic jurisprudence through an analysis of its different forms regarding the relationship between Muslims and pagans, or between Muslims, Christians, and Jews.[5]

Similarly, there is no doubt that the broad politico-religious abilities of the Byzantine and Persian emperors inevitably influenced the Arab legal scholars who progressively developed the theory of the caliphate, which was an integral part of shari'a law, given that the world of these two empires was so familiar to them.[6] Moreover, it is well known that the Umayyad Caliphate kept intact the administrative structures of the Byzantine Empire that reigned in Syria, Palestine and North Africa. Therefore, to study the mental framework of Arabs as if they had lived in a closed world and had invented a new political system and a system of thought from scratch appears to be a hypothesis that is hardly realistic from the perspective of historical truth.

The comparative status of philosophy in Islam and Christianity

Another critique of Tarabachi's criticisms, one that complemented his first criticism, concerned the place of philosophy in Muslim culture, which al-Jabri conflated with Arab culture. Indeed, apart from his brief reference to Aristotle's influence on the third type of mental framework, the demonstrative mind, al-Jabri denied any contribution from philosophy to its development. For him, the Arab mind seems to have totally rejected the heritage left behind by the great philosophers of Arab-Islamic civilisation when Arabic was the language of high culture shared by all the intellectuals of this time, regardless of whether they were of Persian, Arabic, or Central Asian origin. This would imply that there was an incompatibility between the mental framework of Arabs who had become Muslims and those of the ancient Greeks or, later on, the European philosophers. For al-Jabri, Christian Europe was able to assimilate the philosophical heritage of ancient

Greece, whereas Muslims were completely incapable of doing so, with the exception of a few Andalusian jurists.

Georges Tarabichi completely rejected this thesis, and for valid reasons. He developed his criticism in a work that was specifically dedicated to this central question, in the determination of specifically Islamic mental frameworks and systems of knowledge. Its title, 'The Destiny of Philosophy between Christianity and Islam', very clearly expresses the nature of the comparative problematic that Tarabichi attacks.[7] He delineates from a historical point of view the comparative attitudes of Christian and Muslim religious individuals towards philosophy as it was inherited from Greece and from the Hellenistic culture that spread throughout all of Asia Minor. It follows very logically from this that during the first centuries of its existence, Christianity fought violently against this philosophy, which it qualified as pagan and irreconcilable with the new monotheistic faith, whereas converts to Islam had happily accommodated it for several centuries. Philosophy had been a central element of Islamic culture at the time of its splendour when it also included a range of sciences (astronomy, medicine, mathematics – the word algebra comes from Arabic – anthropology, and history).

With the decline that affected the Muslim world during the Crusades, as well as the Mongol invasions and the Turkish Mamluk domination of the eastern Mediterranean, philosophy acquired a bad reputation and was conflated with atheism. Nonetheless, it continued to thrive in Andalusia and in North Africa. In my view, it is possible to consider that the exceptional and multifaceted genius of Ibn Khaldun, who lived in the fourteenth century and who originated from North Africa, represents one of the intellectual summits of Arab-Muslim culture. Muslim philosophy therefore remained a central cultural element for about seven centuries before it was definitively condemned as contrary to religion, since it was believed to lead to atheism, and other non-religious sciences were abandoned.[8] Conversely, in Europe, it was not until the Renaissance that the disapproval of everything related to philosophy slowly began to fade. This was when elements of a return to philosophy, especially Aristotelian philosophy, emerged with the translation of the great Arab philosophers into Latin through contact with Muslim Andalusia. Bolstered by this well-documented historical insight, Tarabichi invalidated al-Jabri's vision of an Islamic mental structure that was closed in on itself, and which denied any contribution from philosophy to the establishment and formalisation of the religious sciences.

The impact of European Islamic studies and Ernest Renan's thought on al-Jabri

At this stage of the summary of this central controversy in the debates on the nature of Islam, its key importance to understanding the perception of the relationships that Muslim societies have with other societies becomes clear. It is also important regarding the cause of freedom of consciousness and the cultural interactions between different ways of thinking within Muslim societies. Indeed, Tarabichi objected to the way al-Jabri had confined Arab thought within the straitjacket of Islamic orthodoxy, a position influenced by European Islamic studies. The latter posited the structures of the Muslim mind as a self-sufficient world that is closed in on itself due to the classical traditional religious sciences of Islam that guarantee Muslims have all the elements of knowledge and rules of behaviour that they need. In particular, he considers that al-Jabri wrote under the influence of the racist theses of Ernest Renan, who analysed Islamic mental structures in the framework of a division of the world between Semites and Aryans. Europe, which was Christian and Aryan, represented for Renan the world of refinement and civilisation founded on philosophical openness and progress. Muslim societies, however, embodied the heaviness and closed-mindedness of the Semitic mind.[9] For Tarabichi, there was no doubt that al-Jabri, despite all of his erudition – which Tarabachi indeed sometimes found to be lacking – was influenced by Renan's thesis, and that only the third type of Islamic mental structure was emphasised, the one qualified as 'demonstrative.' This was the only rationalising structure in the sense that it was more likely to evolve by accepting additional European cultural and scientific contributions.

Along the same lines, Tarabichi faults al-Jabri for submitting to a European ethnocentrism that seeks to monopolise the philosophical mind, whose appearance is exclusively attributed to ancient Greece and whose sole heir is Europe. Although al-Jabri denounced this ethnocentrism several times throughout his work, he was unconsciously influenced by it when he stated that only the demonstrative Arab mind, which he considered to be centred in the Occident of the Arab world (Andalusia and North Africa), had preserved the possibility of recovering the rationality inherited from Greek philosophy, thanks to the Muslim philosophers of Andalusia, to the exclusion of those from the Orient of the Arab world, such as Avicenna. For Tarabichi, the critical work of al-Jabri simply reproduces the discourse of European Orientalism and that of Ernest Renan, who believed the Semitic mind to be incapable of philosophical thought and cultural refinement. Al-Jabri's broad erudition is used to serve an Islamic historicism that excludes the 'Oriental', by far the most important branch of high Islamic culture and thought, dismissing it as something that is not really representative of Muslim culture. Thus, in 'Jabrian' terms, the Oriental branch carried within it too many elements from Persian Manicheism and other mystical and gnostic elements from the Orient.

The artificial opposition between the gnostic Islam of the Orient and the rational Islam of the Occident

Another major objection of Tarabichi to al-Jabri's classification of Islamic mental structures into three different types concerns the somewhat caricatural, or deprecating, description of the mode of thinking of the second mental framework, the gnostic mysticism of Shi'i Islam. In fact, in the conclusion to his second major work on the Arab mental structures created by Islam, al-Jabri also discredits the first system of thought, the declarative or enunciative, stating somewhat carelessly that the latter had remained rather too much on the surface of things, that it was overly formal and therefore somewhat paralysing to the development of the mind. I do not share this stern point of view given that the formative period of Islamic thought was not merely religious. It was also a period during which all of the rules of the written Arabic language were set forth and the language developed its conceptual richness. This allowed it to quickly become the language of high civilisation and science that was adopted by the Persians as well as the Aramean populations of the entire Syro-Mesopotamian region.

The work of al-Jabri was celebrated in the Arab world, and even in Saudi Arabia, presumably because it confirmed all the theses of the followers of fundamentalist Islam who presented it as a system of thought that was sufficient in and of itself and endowed with a distinctive otherness compared to other systems of thought and mental structures. Conversely, within the reformist aspect of al-Jabri's thought, especially in one of the first works he wrote entitled 'Heritage and Us', he strongly criticised the isolation of this heritage. Indeed, he called for it to be renewed and to accept rationality in all of its aspects (understood here to mean modern scientific thinking).[10] It is in his two books written on the structures of the Arab mind that he makes apparent what had barely been touched on in his previous work; that is, the forced comparison between, on the one hand, the structures of the mystical and Platonic Oriental Islamic mind that he claimed were represented by

Avicenna in the philosophical arena, and, on the other, the structures of the 'demonstrative' Occidental Islamic mind, allegedly represented by the Aristotelianism of Averroes. Al-Jabri drew a very sharp contrast between Averroes and Avicenna, and claimed that the latter contributed to corrupting the Oriental Islamic mind. He thus called for strengthening the rationality of mental structures and of the Arab-Islamic system of knowledge. This dichotomy was vehemently criticised by Tarabichi, who saw in it a type of visceral attachment on the part of al-Jabri to the Sunni mind as opposed to the Shi'i mind, specifically the Sunnism of North Africa (or Occidental Islam), which by virtue of being close to Europe was allegedly better suited to reforming the mental structures of Oriental Islam, seen as rigid, mystical, and hardly rational.

When he passed away in 2010, al-Jabri was celebrated as one of the great minds of contemporary Arab culture. Tarabichi, to whom al-Jabri had responded in a rather indelicate manner by characterising him as a Christian incapable of understanding the Muslim mind, even wrote a glowing article praising the importance of his work, and in so doing moved beyond the fierce disagreement that had pitted these two scholars against one another.[11] It is truly regrettable that their dispute has not been the subject of further research and critical analysis. Indeed, it concerns the deep structures of Arab identity and, in this sense, should serve as the basis for demonstrating the diversity of forms of thought within Arab culture, one which cannot and should not be constrained by a kind of straitjacket that allows religion to devour the Arab mind and prevent it from reaching the universality of thought.

What is the cause of the decline of Arabs and Islam, of the resigning mind (al-'aql al-mustaqil) described by al-Jabri in his work? Could this be the singular effect of Oriental heritage, especially the Persian, Babylonian, and Chaldean heritages that allegedly obliterated the divine rationality induced by Islamic religious sciences, but were themselves eroded by mystical Oriental philosophy, that of Shi'i Islam? However interesting this controversy between these two scholars may be, it remains inscribed within a past that is long gone, constrained by an approach to Arab thought and culture that runs exclusively through Islam.

The lesson to be drawn from this scholarly polemic is the importance of moving beyond intellectual isolation within religion in order to escape from intractable debates that pit an Arab national trait against an Islamic trait. Arab culture, as we have seen, is much more varied than can be accounted for by these singular theologico-political variations linked to the role of Islam. It is true that European Orientalism weighs very heavily today in the reflections of Arabs themselves on their past and their heritage, especially due to the large number of students who have performed brilliantly within European and American universities and have become well-respected intellectuals in the Arab world as well as in the United States and Europe. Does Orientalism determine the direction of the critical reflection that Arabs are trying to develop on their heritage and on the relationship they maintain with it? This could be an additional hypothesis to complete the devastating criticism by Edward Said of Western Orientalism, which is alleged to have enclosed the Muslim mind within stereotypical views. Said nonetheless ended up incorporating these views into his efforts to emancipate the Muslim mind, thereby worsening what was already a reflection in a state of paralysis. At the very least, he exacerbated its incorporation into a vicious cycle, since any effort at emancipation of thought regarding Islamic heritage was likely to collide with the constraints of Muslim mental structures.

The dispute between partisans and adversaries of secularism: a religious McCarthyism?

Starting in the 1980s, another dispute related to secularism completed the one related to the structures of the Arab mind and, in fact, stemmed from it. Pitting secular nationalists against religious nationalists, it grew and became more radicalised to the point of taking up a considerable amount of space in Arab thought. This was to the detriment of reflection on other crucial questions, especially the technological and scientific under-development of Arab countries compared to the spectacular economic development of so-called 'emerging' countries, according to the terms of neo-liberal ideology (Brazil, Russia, India, China, and South Africa, grouped under the acronym BRICS, but also including South Korea and Turkey).

This philosophical disagreement, which is still nowhere near being resolved, is of major importance to the future of the Arab world. But the place it has occupied for more than thirty years has become so predominant that it has unfortunately marginalised reflection on the other major problems that paralyse the development of Arab societies. This situation contrasts with those of other formerly colonised countries, where debates on the place of religion in society have become marginal and questions relative to the appropriation of science and technology in order to deal with economic globalisation are more often front and centre in the thought of the intellectual and technocratic elites (see *infra*, Chapter 14).

As previously described, in the context of the disenchantment with secular and modernist Arab nationalist thought, followed by the 're-Islamisation' of Arab societies, a feverishly anti-secular Arab school of thought began to develop.[12] The attacks against the modernising secularism of the previous generations were carried out according to two different modes, that of the Sunni-inspired rigorist Islam that promoted an 'Islamic awakening' to compensate for Arab failures, and that of the ideology of the Iranian religious revolution that theorised about an Islamic democracy. In both cases, and for opposite reasons, modern nationalism was rejected and only utopian Islamic nationalism was considered capable of resolving Muslim identity problems. Subsequently, there was the elaboration of a canonical narrative that attributed the decline of Muslim societies to the importation of secular ideas. Similarly, these ideas were blamed for the unfair and oppressive practices of Muslim states that had presumably adopted the secular positions of Western countries and had forced them on people for whom religious norms supposedly constituted the basis of social life.[13]

The atmosphere that this created in the Arab world was characterised as religious McCarthyism by Yasin al-Hafiz in the 1960s. It was a stifling atmosphere, especially because some thinkers who continued down the path of in-depth Islamic reform were put on trial, while others were assassinated or subjected to assassination attempts. All of the voices within academic circles, the Western media, and NGOs devoted to defending human rights, who had vehemently denounced the imprisonment of members of the Muslim Brotherhood and the death sentences of Sayyid Qutb, now responded in the opposite way by keeping quiet. There was a deafening silence (or at best a timid denunciation) that followed the persecution of reformist and modernising thinkers from then onward. Gilles Kepel's book, *The Prophet and Pharoah*, set the tone for this by presenting Nasser (Pharaoh) and Nasserism as the source of all the problems and of totalitarianism, and Sayyid Qutb (the Prophet) and the Muslim Brotherhood as victims of this dictator.[14]

The secular victims of the religious censorship that descended on the Arab world starting in the 1980s will now be discussed by looking at the cases of Nasr Hamid Abu Zayd and Farag Foda, before exploring another theoretical clash over secularism between two well-known intellectuals in the Arab world.

The tribulations of Nasr Hamid Abu Zayd

The arguments that comprised this dispute can be summarised from the trial of one of Egypt's great critical intellectuals, Nasr Hamid Abu Zayd, who was declared an apostate by an Egyptian court in 1994 based on a complaint brought against him by his colleagues at the Ain Shams University in Cairo. Abu Zayd, an Associate Professor, was subjected to a zealous campaign by his departmental colleagues that led to court proceedings and a ruling in favour of his detractors. He was removed from his university position, and his wife was ordered to separate from him on the grounds that his religious opinions were equivalent to apostasy. In a very thorough work, Abu Zayd describes in detail the context of his disagreement with his university colleagues and very clearly presents his religious positions.[15]

What becomes clear in this work is that the author was blamed for his liberal and open interpretation of Islam, and in particular of the Qur'anic text. His interpretation aligns with that of the famous philosophico-religious school of the Mutazilites. This school challenged the belief in a Qur'an alleged to be 'uncreated' because it emanated directly from God and, that therefore, its formulation had existed since the beginning of time. As such, the Qur'anic text did not emanate from a given historical context. Therefore, it must be read in a literal way and cannot be subjected to interpretations that take into account the historical context of the prophetic event.

For Abu Zayd, this rigid position is what paralysed the use of reason by Muslims and gave rise to the lag in their development that has made them suffer in all areas. In the tradition of the great Arab religious reformists starting with al-Tahtawi, Abu Zayd reiterated that God's message throughout the Qur'an was, on the contrary, a call for the use of reason and reflection. Furthermore, he saw no difference between Muslim thinkers known as 'progressives,' that is, former Marxists who had converted to different forms of Islam, and conservative religious thinkers. Likewise, he saw no difference between 'moderate' and 'extremist' Islamist thinkers. Both currents, in his view, relied on non-negotiable axioms. The moderates confined themselves to attempts to show that the rationalist thinkers were wrong, and the extremists excommunicated them and called on Muslim society to respond by taking action against them, even by using physical means if necessary.

More explicitly, Abu Zayd clearly specifies in this work that which separates rationalist and enlightened Islamic thought from the adherents of a narrow literalist interpretation of the Qur'anic text. The former endeavours to provide a modern interpretation of Islam that is free of traditionalism, for it understands that 'Islam as a historical and social process continues to be alive and to evolve due to its openness regarding the meaning and content of the original texts.'[16] The latter imagines that 'Islam is the first event of the Revelation and that any opening or transformation is only perdition, deviance, and falsification that must be discarded.' Zayd cannot be more explicit when he adds that 'even though the extremist attitude, that of Sayyid Qutb and of Sayyid Abul A'la Maududi, have characterised the history of all humanity, except for the first decades of the history of Islam, as an era of paganism and darkness, the thought of "moderate" Islamists considers that Islamic history extends to the abolition of the caliphate by Mustafa Kemal Atatürk in the twentieth century.' But, he adds, in fact, 'extremists and moderates agree to claim that the meaning of Islam is established and perfect, as Muslim legal scholars (*fuqaha*) and theologians (*mutakallimun*) defined it prior to the era of decline, that is, in the fourth century of the Hegira, and both categories exclude from this definition numerous philosophical, political, and theological orientations.'[17]

Zayd describes the consequences of this way of seeing Islam: 'sanctification of history and the study of history as a means of celebration and honouring, as opposed to the analytical, explicative, and critical method.'[18] It is this approach that has allowed the canonical history of Islam to practically ignore all of the fierce clashes and wars that took place between the companions of the Prophet, who, he adds, are all shown unconditional deference.

Furthermore, according to Zayd, this leads to the sanctification of the jurist-theologians (*al-a'imma*) and to considering their thought as definitive and absolutely relevant. Consequently, any attempt to analyse and evaluate their works is considered to be a pursuit driven by ideology. This is how knowledge itself becomes 'Islamicised,' and that it is this that lies at the heart of Islamist thought since it provides a way to dispense with temporality, history, science, and knowledge. Therefore, claims Abu Zayd, any progress along these lines is a 'step backwards' in time; which also helps to explain the symbolic importance of clothing, the veil, the wearing of beards, and the construction of mosques.[19] It also helps to demonstrate why the Islamist project is a political project that repudiates the state as an instrument of people's oppression; for, allegedly, only the project to establish a regime of 'the sovereignty of God' is able to ensure the fulfilment of *Homo islamicus*. This is far from the godless aspirations to secularism, a notion which is conflated with materialism and an absolute faith in the possibility of subjugating nature purely as a means to material power, thus ruling out any relationship between humans and their creator.

Clarifying his thought, Zayd explains that even the advocates of a middle ground (*al-wasatiyya*) regarding religion seek to shut the secular window, that of the resistance of thought to the closed universe of the Islamists. This is because this thought, according to Zayd, is 'that which resists totalitarianism in all its forms and that which stands in the way of the imprisonment of the present in the chains of the past.' For him, secularism is a reservoir of resistance of thought, but in fact, also a thought oriented by its essence towards knowledge as well as a form of political resistance in terms of its implications and its significance. Secularism, Abu Zayd claims, is not outside of Islam as many intellectuals allege, and 'it is time to lay our cards on the table in order to decide these questions in light of thought.' Thus for him, it is necessary to 'discuss the concept of Islam and the concept of secularism together, for it is possible to conclude that Islam is a secular religion if we know how to reason and how to put the texts, history, and reality in the right order at the same time.'[20]

The assassination of Mahmoud Taha and Farag Foda

Nasr Hamid Abu Zayd's fate was much better than that which awaited two other individuals who were assassinated, each one a major intellectual and reformer. One was killed by the Sudanese regime that condemned him to death for apostasy, and the other by individuals carrying out a sentence for apostasy.

The first of these is Mahmoud Taha (1909–1985), a religious reformer and a fascinating individual. He created the Republican Brotherhood, actively fought for women's rights, and vehemently opposed the application of Muslim law to non-Muslims, a policy the Sudanese regime implemented in 1983. This shift occurred under the influence of Hassan al-Turabi and led to the resumption of the war between the north and the south of the country. Following a summary judgment, Taha was found guilty and put to death by hanging in the central prison of Khartoum in 1985. The silence on the part of human rights organisations was deafening, but even worse was the structural institutionalised ignorance within European and American academia regarding the rich thought of this intellectual. This ignorance strongly contrasted with the extraordinary academic publicity given to the work of Sayyid Qutb, the major source of inspiration for the Muslim Brotherhood and for the most radical form of Islamic fundamentalism, along with the works of other Islamist thinkers admired by a large number of Arab and non-Arab intellectuals.

The epic tale of the life of Mahmoud Taha reveals an exceptional individual who was able to gather together all of the conquests of political modernity into a thought that remained authentically Muslim.[21] Certainly, it required exceptional courage to fight for the re-establishment of Muslim liberalism in the political context of Sudan at that time when the regime was evolving from a secular and socialist-style Nasserism towards a religious fundamentalism that could conveniently silence all opponents.

A few years later, the assassination of Farag Foda in Cairo on 8 June 1992 marked a major turning point in the policy of intimidation carried out by Islamic movements in this key capital of the Arab intellectual world ever since the assassination of President Sadat in 1981.[22] The story of this assassination clearly demonstrates the atmosphere of religious intolerance that constituted a major diversion from the real problems facing Arab societies – growing social inequalities, unemployment and exclusion, and the indispensable entry into industrial modernity.

Born in rural Egypt in 1945, Farag Foda became an agronomist and nothing predisposed him to take an interest in the politico-religious questions that were stirring up Arab thought. It was the rise of Islamic movements that pushed him to learn more about religious prescriptions and how they had developed throughout history. He acquired a vast amount of learning on the judicial heritage of Islam in order to be able to denounce, on the basis of in-depth knowledge, the rigid and dangerous vision of these movements. At the same time, even as he continued to carry out his profession as an agronomist, Foda became more and more involved in politics. At first he joined the major, historical Wafd party, which he subsequently left when it aligned with the Muslim Brotherhood during the 1984 legislative elections. He then tried to form his own party, the Party of the Future, but he was not granted permission by the Ministry of the Interior, most likely due to pressure from conservative Islamic circles.

With the escalation of events that were rattling Egypt, in particular the assassination of President Anwar Sadat in 1981, but also the entire Middle East region following the takeover of power by the clergy in Iran in 1979, Foda felt a pressing desire to write. He published major pieces in the Egyptian press and substantially contributed to the debate between conservative Islamic movements and classical, modernist Muslim reformism. He published several successive volumes of his collected articles and studies covering all of the major themes of the debate between these two contradictory forms of thought. Making no concessions to the aura that a dose of political Islam could have provided to an Arab intellectual career starting in the 1980s, Foda kept on course throughout his political life.

Between 1983 and 1992, he published at least ten books that organised his works according to different themes, such as 'The Wafd Party and the Future' (1983), 'Before the Fall' (1984), and 'The Absent Truth' (1984). His most scholarly work dealt with the ignorance of the new radical wave of preachers and issuers of fatwas compared to the modes of subtle and rational reasoning within classical Islamic jurisprudence. Additionally, in 'Crooks' (1985), he denounced the scandal of Islamic financial firms that took advantage of the naiveté of pious depositors who lost large parts of their savings. In 1990, he also denounced the introduction of the 'marriage of convenience' (*zawaj al-mut'a*), which led to a type of legalisation of the sale of women's bodies. Again in 1990, he published 'To Be or Not To Be'; and finally, in 1992, 'So That Our Words Will Not Be Empty.' Prior to this, in 1988, he published the results of his research on the Islamic terrorism that was thriving in Egypt at that time in a book entitled 'Terrorism'; and in 1989 he published another entitled 'The Warning'. In 1985 he published his writings on secularism in a volume entitled 'Dialogue on Secularism.'[23] He did not consider secularism to be in any way opposed to the content of Islam.

In all of his writings, and during his appearances on various television shows, Foda consistently defended a secular concept of the state that was not forbidden by anything in Muslim society. At the same time, he deconstructed the three main tendencies that he had very creatively diagnosed within political Islam. The first of these was the traditional tendency of the Muslim Brotherhood, which was outwardly moderate and accepted participating in the electoral process, but whose ideology was in reality totalitarian and contained a branch that practiced political assassination. The second was that of armed, radical Islamic movements that emerged in the last third of the twentieth century and which rejected the very notion of a constitution and democracy. Finally, the third tendency was one that Foda characterised as one of 'financial fortune' (*al-tharwawi*), which included everyone who had made a fortune in Saudi Arabia and Egypt after Nasser's death due to President Anwar Sadat's more open economic policies, which had initiated an era of major corruption.

Foda's main concern, one he shared with all Arab Muslim reformers since the nineteenth century, was to awaken rationality and recall the openness of

Islamic heritage to other cultures, on the one hand, and to European achievements of modernity, on the other. As this modernity had now acquired a universal character, it would be vain and harmful to be isolated from it. Similarly, unlike the fundamentalists, he showed the richness and diversity of Islamic jurisprudence, which they had passed over in silence. Indeed, the fundamentalists were only committed to rigid and pernicious interpretations of the Qur'an or of the 'sayings and deeds' of the Prophet (*sunna*) that tended towards rigidity. Moreover, it was not clear whether these 'sayings and deeds' were authentic or if they were invented to suit the needs of a particular set of circumstances in the beleaguered history of the early centuries of Islam.

Foda was also a virulent critic of the Iranian revolution, which had allowed religious clerics to seize power and to claim that they had established an Islamic regime. For him, this revolution contributed to creating the desire for an Islamic state in the Arab world, which encouraged the Islamic movements to become more and more animated and radical. Given the circumstances in Egypt at the time, during which some Islamic movements had resorted to violence following the assassination of President Sadat, the high profile acquired by Farag Foda put him in even more danger than that which Nasr Hamid Abu Zayd faced a few years later. Following a series of television appearances in March 1992 during which he had debated the issue of a state of a civil nature (secular) versus a state of a religious nature, an association of ulama who had studied at Al-Azhar declared him an apostate, that is, someone who was to be punished by death, on 3 June 1992. Five days later, on 8 June, he was assassinated by two men on motorbikes in front of his young son as he was leaving the Egyptian Society for Enlightenment, an NGO he had founded. From that point onwards, it was an absolute certainty that accusations of apostasy loomed for any free thinker, especially a thinker who remained a devout Muslim and understood the classical texts of Islam.

There are other authors who need to be mentioned here, especially Fouad Zakariya (1927–2010), who will also be discussed in Chapter 14. He was a well-respected Egyptian philosopher who taught at Cairo University, and subsequently at the University of Kuwait. In two of his very courageous works, 'Truth and Illusion in Contemporary Islamist Movements' and 'The Islamic Awakening in the Mirror of Reason',[24] he questioned the aims of Islamic movements and showed how dangerous they were for the future of Arab societies. Similarly, the radical critique by the Egyptian career magistrate,

Muhammad al-Ashmawy, should also be highlighted. Among the many books that he has written, one has been translated into French.[25] In addition, there is al-Sadiq al-Nayhum, a Libyan born in Benghazi (1937–1994), who published a diverse collection of articles and studies in a volume that was eloquently entitled 'Islam versus Islam: A Paper Shari'a.'[26]

The debate between al-Azmeh and al-Messiri

Another important window into the dispute over the possibility of establishing a civil state separating politics and religion can be found in a work with two voices, one Islamist and the other secular, by two major Arab intellectuals.[27] I refer here to Aziz al-Azmeh, a Syrian modernist with extensive university training and author of a remarkable work entitled 'Secularism from a Different Perspective', and Abdel Wahhab al-Messiri (1938–2008), a highly prolific Egyptian intellectual and a convert to the Islamic worldview. What is interesting about this work is that it presents one long essay by each of the two authors, the first extolling the virtues of secularism and the second denigrating it. This is followed by each author's commentary on the text of the other. What this does is to lay out all of the possible arguments imaginable in favour of secularism as an opening of the mind and source of creativity and energy or, on the contrary, to denounce secularism as a source of intolerable materialistic decline that destroys the human spirit, social connections, and eliminates all spirituality within human beings.

In the book's opening essay entitled 'The Notion of Secularism', Messiri builds his case against secularism by making ample references to European philosophical and theological sources that have denounced secularism as an impoverishment of the human mind that causes it to degenerate into a nihilistic type of materialism exemplified by Marxism. This, he claims, would result in the death of civilisation and civility. He then denounces the leisure industry (*qita' al-lidhdha*, or pleasure activities). For Messiri, these are represented in particular by American films and television programmes whose 'values are relative, psychological, functional, and pragmatic, with no relation to good or evil, values that are completely self-centred and which do not distinguish between interiority and exteriority.' This odd conclusion is drawn from the author's interpretation of the very popular Tom and Jerry cartoons about a cat and a mouse.[28]

Secularism as the source of all the woes of the modern world in the work of al-Messiri

In order to really understand its danger, according to al-Messiri, secularism needs to be recognised as something that has produced a complete social and political structure, and should not be viewed as something that is just a movement of thought. To do otherwise would be naïve. Using this as his starting point, it is easy for him to blame secularism for all the flaws of the modern consumer society that has uprooted individuals, driven them away from religion and spirituality, and led them down the path of sensual pleasures. As he sees it, even European humanism of secular inspiration is only a superficial doctrine that hides the profound materialism and individualism into which Western society has fallen.[29] This is followed in Messiri's presentation by a completely biased analysis of Western thought and the human sciences it developed, whose ethnocentrism he rightly denounces. In short, for him, secularism is the equivalent of the degeneration of the social body and the depletion of human qualities. In over 140 pages, the author creates a conceptual world of his own and argues that we have entered into a 'post-secular' era, as secularism is losing all of its appeal due to a need to return to a warm, organic community irrigated by collective religious sentiment.

But Messiri goes much further. For him, even colonisation, imperialism, and Zionism are the result of the secular structure of society. These phenomena, in their essence, are the result of secular Darwinism.[30] The following excerpt from the author's anti-secular pleading might just summarise the profoundly conservative approach that animates the author's Islamic view and which can be found in the perspective of many Islamist thinkers:

> In my view, man is not able to assimilate the increased pace of consumption due to his nervous system and the limits of reason. This is why, instead of experiencing a feeling of total mastery, man feels that his dominance is disintegrating and that he is being subjected to processes he cannot control. Progress is thus comparable to a train launched at high speed whose destination is not known by anyone, which produces a feeling of imbalance, a loss of mastery, and the disappearance of boundaries; but also, on the philosophical level, the appearance of post-modernity and philosophical nihilism. On the level of society, this has led to the increase in criminality and in divorce, but also to a decrease in births, the break-down of the family and of morals (illegitimate children, teen-age pregnancy, AIDS, etc.) as well as all of the woes considered to be the 'inevitable and reasonable cost of progress.'[31]

Secularisation of the Arab world 'from another angle' in the work of al-Azmeh

Whereas Abdel Wahhab al-Messiri became famous for converting from a modernist position to one in support of the need for a defensive inward turn of Arab society towards religious identity and the sacred text as a reference, Aziz al-Azmeh became known for three successive works in which he sought to demonstrate the entrance of the Arab world into modernity. This implies the secularism of many new institutions as well as the evolution of behaviour and customs in a modernist direction. His works denounced the position of Arab intellectuals who made Muslim religious culture the reference point of any individual or collective life, as if time had stood still in the midst of the perfection of the divine Revelation. The text that he wrote for this two-voiced work was largely inspired by his previous publications. His seventy page contribution, considerably shorter than Messiri's, was entitled 'Secularism in Contemporary Arab Discourse' and took the opposite direction to Messiri's text. His goal was to show that contemporary Arab thought was very well suited to the 'secularisation' of the world.

Unlike Messiri, al-Azmeh explained in his response that 'modernity – just like secularism – is not a ready-made recipe and cannot be summarised within the modernising trend within art and painting. Instead, it designates the objective process of evolution, within effective history, of the political, the societal, the law, and knowledge.' 'The era of modernity', he adds:

> [E]ven if its origin is European, led to considerable and profound transformations on every continent. The decisive factor of all these transformations was the state. The modern state, of European origin, has been established and has taken root everywhere, in our homelands (Arabs) as well as in the lands of other people, when the Ottoman Empire itself undertook reforms (*Tanzimat*) of a political, administrative, and economic order based on the European model, with all of its additional features in the legal, educational, cultural, and intellectual domains. This was done both under external military and economic pressure and through the growing awareness of the need to usher in the changing times and history. Thus adaptation to historical developments is a normal phenomenon in all eras and in all human societies.[32]

For him, fully-fledged secularism was like history, open to change and social developments:

> It is in the image of world history, which has become a unified whole over the past two centuries and which has affected the West and the East and every single

country. This is why it is fitting to approach it in this way, through the lens of comparative history, instead of remaining isolated and floundering within the specificity of Arab societies, cloaking them exclusively with their religious characteristics in such a way as to give them the appearance of being an imaginary exception, a situation that does not respond to the laws of human society and to the workings of the historical spirit and sociological considerations.[33]

Al-Azmeh then explains how the notion of time became secularised, along with the notion of places that became national spaces. He of course also claims that knowledge became secularised by 'disconnecting from the referent of the sacred texts', along with political power. Henceforth, political power was based on a constitution, the separation of powers, and popular participation; and no longer based on the notion of 'God's Vicar on earth.'[34]

In short, although these two authors, both of whom were equally steeped in European culture, were in agreement regarding the importance of secularism in today's world; Messiri cursed it and blamed it for all of humanity's woes and for modern and post-modern society, whereas al-Azmeh saw in it the opening of the mind and the reign of reason. These two points of view, those of an Islamist traditionalist and a liberal modernist, are completely irreconcilable. This is why the polemic aptly sums up the intolerable contradiction that has been tearing apart Arab thought for the past half century. In order to strengthen his position, Messiri blends in arguments that refer to Edward Said's denunciation of Western discourse on the Muslim Orient and his analysis of the relationship between European culture and imperialism. Al-Azmeh objects to Messiri's cultural essentialism, one that petrifies Arab thought into a rigid religious heritage which prevents it from adapting to the requirements of changing times. Messiri demonises so-called Western civilisation, and al-Azmeh points out that all societies change and evolve, reiterating the fact that although modernity was initially European, this did not prevent other societies from modernising in turn.

Ultimately, this discussion is not new. At the beginning of the twentieth century, in 1902 when Egypt was the centre of Arab thought, a similar polemic shook up the intellectual elites of the time. It opposed the great Egyptian Muslim reformist, Muhammad 'Abduh, to Farah Antun, who was originally from Lebanon and who was also a reformist and an admirer of the Andalusian philosopher Ibn Rushd (Averroes), of Darwin and of European positivist thought, especially French thought.[35] Also of interest are the polemics between 'Abduh and Gabriel Hanotaux (1853–1944), and between Jamal al-Din al-Afghani and Ernest Renan. Be that as it may, the civility apparent in their exchanges is exemplary, especially compared to the assassinations and attempted assassinations that modernists were subjected to in their opposition to traditionalists at the end of the twentieth century.

To conclude this chapter, it is useful to briefly analyse Aziz al-Azmeh's reflections on the secular phenomenon in the world as discussed in his major work 'Secularism from a Different Perspective.'[36] This is a serene and brilliant reflection on the trajectory of secularism in today's world, and in particular in the Arab world. The work of this author, Professor Emeritus in the Department of History at the Central European University in Budapest, Hungary, provides a critical and reasoned assessment of the circulation of secular ideas and behaviours in the Arab world and the barriers that rulers and Arab intellectuals placed in their way almost everywhere, naturally for non-religious reasons.

The value of all these reflections is that they draw on anthropology and comparative historical politics in their approach to ascertaining the political significance of secularism as it appeared in the West and was spread to the Orient. In this work the author is far removed from the cultural essentialism practiced by classical Orientalism and expanded by contemporary neo-Orientalism. He shows with great precision, beyond the rigidity of the founding texts, the multifaceted diversity of politico-religious behaviours and their historicity. This basic methodology yields prodigious results throughout the author's historical analysis because it is based on very thorough knowledge of the major historical upheavals experienced by the Arab world, which are continually shown in relation to religious exegeses and the practices of rulers.

The heart of this work is devoted to presenting the contradictions experienced by rulers and political thinkers from the period of reform in the Ottoman Empire (*Tanzimat*) through to the intolerable tensions that most Arab states live with today in relation to the Islamist movements which they themselves initially encouraged following the major defeat of the Arab armies by Israel in 1967. The author demonstrates with clockwork precision how even the most revolutionary governments neglected every opportunity to definitively align formal value systems and legal systems with secular practices that had become increasingly widespread from the middle of the twentieth century onwards. As hope faded for the achievement of a liberal state and as the failures of the authoritarian 'progressive state' became more obvious over the course of the past half century, the author shows how Arab governments all played with fire by allowing, and more often than not actually encouraging, formal religious structures to put a stop to the growing secularisation of behaviours and lifestyles throughout the Arab world.

In his work, al-Azmeh denounces Arab intellectuals whose writings have fuelled a specifically Arab 'schizophrenia' and uses extensive quotations to support his case. This schizophrenia resulted from a dichotomy between, on the one hand, the rapid secularisation of social and political behaviours, and on the other, the cheap cultural metaphysics of Islamic identity that these intellectuals helped to spread, particularly over the past few decades. Like other Arab thinkers, through his work al-Azmeh makes it easier to understand the complexity of the causes of the regression experienced by the Arab world. In spite of this regressive inward turn, the author calls for hope in the event that secularising currents are able to gain ground in their countries of origin. Indeed, as he aptly explains, 'secularism does not materialise as one single form and cannot be reduced to a single slogan. On the contrary, it is a historical conquest that can serve as a starting point for questioning and examining our reality in order to build a democratic future.'

This analysis of the disputes and polemics generated by the hardening of a radical Islamic thought intent on embracing all those disillusioned with nationalism and with socialist and modernist forms of progressivism thus illustrates the reduced scope for freedom and breathing room within Arab thought. The threat of violence and the risk of being subjected to the wrath of Islamist circles have obviously contributed a great deal to suppressing or marginalising the great movement of reformist thought examined in Chapter 7, nationalist thought (see *supra*, Chapter 8), and by extension the serious critical thought that followed the defeat of the Arab armies by Israel in 1967 (see *supra*, Chapter 10). In the following chapter, the other trends in Arab thought will be described, particularly those that seek to reconcile Western-style democracy and the dominant version of Islam, which has become radical; but also those trends that call for moving beyond ideological disputes.

CHAPTER 13

Intellectual attempts at ideological conciliation

The liberal thought that dominated the era of the *Nahda* was subsequently suppressed by the rise of revolutionary Arab radicalism as well as by theologico-political Islam. It began to reappear, timidly at first, following the 1967 defeat. It then made a more widespread comeback in the 1990s when the 'American superpower' intervened directly and openly in Arab affairs following the Iraqi occupation of Kuwait in 1990. Starting with the presidency of George W. Bush and his ambitious programme to reshape the Arab world and to force it to enter into the vicious cycle of democracy, this liberal school of thought was adopted due to American and European support. Paradoxically, it was incorporated into the ultra-conservative press and by media outlets financed by the emirates and kingdoms of the Arabian Peninsula. Arab intellectuals who had emigrated to the United States or to Europe were very active in this regard and were overtly supported by the Western media.

Very often, after having spent relatively extensive periods of time in Europe or the United States, some of these intellectuals occupied influential positions in their home countries through a network of NGOs and local think tanks that they set up with external European or American financing. However, they were also recruited by large Western NGOs and think tanks that opened satellite offices in major Arab capitals. The career of one major Lebanese intellectual, Fouad Ajami (1945–2014), attests to these developments. Born in a poor village in southern Lebanon, his ideological route led from militant Arab nationalism working in defence of Palestinian rights to a stunning conversion to the neo-conservatism of the United States, to where he emigrated in 1963 for his studies. He subsequently built his career in United States government circles, particularly during the presidency of George W. Bush, at which time he became an advisor to Condoleezza Rice and Paul Wolfowitz.

When he passed away, he was lauded by major American newspapers for having denounced Arab dictatorships, especially the regime of Saddam Hussein, and for encouraging the American government to invade Iraq in order to establish a 'democratic' state. The *New York Times* and the *Washington Post* published glowing articles about him. His works garnered an enthusiastic reception from the media and within the academy. In them, he described his disillusionment with Arab nationalism as well as his Shi'i origins and the marginalisation of his community by the Sunnis. He also described the journey of Imam Musa al-Sadr, an Iranian cleric of Lebanese descent who came to live in Lebanon, where he undertook to raise awareness among the Shi'i population of their own identity and to found the Movement of the Deprived.[1] He is the most prominent Arab intellectual to have completely veered to the side of the American superpower and to boast about it. There are many others that could be discussed here, but there is no use in doing so. Ajami is, however, undeniably the intellectual who paved the way for numerous others to dramatically change their opinions, and provide the template for a 'conversion' to the benefits of submitting to the United States. It was thus important to mention him here as a leader of new liberal Arab thought.

The new 'liberal' Arab thought

The political philosophy which resulted from this trend consisted of preaching about the need to build an Arab civil society, seen as the requisite way forward towards democracy and respect for human rights. The oppressive 'Leviathan' state built by Arab dictatorships had to give way to a modest and respectful state with public freedoms and minority rights. Within this somewhat summary vision, the demagogic Arab nationalist state was to be succeeded by a state that retreated and privatised the public sector, a domain subjected to dogmatic claims about its wastefulness and inefficiencies. This state was to encourage private enterprise and create an 'investment climate', to use dominant neo-liberal terminology. It should encourage the influx of foreign capital and a regime favourable to new investments that the local and international business world could utilise. Multinational firms that had been so despised and feared by previous generations of Arabs, rich Arab tycoons who had sprung up like mushrooms amidst the explosion of petroleum revenues and their monopolisation by princely and royal rulers, or their privileged intermediaries, all needed to be welcomed with open arms.[2] These new actors on the Arab political scene would be able to advance the cause of democracy and civil liberties through the financing that they alone could provide to the new institutions that were required to assist with the development of civil society, an indispensable intermediary mechanism between the state and the citizen.

There is a collective work that reflects this new vision of the Arab world in need of being saved from totalitarian demons through economic liberalisation, a reduction of the role of the state in the economy, and the encouragement of investments. This work focused on the economy of peace in the Arab world and appeared at about the same time as the Oslo Accord (1993) between the PLO and Israel, an agreement that led many to believe that peace in the Middle East was imminent.[3] The entrepreneur is described in this work as a 'determining player' in the required changes necessary for the Arab-Israeli peace that many believed to be on the horizon, as well as for the transition to democracy.[4] But the entrepreneur is also described as someone who needs to show allegiance to political Islam in order to compensate for a 'detestable and dangerous political image.' In his contribution to this work, the French political scientist Rémy Leveau (1932–2005) clearly expressed how this entrepreneur would create religious foundations, construct numerous mosques and Qur'anic schools, and award scholarships to students in order to send them to European capitals or to the United States.[5] This entrepreneur would enlist ulama to join corporate boards, but would also finance political movements aligned with Islam. In short, the different contributors to this collective work believed that the transition to peace and democracy required the liberalisation of the economy and the promotion of new entrepreneurs, no matter how obscure the origins of their fortunes, their relationships with the mechanisms of power, or their associations with Islamic movements.[6]

Abundant evidence of this can be found in the important work of another Arab intellectual, Larbi Sadiki, who was born in Tunisia and educated in Australia. He wrote a very lengthy work, *The Search for Arab Democracy*, published by the prestigious Columbia University Press,[7] which contains a great deal of rich and informative material and an extensive bibliography. Most of the authors listed in it are American; some of whom focus on democracy itself, but most of whom address the need for the Arab world to accept a 're-Islamisation' of thought and society, which is seen as the only way forward towards achieving forms of democracy that are acceptable to the Arab psyche, a popular theme in American thought on the Middle East.[8] For the past few decades, this theme has also been very prevalent within French Islamic studies, where colonisation and post-colonial modernity are considered to have violated the Muslim psyche, and for this reason to have alienated Arabs. The extremist currents of Islamic movements embodied by Al-Qaeda and other similar organisations are allegedly nothing more than the result of this 'anthropological' violation carried out by the modernist Arab elites who have ruled since independence.[9]

This is why Sadiki starts his work by stating that 'secularism must be rethought within societies where pervasive religiosity contradicts with the privatisation of religion as in the West.'[10] He argues that Orientalist thought, just like 'Occidentalist' thought, is essentialist and reductionist. For him, Eurocentrism, sexism, racism, colonialism, Orientalism, and Occidentalism have uprooted Muslim societies, and they therefore need to establish new foundations. Until now, in his view, there have only been truncated interpretations of Islam, which has been presented as a 'totalitarian order', without seeing all of its 'democratic potential.'[11] To justify this statement, he analyses the positions of several thinkers and political leaders who are convinced of the necessity to re-Islamise Arab societies in order to liberate their energies and provide them access to development in the Islamic mode. These include, in particular, Hassan al-Turabi (Sudan), Hassan Hanafi (Egypt), Rachid al-Ghannouchi (Tunisia), and even Roger Garaudy, a French communist who converted to Islam.

For Sadiki, Islamists are major thinkers who have come out against Eurocentrism and Orientalism. In support of his argument, he relies on the work of John Esposito and John Voll, both of whom he often quotes. He argues that Islamists 'hope to recover through democratisation numerous revered institutions in order to establish a just and accountable Islamic regime. Through Islamisation they hope to reclaim and operationalise concepts of justice, consultation, legality, accountability and probity in the management of economy, polity and society.'[12] With surprising naiveté, he believes that the development of communication technologies will contribute significantly to reducing the influence of the ulama as the guardians of Islamic orthodoxy.[13] This development has clearly had the opposite effect, thanks to Arab satellite television channels, especially those belonging to oil-producing emirates and kingdoms. Religious preachers and shaykhs prone to publishing fatwas soon became a constant presence on television screens. Far from reducing their authority, as Sadiki stated this would do, they instead acquired widespread popularity and became real media stars, such as Shaykh Youssef al-Quradawi on Al-Jazeera television.

All doubts are dispelled in the book's conclusion: 'Democracy has joined Islam in jostling to inform the political process in many Arab societies as a normative standard. Their struggle is against a brand of secular-nationalism embodied today in decaying authoritarianism, clan or family-based politics, delegitimised rule, failed states and bankrupt revolutions.'[14] This now canonical conception dominates the scene of liberal thought today. What is strange is that this thought only attacks dictatorial republics that promoted anti-imperialist Arab nationalism during the Nasserist period. No references are ever made to the diverse social policies carried out in the areas of health and education, or of the agrarian reforms of the 1950s that aimed to reduce the enormous socio-economic inequalities that reigned in these societies.[15] In contrast, the neo-patrimonialist regimes (kingdoms and emirates) that exploit oil windfalls to benefit the ruling families are never mentioned. With only minor exceptions, these regimes are just as repressive as the republican ones, but have managed to place themselves under the protection of Western powers whose policies they faithfully execute within the region. This is why the narrative produced by this thought is so monotonous: all of the woes of the Arab world are allegedly due to this 'cursed' period of demagoguery and fascism, even totalitarianism, as represented by the dominance of Arab political regimes that have been strong-willed in their approach to regional geopolitics (especially Egypt, Syria, and Iraq).

In addition to those authors who enjoyed advanced university training and who 'converted' to the benefits of Islam and democracy, an impressive number of former Marxists and Arab nationalists also transformed themselves into virulent editorialists for the pan-Arab press, in particular the two major daily newspapers *Al-Hayat* and *Asharq Al-Awsat*, both financed by oil monarchies, led by Saudia Arabia.[16] This is why it is simply astonishing that the frequently unbridled authoritarianism and neo-patrimonial mechanisms of the economies of the oil monarchies are all passed over in silence within these narratives, as if Saudi Arabia or Qatar were advanced democracies along the lines of Scandinavian countries. Moreover, many of these intellectuals are close to Arab billionaires, most of whom made their fortunes in the oil monarchies and finance religious foundations, journals, university scholarships and new professorial chairs in major English-speaking universities.[17] This category of new propagandists and flaming ideologues of the neo-liberal trend in economics can be found just about everywhere occupying important positions within international organisations such as the World Bank and the International Monetary Fund, as well as within major American and European think tanks, such as the Carnegie Foundation.

The silent continuation of the critique of formal 'Islamic reason'

It is now clear that rationalist heritage played an important role in what has been called 'Islamic Enlightenment', in reference to the influence of European Enlightenment philosophy on numerous Muslim thinkers of the nineteenth century. These thinkers were often individuals who had studied at the prestigious Al-Azhar University, the guardian of the Muslim faith. Starting with the turning point of the 1967 defeat by Israel and the weakening of Arab nationalist thought, the groundswell of political Islam as a substitute ideology of identity, but also the escalation of ceremonial religiosity and the creation on this basis of an irreducible otherness in relation to the rest of the world, succeeded in most efficiently marginalising, if not eliminating, the strong rationalist tradition within the interpretation of the Qur'anic message. This tradition has been almost completely overlooked within French academic research, and more generally in the West. In the Arab world, books by the thinkers who have kept this tradition going are hardly ever the subject of in-depth studies, despite some of them becoming very well-known thanks to the wide distribution of their books. These include, for example, the Syrian intellectual, Mohammed Shahrour (born in Damascus in 1938), or the Egyptian scholar Nasr Hamid Abu Zayd.

Their undertaking is not without risk, because they could be accused of apostasy at any moment by the new class of clerics who have access to the Qatar and Saudi Arabia-influenced pan-Arab media, such as, for example, Shaykh al-Qaradawi. It is important to reiterate that in Egypt, Farag Foda was assassinated because he stood up to the ignorance and obscurantism of the clerics, Naguib Mahfouz was the victim of an assassination attempt, and Nasr Hamid Abu Zayd ran into so many problems that he had to go into exile in Europe. In 2012, Ziad Hafez, a long-term supporter of Arab nationalism from Lebanon, published a highly scholarly work presenting an impressive overview of the persistence of critical thought in Islam in spite of all of the direct and indirect pressures that are brought to bear on it in the Arab world.[18] This book is further enhanced by an explanation of the reasons why this critical thought is overlooked in European and American academic research and presents a detailed picture of the often considerable work of many of these unrecognised authors. In so doing, Hafez re-inserts this tradition of critical thought within the historical context in which it appeared, that is, the long intellectual tradition of critical exegesis, and theological, philosophical, and political inquiry that developed as a result of the Qur'anic Revelation after it first appeared. This is why it is useful to acknowledge this, as it represents a beneficial and pioneering new work, along the lines of Albert Hourani's in 1962, allowing a better understanding of the geopolitical and local issues of the political contexts and the richness of an unrecognised Arab thought, which alone, unpopular, and mistreated, has to face these issues and contexts.

In his introductory chapter, Ziad Hafez denounces the manipulation and instrumentalisation of religion in which Western powers are engaged. Even in the preface to his book, he does not mince words when on several occasions he refers to the 'spectre' and the 'Western imperial project'. He then goes on to describe the historical political context of the relations between Arab and Western countries. In his work an approach of resentment can be found which was developed in works such as Edward Said's *Orientalism*, in which Western discourse on the Muslim Orient is severely criticised and deconstructed. What also makes Hafez's work appealing is the way he looks back at the major theologico-political debates within Arab Islam of the classical period, the time when Arab-Islamic civilisation was built. This is followed by an explanation of the reasons why the Arab renaissance was 'taken hostage' due to the instrumentalisation of Islamic fundamentalism within the evolution of global and regional geopolitics. The author then provides a comprehensive overview of contemporary Muslim reformists who have been ignored by today's academic research. This disdain is very surprising in light of the fact that some of these thinkers were often persecuted by local governments to the extent of being sentenced to death. This was the case of the outstanding intellectual Mahmoud Taha (1909–1985) in Sudan, whose case was previously discussed and whom Hafez characterises as the 'Gandhi of Islam' and to the broad scope and originality of whose religious views he brings well-deserved recognition.

Another innovative reformist of Qur'anic interpretation whose thought Ziad Hafez analysed was Muhammad Shahrur of Syria. His work, just like that of Taha, has practically been ignored by European and American Islamic studies. Nonetheless, it had enormous repercussions in the Arab world. Born in Damascus in 1935 and an engineer by profession, Shahrur became interested in linguistics and in the meaning of words as they might have been understood during the lifetime of the Prophet in the seventh century. This led him to challenge all the interpretations of the verses of the Qur'an influenced by the political evolutions and interests of the ruling elites. Published in 1990, his major work, *al-Kitab wa'l-Qur'an*, was followed by numerous other works on Islamic values and their influence on political and social organisation.[19] Shahrur's work seeks to provide a contemporary reading of the Qur'an and Muslim institutions, a radical update to the interpretation of this text and the Qur'anic Revelation that does not betray the genius of the Arabic language nor its precision, and in so doing is able to make apparent all of the subtlety of the Qur'anic text and its potential for adaptation.

According to Shahrur, the Qur'an actually contains two very different types of verses: those from the divine Revelation (*al-kitab*, the book) that pertain to knowledge of the universe and the nature of God; and those that pertain to the message that God gave to the Prophet in order to preach this Revelation (*al-risala*, the message). For the author, only the verses from the Revelation are atemporal and absolute, whereas those related to the message are circumstantial and attached to the historical period of the life of the Prophet, and thus do not have any absolute value.[20] This of course represents a complete revolution in the way the Qur'an is read and complements the one suggested by 'Ali 'Abd al-Raziq seventy-five years earlier in 1925, when he demonstrated that the Qur'an did not contain any prescriptions regarding which political regime to adopt. Moreover, the prescriptions contained in the verses that deal with social life (marriage, dietary restrictions, veiling of women and control of their behaviour) were contingent and marked the major progress that had been made since this era; but just as importantly, they needed to be read in light of God's mercy and compassion, two divine attributes that are pervasive within the Qur'anic text. Unlike Taha, who was imprisoned, sentenced to death, and executed, Shahrur has lived a very peaceful life in Damascus until now, a place where Muslim fundamentalism and its political organisations have hardly been encouraged or instrumentalised as has been the case in other Arab regimes, particularly in Egypt by the two presidents Sadat and Mubarak.

For Hafez, the work of these two major authors represents what he calls the 'new readings of the [Qur'anic] text'. He thus chose these two key thinkers as illustrations of these critical readings, ones he situates within the continuation of the movement of reformist Islam, or rather, 'enlightened' Islam (*al-Islam al-tanwiri*), according to Arabic terminology. He clearly shows the debt of this movement to the *Nahda* of the nineteenth century, the roots of which extend back to the Qur'anic Prophecy and some of the schools of interpretation of the early centuries. For him, the work of these two influential authors is an example of a true return to the sources of Islamic thought, unlike the work of fundamentalist authors.

Following this, Ziad Hafez gathers together the works of several other authors in what he calls a 'new reading of heritage,' a critical reading of the enormous jurisprudential and theologico-political corpus (shari'a law) built up over centuries around the interpretation of the Qur'anic verses. He provides an overview of the work of the famous Egyptian writer, Taha Husayn, who has already been discussed at length, that challenges the very notion of *Jahiliyya* (the time of ignorance, and absence of civilisation and institutions) as opposed to the time of the Qur'anic Revelation, which serves as the basis of numerous rigid and sterile interpretations of heritage. In addition to Nasr Hamid Abu Zayd, also previously discussed, Ziad Hafez focuses on two other Egyptian authors, Khalil Abdelkarim (1930–2002) and Sayyid Mahmoud al-Qimny (born in 1947), who are not well known and even less well appreciated. Throughout their courageous and scholarly works, both authors aim to re-establish the continuity of Arab history between the time prior to and after the Qur'anic Revelation in order to demonstrate the legacy of the pre-Islamic period in Islam. In the same vein, they provide a profane reading of the early years of Islam and of the behaviour of the Prophet's companions that is far removed from the myths of traditional sacred history. For al-Qimny, this led to a denunciation of his work as heretical as well as to death threats in 2005 by terrorist organisations claiming to defend Islam. In response to this, he published a letter in the press in which he disavowed his writings and committed to stop writing about religious topics.[21]

What is commendable in Ziad Hafez's meticulous and precise work is his overview of numerous other works that are, for the most part, largely unknown. It also reflects the contentious controversies raised by critical readings of the Qur'anic text and the shari'a corpus. In contrast with the open reading of reformers, it is the literalist reading of shari'a law asserted indiscriminately by fundamentalists in order to justify their conservative views that imprison society and facilitate the ideological control over the population through political power. This is clearly demonstrated by Hafez in his very thorough survey of the various currents of Arab thought, whilst at the same time emphasising those works considered to be the most significant within Arab critical religious thought.

This allows the issues at the base of these theologico-political and philosophical disputes to be made clear, and leads to a better understanding of the relevance of the age-old debates that permeate Arab religious thought, torn between authoritarian and fundamentalist forces, as well as forces for progress and change. Through his in-depth knowledge of the Qur'anic text, Ziad Hafez leads the reader to attempt, alongside him, to understand the countless ways of reading it; from literalism and the narrowest form of dogmatism to philosophical openness and the most astonishing political liberalism. Nothing could be more beneficial than this exercise of comprehending a passionate intellectual world, one that has been broadly concealed by obviously self-interested complicity – most likely unconscious – between governments and academic settings, and government circles and the Arab media. They have set up barriers against the expansion of any ideology that allows conciliation between faith and reason. The latter would mean opening an irreversible pathway towards liberty and access to full-fledged Arab citizenship, which would endanger the interests of the major powers as well as those of current Arab regimes.[22]

To follow the route proposed by Ziad Hafez is to discover another Arab world that is far removed from the one served up daily by political events, academia, and the news media; that is, a world of despair. Indeed, the relevance of this work became fully apparent with the Arab revolts of 2011, which led to numerous external interventions and the instrumentalisation of fundamentalist currents in order to prevent the emergence of new forms of power, which again provides proof of the intense manipulation of religion in the Arab world.

Many other overshadowed contemporary critical thinkers

It is fitting here to discuss other thinkers who are critical of traditionalist approaches to religious heritage, but who are mostly outside of the field of vision of writings on the religious dimension of Arab thought. This concerns Gamal al-Banna (1920–2013), who was known for his forceful personality. He was the brother of Hassan al-Banna (1906–1949), the founder of the Muslim Brotherhood. At first, he was an admirer of his older brother Hassan, but he gradually distanced himself to join the group of liberal reformers that criticised the dogmatic and rigid approach of fundamentalist movements, such as that of the Muslim Brotherhood. Through his numerous articles and writings, Gamal al-Banna kept this critical tradition in Islam alive. Just like everyone else who was part of this school of thought, he received no academic attention or media coverage, unlike, for example, the two brothers, Tariq and Hani Ramadan, who through their mother were the grandsons of Hassan al-Banna.[23]

Al-Banna's works take on heated subjects, on which he takes positions that are radically liberal, especially on issues such as the veiling of women, and equality and brotherhood between Muslims and non-Muslims (particularly the Copts in Egypt). He also raises the fact that Islam is both a religion and a religious community, but not both a religion and a state. In his view, apostasy should not be punishable by death, and corporal punishment is not compatible with the spirit of the Qur'an. Indeed, he claims that there is nothing in the Qur'an to oppose the establishment of secularism, and that the corpus of 'sayings and deeds' of the Prophet (*hadith*) is unreliable.[24] On this last point, al-Banna's views are consistent with another reformist who is not well known but who is no less important, Zakaria Ouzon of Syria. He is the author of a scathing work on the veracity of the thousands of narratives on the deeds and actions of the Prophet that have been transmitted for generations and which served to establish the vast corpus of shari'a law.[25]

The same approach can be found in the excellent work of Sadok Belaïd, a Professor in the Faculty of Legal, Political and Social Sciences at the University of Tunis (Tunis II) who advocates a new reading of the prescriptive parts of the Qur'anic text in the tradition of the great reformists, especially that of 'Ali 'Abd al-Raziq.[26] At the end of his rich and well-documented analysis of the conditions in which the Qur'anic text appeared, and the geographical and historical contexts in which it was interpreted by jurists, he calls for an end to 'self-confinement' and to the 'blockage of perspectives.'

All of this very important ongoing religious criticism is of course often hidden from view in the Arab world, as it is in Europe and the United States. One of the rare works on this issue published in France was written by a modernist Moroccan intellectual, Abdou Filali-Ansary, the French-language translator of one of 'Ali 'Abd al-Raziq's most important books, *Islam and the Foundations of Political Power*. Filali-Ansary chose to examine the thought of several intellectuals, both Arab and non-Arab, on the issue of reform in Islam. His book also includes an analysis of the positions of some of the well-known Orientalists such as Maxime Rodinson, Jacques Berque, Ernest Gellner, and Marshall Hodgson.[27]

Abdellilah Belkeziz is another highly respected Moroccan intellectual whose thought merits discussion here. He is the author of a large body of critical work focused on the deconstruction of contemporary Arab discourses on many issues.[28] These include the connection to ancient Arab intellectual heritage, the relationship between religion and the state, as well as the problems of political legitimacy, the dialectic of authenticity and modernity in the Arab world, the rivalries and disputes in the exercise of political power during the Arab conquests, and the critique of nationalist thought. Belkeziz's work is encyclopaedic in scope and provides an objective and detailed review of all of the major controversies that have concerned Arab thought over the past half century. The author makes no attempt to hide his 'desire for modernity,' and deploys his in-depth knowledge of Muslim and Arab history, and the fact that his work is based on extensive knowledge of this intellectual heritage, to critique the works of many other Arab intellectuals in a way that is both measured and firm. One of these intellectuals is his compatriot, Al-Jabri.

It is of course unthinkable to conclude this analysis of religious criticism without discussing the thought of Mohammed Arkoun (1928–2010), who was recognised and honoured in France as one of the main religious reformists of the past half century. The municipal library in the Fifth Arrondissement of Paris was renamed in his honour following his death. Arkoun, of Algerian descent, had an impressive academic career and left behind a vast body of work that aimed to re-establish an 'Islamic reason' appropriate for modern times, instead of one that remains stubbornly confined within an inflexible past. Many of his works have been translated into Arabic as well as other languages.[29]

It is worthwhile mentioning here one of Arkoun's works on 'Present-day Islam Confronting its Tradition and Globalisation,' which appeared in a collective volume in 1998.[30] In this article, he faults many modernist intellectuals, such as Taha Husayn and other great names from the reformist period, for the concessions they made to fundamentalists starting with the emergence of the Muslim Brotherhood movement in Egypt in 1928. He also tries to resituate Islamic fundamentalism within the globalisation movement and relies on the work of Benjamin Barber, who pits the two notions of Jihad and McWorld against each other.[31] Fundamentalism, Arkoun claims, is a 'search for [the] meaning' that consumerist logic has eliminated within an atmosphere of 'disposable thought' that prevents the 'production of inspirational intellectual and spiritual values.' For Arkoun, in its reactive stance towards modernity, the Islamic revival is in fact a response to globalisation.

In my view, it is possible to consider Arkoun's approach part of the new canonical narrative concerning the need for Arabs to re-appropriate Islam, which has been disfigured by secularism and modernity. Certainly Arkoun, whose thought embodies the continuation of religious reform, is himself far removed from fundamentalism. However, by subscribing to the thesis of a quasi-biological reaction on the part of this hypothetical being that is Islam in the face of globalisation, he glosses over all of the Arab political contexts and all of the geopolitical contexts of the Middle East that I have described here. These are the contexts that substantially fuelled modern Islamic fundamentalism, which was still very marginalised in the early twentieth century. This was before the creation of the Saudi kingdom and the Muslim Brotherhood movement, but also before the historic step of the instrumentalisation of religion during the Cold War.

Now that the different ways of thinking in the Arab world have been broadly outlined, it is useful at this stage to review the work of two original thinkers, one from Bahrain and the other from Lebanon. Both of them focused on completely contradictory currents of thought in Arab societies.

Reflections on serious tensions within Arab thought

It was these acute contradictions between the supporters of an inward-turn of Arab thought towards religious heritage and the secularist-leaning modernists or religious reformers, who reread the Qur'anic text outside the convention of tradition, which led two intellectuals to reflect on the continuous development of this contradictory phenomenon and to try to provide a life-saving diagnosis. I refer here to Mohammed Jaber al-Ansari, born in Bahrain in 1939, who had both a political and academic career in his home country, and Muhammad Dahir, a Lebanese citizen who was a career diplomat and who currently runs a publishing house (El-Biruni) that publishes many books translated into and from Arabic. These authors overlap in their desire to move Arab thought beyond its apparently insurmountable contradictions, ones which have generated so much existential tension among Arabs.

Mohammed Jaber al-Ansari's critique of the spirit of conciliation

In a major work entitled 'Arab Thought and the Struggle between Contraries', published in 1996, al-Ansari, much like Aziz al-Azmeh (who was not cited in his bibliography), denounced the schizophrenia that results from, on the one hand, individual behaviours that are mainly secular, sometimes to the point of being atheist or agnostic, and, on the other hand, obsessively clinging to

Islamic identity as a form of otherness versus Western modernity.[32] From this point onward, al-Ansari delved deeply into the major themes of contemporary Arab thought to explore the continual attempts at accommodating this particular ancient heritage and integrating it with the secular values of modernity, attempts which dated to the beginning of the Arab renaissance in the early nineteenth century. In this respect, al-Tahtawi had already instigated what al-Ansari refers to as this 'conciliatory' way of thinking.

The author devotes a lot of time to discussing the works of those Arab thinkers of the renaissance who tried to find democratic roots within Islam, a religion that is alleged to be the bearer of values that are not materialistic, selfish, or individualist like those of the West. However, he considers that the critical thought and rationality expounded in the works of the renaissance thinkers, which culminated with the generation spanning the end of the nineteenth and beginning of the twentieth centuries, very quickly fell into decline. This occurred when nationalist thought that was rationalist and secular, and according to al-Ansari best exemplified by the work of Sati al-Husri, clashed with the harsh realities of the fragmentation of Arab states. He thus believes that it was the headlong rush into revolutionary romanticism that contributed to the decline of rationality and secular critical thought.[33]

Interestingly, Al-Ansari does not consider this school of Arab thought to be the equivalent of any of the non-Western models he cites: Japan, which achieved a successful technical revolution whilst preserving its traditional character; the radical and global revolution in China; and finally, India, which became a modern democratic state while preserving its spiritual heritage and its traditional nature.[34] The author painstakingly demonstrates how critical and rationalist thinkers began to backtrack from their initial radical attitudes at the end of the 1930s and began to integrate Islamic religious heritage and its main protagonists into their worldview. Likewise, he shows how fundamentalist thinkers began to gain strength at the same time, eventually materialising with the creation of the Muslim Brotherhood movement in 1928.

For al-Ansari, the Baath party doctrine represents the best example of the new conciliatory spirit, one that renounced the doctrine of scientific socialism, positivism, and abstract ideas, which Michel Aflaq, the party's founder, had contrasted with the spiritual roots of Arab civilisation, the central core of which was, of course, the Qur'anic Prophecy.[35] The author similarly criticises the thought of Constantine Zurayk, and is amazingly clear-sighted and accurate in his meticulous analysis of these texts, as well as those of Nasserist thought, which also attempted to conciliate heritage and modernity. As I have also done in this and other previous works, al-Ansari does not fail to note the influence of the European Romantic and nationalist movements, especially Italian and German, on the development in Arab thought towards renunciation of the positivist and rationalist spirit. He concludes:

> Arab romanticism, like its European predecessor, not only marked the literary movement that it initially influenced, but gradually transformed into a general social phenomenon. This blended into the new national sentiment, with support from the new developing religious sentiment, and influenced the renaissance of religious culture (after 1930) through its character of idealistic consciousness. Likewise, it influenced the creation of new parties and movements dominated by the romantic view of history, politics, and society.[36]

'This romantic revolution,' adds al-Ansari, 'which left a much greater mark on Arab culture than the rationalist movement was ever able to do, went through several stages before becoming a widespread national phenomenon.'[37] It is interesting to see how the author defines these stages, since he begins with the influence of scholars who emigrated to North America, especially Lebanese and Syrian Christians, including the great novelist Mikhail Naimy and Khalil Gibran, the scholar and poet celebrated in both the United States and the Middle East. In his view, humanist romanticism was pervasive in their works.[38] When transposed into the Arab world, this romanticism is identified with Arab nationalist thought and its sense of attachment to Islamic heritage. Consequently, he adds, romanticism was Arabised at the level of national, political, and cultural consciousness. Finally, in the third stage of this romantic revolution, which is less clearly defined, he claims that romanticism entered poetry and prose.[39]

At this stage of his analysis, the author considers that the conciliation thus achieved by the two major Arab national movements, Nasserism and Baathism, was responsible for the fact that the debate between romanticism attached to heritage and an irreversible integration into modernity was not settled during this time period. In arguments that are very close to those made by Marxist critical thinkers, al-Ansari also considers that the nationalist movements gave rise to a new petite bourgeoisie that reconciled the two extremes of Arab thought represented by fundamentalism and Marxism. This barred the way to a radical revolution that would have pivoted the Arab world into modernity, as had been as the case concerning the Russians, the Chinese, and the Vietnamese, for example.[40]

It is obviously not possible here to account for the richness and in-depth scholarship of this work. Nonetheless, the author goes to the root of the positions of conciliation between reason and the Revelation, including the time before the appearance of Islam. He also shows how classical Arab-Islamic culture endeavoured to successfully bring this conciliation to fruition, especially between philosophy and divine Revelation. Reconciling Aristotle and Plato, but also philosophy with the divine Revelation, was considered by Arab philosophers to be the route to society's happiness and an easing of tensions. These reconciliatory efforts were also made within European and Arab Christianity, which al-Ansari describes at length.

In his work, the author thus provides an exhaustive overview of different currents of thought, which he organises according to their efforts to blend with opposing points of view. But al-Ansari goes even further, for he considers that within Arab romanticism there is an obsession with the figure of an enlightened guide or a charismatic personality who is able to reconcile modernist ideas and fidelity to historical heritage, a role played, in his view, by Gamal Abdel Nasser. This might provide, according to him, a basis for understanding the proliferation of dictatorships in the Arab world, which have contributed to paralysing the radicality of popular movements seeking to bring about a complete revolution. It is this revolution that would allow a decisive and irreversible step forward towards modernity, without any possibility of a regressive return to traditionalism, even at the cost of bloody confrontations.

In short, for al-Ansari, it is the spirit of reconciliation that paralysed the evolution of the dialectics of history described by Hegel and Marx according to different registers; and it is this paralysis that impedes the progress of the human mind. He considers that in order to succeed in a process of conciliation between two essentially opposite positions, it requires considerable efforts of thought to get to the heart of contradictory evidence and its meaning. This would make it possible to achieve a synthesis of two opposite poles within a lively new and active organic fusion. If this cannot be accomplished, we are left with a sterile eclecticism which, according to al-Ansari, is what most of the thinkers of the Arab renaissance produced. This fusion is only possible when we recognise the existence of a major struggle whose contradictory premises must be acknowledged in order to fully and completely pursue an intellectual breakthrough.[41] In contrast to the 'conciliationism' that characterises the thought of many Islamic reformers, the author underscores the clear stance taken by political Islam as embodied by Sayyid Qutb and Ibn Taymiyyah. In their view, the definitive norm is the one provided by the divine Revelation through the Qur'an, which excludes any other referent for the organisation of human society. For al-Ansari, this clearly shows that the attempts at conciliation have until now been inadequate.

Al-Ansari's conclusion is uncompromising:

Today's Arabs are either living in the past and are prisoners of their own heritage, or they are secularists under the influence of the West, or, most frequently, they are conciliators who try to create a practically impossible balance between their heritage and the West. In all three of these cases, they are prisoners of that which is exterior to their deeper subjective being in the present. They are prisoners of this exterior in place and time, because the West is foreign to them due to its geographical distance, and their past is just as foreign to them due its distance in time.[42]

This is why the Arab personality is a 'shattered' one, a kind of schizophrenic personality in which those who cling to religious heritage do so as a form of imitation or out of fear of being subjected to disdain or accusations of impiety. This is also a way of clinging to an Islamic identity in response to the West as a last refuge in the face of the collapse of a modernising national identity. At the same time, it is possible to observe people who live and behave in a secular manner calling for a return to the application of shari'a law, even at the risk of becoming victims of it.[43]

The author suggests that 'these two opposing positions have lost their authenticity and have invaded the contemporary life of Arabs in two fragmented and corrupted ways. This means that the issue has come down to conciliation between a fragmented modernity and a heritage whose authenticity has been irreparably harmed.'[44] In order to escape from this alienation, today's Arabs must break from the grip of these two debilitating positions and escape the trap of 'conciliationism' through a return to 'the innocence of a free being and his natural ways, far from the chains of both heritage and tradition.' 'It is necessary', the author adds, for today's Arab

to rely on his personal torment, his being, his woes, his desires, and his unique position in time and space to make of this the only base value for determining what he can accept from both tradition and modernity, rather than having his personality subjected to the duality of values from two sources that are alien to him in both space and time... Because heritage, in reality, is present in each one of us, either positively or negatively, and modern civilisation is the most obvious truth of our time. We can neither deny one or the other, nor can we abandon them, because what would then remain of Arab identity? It is better, therefore, to discover the existential void within each one of us [Arabs] and to fill this void through authentic creativity rather than remain continually torn between two contradictions. We have nothing to lose or to fear in so doing, given the succession of "collapses" that the conciliatory spirit has been unable to prevent for the past 150 years.[45]

The remaining question is whether this stirring call for individual liberty alone measures up to the challenge that al-Ansari analysed so well and the uncompromising demonstration he provides throughout the book of the incompatibility of traditionalist and modernist positions. While it is possible to completely agree with his invitation to liberty and free will, can the solution to the split of the Arab personality between these two currents, given the failures so many Arab thinkers have experienced in their attempts to reconcile them, be found in a kind of do-it-yourself free individual? Given the intimidation of free thought in most Arab societies by the currents of political Islam, there must be other actions to undertake in order to break free of this grip. What might be done will be considered in the conclusion to this analysis of the major currents of political and philosophical Arab thought, within the historical framework I have provided.

Muhammad Dahir: on the need to return to the modernist, secular experiment of Muhammad 'Ali and Nasser

The other important work on the disagreement between religious and secular currents of contemporary Arab thought comes from the pen of Muhammad Dahir.[46] It was published in 1994, two years before the publication of al-Ansari's work on the same theme. It is significant to point out that this book is dedicated to 'all those who engage in free thought in the Arab world and in the Muslim world', which gives us insight into the author as a free thinker. In the preface to the second edition, the author states that the goal of his book is to 'work towards progress for the Arab man, the development of his critical and liberating consciousness as well as the identification of real means for his progress, which an elite group of thinkers from the Mashriq to the Maghreb have fought for, and to whom I dedicate this work.'[47]

Unlike al-Ansari, Muhammad Dahir's interpretation is not focused on denouncing conciliatory thought for having prevented Arabs from definitively and concretely achieving modernity and all of its advantages. It reads more like a defence of secularism and a denunciation, on the level of thought, of fundamentalism; but also like a reminder of the importance of the secular political experiments inspired by Arab nationalism, especially those of the first pan-Arab revolution initiated by Sharif Hussein during the First World War, and the Nasserist experiment. Similarly, the experiment of Muhammad 'Ali in Egypt is discussed at length along with the impressive work of al-Tahtawi and that of Mustafa Kemal in Turkey. For Dahir, the reign of Muhammad 'Ali was the first Arab political regime to put in place all of the elements of secular modernity.

Muhammad Dahir's work is more subtle than the work of al-Ansari, for he brings out the reformist radicality of many thinkers with their claims about Islamic thought, whereas al-Ansari sees this as weak because it is conciliatory or eclectic. He wastes no time qualifying religious fundamentalism as counter-revolutionary by stating this in the title of Chapter 8. Conversely, he highlights the experiment of Muhammad 'Ali early on in Chapter 2, in addition to that of Ahmed 'Orabi in Chapter 3. Born in rural Egypt, 'Orabi rose to the rank of officer in the Egyptian army, and in 1881 courageously launched a major revolt against the British occupier. This revolt, as Dahir clearly shows, sparked both nationalist and modernist popular demands that had been brewing in nineteenth-century Egypt, ever since the reign of Muhammad 'Ali. He recalls that after a brief period of reaction by religious fundamentalists to the death of Muhammad 'Ali during the reign of his successor, Khedive 'Abbas, the wave of modernist enthusiasm returned, especially under Khedive Ismail, during which time the Suez Canal was built.

'Orabi's revolution, as the author very correctly concludes, was both a nationalist reaction against the domination of Egypt by the Europeans, led by the British, and a constitutional revolution to bring an end to the arbitrary rule of the local sovereign.[48] It led to the formation of the National Party, which demanded that a parliament be established and that basic public freedoms be granted to Egyptians, all of which was achieved. Dahir also clearly explains how the Egyptian nationalists at that time, who were strongly influenced by the ideas of the French Revolution, allegedly wanted the establishment of a republic. Nonetheless, in order to avoid too much upheaval of the traditional mentalities of those accustomed to rule by divine right, the demand they formulated was for a constitutional monarchy whose powers were limited by the existence of a General Assembly and the principle of separation of powers. He also very effectively recalls that most of the great reformist and nationalist thinkers from this period were Freemasons, for all of them wished for a separation of state and religion. Even al-Afghani appears to have promoted a closer alliance of the three monotheistic religions, all of which originated from the same source; since, as Dahir explains, for al-Afghani, 'the disagreements among them can be attributed to the leaders of these religions who profit from them, which is what made these disagreements worse.'[49]

The author also discusses at length the experiment of Gamal Abdel Nasser, to whom he devotes extensive passages (Chapter 9) in which he explains the causes of Nasser's rift with the Muslim Brotherhood, which had nonetheless initially welcomed the military coup d'état. For Daher, the Muslim Brotherhood's initial support of the coup was based on the social reform programmes proposed by the military officers, especially the programme supported by Nasser. This makes sense because in the ideology of the Muslim Brotherhood, the issue of social justice occupies a very important place. However, as time went on, the Brotherhood's desire to become the guide of the military council and to impose their theologico-political views led to the split and the subsequent attempt by the Muslim Brotherhood to assassinate Nasser in 1965. Dahir summarises the situation quite well when he writes, 'Abdel Nasser wanted to build a modern state based on science, technology, democracy, and social justice. The Muslim Brotherhood, in contrast, wanted to achieve an Islamic society in which the prescriptions of the Qur'an and shari'a law would be applied, even by violence and force.'[50] He recalls that Nasser had allowed Sayyid Qutb's book against his regime to be printed and reprinted several times, and that the response to this book had come from an Azhari shaykh, Abdel-Latif al-Sabki, who denounced the book's inflammatory character and its demagogical exploitation of religion aimed at the underclasses. In short, according to Dahir, the Muslim Brotherhood wanted to lead a counter-revolution and cause a split within Egyptian society.[51]

Dahir describes how Al-Azhar University was modernised under Nasser, the second modernisation after the one initiated by Muhammad 'Ali. He also explains how Nasser directed the work of the commission in charge of drafting the Egyptian National Charter in order to give it a more modernist orientation in which religion was only called upon to be used as a factor of progress, social justice, and economic development; but not as a supreme norm for the management of society.[52] Dahir concludes that 'if the Nasserist experiment had been able to continue, it would surely have settled the debate once and for all in favour of the secular current, while at the same time preserving the rationalist and enlightened qualities of religion, and its position as a source of ethical values and ideals for life, as well as its support for the issues of progress, liberation, development, and modernisation.'[53]

It is now clear that Dahir's position differs from that of al-Ansari since he considers that the heritage of Enlightened Islam was adequately constructed and, thus, was not a conciliatory school of thought, as denounced by al-Ansari. Indeed, Dahir gives greater importance to the political context and developments within it to explain the fall of liberal and reformed Islam since the reign of Muhammad 'Ali. His interpretation of the texts by religious reformist thinkers clearly shows their modernist and secularising content, which al-Ansari tended to minimise in support of his main thesis on the shortcomings of conciliatory thought.

By examining in the final pages of his book (Chapter 10) the causes of the collapse of secular Arab discourse in favour of reactionary and anti-modernist discourse, Dahir denounces the canonical narrative of those who support a major role for Islam in the management of society. According to this narrative, the adoption of secular reforms supposedly led to the disintegration of the coherence of Muslim societies, which were allegedly founded on the pillar of religion, but also to the phenomenon of dictatorships and the inability to make progress or deal with Israel. At the time this book was written (1994), he already considered that the virulence of the Islamists' positions could lead to a situation that was ripe for civil war in the Arab world in the absence of a free and stable democratic regime that could provide an outlet for debate. He called for 'calm' dialogue between both currents in order to find solutions to the persistent underdevelopment. He was also convinced that only the application of the norms of modernity, described at length in the first chapter of his book, could solve the problems of the Arab world. He did not fail to emphasise the scandal of the persistence of widespread illiteracy in some Arab societies.[54]

In his view, the secular current is on the same side as reformist Islam, whereas the fundamentalist current is extremist, irrational, and disconnected from the present moment and from the evolution of history. For this reason, it impedes the proper understanding of Islam and its principles. For Dahir, the problem of identity posed by the rivalry between these two currents, secular and modernist, on the one hand, and traditionalist and fundamentalist on the other, can only find a solution within an open Arab nationalism, one that accepts that Arab society is a pluralistic one that includes Christians and Jews as well as Amazighs and Kurds.

Clearly, these are two major works that seek to provide keys to understanding the extreme tensions in Arab societies. The narratives developed here provide a stark contrast to all of the academic literature, both Arab and non-Arab, on the importance of political Islam as the only possible vector of modernisation. What gives credibility to these analyses is the high calibre of their authors, both of whom are involved in the political and diplomatic life of their respective countries. Both are also accomplished intellectuals who have an in-depth understanding of the problems of their societies and who have mastered the historical background necessary to assimilate the virtues of modernity, something which no society can escape.

Wasatiyya: An attempt to counter radical and fanatical Islamic thought

It is also important to highlight the attempts made by some well-known Arab figures to establish a school of Islamic thought known as *wasatiyya*, 'the middle way'. This approach was mainly spearheaded by two well-respected individuals who are both politicians and intellectuals. The first of these is Prince Hassan bin Talal of Jordan. Born in 1947, he is the grandson of Sharif Hussein, the head of the Hashemite family who were the guardians of the holy sites of Mecca and Medina before being chased out of the Hejaz by the military in the 1920s at the behest of the Saud family, founders of the Kingdom of Saudi Arabia. Prince Hassan, a highly cultured and well-read individual, founded the Arab Thought Forum (Muntada al-Fikr al-'Arabi) in 1981, headquartered in Amman, Jordan.[55] This institution promotes religious dialogue between the Arab world and other regions of the globe, in addition to dialogue among Arabs, on the major problems tearing apart this region.

Wasatiyya was also spearheaded by Sadiq al-Mahdi – the Mahdi being the one inspired by God and whose mission it is to lead Muslims out of a period of decline. Born in 1935, al-Mahdi was the leader of the prestigious Al-Mahdiyya, a Sudanese religious movement created in 1881 to lead the fight against the British coloniser. He is a descendant of the movement's founder, and in the early 1980s he started the National Umma party. He served as the prime minister of Sudan several times during its brief democratic interludes, and was also imprisoned following military coups, including the one in 1989 that ushered in the dictatorial Islamist regime of Omar al-Bachir, who remains in power at the time of writing (March 2019).

This school of thought invokes a verse in the Qur'an (2:143) in which God announces to the Prophet that he has made the Arabs a nation of the 'middle way' (*'Ya'alnakum ummatan wasatan'*) – presumably, the middle way between different peoples and religions, especially Judaism and Christianity. This school also invokes the verse that states, 'No coercion in religion' (2:256) and another that leaves humans free to believe in the message of the Qur'an or to refute it. It aligns itself with the Islamic tradition that condemns overreach in religious matters (*la ghuluw fi'l-din*) and emphasises several verses that call on believers to be 'modest' in their behaviour, to abstain from ostentation in their religious practice, in addition to avoiding ostentatious displays of wealth and consumption of food and pleasure. This is one aspect of Islam that is not well known, or has perhaps been forgotten due to the growing religious ostentation that began at the end of the 1970s (see *supra*, Chapter 11).

Wasatiyya was launched through several successive colloquia, the first of which was held in Bahrain in 2005 and inaugurated by Prince Hassan. Its theme was '*Wasatiyya* in theory and in practice.'[56] The second took place in 2006 in Amman and was organised by the Arab Thought Forum.[57] A third colloquium in 2006 in the Lebanese city of Tripoli focused on 'the role of information technologies in reinforcing the culture of the middle way.' A fourth international colloquium on *wasatiyya* took place in 2010 in Beirut and was opened by Sadiq al-Mahdi. These colloquia were attended by intellectuals of many different ideological orientations, including Marxists such as Tayyeb Tizini (see *supra*, Chapter 10), and the talks given were rich and varied. All of them reiterated the need to read the Qur'anic text in an open way and to account for the diversity it contains. The impoverished reading that reduces it to a few verses taken out of context, which is the way in which it is read by radical Islamic movements, is completely rejected. The two intellectuals who inspired this movement, Prince Hasan and Imam al-Sadiq, have emphasised its international scope. They believe that it can nurture dialogue among cultures and foster the construction of a humanism that is the subject of a broad consensus. It is thus unfortunate that these laudable efforts have been largely ignored by the media and by European and American academic research that is more often than not consumed by the manifestations of so-called 'radical' Islam.

Thought that claims to be rooted in Arab Christianity

It would not be possible to conclude this broad outline of the major currents of Arab thought without discussing two Lebanese thinkers who claim Christian values. It is important to do so, because it shows the extent to which they too face the general issues that Arab thought has had to face. It also disproves the idea that there is a specificity of thought among members of religious minorities in Arab societies. Their thought has obviously been highly influenced by the specific context of Lebanon, which is one of very profound secular interpenetration between religious communities, both Muslim and Christian. Lebanon is, of course, not the only Arab country with a high level of religious diversity. This is also the case in Iraq and Syria, but also in Egypt, whose Coptic community descends directly from Pharaonic civilisation.

It is important to note that the Christian communities of the Arab Levant are the descendants of the original populations that existed before the arrival of Islam and their gradual Arabisation. Lebanon presents a unique case to the extent that it is the country that suffered the most from the instrumentalisation of religious communities, both by European colonial powers starting in 1840, and by the Ottoman Empire as a response to Europe. This instrumentalisation led to the institutionalisation of the country's major communities within the political order through a system that distributed civil and military functions between them. This was established through the National Pact of 1943, then renewed by the Intercommunity Agreement reached in Taif, Saudi Arabia in 1989, following several years of violence in Lebanon between 1975 and 1990.

This is why this school of thought has several different facets. Among the Lebanese thinkers who align themselves with Christianity, their writings are marked by fear of Islam. There is also a tendency to magnify the experience of communitarian differences and to present these in an essentialising anthropological framework, in spite of the shared language, history, and culture that unite the Lebanese regardless of their religious faith. This literature tends to draw on European and American theories on the governance of pluralistic societies, such as Canada and Belgium, that have promoted the model of harmonious society and consensus democracy among heterogeneous linguistic or ethnic elements, sometimes even calling for a type of federal system among communities. Two highly prolific thinkers are of note here.

The first of these is Michel Chiha (1891–1954), a prosperous businessman of Iraqi origin who was close to the political and financial power centres of Lebanon. He was probably one of the most famous Francophone writers in Lebanon and regularly published articles in the French-language Lebanese press that played a role in forging the political sensibilities of the Francophone elite. Three main themes pervaded his work.

The first was the need for political moderation in a country that is above all a 'mosaic' of communities and which, consequently, must be governed in a way that includes all of these in the management of power. The idea that Lebanon is a federation of communities is very pervasive in his work. This idea of community democracy became widespread within the Francophone elite of Lebanon. The second theme is the need for free trade and for the state to play a modest role in the economy, but also for the Lebanese economy to develop exclusively as a centre for commerce and services and as an intermediary between developed European, and its neighbouring underdeveloped Arab, economies. Chiha showed himself to be an early neoliberal, before the term was coined. He justified this position that went against the grain of prevailing views in political economics at the time – which promoted the state's intervention to ensure development – by appealing to Lebanon's prestigious Phoenician past. He presented the Phoenicians as a people essentially composed of merchants and voyagers.[58]

Finally, Chiha's third line of thought was perhaps his most prophetic; it concerned the future disaster of Palestine, which at that time was already underway, and the tragic consequences for Lebanon that would result from the emergence of a state that practiced religious exclusionism, something that would severely strain the Lebanese system of community harmony. Michel Chiha's thought had wide repercussions in Lebanon. Even though he wrote exclusively in French, his work permeated a large part of the intellectual elite.[59]

Another major Lebanese figure who wrote in both French and Arabic was Antoine Messarra. Born in 1938, he had an influential academic career, and his work was devoted to lauding the merits of the system of consensus democracy theorised in Europe, the United States, and Canada by political scientists such as Charles Taylor and Arend Lijphart. He was a staunch activist for the re-establishment of civil peace after the tragic events that tore Lebanon apart between 1975 and 1990.

In contrast, or as a counterpoint to this conservative approach to the situation in Lebanon that sought to maintain and even to exaggerate communitarian specificities, a whole current of courageous and innovative thought existed that fought to deconstruct the negative images of Islam. More often than not, these images were inherited from ancient polemics of European Christianity against Islam; and subsequently from a certain type of French colonial literature that was eager to maintain the myth of France as a protector of Christians in the Orient confronted by 'Islamism' or unitary Arab nationalism. With respect to this issue, I have chosen here to focus on the influential works of four churchmen, especially two priests from the Maronite community whose works essentially aim to better understand Islam and the role of Lebanon in the Arab East as a land of dialogue and religious pluralism.

The first is Youakim Moubarac (1924–1995). Originally from North Lebanon, he had a very successful academic career in France and Belgium as a specialist of Islam. His substantial body of written work reflects three major aspects of his personality as well as his tireless activities: a knowledgeable historian of the churches of the East, especially the Maronite Church, and the central figure in their reconciliation, all of which emerged from a common heritage that he defines as 'Antiochan,' since the institutionalisation of most of these took place in the city of Antioch in Syria;[60] the best guide to understanding the Qur'an in light of the disagreements between Jews and Christians, but also between the churches of the East, and therefore the most enlightened promoter of Islamo-Christian dialogue; an ardent defender of the Palestinian and Lebanese causes, and the deep bonds that unite them in the face of Israeli aggression and Zionist ideology, as well as the blindness of Europe and the biased position of the United States.

He was the author of three doctoral theses on Islamo-Christian relations since the Middle Ages, which constitute a major contribution to the explanation of theological, sociological, and psychological misunderstandings between these two great monotheisms.[61] He was an ardent defender of the rights of Palestinians, and he developed extensive arguments in favour of Lebanon's inclusion in Arab cultural identity, what he called 'urba, in order to differentiate it from classical Arab nationalism or 'uruba.[62]

Another Maronite priest, and a contemporary of Moubarac, was Michel Hayek (1928–2005). Like Moubarac, he was also a very learned man whose work focused on integrating Islam within the broader framework of monotheism and recognising it as a new and final version of monotheism that cannot be dismissed or considered foreign to Christianity. He too was the author of a large body of work.

The third major thinker inspired by Christianity is Grégoire Haddad. Born in 1924, he was a priest and bishop of the Greek Catholic community in the city of Beirut from 1968 to 1975. He was at that time a strong supporter of secularism as the only solution to the communitarianism that was consuming Lebanon and other Arab societies, a defender of the oppressed inspired by liberation theology, and a supporter of the profession of the Islamic faith which, according to him, was not offensive to Christianity. This got him into trouble with the hierarchy of his community. They suspended him from his pastoral duties and tried unsuccessfully to get the Vatican to condemn his courageous theological positions. Haddad also founded the periodical *Afaq* (Horizons) in 1975, which became known for its secular and modernist orientation. In Lebanon, this publication played a major role in spreading knowledge and understanding of the benefits of secularism.

A fourth thinker is Georges Khodr (born in 1924), who was the bishop of the Greek Orthodox community. He wrote numerous editorials for the Arabic-language Lebanese newspaper *Al-Nahar*, in addition to his articles and research on the relations between Christianity and Islam, all of which greatly contributed to maintaining a productive dialogue on Islamo-Christian relationships in Lebanon.

An impressive synopsis of the works of these intellectuals who identify as followers of the Christian faith was published in 2011 by Antoine Fleyfel, a young Lebanese scholar in Paris who edited a collection for a Parisian publisher entitled 'Pensée religieuse et philosophique arabe' (Arab Religious and Philosophical Thought).[63] Another Lebanese scholar of theology and philosophy, Mouchir Aoun, wrote extensively on Arab Christian thought.[64] In addition to his book on Paul Khoury cited in Chapter 3, he is the author of several works on Islamo-Christian dialogue, on the comparative anthropology of the Christian and Muslim religions, and even a reflection on Heidegger and Arab thought.[65]

This brings to a close the broad outline of those major currents of Arab thought that have reflected on the decline that has affected Arab societies, its causes, and the ways to remedy it. These currents are simultaneously modes of self-reflection as well as reflection on the Other, that is, Europe as both coloniser and a developmentally advanced society. In order for this overview to be complete, the final chapter of this book will be devoted to a brief foray into the domain of Arab thought in the human and social sciences, particularly history, sociology, philosophy, and economics.

CHAPTER 14

An overview of contemporary Arab thought in the human and social sciences

The previous chapters have provided an overview of the wide variety of ways that Arab thought has responded to the three major questions it has faced since the nineteenth century; that is, the Arab world's persistent decline, its underdevelopment, and its inability to create a modern nation that includes all of the building blocks required for a stable and respected sovereign entity, an entity that is capable of achieving equal footing with other great nations, for this is what would prevent the fragmented states falling prey to various forms of dependency on the major powers that covet the region's wealth and its position as a major geographical and geopolitical crossroads. It has been demonstrated that although Arab thought is very rich in many areas of knowledge, including academic ones, it is clear that the issue of religion and its relationship to national identity has continued to occupy centre stage, thus becoming a source of severe conflicts. This has paved the way for a mode of framing the Arab world, promoted by academia and the media in Europe and the United States, to become dominant. With their growing contingent of Arab intellectuals, European and North American media and academia posited the view of an Arab mind that was for the most part invariant and seemingly dominated by Islam.

Given the unprecedented increase in the number of inward-looking theologico-political controversies in the Arab world since the decline of national thought and its openness to modernity, it should come as no surprise to see a weakening of the human and social sciences in the region. Many areas of Arab thought have been examined in previous chapters, but the production of Arab intellectuals within these areas has not been a specific focus, especially in philosophy, history, anthropology, sociology, and economics. It is true that their intellectual forebears were steeped in high culture and engaged in all areas of knowledge of interest to the human spirit in the contemporary world, especially the philosophy of history, political systems, and the effects of contact between cultures and civilisations. Subsequent generations have been subjected to the effects of the compartmentalisation of knowledge and the rigid system of specialisation within the various disciplines of the human and social sciences.

The goal here is obviously not to provide an overview of Arab intellectual production within all of these disciplines. Rather, I will limit this discussion to the major players who have emerged within these domains. I do so in the hope that future scholars will produce more detailed accounts within the context of academic research, especially since, to my knowledge, there have been no specialised studies of the status of the human and social sciences in the Arab world.[1] The relative paucity of Arab production within the human sciences can be largely attributed to the limited research budgets of Arab universities, difficulties involved in undertaking fieldwork, as well as to the fact that application of Western sociological methods in local Arab contexts is not always effective. In contrast, foreign universities and the major centres of academic research in Europe and the United States, along with their establishment in the capital cities of certain Arab countries (specifically Beirut and Cairo), have much greater financial means than local universities. But in the latter, research is often designed to respond to the needs of the political and economic agendas of Europe and the United States; and it is not intended to contribute solutions to the internal problems of Arab societies or to produce a better understanding of them. Nonetheless, as I hope to show in this chapter, some thinkers have made very substantial contributions within various domains of the human and social sciences.

Philosophical and anthropological thought

After a hiatus of several centuries, we have seen how the philosophical spirit re-emerged in Arab thought with the arrival of the *Nahda*. Inspired by the major European philosophical currents, especially the different schools of Enlightenment philosophy, many thinkers contributed to the introduction of these schools to the Arab world and to their appropriation in order to develop a new worldview, different from that which had emerged during the long-lost flourishing of Arab-Islamic civilisation. Moreover, as discussed previously, a major movement of translation was initiated by al-Tahtawi in the first half of the nineteenth century and is still going strong today (see *supra*, Chapter 7). In order to avoid including too much in this book, the philosophical positions of the great thinkers from the renaissance period have not been described at length. The argument can be made that many Arab thinkers of the twentieth century integrated a philosophical dimension into their work, or that they analysed the situations in their respective societies from specific philosophical positions. This was especially true of the Marxist thinkers whose works I have described in broad strokes. For this reason, and given the limitations of this book, regarding the second part of the twentieth century, I will limit my discussion to the work of those philosophers who are best known and whose work in my view had an important impact in the Arab world and which contributed to expanding modern Arab philosophical heritage.

Abdel Rahman Badawi, a prolific 'go-between'

The first of these philosophers is Abdel Rahman Badawi (1917–2002), due to the sheer volume of his work and the significance of his contribution to the development of philosophical knowledge. He was an Egyptian who undeniably holds the record for authoring the greatest number of works in the area of pure philosophy.

Heavily influenced by existentialism, he devoted his doctoral thesis to this topic (1944) and took an interest in a broad array of subjects. These varied from ancient Greek philosophy, especially Platonism, to the Arab philosophy that developed from it, as well as Sufism and different Islamic sects, and atheism in Islam. He also studied German philosophy and translated several philosophical works from German into Arabic. He was a very prolific author who produced roughly 120 works, including translations of German philosophers.

His work is more of a bridge between contemporary European philosophy and Arab and Muslim heritage, especially its philosophical components, rather than a foundation for an Arab philosophical system that creates new rules for understanding the world that are appropriate for the complex contexts that Arab thought has been grappling with since the nineteenth century. Nonetheless, Badawi's works enriched Arab culture in an impressive way.

The innovative thought of Nassif Nassar

The work of Nassif Nassar is something else entirely. Born in Lebanon in 1938, he is arguably one of the greatest thinkers of political philosophy in the Arab world, and his book on the search for Arab philosophical independence has been mentioned previously. He dedicated his life to university teaching and to writing about all of the major issues that trouble contemporary Arab political and philosophical thought. His objective was to develop a philosophical conception that would allow the situation of Arab societies to be grasped in an independent-minded way and to be analysed within the framework of the shifting context of the modern world.

Nassar began his intellectual career with a doctoral thesis on the thought of Ibn Khaldun, which was published in France in 1967. It became a major reference for anyone interested in the genius of this major figure of Arab thought.[2] Following this, Nassar's work was heavily driven by various themes related to the issues of change in the Arab world and their relationship to the culture of the modern world. In so doing, he expanded on the work Constantine Zurayk had devoted to Arab nationalist thought, which was discussed in Chapter 4. Moreover, it is possible to place Nassar's work, like the work of Laroui, in the category of nationalist thought. However, critical thought dominates in his work as well as thought related to social, cultural, and philosophical renewal.

In 1970 he published a reformist manifesto in support of a new society in Lebanon. It was a stirring appeal for the establishment of secularism in place of the communitarian system that was paralysing the country's civic forces.[3] Nassar subsequently published an excellent scholarly work focused on a concept with multiple meanings in Arabic, that of 'umma', and began by identifying all of the verses in the Qur'an that use this term to mean community of believers. He then examined its use by the great tenth-century philosopher al-Farabi, followed by its use by the famous historian, geographer, and astronomer born in Baghdad, al-Mas'udi (896–957), as well as by other thinkers of the classical Islamic period, in particular Ibn Khaldun.[4] In the preface to his work, the author explains that the goal of his research is to highlight the fact that many philosophers, historians, and legal scholars from the classical period clearly distinguished between the religious concept of the *umma* and the social concept as it applied to the nation. For him, the great classical thinkers had very aptly conceived of the unity of the nation and, consequently, it was appropriate for him to denounce the false notion that prior to European progress nobody had thought of it. This work was completed by another one dedicated to the modern concept of the nation.[5] One of the major themes of Nassar's thought was thus the issue of the Arab nation, which he approached from a philosophical and a conceptual perspective.

There are three other major complementary themes that make up Nassar's work: historical presence, liberty, and secularism. In 2003, he published an important book on the first theme, to which he gave the suggestive title, 'The Gate of Freedom.' It called for a new Arab renaissance that was able to absorb and finally move beyond the binary divide between heritage and modernity by adopting a positive stance toward globalisation due to a greater openness to freedom.[6] Nassar called here for a reform of Western-style liberalism and for this new liberalism to be grounded in more solid philosophical principles. For him, there were four main principles of this reform: the natural sociability of the individual and of dialectics; the connection between liberty and rationality; between liberty and justice; and, finally, between liberty and authority (in the sense of enforcement of power).[7] In this work, Nassar correctly analyses the inadequacy of the notion of the social contract for the establishment of liberty as well as the sterility of the debates that pit the individual against community. Along the same lines, he criticises Western neoliberal philosophy. For him, freedom is not an end in and of itself, but rather, it is simply the precondition of individual and societal action.

Nassar's thought in the area of political philosophy fully unfolds in a book published in 2008 and beautifully entitled 'The Self and Presence.'[8] In the preface to this work, he warns the reader that he is in fact deepening rather than bringing closure to his reflection on 'existence' (*al-wujud*, the fact of existing or of being present), 'action' (*al-fi'l*), and on the meaning of a human being's self-construction through action, which is what allows an individual to exist. The book is a lengthy and lucid essay on the why and how of each human being as a moment of encounter between past and present, and a projection into the future. It begins with three chapters that decipher the nature of the present in each individual's consciousness, their consciousness of existence, and seeks that which might make this present more effective. This is followed by eight chapters on the notion of presence (*al-hudur*) in relation to reason and values. Here he provides an overview of the different values an individual may have to face (the good, dignity, work, health, justice, truth, affection). He ends this fine philosophical treatise with three chapters that focus on 'the present and that which preceded it', and three chapters on 'the present and what will come after it.'

The depth of his reflection in these two works also draws on some of Nassar's other works, such as his treatise on 'the logic of power' (1995), a lengthy reflection on how power works and its relationship to reason, justice, and religion.[9] In 1986, Nassar published a book on the same theme in which he proposed nine 'theses for the engaged mind,' some of which were theoretical while others involved issues that were faced by Arabs.[10] In it, he explained the importance of philosophy for rebuilding Arab rationality as well as the need to integrate the rich European heritage of political philosophy. However, he emphasised the importance of critiquing it, as well as critiquing Arab political reality without slipping into ideology or Sufi mysticism. He also dealt with the question of the relationship between the power of religion and that of the state.

In 2000, Nassar published a major work on the link between education and politics and suggested a way to make individuals into citizens.[11] In 2011, he published a volume of collected writings that dealt with intersecting themes, and in so doing articulated general problematics of Arab thought in the face of modernity.[12] The work opens with an impressive study of Ibn Khaldun's writings on historical change and ends with a passionate appeal for secularism, a basic component of justice. Two other important pieces are also included here: a lecture on the dialectics of universalism and specificity; and a description of the philosophical roots of the Universal Declaration of Human Rights.

What we have here is a vibrant and cogent body of work enriched by the author's considerable erudition, which spans both Arab and European culture. Nassif Nassar's thought is never purely speculative and abstract, for it is driven by questions that Arab thought has been grappling with since the *Nahda*, that is, how to develop an ability to adapt to the triumph of European modernity in a way that is positive and innovative. Like Constantine Zurayk, Aziz al-Azmeh, and Abdallah Laroui, Nassar seeks philosophical independence and sees it as the only gateway to Arab cultural renewal. In February 2014, the importance of his work was recognised through a conference held in the Faculty of Arts and Humanities at the Hassan II University in Casablanca.[13]

A broad diversity of contemporary thinkers

Another philosopher whose works have been very well received is Zaki Naguib Mahmoud (1905–1993), an Egyptian intellectual and author of a large number of widely read books. Like Badawi, Mahmoud was interested in contemporary European philosophy, especially positivist philosophy and the philosophy of science. He sought to make Arab readers more familiar with this philosophy, especially in a two-volume work on formal logic as well as a biography of Bertrand Russell. Subsequently, he became interested in Arab religious heritage and called for rules of reason to be applied to it.

Fouad Zakariya is another important philosopher of the last fifty years who also comes from Egypt. Two of his works that challenge Islamic movements have already been mentioned. His interest in philosophy was expressed through numerous works that covered a wide array of different topics such as the theory of knowledge, scientific reasoning, the thought of Nietzsche as well as that of Herbert Marcuse, humans and civilisation in the industrial age, and the various areas of philosophy. Zakariya also translated several works by Spinoza into Arabic. He wrote three books on music; one was a treatise on the nature of music, another was entitled 'With Music: Memories and Studies', and the third was a biography of Richard Wagner. In the realm of politics, he wrote an essay on the crisis of Arab thought ('How Long Will the Age of Anger Last?'), and another entitled 'A Speech Addressed to the Arab Mind', a book on Nasser and the Egyptian left, as well as a collection of articles and essays entitled, 'The Era of Ideology.' Fouad Zakariya can be counted among the great modern Arab thinkers, but his work is too often overlooked in the rare studies undertaken on Arab philosophical thought.

Paul Khoury, the Lebanese intellectual born in 1921, has also been previously discussed. It is fitting here to mention his philosophical work as well as his work in the comparative anthropology of Islam and Christianity. He has been called the philosopher of incompleteness, or of incompletion, within the framework of his rich thought denouncing vanity of attempts by human beings to achieve the 'absolute', and their disappointment when they become aware of their limits. As a result this philosopher has rejected all of the major religious and philosophical systems that claim to grasp that which cannot be grasped, whether divine transcendence or the search for a philosophical system to explain the order of the world.[14] Based on this awareness of human incompleteness that no religion or system of thought is capable of remedying, it becomes possible to develop a truly universal humanism.[15] Khoury approaches the issues of Islamo-Christian dialogue through this framework, much like the issue of the tension between tradition and modernity (see *supra*, Chapter 3). Although he was trained as a Christian theologian, Khoury appears to be agnostic, something which helps him to identify the areas where the two religions overlap. At the same time, he argues that the Islamic aspect of Arab culture must move beyond traditionalism and its attachment to a rigid concept of heritage to find those values it shares with Christianity in a joint effort to prioritise the humanist values of both religions.[16]

On the same list of Lebanese intellectuals, it is important to note the great legal scholar Soubhi al-Mahmassani (1909–1986). Throughout his vast body of work, he sought to bring traditional Islamic law (shari'a) more in line with the modern principles of public law and human rights. He is especially known for a book he wrote on the philosophy of Islamic law,[17] which has been translated into several languages, in addition to a book entitled 'The Constitution and Democracy',[18] as well as a very fine comparative study of the pillars of human rights.[19] Subhi Mahmassini's son, Maher Mahmassini, is also a legal scholar. In 2014 he published a major work that recalled the reality of the message of Islam and situated it within the historical context of monotheism and its prophetic tradition. He illustrates the secular nature of power in Islam and denounces the 'myth of a divine theory of the state' by highlighting the fact that the notion of liberty and equality as fundamental rights is contained in the Qur'anic Revelation.[20]

It is also fitting to mention the work of Hassan Saab (1929–1990). A native of Beirut, he was both an academic and a diplomat who published a large number of works in a variety of areas. Among these is an excellent book on Islam and liberty[21] as well as another on the challenges facing Arab societies as a result of the technological scientific revolution.[22] In Lebanon he founded the Society of Development Studies, which held several conferences on all aspects of the modernisation of the Lebanese economy, including rural areas, in the framework of justice and social cohesion. An endearing individual, Saab has been largely forgotten today, even in Lebanon.

Moving onward to the countries of the Maghreb, it is clear that the harvest was equally bountiful there. Nobody could fail to mention the thought of Malek Bennabi (1905–1973), an Algerian intellectual born in Constantine. Firmly devoted to his Islamic faith, he sought throughout his entire body of work to call Muslims to an 'awakening'. As someone whose life was spent between Algeria, France, and Egypt, his first books were published in French, particularly *Vocation de l'islam* (The Vocation of Islam) (1954) as well as *Les conditions de la renaissance* (The Conditions for the Renaissance) (1949).[23] He put forth the notion of 'coloniability', something that affected declining societies. Bennabi actually contributed more to the development of a Muslim consciousness than an Arab one. Moreover, he wrote a book entitled *Le problème des idées dans le monde musulman* (The Problem of Ideas in the Muslim World) (1970).[24] Another work on the idea of an Islamic commonwealth (*L'idée du commonwealth islamique*, 1959) appeared ten years before Saudi Arabia made this materialise in 1969.[25] His devotion to his calling as an 'Islamic' philosopher is illustrated in his final works published in 1972 on Muslims in the world of economics (*Le musulman dans le monde de l'économie*)[26] and on the role of Muslims in the late twentieth century (*Le rôle des musulmans dans le dernier tiers du XXème siècle*).[27]

Other major philosophers from the Maghreb made important contributions to Arab philosophy in their search for more openness to the universal, unlike the philosophy of Bennabi, who sought to be Islamo-centric, although this was done in an effort to be more open-minded rather than closed-minded. The first of these is the brilliant Tunisian academic, Fathi Triki, who was born in Sfax in 1937. Since 1997 he has held the United Nations Educational, Scientific and Cultural Organization (UNESCO) Chair of Philosophy for the Arab World. As indicated by the title of his inaugural lecture of this chair, he has sought to be the theoretician of the 'philosophy of living together.'[28] Through his numerous works, which include titles in both Arabic and French, Triki shows himself to be the philosopher of modernity and of the diversity of the world. His essay entitled *Stratégie et identité* (Strategy and Identity) is a very insightful deconstruction of essentialist thought concerning questions of identity and the development of alterity.[29] In it, he connects the strategies described with political, economic, and geopolitical developments around the world, in particular the development of globalisation and modern means of communication. He also simultaneously deconstructs the arguments of the Islamists and those of Huntingdon on the clash of civilisations. It is fitting to mention here the books he wrote in Arabic whose titles translate as 'Reason and Liberty,' and 'Writings on Philosophy and Diversity.' In addition, together with his wife Rashida Triki, he wrote a book entitled 'Philosophy and Modernity,' and with Muhammad Ali al-Halwani, 'Philosophical Approaches to the History of Arab Sciences.'

Along the same lines, but in the area of literature and poetry, Abdelkebir Khatibi (1938–2009) became a figurehead for incorporation and openness to the other. Born in Morocco, he was a true bilingual speaker of Arabic and French who became a university teacher and author of a large body of rich and complex literary works. Just like Triki, he dealt with alterity, diversity, and hybridity in his thought, and he readily navigated the intricacies of the Arab-Islamic and European psyches. The titles of some of his main works clearly reflect the expression of his thought: *La mémoire tatouée. Autobiographie d'un décolonisé* (Tattooed Memory. Autobiography of a Decolonised Person),[30]

Amour bilingue (Bilingual Love),[31] *Maghreb pluriel* (Plural Maghreb),[32] *Figures de l'étranger dans la littérature française* (Figures of the Foreigner in French Literature),[33] and *Imaginaire de l'autre* (The Imaginary of the Other) (1987).[34]

Finally, in 2014, Mondher Kilani, a Tunisian sociologist and anthropologist who teaches in Switzerland, produced a very fine synthesis of philosophy and anthropology that constitutes one of the best and most original critiques of the ethnocentrism inherent in European anthropology. It is an exemplary reflection of how Arab thought is open to the world and to modernity, while at the same time remaining critical with respect to those aspects of modernity whose criteria were produced in Europe and the United States. The goal of Kilani's work is to 'highlight the paradox that consists of formulating the universal from a particular point of view.'[35] In doing so, he expresses the aspiration of generations of Arab thinkers to explore a universalism free of the Euro-American ethnocentric point of view.

Arab thought in sociology and history

Hardly any works of major importance exist in sociology and history. This is mainly because most efforts have been channelled into writing articles for publication in European and American journals specialising in the Middle East, which play a crucial role in establishing a scholar's reputation in the field. Nonetheless, many articles are also written for local journals in the human sciences, particularly those published by the Centre for Arab Unity Studies and the Institute for Palestine Studies (see *supra*, Chapter 9). Specific mention should also be made of the *Revue arabe des sciences sociales* (Arab Social Sciences Review) and the *Revue des études économiques arabes* (Review of Arab Economic Studies). For this reason, the discussion here will be confined to those works and authors that are most noteworthy.

Such is the case with the impressive work of Hanna Batatu (1926–2000) in political sociology on the interplay of social classes in Iraq and its relationship to the creation of major revolutionary parties in that country.[36] This is truly a monumental work, comprising 1,283 magnificently documented pages in fluid prose. It offers a grand panorama of the political, economic, and social history of Iraq from the period following the First World War, during which time the country was created, to Saddam Hussein's seizure of power in 1975. Batata authored another important work on rural societies in Syria.[37] Mention should also be made of the fine work by Mansour Khalid, which is similar to that of Batatu. Born in 1931 in Sudan, Khalid's work focuses on the tormented history of his country.[38] A courageous intellectual, he is also the former Minister of Foreign Affairs of Sudan and was counsellor to John Garang, the leader of the rebellion in South Sudan. He sided with Garang when the regime imposed shari'a law in this part of the country where the population is mainly Animist and Christian, and was the major architect of the peace accords signed in 2005. For several years now he has been living in exile in Cairo. He also became known for his efforts in support of sustainable development and was, in fact, the first Vice President of the Brundtland Commission tasked by the UN to study issues of development and environment.

One of the most important sociologists of the Arab world was the Iraqi, 'Ali al-Wardi (1913–1995). He wrote an eight-volume social history of Iraqi society as well as many other works critical of outdated socio-political customs hindering progress and development. One of these directly attacks the influence of religious men, referred to as 'the sultan's moral preachers', that is to say, preachers of power. 'Ali al-Wardi argued in favour of moving beyond 'the great discord' between Sunnis and Shi'is, and called for it to be considered a distant historical fact with no relationship to the present. He also believed that maintaining these two separate identities simply prolonged the ruthless wars waged by the Ottoman Empire and the Safavid monarchy over the control of Mesopotamia. The Ottomans exploited Sunni identity while the Safavids played on that of the Shi'is.[39] He also wrote a book that focused on the importance of Ibn Khaldun's work in sociology.

Still within Iraq, in the area of religious criticism, it is important to mention Maruf al-Rusafi (1877–1945), who was a great poet and author of a devastating critique of the way in which the 'sayings and deeds' of the Prophet were scandalously distorted in order to serve the aims of the caliphs and the sultans. He held a rather peremptory view that history is often nothing more than pure invention and that it cannot be trusted. This is why he called for freedom of thought and thus for the freedom to criticise canonical literature on the development of Islam and the political regimes that laid claim to it. His major work, 'The Book of the Muhammadan Personality', is still banned in most Arab countries today and is sold under the table in only a handful of bookshops.[40]

Two of the greatest historians of the Arab world also came from Iraq. The first of these is 'Abd al-'Aziz al-Duri (1919–2011), who from 1963 to 1968 served as President of the University of Baghdad. He was an Arab nationalist whose work focused on the classical period of the Muslim empires from the perspective of political, economic, social, and fiscal institutions. He is the author of a key work on the historical constitution of the Arab nation, in which he marked the stages of the formation of a cultural consciousness, followed by the transition from an Islamic to a modern national consciousness.[41] He is also the author of a book entitled 'Introduction to Arab Economic History.'[42] The second historian is Jawad 'Ali (1907–1987), who was the author of an eight-volume work on the history of the Arabs before Islam that was published courtesy of the Iraqi Ministry of Culture between 1956 and 1960. Other works of history that he wrote include one on the history of prayer in Islam, a description of the idols that were objects of worship for the Arabs, and a history of the Arabs in Islam. He spent his entire career in Iraq in education and culture.

In the Maghreb, Abdallah Laroui published an excellent overview of Maghrebi history,[43] Mostefa Lacheraf wrote a history of Algeria,[44] and the pioneering work of Mohammed Harbi on the origins of the Algerian National Liberation Front (FLN) should also be mentioned.[45] Although Batatu's work highlighted the importance of the rural world and the interplay of social classes, very few works exist on the rural Arab world in spite of its socio-economic importance in almost all of the countries in the region, with the exception of the monarchies and emirates of the Arabian Peninsula. This is why the work of Claudine Chaulet (the wife of French resistance fighter Pierre Chaulet who joined the FLN)[46] on the rural world of Algeria is so important.[47] Indeed, it is easier to find useful descriptions of the problems of the rural Arab world, and their intensity, in the works of Arab novelists.[48] In 2012, the French academic Pierre Blanc published a very interesting work that related the nature of the agricultural reforms in Egypt and Syria and how they were followed by counter reforms that deprived farmers of the benefits that the initial reforms were supposed to provide.[49]

The shortcomings of Arab thought in economics and technology

While the preceding chapters have contextualised many areas of Arab thought, I have not yet developed any extensive descriptions of economic thought, except in those instances where thinkers were influenced by Marxism. However, their thought was directed more towards interpreting the past than building the future. Certainly, it is appropriate to admire the timely critiques of Elias Morcos, Mahdi Aiel, Samir Amin, and Fawzi Mansour on the causes of persistent stagnation and decline, or those of Tayyeb Tizini and Husayn Mroué, who reinterpreted the long history of Arab society by analysing the evolution of socio-economic structures. However, this thought was unable to construct a pathway to the future that made sufficient use of all of the intellectual capabilities of the Arabs. As for those thinkers who specialised in economic research on the contemporary Arab world, I wonder how effective they have been and whether they have identified solutions to move Arab economies beyond their persistent lag in relation to the rest of the world. And if this is not the case, what has caused this failure? These are the questions I will try to answer here, but a few prior remarks are in order.

First of all, there are very few professional economists who have contributed major intellectual works that could have influenced the outcome of Arab political life and led to a favourable change of context. The intellectual efforts that have been devoted to issues of Arab identity and national consciousness, to reformist and conservative Islam, and to critical interpretations of heritage are often of encyclopaedic proportions and of a very scholarly nature. By comparison, very little attention has been paid to economic factors, in spite of the enormity of this field. For what we have here is not just a society in long decline, but a society that has neglected to embrace technology and applied science and that has refused to engage with the main schools of political economy from countries that have achieved industrial modernisation of their socio-economic structures. These include Europe and Japan as well as more recently modernised countries such as South Korea, China, Taiwan, and Singapore. In this regard, there is a major risk of passively espousing the European or American theoretical approaches to this branch of social sciences and their successive schools – including their inconsistencies.

Next, it is appropriate to note that the theoretical approach of political economy, utilised by countries that have reached industrial maturity, is hardly appropriate for societies that have not undergone profound and dramatic transformations of their social and political structures, similar to the upheavals experienced by European societies during the industrial revolution and which included, for example, bourgeois capitalism, violent authoritarianism in Soviet Russia, Maoist China, and in Germany under the Third Reich, as well as, closer to our own time, the case of Chile under the iron-fisted criminal rule of its putschist generals. Indeed, the societies that have remained on the side-lines of this industrial modernity have remained so for a variety of reasons, including colonial and imperialist domination as well as protection of old systems of power and distribution of wealth, and the formula they need for accelerated industrialisation cannot be found in either capitalist or socialist political economy.

What these theories of political economy do provide, however, are highly ideological descriptions of institutions that would favour economic development, bourgeois capitalist on the one hand and proletarian socialist on the other. They cannot, however, provide a magic formula to set in motion a cumulative process of agricultural inventions capable of increasing production capacity and industrial inventions suitable for producing the equipment necessary to facilitate this, as well as an increase in the number of products and services that could rapidly become objects of mass consumption or formidable weapons sowing death and destruction. There is, in fact, very little consensus among economic and scientific historians regarding what this magic recipe should include. The causes of the industrial revolution have given rise to an enormous amount of scholarly literature in Europe and the United States. More importantly, some economists have focused on the challenges of industrial development for countries that have remained 'underdeveloped' or 'backwards' in this regard, especially in Germany and Russia. All of this literature has for the most part been ignored in the Arab world; or perhaps many economists simply considered that colonial plunder was the only relevant cause of the accelerated development of Western Europe, and of the underdevelopment of their own countries, because it closed the door to similar development in societies dominated by European colonialism. The Marxist theory of 'Asian despotism' – challenged by Arab intellectuals, with just cause – based on the notion of 'hydraulic societies' in which government authority was brought to bear at every level of the economy, suggests that this is the cause of the persistent decline in Arab, Indian, and Chinese contexts. However, this theory never really offered a theoretical or practical alternative for societies that were lagging behind in their development.

Overall, Arab intellectuals have paid little attention to the details of the history of European science and technology, nor have they closely examined the history of the mechanisms of technological innovation in the production and development of the complex machinery needed to increase the 'forces of production', to use a Marxist term.[50] This lack of attention applies to Europe since the Middle Ages, to China and the Abbasid Empire at the height of their respective grandeur; or, closer to our own time, during the Meiji era in Japan at the end of the nineteenth century, and in South Korea and Taiwan at the end of the twentieth century. It is no exaggeration to state that, with a few rare exceptions, Arab thought has not focused on this problem and has not developed specific knowledge of the mechanisms that have allowed underdeveloped societies to overcome this gap. This thought has held on to the division that prevailed for so long between a political economy that was Marxist, and therefore socialist, and one that was 'liberal', and therefore capitalist. The battle of ideas in the Arab world around this issue very simply mirrored the same debate on a global scale over the two systems that dominated the world economic order between 1917 and 1990. These were ideological disputes with little emphasis on finding a formula for societies to achieve broad progress. Even Ibn Khaldun's powerful vision of prosperity and the blossoming of civilisation (*'umran*, which comes from the verb meaning 'to build, construct'), was hardly utilised, despite the fact that it showed how political, sociological, and cultural factors interact to produce dynasties and sovereigns who are capable of ensuring a blossoming civilisation.

As a result, Arab economic thought, which was bitterly divided, completely avoided moving beyond ideologically based disagreement over the issue of whether the economic institutions that were to be set up should be capitalist or socialist. This prevented it from engaging in a deeper reflection on the ways in which the development and wellbeing of societies and the creation of rich and powerful civilisations might be achieved. Since the time of the *Nahda*, and even more so since the middle of the twentieth century, the polarisation of Arab intellectual efforts around the need for religious reform and the major position attributed to Islam in Arab identity has prevented the development of in-depth knowledge about the economic history of the Arab world, its specificities, and especially the reasons for the tremendous expansion of classical Islamic civilisation that achieved major progress in all areas of science and technology, including everything from astronomy, mathematics, and medicine, to hydraulics and irrigation.

However, one would have thought that the acute awareness of underdevelopment that broadly characterised contemporary Arab thought would have moved it in a more positivist direction, and not in the direction of the idealism that tended to predominate, and which had been strongly denounced in the critiques of Arab Marxist thinkers. But these thinkers in turn became wrapped up in this critique – which was most enlightening nonetheless – of so-called bourgeois thought and interpretation of the general history of Islamic civilisation taking into account the structures of production and class relationships. However, Samir Amin, a major intellectual, who worked specifically in the framework of internationalist humanism, looked at the relationships between the developed 'centre' of capitalism and its 'underdeveloped' peripheries kept in a state of dependency. For the other Arab Marxist thinkers already discussed, it was this situation that produced the ideology of the Arab petite bourgeoisie, an ideology which was inadvertently influenced, through the impact of certain European philosophies, by an essentialist understanding of religion and its immutable world view, behind which this petite bourgeoisie managed to conceal its narrow class interests.

Arab economists who have made substantial contributions

Nonetheless, in the 1970s in a fine study of the evolution of Arab economies, the Egyptian economist Galal A. Amin, the son of the famous religious reformer Ahmad Amin, provided a devastating diagnosis of what he called the 'modernisation of poverty'.[51] He showed that everywhere, behind the facade of modernisation, the reality of the economies of Arab countries remained one of rural societies that were increasingly impoverished, of a predominance of foreign interests in other forms, and of waste and inefficiency. In 2006, he updated this work in a new book on the 'illusion' of progress in the Arab world,[52] followed in 2008 by a book critiquing the philosophy of economics in which he denounced the bias of major economists, one that reflected the evolution of the capitalist system.[53] Galal Amin also got caught up in the debates over modernity versus authority, the critique of Nasser's secular modernism, and the need for cultural resistance to the West.[54] But in the specific area of economic thought, his work is very rich and includes a critique of Marxist economics, several books on the Egyptian economy (one of which focuses on the shortcomings of the state), and another on the lives of illustrious Arab personalities. His books address many different themes, including the attitude of Arab intellectuals towards Israel, economic globalisation, globalisation of oppression (a study of Arabs and Muslims in the United States before and after 9/11), and even the mythology of development and the hypocrisy of economic theories of development. He also wrote an autobiography entitled 'What Life has Taught Me'. He is a complex individual with a strong personality whose abundant body of work is unfortunately not well known and has not received sufficient scholarly attention.

Youssef Sayegh's premonitory analysis of the failure of
Arab development

Altogether different are the career paths of two great Palestinian economists, Youssef Sayegh (1916–2004) and Burhan Dajani (1921–2000). The former was the son of a modest Protestant pastor. He lived in both Lebanon and

Syria, worked as a professor at the American University of Beirut, and later became a member of the Palestine Liberation Organization (PLO). For a long time, his work was an essential reference, but it has fallen into oblivion today. He wrote a book that unquestionably provides the best description of the state of Arab economics at the end of the 1970s. It was published in 1978 in two volumes, the first of which gave an overview of the structure and evolution of the economy of each Arab country, and the second described the general conclusions he drew from this analysis, conclusions that he called 'determinants of Arab economic development'.[55] This is a meticulous study that deals with all Arab economies as a whole, the challenges faced by each individual country, as well as the evolution of inter-Arab cooperation. Thirty-six years later, this extensive overview is still unmatched, and in retrospect his sharp insight is all the more apparent as the shortcomings he identified within Arab economic policies have turned out to be so accurate.

In the second volume, he enumerates at length the challenges facing the economies of the region if they are to produce an efficient and socially just self-reliant development strategy. In the volume that addresses the determinants, these challenges are organised according to nine broad themes. The first concerns the 'content and philosophy of development', in which the author warns against an overly mechanical view of development that fails to take into account the needs of the population and the mechanism for distribution of national income. He also warns against a fragmented approach to development that blatantly disregards social needs and the dignity of the population. The second concerns the social forces of development in which the author identifies the risk of exclusion of the population and the creation of a 'new class' of leaders who in turn become exploitive. The third challenge involves the need to establish a solid redistributive justice between regions and social groups without negatively affecting economic efficiency. The fourth challenge is that of education and the dilemmas faced by developing societies in this regard (quantity to the detriment of quality, universal education or specialised vocational education, education for all or the privileged few). The fifth challenge, and one that is rarely mentioned in the work of Arab economists, is the appropriation of technologies, how to distribute them within the social body, which technologies to adopt, and how to adapt them to local needs.

The sixth challenge is that of economic self-reliance and the distribution of available resources between consumption and investment, and between civilian and military needs. The seventh concerns the population and the work force and addresses a variety of issues including birth control, and unemployment and underemployment, which may be exacerbated by poor technology investment decisions as well as the brain drain which particularly affects the Arab world. The eighth challenge concerns public administration. The ever-expanding role of administrations requires the increased professional competence of civil servants; however, in some countries, loyalty to the party or to members of the political class are often the main criteria for recruitment and promotion. Finally, the ninth and last challenge is the development of inter-Arab regional cooperation. Which institutions would best support this and how can the free circulation of people and goods be liberalised? And more importantly, how can the vast energy resources be made available for use by all of the economies of the region?

In both volumes, Sayegh shows how industrialisation policies in Arab countries are incoherent, fragmented, inadequate, sluggish, and mostly driven by the desire to appear 'modern' and 'advanced', or the desire to conform to a pre-established ideological model.[56] He is one of the few Arab economists to focus on the implementation of technology appropriation policies, but also on issues of social justice, at the level of individuals as well as of the inequality of development between the different regions of each country, and the development of excessive consumption, especially in oil-producing economies. Already in the 1970s, he expressed deep concerns about issues of unemployment and underemployment, technological stagnation and lack of innovation, political authoritarianism and the absence of participatory democracy, all of which were major issues that contributed to unleashing the revolts of 2011.

In 1961, Youssef Sayegh published his first book entitled 'Bread with Dignity', the title of which resurfaced in the slogans of the 2011 protests.[57] He also published a book on 'unregulated' development in 1991, in which he revisits the major themes of his economic thought and, following the collapse of the Soviet Union, warns against questioning social reforms in Arab countries.[58] He makes the case for maintaining socialist ideals and argues that their flawed application should not doom their grand principles concerning human dignity. Sayegh believed it was possible to reconcile the principles of a socialist economy with the existence of a large private sector.[59] In this work, he does not mince words in his criticism of the numerous Arab economists who switched sides as the winds began to shift in a different direction. Once fervent partisans of socialism, they became staunch defenders of the new global capitalism. For him, the major problem is how to break free from the mechanisms of economic dependency to establish a self-reliant economy built on the unique strengths of Arab countries themselves, given that they are endowed with all of the necessary natural factors. An Arab nationalist, Palestinian activist, and socialist humanist, it is clear that Sayegh represents the epitome of the engaged intellectual. He was a top-notch economist, and it is unfortunate that his work has not been given the honour it deserves and that there is really nobody among the new generation of economists who can carry on his work. So many of today's economists have been won over by neoliberal theories, as well as lacking precise knowledge of the problems of Arab economies and their barriers to inter-cooperation.[60]

Unlike Sayegh, Burhan Dajani did not author key works on the Arab economy, but instead tirelessly advocated for the advantages of integrating Arab economies, and developing their complementarities, despite the absence of a formal economic union. His numerous writings on this issue were published in 2004 in a two-volume edition by the Institute for Palestine Studies.[61]

Numerous other useful economic contributions

Several other Arab economists who have produced significant work should also be mentioned. Firstly, Abdelkader Sid-Ahmed, an Algerian who very early on warned against the harmful effects of the petroleum-based rentier economy.[62] In addition to founding and directing the Parisian publishing house Paris-Sud, which published many good works, he also had a university career in France. Another particularly brilliant Algerian economist is Ahmed Henni. He was both a university teacher and director of taxation in Algeria before going into exile in France following the destabilisation of Algeria in the 1990s, where he taught at the Université d'Artois in Arras. In his work, Henni deftly combines anthropology and economics, both in his work on Algeria as well as his writing on the global development of the rentier economy and how the Islamist movement fits in with this.[63]

The Egyptian academic Mahmoud Abdel-Fadil is also part of this same progressive nationalist trend. He is the author of an interesting work that provides an overview of the different currents of Arab economic thought regarding the problems facing Arab societies, such as national unity, planning and development, socialism, and so forth.[64] In this book the author also looks at how external schools of economic thought have influenced Arab economic thought, which he describes as being in a state of crisis. He is also one of the few Arab economists to have focused on the successful experiments of South-

East Asian countries and to have looked at what regional economies can learn from this.[65] As for the Lebanese historian Massoud Daher, he is the only Arab thinker who has compared the experience of nineteenth-century Japanese development during the Meiji era with that of Egypt fifty years earlier during the reign of Muhammad 'Ali.[66] Moreover, Daher produced an enormous body of work, particularly on the social and communitarian history of Lebanon, but also on rural history and the difficulties with modern state building in the region. He has received several prizes for his work in the Arab world as well as Japan's highest academic distinction.

Antoine Zahlan's analysis and the causes of Arab technological powerlessness

I will finish this brief overview of Arab economic thought by mentioning the important work on Middle Eastern economic history by Charles Issawi (1916–2000), an Egyptian who emigrated to the United States where he enjoyed an outstanding academic career.[67] The work of Antoine Zahlan will also be highlighted, a physicist of Palestinian origin who was born in Haifa in 1928 but who lived most of his life in Lebanon. He taught for many years at the American University in Beirut before devoting himself to full-time economic consultancy for international organisations and Arab governments. His work is interesting due to the precise way in which he identified the causes of scientific and technological stagnation in Arab societies, despite the fact that they had been open to European modernity for the previous two centuries. In his work, Zahlan identified the barriers to the development of local technological capabilities. These included, among others, brain drain; failure to stimulate the scientific and technical capacity of local engineering consultants, thus favouring foreign companies;[68] the dispersal of those scientific and technical capabilities that existed locally;[69] and poor industrial planning.[70] He went on to explain how to plan and successfully implement industrial growth, and described the shortcomings of public policies on science and technology. In one of his latest books, published in 2012, he addresses the relationship between sovereignty, science, and development in the Arab world. This work comprises a synopsis of all of the knowledge acquired by the author throughout his long career, knowledge which he devoted to issues neglected by most Arab economists, particularly those of the younger generations.[71] After the Israeli-Palestinian Accords were signed in

Oslo in 1993, Zahlan authored a development plan for the Occupied Palestinian Territories following Israel's planned evacuation.

This brings to an end the much too brief survey of Arab thought in the human and social sciences. I have tried to do justice to a certain number of thinkers whose work is important enough to bring to the attention of the reader. This overview is certainly far from being exhaustive. For each specialisation within the human and social sciences, an entire volume would be needed in order to provide a detailed overview of all of the works published, their content, and their leanings. This is obviously not possible in the framework of this book. However, this final chapter at least clearly shows that we are not dealing with a lack of thought in the different disciplines discussed. Therefore, having journeyed through the different facets of Arab thought, we can now turn to the conclusion.

CONCLUSION

Vibrant thought, decaying politics

Having come to the end of this journey through the intricacies and richness of Arab thought, is it possible to take stock of what has been found and to summarise the relationship between politics and thought in the Arab world? Modern Arab thought has been open to the search for common universals from the time of al-Tahtawi to the present day. Should it therefore be blamed for the phenomena of dictatorships, regression, and the dislocation we have witnessed in Arab societies since the wave of popular revolts in 2011? Should the search for an unattainable Arab unity, or for an Arab socialism with a human face, be called into question? Or, rather, is there cause to indict the different forms of political Islam? These, after having been marginalised in modern Arab political culture, have now not only invaded and overwhelmed it, but also infiltrated political power at various levels in most Arab states only to devolve into increasingly bloody terrorism.

The hegemony of the radical Islamic thought of a few writers, thought that is completely incompatible with the universals around which the human species might unite, has been preached as a solution to all of the problems of Arab societies. And yet, is it perhaps fair to say that this dominance has been imposed through the powerful channels of material influence coming from the oil-exporting countries of the Arabian Peninsula and from European and American academic institutions? Is it therefore really the reflection of a collective Arab psychology and of an Arab-Islamic culture presumed to be invariant? Does the complicity of a new Euro-American Islamic studies focused on political Islam not reproduce a carceral hegemony already denounced by Edward Said, but which has become even more formidable and totalitarian as numerous Arab regimes and many intellectuals join in?

If this is the case, the central question is how to escape this dark tunnel in which we find ourselves. Many of the authors discussed here have studied the contradictions of Arab political thought, and have all denounced conciliatory thought, which would have led modernist intellectuals to making too many concessions to proponents of an Islamic cultural essentialism alleged to be the invariant aspect of the Arab mind. But the events that have taken place since 2011 show the partial collapse of the social consensus that has governed life in Arab societies since the period of independence. This collapse is largely due to the ambitions of the Islamic movements, but is also due to the numerous ways in which they were manipulated by Arab regimes themselves as well as by regional powers such as Turkey. This manipulation also took the form of direct or indirect support of some of these movements by Europe or the United States, as well as the media attention they received.

This collapse can also be clearly seen today on the ground in Libya, Syria, Iraq, Sudan, and Somalia, not to mention Algeria in the 1990s and Lebanon between 1975 and 1990. It is still contained in Egypt and in Lebanon, whose governments are subjected to strong pressure from terrorists. Its source can perhaps be attributed to the rising power of the transnational Muslim Brotherhood movement from the beginning of the last century onwards, a movement whose creation coincided with the emergence of the Kingdom of Saudi Arabia. This is the only Arab state to bear the name of a family (the Sauds) and to have a 'national' flag that bears the Islamic profession of faith underlined by a sword.

Arab political thought, whether of the religious reformist variety or of the nationalist, anti-imperialist, and progressive variety, is therefore, in my view, not responsible for this major ideological swing to various forms of political Islam. There is certainly reason to criticise the excessive idealism of modernist Arab thought as well as its somewhat naïve belief in a 'historical direction' that will succeed in leading formerly colonised peoples to free themselves from both colonialism and neo-colonialism as well as from internal reactionary and anti-modernist forces. This has in fact been addressed by critical Arab thought, which has undergone considerable development and which is still going strong. The problem is its lack of visibility, given that all other academic research for the past several decades has concentrated on the question of the specificity of Arab-Islamic identity and on how modernity and secularism allegedly constitute a violation of this identity due to its presumed invariance since the time of the Prophet in Medina.

As demonstrated in the previous chapter, it is unfortunate that the appropriation of science and technology has not been given more attention within Arab thought. This is particularly the case concerning the past few decades, given that in that time two major Arab economists (Youssef Sayegh and Antoine Zahlan) produced very relevant analyses of this topic and identified solutions to the technological stagnation of Arab societies. I think that the lack of interest in these issues results from two factors which together produce a combined effect: on the one hand, the concentration of intellectual efforts on the same circular, sterile, and futile questions concerning the continual assertion of civilisational authenticity and specificity (that of so-called Arab-Islamic civilisation); and, on the other hand, the incursion of neoliberal economic ideology that rejects the idea of technology as a key variable in development, which allegedly only results from the free market and from private enterprise. As the twenty-first century begins to take shape, Arab students are following a university curriculum that is completely pervaded by an ideology that is both superficial and harmful.[1]

Today, most Arab societies offer a sorry political spectacle that now more than ever consists of a confrontation between open- and closed-minded thought. Indeed, on one side is open, secular and essentially secular thought as well as enlightened religious reformist thought that is deeply rooted in the work of its nineteenth and early-twentieth century intellectual forebears. On the other side is the closed thought encapsulated by the imaginary theologico-political heritage of the early centuries of Islam, a heritage which according to this school of thought should be revived. As a result of discussing theology and the specificity of Islam for the past fifty years, as well as promoting such discussions in every academic and media environment in Europe, the United States, and the Arab world, the political scene is currently completely overrun by such debates. The Arab Spring of 2011 was a revolt against social injustice, exclusion, widespread unemployment, the corruption of leaders, and their authoritarianism. It allowed the forces of 'religious McCarthyism', already denounced in 1965 by the influential thinker Yasin al-Hafiz, to pursue political power in those states where it was no longer possible to stop this new revolutionary wave.[2]

This development resulted in the encouragement of all sorts of 'sectarian' shifts, especially between Sunnis and different denominations of Shi'is, and also revived a dying tribalism that had been fading away under the influence of economic modernisation, however limited. Above all, it encouraged profound social changes, massive and chaotic urbanisation, and the 'ruralisation' of cities, all of which have affected Arab societies since the end of the Second World War. The 'end of the rural way of life' and the 'grand transformation' of Arab economies during the last half century in the framework of the emergence of fragmented states from colonial arrangements that materialised and were formalised during the First World War opened the floodgates to all the violent shifts we have witnessed since the end of 2010. These are shifts in which Western powers have often been implicated, the most flagrant cases of which include those in Iraq, Syria, and Libya. Moreover, as has been shown, rentier and neopatrimonial economics have prevented a positive transformation of these economies.

Whether Arab or Islamic, there is simply no anthropological specificity to be found here. Europe, Asia, and Latin America have all experienced similar shifts, but on a much greater demographic and geographical scale than those that have occurred in Arab societies: Nazism and fascism in Europe during the inter-war period, fierce and bloody civil war in Russia after the First World War, seizure of power by Communists in China, Vietnam, and across half of the Korean Peninsula as well as in Cuba. The events in Cuba led to a wave of fascist military coups in Central and South America during the 1970s and to the creation of armed opposition movements of different ideological allegiance (Tupamoros, Shining Path, FARC, etc.). The same phenomenon can be found in Indonesia, Pakistan, and Myanmar where military coups established repressive authoritarian regimes. Included in all of these violent events are the genocides that have affected sub-Saharan Africa as well as Cambodia, the civil war in Bangladesh, the long drawn-out revolt of the Tamils in Sri Lanka, the Cultural Revolution in China, and the two wars in Afghanistan (1979–1989 and 2001 to the present day), which gave rise to the Taliban.

The violent upheavals experienced by the Arab world over the past several decades need to be interpreted within this context. The same applies to the series of military coups (or attempted coups) that have been a regular feature of the history of Arab states since the period of independence; the long and deadly unrest in Lebanon between 1975 and 1990 that involved local militias, both the Syrian and the Israeli armies, and armed Palestinian resistance movements seeking to liberate the territories occupied by Israel; the destabilisation of Algeria in 1992 that turned into a ruthless war lasting until 2000 between the Algerian army and different armed Islamist movements;

and the Iraq-Iran war (1980–1988) and the numerous tragic fallouts it produced, including the Iraqi invasion of Kuwait in 1990 followed by the 1991 war to liberate this oil-exporting emirate prosecuted by a formidable military coalition led by the United States. Following this, the Oslo Accord on Palestine was signed in 1993, which never led to the self-determination of the Palestinian people, but rather, to even greater expansion of Israeli settlements in the occupied territories. In September 2001, the deadly terrorist attacks on New York and Washington, D.C. that were attributed to Al-Qaeda led to the invasion of Afghanistan in the same year; and to the invasion of Iraq in 2003 by Western forces firstly under NATO command, and subsequently under US command. In 2011 it also led to substantial direct military intervention in Libya by Franco-British forces, and in the same year indirect intervention by France and Great Britain in Syria with the support of the member states of the Arab League, especially Qatar and Saudi Arabia, as well as Turkey.

It is hard to imagine the consequences of this succession of violent upheavals in many parts of the Arab world. Ultimately, they have dismantled the societies in these regions and have caused them to lose any rational and unified reference point. In the midst of such stormy seas, reformist Arab thought (religious and secular) nonetheless continued onward. Some thinkers paid with their lives after calling for an emancipation from the ideology of political Islam, which had become increasingly overbearing and constraining in the life of Arab societies. The major problem of secular or modernist thought was not its failure to conform to the realities of the Arab world. On the contrary, I think as a whole it accurately identified the Arab world's intellectual, social, and economic problems and challenges. Rather, its near total invisibility in academia and the media, both Western and Arab, is unquestionably what stifled it in favour of debates that were exclusively theologico-political, redundant, and circular. Whether they were portrayed positively or negatively, these debates continued to be the focus of what bordered on being a marketing campaign to promote the different Islamic movements and their leaders as if they constituted the main political and social force in the Arab world. This state of affairs led to a vicious self-perpetuating cycle.

Leaving aside the debate over the existence of a moderate political Islam, supposedly the only source of a workable modernity, and which could oppose so-called 'radical' Islam, it seems to me high time to recognise that, starting with the 'great discord' of the first two centuries of Arab-Islamic civilisation, and up to the events of the past fifty years, the instrumentalisation of religion as part of the political administration of Arab societies has only led to catastrophic results. Indeed, this instrumentalisation did not yield better results in the history of Christianity either. In the West, the excesses of the temporal power of the papacy, especially the persecution of 'heretics' by the Inquisition, the conflicts surrounding papal succession, and the conspicuous wealth of the Church which went so far as to sell 'indulgences' providing access to heaven, gave rise to the Protestant revolt. This was followed by more than a hundred years of continuous civil war in European societies, and it would take more than two centuries to achieve peace and move beyond these conflicts through the gradual secularisation of societies, followed by the secularisation of political institutions.[3]

Regarding the creation of a Jewish state in Palestine, an objective assessment clearly shows its limitations. Israel has not even been able to attract a majority of those belonging to the Jewish faith. More importantly, there are many religious and secular Jews who are opposed to the very principle of the creation of this state. However, their voices, like those of the Arabs who do not subscribe to politico-religious aspirations, have been strongly attacked and marginalised in both academic and media circles. On the side of the victims of this undertaking, the violence and suffering endured by the Palestinian population over the past seventy-five years has taken on inhumane proportions and is in any case contrary to all the principles of international and humanitarian law. To this can be added the tens of thousands of victims of the major Arab-Israeli wars (1948, 1956, 1967, 1973) and the suffering inflicted on the Lebanese population and the Palestinian refugees in Lebanon from 1968, the date of the first major attack against Lebanon by the Israeli army, to 2006, the year of the thirty-three day war marked by intense land, sea, and aerial bombing in an attempt to eradicate Hezbollah.

If we turn to the Indian Peninsula, a place outside the Arab world where Islam has nonetheless flourished and built sultanates, one of which was the Moghul Empire (1556–1857), we see that the creation of Pakistan through the secession of Muslim Indians did nothing to ensure civil peace and prosperity within this country where a hard-line version of shari'a law has been implemented. Nor did it prevent the bloody secession of the province of Bengal (East Pakistan), which later became the state of Bangladesh.

The time has therefore come to break with the instrumentalisation of the three monotheistic religions, which has caused so much hardship for so many people without ever providing civil peace within those countries that sought to 're-Islamise' their customs and laws on the grounds that this reflects the authenticity of their identity – a notion that has become high-value intellectual merchandise given the success it provides in academia and the media. Parallel to this, it is time to take a good look at the outlandish material fortunes that have been built in the Arab world,[4] Europe, and the United States based on the diversion of oil revenues. While at the same time, poverty, exclusion, illiteracy, massive unemployment, and the lack of mastery of science and technology have created fertile ground for the rise of violent nihilistic movements that invoke Islam to accelerate the dismantling of Arab societies. Supplied with arms and material support, these movements are scandalously manipulated by regional and international entities seeking political dominance.

I therefore call on the young generation of Arabs, those living in their own countries as well as those who have emigrated to another, to liberate themselves from the intellectual restraints placed on them by Islamophiles as well as racist Islamophobes, and from the canonical narratives invoked by each to justify their positions. Indeed, Islamophiles have found in political Islam a substitute for their lost romanticism and Third-Worldist exoticism, which have been replaced by a terrifying fascination with armed theologico-political movements aligned with a radical and anti-modernist conception of Islam. On the other hand, in the face of atrocious terrorist acts carried out by these movements, Islamophobes feel perfectly justified in resorting to the grand racist traditions of Europe that pit a refined and superior Aryan world against a Semitic world embodied by Islam and a tribalism that is incompatible with any form of modernity. It should come as no surprise that Huntingdon's theory of the clash of civilisations received so much attention in the media and in the academy; for it simply provided a pseudo-academic theoretical framework for the old racist ideology of nineteenth-century Europe.

It is for this reason that the only path to salvation for Arab culture and thought is to break free of these unhealthy intellectual paradigms without vision. This would provide a long overdue opportunity for measured reflection on the way forward towards economic and social development strategies that differ from those that emerged from these paradigms, one a religious anthropology based on a virulent essentialism, and the other a neoliberal economic paradigm embodied by a ready-made formula provided by large international economic and financial bureaucracies. Embarking on this path would require an enormous amount of new collective action in order to implement policies to quickly eradicate illiteracy and focus priority attention on neglected rural areas and underserved populations in large cities. This would mean bringing an end to the neoliberalism that has shored up the rentier economy, expanded the field of unemployment, and created social inequalities of unprecedented proportions. This inequality is a source of deep animosity that has led to an escapist strategy of refuge in millenarianisms and the unprincipled invocation of religion.[5]

It is also time for Arab intellectuals to move beyond their ideological disputes, which in some cases reproduce those related to the ambitions of influential states, and to examine the inability of their societies to integrate the world of science and technology, particularly since many other peoples have managed to do so. Moreover, the Arab world possesses enough natural resources and material wealth, and should not have to continually beg for international investment and assistance from international financial institutions whose bureaucracies largely dominate Arab state structures.

Finally, Arab youth should denounce the power games played by those Arab states with access to oil wealth, as well as those of regional importance, not to mention of course the political and military omnipresence of the European Union and the United States. Along the same lines, Arab universities should refocus their curricula and receive much greater financial support. The goal here would be twofold: to improve the ability of students to better understand the needs of their own societies and the numerous underprivileged classes in both rural and urban areas; and to produce technicians and scientists whose knowledge matches the actual social and economic needs of their societies. But this should also be done with a view to restoring and deepening knowledge of the different facets of Arab thought – largely ignored today – that I have presented in this book.

The revolts of 2011 re-established the unity of Arab consciousness. The counter-revolutions created problems with violence in every society, and by creating deadly regional, tribal, communitarian, and sectarian sub-identities, succeeded in temporarily fracturing this unity. The future of the Arab world is now more than ever a great unknown. The Arab thought of the future should therefore concentrate on discovering pathways to philosophical independence, which is the only way forward towards the construction of a system for a coherent perception of the evolution of the world and the place that Arab societies wish to occupy within it. We have seen how many thinkers have already paved the way. It is therefore now necessary to break free of the various stereotypical narratives circulating in the Arab world and its relationship to religion. The schizophrenia inherent on the attitude towards

'Euro-American civilisation' which at once hates and admires it should give way to a broad and dynamic movement to rebuild thought in all of its richness along with the social frameworks of historical memory. Today, these frameworks have disappeared under the influence of the financial fallout of oil revenues and their instrumentalisation in support of a radical religious conservatism opposed to liberty.

This is the task for the young generation of Arabs, whether they have emigrated elsewhere or are living in their own country. Given the scale of the civil wars in the Arab world that are increasingly of a sectarian and religious nature, it may be hoped that fatigue will put an end to these religious and sectarian debates and anathema. This would free up more energy to reflect on a different future without being restrained by virulent theologico-political arguments; or by European, American, and Israeli agendas concerning the Arab world and their Faustian desire, since the collapse of the Ottoman Empire, to remake it.[6] In comparison to Turkey and Iran, which constitute two massive entities in the Middle East, the fragmentation of Arab societies despite all of the cultural and historic ties that unite them acts as a self-perpetuating mechanism to produce more and more violence and conflict. It also attracts increasing external intervention by regional and international powers in the tragic destiny of these societies.

It is time to take stock of rich contemporary Arab thought in contexts outside of the academic canons of major European and American institutions, and the media channels heavily influenced by oil revenues which are subservient to the interests of a few patrimonial-style Arab states as well as the interests of European and American diplomacy. This is what I have sought to do in this book, in an attempt to open a way for the younger generations to free themselves from the intellectual constraints and truncated canonical narratives on the realities of Arab thought and its complex relationship with the cruel games of regional and international geopolitics. To live with dignity within modern productive societies should be the main objective, and if this were achieved it would bring an end to internal violence, inter-Arab conflict, and to unchecked emigration by Arabs who choose to cross the Mediterranean Sea illegally, leading to the tragic loss each year of thousands who perish along the way.

The revolts of 2011 paved the way for this type of change, but it was immediately stymied by the winds of counter-revolutions with their convoys of external interference. It is time to get back on this difficult but exhilarating road and, strengthened by the lessons of experience, rebuild societies based on economic and social justice, full employment, and the fight against corruption, the appropriation of science and technology, and the refusal to accept external interference. This is what other non-European societies have, in fact, accomplished; and they too were formerly victims of the most brutal forms of colonialism. This is why I am calling for a sense of human dignity to re-emerge in Arab societies and for an active 'collective intelligence' to form, as was the case during the now-forgotten modern renaissance (1850–1950). This would usher in an irreversible qualitative and positive change in how to think about and build a different future, one that breaks from the dynamic of failure affecting Arab societies. I have described this unfortunate dynamic at length in the successive editions of my book, *Le proche orient éclaté* (The Shattered Middle East) (first published 1983). In order to accomplish this, it is now more imperative than ever for Arab thought to break through all of the intellectual, philosophical, and political barriers that have developed over the past fifty years, and which are also the result of older developments dating back to the collapse of the Ottoman Empire and the fragmentation of Arab states imposed by the colonial powers after the First World War, not to mention the harmful effects of soaring oil revenues in the latter part of the twentieth century. Eradication of this terrorism that falsely aligns itself with Islam can only come from within Arab societies by changing the sterile intellectual paradigms that fuel these authoritarian and hegemonic shifts on both sides of the Mediterranean. These paradigms seek to petrify and paralyse Arab thought by concealing or marginalising the thousands of different facets of critical thought and finely crafted knowledge that I have endeavoured to present here.

NOTES

FOREWORD

1. Reinhart, Tanya, *Israel/Palestine: How to End the War of 1948*, New York: Seven Stories Press, 2002; *The Road Map to Nowhere: Israel/Palestine Since 2003*, London: Verso, 2006.
2. Pappé, Ilan, *The Ethnic Cleansing of Palestine*, Oxford: One World Publications, 2006.
3. Sand, Shlomo, *The Invention of the Jewish People*, London: Verso, 2009; *The Invention of the Land of Israel*, London: Verso, 2012; *How I Stopped being a Jew*, London: Verso, 2014.
4. Corm, Georges, *La Question religieuse au XXIe siècle. Géopolitique et crise de la postmodernité* (The Religious Question in the 21st century. Geopolitics and the Crisis of Postmodernity), Paris: La Découverte, 2006.

INTRODUCTION

1. Rodinson, Maxime, *Europe and the Mystique of Islam*, transl. Roger Veinus, Seattle: University of Washington Press, 1987.
2. See notably, Hudson, Michael, *Arab Politics. The Search for Legitimacy*, New Haven, CT: Yale University Press, 1977; Ayubi, Nazih N., *Over-stating the Arab State: Politics and Society in the Middle East*, London: IB Tauris, 1995. In contrast, there are many books that describe and denounce the way dictatorships function, and the human rights violations of the republican regimes, although more rarely in monarchical regimes (with the exception of Morocco during the reign of King Hassan II). However, the courageous work of Jean-Michel Foulquier should be mentioned: *Arabie saoudite. La dictature protégée* (Saudi Arabia, the Protected Dictatorship), Paris: Albin Michel, 1995 (book written under a pseudonym).

3.   See Abdou, Mohammed, *L'Islam: religion, science et civilisation* (Islam: Religion, Science, and Civilisation), Beirut: Dār Al-Bīrūnī, 2003.

CHAPTER 1

1.   Not to be confused with the first president of the independent Lebanese Republic (1943–1952) of the same name, who was also very learned in Arab culture.

2.   As illustrated, for example, by the work of the French historian Sylvain Gouguenheim, *Aristote au Mont Saint-Michel. Les racines grecques de l'Europe chrétienne* (Aristotle at Mont Saint-Michel. The Greek Roots of Christian Europe), Paris: Seuil, 2008. Contrary to the evidence, this author denied the role of Arabic translations in the European rediscovery of Greek knowledge in the Middle Ages. Many erudite historians (such as Alain de Libera, among others) have vigorously objected to this negationist enterprise.

3.   Quadri, Goffredo, *La Filosofia degli Arabi nel suo fiore,* Florence: La Nuova Italia, 1939 (French translation: *La Philosophie arabe dans l'Europe médiévale. Des origines à Averroès* (Arab Philosophy in Medieval Europe: From its Origins to Averroes) Paris: Payot, 1947).

4.   See de Libera, Alain, *Penser au Moyen Âge* (Medieval Thought), Paris: Seuil, 1991.

5.   We should mention the very fine translation by Abdessalam Cheddadi: Ibn Khaldun, *Le Livre des exemples* (The Book of Examples), Paris: Gallimard, 2002.

6.   Ibid., p. 251-252.

7.   On this topic see Hallaq, Boutros (ed.), *Histoire de la littérature arabe moderne. 1800–1945* (History of Modern Arab Literature. 1800–1945), Arles: Actes Sud, 1987; among the many useful articles in this volume we should mention the one by Yves Gonzales-Quijano, "La renaissance arabe au XIXe siècle: médiums, médiations et médiateurs" (The Arab Renaissance of the Nineteenth Century: Mediums, Mediations, and Mediators), which clearly demonstrates the role played by the rapid development of the Arab press.

CHAPTER 2

1.   An interesting article by Maxime Rodinson is referred to here, based on a lecture he gave at Inalco in November 1992 ('Islam arabe/islam non arabe" (Arab Islam/Non-Arab Islam), *Les Annales de l'autre islam*, Publications de l'ERISM, no 1, Paris, 1993), in which he analyses the causes of the "confusion between Islam and Arabism" by European Orientalists, causes "that may explain it," he says, "but not legitimise it." He also discussed the "ambiguity of Muslim ideology itself on the relationship between ethnicity and religion."

2.   Hourani, Albert, *A History of the Arab Peoples*, London: Faber & Faber, 1991.

3.   Djaït, Hichem, *La Personnalité et le devenir arabo-islamiques* (The Arab-Islamic Personality and Future), Paris: Seuil, 1974.

4.   Djaït, Hichem, *La Grande discorde. Religion et politique dans l'islam des origines* (The Great Discord. Religion and Politics in Islam at its Origins), Paris: Gallimard, 1989. As will be shown, this title is based on one of the major works of the great Egyptian thinker Taha Husayn, who wrote a book on the same theme of a "major" dispute.

5.   Arkoun, Mohammed, *La Pensée arabe* (Arab Thought), Paris: PUF, 1975.

6.   Fahmī Jad ʿān (Fahmy Gedaan), *Usus al-taqaddum ʿinda muffakirī al-islām fi'l-ʿālam al-ʿarabī al-ḥadīth* (The Foundations for Progress in Muslim Thinkers of the Contemporary Arab World), Beirut: al-Mu'assasa al-ʿarabiyya li'l-dirāsāt wa'l-nashr, 1979.

7.   Djaït, Hichem, *La Grande discorde*, p. 10.

8.   The word *fitan* (plural of *fitna*) means deep disagreement, which could be violent.

9.   Djaït, Hichem, *La Grande discorde*, pp. 412-413.

10.   Djaït, Hichem, *La Personnalité et le devenir arabo-islamiques*, p. 16.

11.   On this point, the brilliant essay by Hélé Béji on the veil should be referred to: *Islam pride. Derrière le voile* (Islam Pride. Behind the Veil), Paris: Gallimard, 2012.

12.   Wahhabism is the extreme puritanical form of Sunni Islam spread by Muhammad ibn ʿAbd al-Wahhab (1703–1792), who lived in Najd and who allied with Muhammad ibn Saʿud in 1747 to spread this doctrine by the sword. In 1810, in order to gain control of this movement, the Ottoman Sultan, whose army had reached as far as Iraq, sent an Egyptian military expedition. Due to its extreme nature, Wahhabism was for a long time considered to be heretical in Islam, up until the time of the creation of the Kingdom of Saudi Arabia in the 1920s under British protection. Subsequently, the Kingdom's petroleum wealth allowed it to extend the influence of the Wahhabi doctrine to other Sunni Muslim communities throughout the world. Likewise, the Saudi system of state management of wealth and resources ended up influencing other Arab societies through various channels as the Kingdom expanded its influence in the Arab and Muslim worlds.

13.   Said, Edward, *Orientalism*, New York: Pantheon Books, 1978.

14.   Carré, Olivier, *Le Nationalisme arabe* (Arab Nationalism), Paris: Fayard, 1993.

15.   See Carré, Olivier, and Seurat, Michel, *Les Frères musulmans (1928–1982)* (The Muslim Brotherhood (1928–1982)), Paris: Gallimard, 1983; Kepel, Gilles, *The Prophet and the Pharaoh*, London: Saqi, 1985; Carré, Olivier, *Mysticism and Politics: A Critical Reading of Fi Zilal Al-Qur'an by Sayyid Qutb (1906–1966)*, Leiden: Brill, 2002; Roy, Olivier, *Islam and Resistance in Afghanistan*, Cambridge: Cambridge University Press, 1990; Étienne, Bruno, *L'Islamisme radical* (Radical Islamism), Paris: Hachette, 1987; Seurat, Michel, *L'État de barbarie* (State of Barbarism), Paris: Esprit/Seuil, 1989; Burgat, François, *The Islamic Movement in North Africa*, transl. William Dowell, Austin: University of Texas Press, 1997 (as well as *Face to Face with Political Islam*, London: IB Tauris, 1999; and *Islamism in the Shadow of Al Qaeda*, Austin: University of Texas Press, 2008).

16. It should be noted that this deep divide between Islamophiles and Islamophobes also corresponds to two schools of thought in the politics of the United States regarding the Arab world, that of researchers, diplomats and politicians who can be qualified as "accommodating" to political Islam and those who, conversely, consider it as a "green peril" that needs to be vigorously fought. See the description of the two schools in Do Ceu Pinto, Maria, *Political Islam and the United States. A Study of U.S. Policy towards Islamist Movements in the Middle East*, Reading: Garnet Publishing, 1999.

17. As Hudā Naʿma (Hoda Nehme) has done in *Abraz masālik al-fikr al-ʿilmānī waʾl-iṣlāḥī al-ʿarabī* (The Main Movements of Secular and Reformist Arab Thought), Kaslik, Lebanon: Publications de l'Université du Saint-Esprit-Kaslik (USEK), 2013.

18. Hourani, Albert, *Arabic Thought in the Liberal Age, 1798–1939*, Cambridge: Cambridge University Press, 1962.

19. Hudson, Michael, *Arab Politics: The Search for Legitimacy*, New Haven: Yale University Press, 1977, p. 2.

20. Ibid., p. 5.

21. Ibid., beginning on page 7.

22. Ayubi, Nazih N., *Over-stating the Arab State: Politics and Society in the Middle East*, London: IB Tauris, 1996.

23. Ibid., Chapter 1.

24. See Corm, Georges, *Le Proche-Orient éclaté. 1956–2012*, Paris: Gallimard, 1983, pp. 843-893.

25. See Henni, Ahmed, *Le Syndrome islamiste et les mutations du capitalisme* (The Islamist Syndrome and the Mutations of Capitalism), Paris: Éditions Non Lieu, 2008; an original reflection expanded in another work: *Le Capitalisme de rente. De la société industrielle à la société des rentiers* (Rentier Capitalism. From an Industrial Society to a Rentier Society), Paris: L'Harmattan, 2012.

26. See Sid-Ahmed, Abdelkader, *L'Économie arabe à l'heure des surplus pétroliers* (The Arab Economy at a Time of Oil Surpluses), Paris: ISMEA, 1975.

27. See Jūrj Qurm (Georges Corm), *Fī naqd al-iqtiṣād al-rayʾī al-ʿarabī* (Critique of the Arab Rentier Economy), Beirut: Markaz dirasāt al-waḥda al-ʿarabiyya, 2012.

28. See Ghandour, Abdel-Rahmane, *Jihad humanitaire. Enquête sur les ONG islamiques* (Humanitarian Jihad. Enquiry into Islamic NGOs), Paris: Flammarion, 2002.

CHAPTER 3

1. Corm, Georges, *L'Europe et le mythe de l'Occident*, Paris: La Découverte, 2009.

2. Boullata, Issa J., *Trends and Issues in Contemporary Arab Thought*, Albany, NY: State University of New York Press, 1990.

3. See also Corm, Georges, "Aux origines de l'instrumentalisation des trois monothéismes", (The Origins of the Instrumentalisation of the Three Monotheisms), *Diplomatie*, 16, August September 2013.

4. Zaydān, Yūsuf (Yusuf Zaydan), *Al-Lāhūt al-ʿarabī wa uṣūl al-ʿunf al-dinī* (Arab Theology and the Sources of Religious Violence), Cairo: Dār al-Shurūq, 2009 (several successive editions). This author also wrote a remarkable novel published by the same publisher in 2008, *ʿAzāzīl*, which describes the wanderings and torments of an Egyptian monk in the fifth century, who witnesses the end of Paganism and tries to find his way in the violent theological disagreements on the nature of Christ that were tearing apart the rival Eastern churches at the time.

5. On this dispute see Daniel Lancon, "Al-Afghani contre Ernest Renan: paroles orientales au coeur de l'empire, migration intellectuelle, traduction et transferts (1883–1884)" (Al-Afghani versus Ernest Renan: Oriental Theology and the Sources of Religious Violence (1883–1884)), in Ridha Boulaâbi (ed.), *Les Orientaux face aux orientalismes* (The Orientals in the Face of Orientalisms), preface by Georges Corm, Paris: Geuthner, 2013, pp. 41-66. This work is particularly rich in illustrating the mirror play of Orientalisms and counter-Orientalisms that I have discussed.

6. Edward Said, *Orientalism*, op. cit.; on this point see Nadīm Najdī (Nadim Najdi), *Athar al-istishrāq fī'l-fikr al-ʿarabī al-muʿāṣir* (The Influence of Orientalism on Contemporary Arab Thought), Beirut: Dār al-Fārābī, 2005.

7. See ʿAbd Allāh Ibrāhīm (Abdallah Ibrahim), *Al-thaqāfa al-ʿarabiyya waʾl-marjaʿiyyāt al-mustaʿāra* (Arab Culture and Imported Referential Norms), Rabat/Beirut: Arab Scientific Publishers/Dār al-Amān, 2010.

8. On this subject see Chibber, Vivek, 'Contre l'obsession des particularismes culturels: l'universalisme, une arme pour la gauche' (Against the Obsession with Cultural Particularisms: Universalism, a Weapon for the Left), *Le Monde diplomatique*, May 2014.

9. See in particular Sharabi, Hisham, *Arab Intellectuals and the West. The Formative Years, 1875–1920*, Baltimore: Johns Hopkins University Press, 1970.

10. Miquel, André, *L'Islam et sa civilisation, VIIe-XXe siècle* (Islam and its Civilisation: 7th to 20th Century), Paris: Armand Colin, 1968.

11. Edward Said, *Orientalism*.

12. In France, this is particularly the case regarding Michel Seurat, Bruno Étienne and François Burgat, who have assumed the role of defenders of the various movements of political Islam.

13. See Corm, Georges, *Orient-Occident. La fracture imaginaire* (East-West. The Imaginary Fracture), Paris: La Découverte, 2005.

14. See Naba, René, *Guerre des ondes… guerre des religions. La bataille hertzienne dans le ciel méditerranéen* (War of the Waves…War of Religions. The Hertzien Battle in the Mediterranean Sky), Paris: L'Harmattan, 1998. We cannot fail to mention in this regard the role played by Al-Jazeera over the past few years

through its weekly show hosted by the Syrian journalist Faisal Al-Qassim. He brings together two Arab intellectuals with completely opposing political views and gets them so worked up that they end up at each other's throats. The viewer witnesses a veritable cockfight in which the impossible reconciliation of points of view is mocked. This mockery attacks ideas and discredits thought itself. The mediocrity of this show contrasts with the atmosphere of dignity and respect that characterises the numerous interviews with the figureheads of religious fundamentalism, who are frequent guests of this channel's programs, such as the Shaykh Yusuf al-Qaradawi.

15.   This phenomenon has been accentuated by the predominant role played by European and American think tanks in contemporary knowledge production in the Arab world. A study of the think tanks that specialise in this region of the world undertaken at my request in 2014 by the Lebanese scholar Christian Bassil identified 255 foreign institutions. Of these, 40 per cent had their main offices located outside the Arab world and 32 per cent in the Arab world, and 60 per cent of them were American. They have far greater financial resources compared to local NGOs or think tanks, and they have existed for a much longer time. The average age of the foreign centres that study the Arab world was thirty-six years (forty-two for the United States) compared to eighteen for the Arab centres. This shows the imbalance in capacity to undertake research and produce studies that are aligned with the geopolitical interests of states.

16.   See Nāṣīf Naṣṣār (Nassif Nassar), *Tarīkh al-istiqlāl al-falsafī. Sabīl al-fikr al-ʿarabī ilā'l-ḥurriyya wa-l-istiqlāl* (The Road to Philosophical Independence. The Movement of Arab Thought towards Freedom and Creativity), Beirut: Dār al-Ṭalīʿa, 1975. This was a highly successful book.

17.   This is not the case in English, in which, as will be shown, several works have attempted to provide overviews of the most recent intellectual trends.

18.   Abdel-Malek, Anouar, *Contemporary Arab Political Thought*, London: Zed Books, 1984.

19.   Hourani, Albert, *Arabic Thought in the Liberal Age, 1798–1939*.

20.   Arkoun, Mohammed, *La pensée arabe*, Paris: PUF, 1975.

21.   Serouya, Henri, *La Pensée arabe* (Arab Thought), Paris: PUF, 1960.

22.   Monteil, Vincent, *Clefs pour la pensée arabe* (Keys to Understanding Arab Thought), Paris: Seghers, 1974.

23.   Berque, Jacques, *The Arabs: their History and Future*, London: Faber and Faber, 1964.

24.   See Al-Mūḥāfaẓa, ʿAlī (Ali al-Muhafaza), *Al-ittijāhāt al-fikriyya ʿind al-ʿarab fī ʿaṣr al-nahḍa 1797–1914. Al-ittijāhāt al-dīniyya wa'l-siyāsiyya wa'l-ijtimāʿiyya wa'l-ʿilmiyya* (Intellectual Orientations of the Arabs at the Time of the Renaissance. Religious, Political, Social and Scientific Orientations), Beirut: Al-Ahliyya li'l-nashr wa'l-tawzīʿ, 1975 (several successive editions).

25. Dakhli, Leyla, *Une génération d'intellectuels arabes. Syrie et Liban (1908–1940)* (A Generation of Arab Intellectuals. Syria and Lebanon (1908–1940)), Paris: IISMM/ Karthala, 2009.

26. See Hervé-Montel, Caroline, *Renaissance littéraire et conscience nationale. Les premiers romans en français au Liban et en Égypte (1908–1933)* (Literary Renaissance and National Consciousness. The First Novels in French in Lebanon and Egypt (1908–1933)), Paris: Geuthner, 2012.

27. Ibid., p. 526.

28. Ibid., p. 527.

29. Abdel-Malek, Anouar, Belal, Abdel Aziz, and Hanafi, Hassan (eds.), *Renaissance du monde arabe* (Renaissance of the Arab World), Louvain: Ducoulot, 1972; and Chevallier, Dominique (ed.), *Renouvellements du monde arabe, 1952–1982* (Renewals of the Arab World, 1952–1982), Paris: Armand Colin, 1987.

30. Khoury, Paul, *Tradition et modernité. Thèmes et tendances de la pensée arabe actuelle*)Tradition and Modernity. Themes and Trends in Current Arab Thought), Beirut/Jounieh: Librairie Saint-Paul, 1983.

31. Khoury, Paul, *Tradition et modernité. II. Matériaux pour servir à l'étude de la pensée arabe actuelle. Inventaire sélectif de la production littéraire arabe* (Tradition and Modernity II. Materials to Use for the Study of Current Arab Thought. Selective Inventory of Arab Literary Production), Beirut/Jounieh: Librairie Saint-Paul, 1984.

32. Khoury, Paul, *Tradition et modernité III. Matériaux pour servir à l'étude de la pensée arabe actuelle. Analyse descriptive d'ouvrages arabes typiques* (Tradition and Modernity III. Materials to Use for the Study of Current Arab Thought. Descriptive Analysis of Typical Arab Works), Beirut/Jounieh: Librairie Saint-Paul, 1985.

33. Khoury, Paul, *Tradition et modernité I. Instruments d'enquête* (Tradition and Modernity I. Instruments of Investigation), Münster/Jounieh: Librairie Saint-Paul, 1981.

34. Khoury, Paul, *Une lecture de la pensée arabe actuelle. Trois études* (A Reading of Current Arab Thought. Three Studies), Münster/Jounieh: Librairie Saint-Paul, 1981.

35. In 2010, the Antonine University in Lebanon paid tribute to Paul Khoury and his work by publishing a collective volume of his writings: Pascale Lahoud (ed.), *Boulos Khoury. Faylasūf al-lākāmil* (Paul Khoury, Philosopher of the Unfinished), Baabda, Lebanon: Publications de l'Université Antonine, 2010.

36. Elizabeth S. Kassab, *Contemporary Arab Thought. Cultural Critique in Comparative Perspective*, New York: Columbia University Press, 2010.

37. Boullata, Issa J., *Trends and Issues in Contemporary Arab Thought.*

38. Ibid., p. 6.

39. Ibid., p. 12.

40. Ibid., p. 163.

41. Khalīl, Khalīl Aḥmad (Khalil Ahmad Khalil), *Mawsū'at a'lām al-'arab al-mubdi'īn fī'l-qarn al-'ishrīn* (Encyclopaedia of Creative Arab People), Beirut: al-Mu'assasa al-'arabiyya li'l-dirāsāt wa'l-nashr, 2001.

42. See Al-Anṣārī, Muḥammad Jabir (Mohammed Jaber Al-Ansari), *al-Fikr al-'arabī wa ṣirā'at al-aḍdād* (Arab Thought and the Struggle of Opposites), Beirut: al-Mu'assasa al-'arabiyya li'l-dirāsāt wa'l-nashr, 1996. This work has two long subtitles on its cover: "How the approach to compromise contained the forbidden struggle between fundamentalism and secularism and delayed the solution between Islam and the West. A diagnosis of the situation of uncertainty in Arab life and absorption by compromise of forbidden dialectics." See also Muḥammad Ḍāhir (Muhammad Dahir), *Al-Ṣirā' bayn al-tayyārayn al-dīnī wa'l-'ilmānī fī'l-fikr al-'arabī al-ḥadīth* (The Struggle between the Two Religious and Secular Currents in Contemporary Arab Thought), Beirut: Dār Al-Bīrūnī, 1994; as well as Aziz Al-Azmeh, *Secularism in the Arab World: Contexts, Ideas and Consequences*, Edinburgh: Edinburgh University Press/Aga Khan University Institute for the Study of Muslim Civilisations, 2019.

43. Ra'īf Khūrī (Raif Khoury), *Al-fikr al-'arabī al-ḥadīth. Athar al-thawrat al-faransiyya fī tawjīhihi al-siyāsī wa'l-ijtimā'ī* (Modern Arab Thought. The Influence of the French Revolution on its Political and Social Orientation), Beirut: Dār Al-Makshūf, 1973 (2nd edition).

44. Mārūn 'Abbūd (Maroun Abboud), *Ruwwād al-nahḍa al-ḥadītha* (The Vanguards of the Modern Renaissance), Beirut: Dār Al-Thaqāfa, 1966.

45. Hisham Sharabi, *Arab Intellectuals and the West: The Formative Years, 1875–1914*, Baltimore: Johns Hopkins University Press, 1970. The Arabic edition of this book (*Al-muthaqqafūn al-'arab wa'l-gharb*, Beiruth: Dar El-Nahar, 1971) went through several editions.

46. See Corm, Georges, *Histoire du pluralisme religieux dans le bassin méditerranéen* (History of Religious Pluralism in the Mediterranean Basin), Paris: Geuthner, 1998.

47. Several years ago, during one of my meetings with Sharabi in Beirut, I had the opportunity to directly express my critique of the extreme oversimplifications contained in his work and to ask him to issue an amended edition. He acknowledged that the dichotomy between Christians and Muslims that he had adopted was not as relevant as he had believed it to be at the time. In reality, the entire framework of this book required revision. But the declining health of Sharabi, who was an endearing individual far removed from any religious fanaticism, rendered this impossible.

48. On the notion of universals see Kilani, Mondher, *Pour un universalisme critique. Essai d'anthropologie du contemporain* (Towards a Critical Universalism. An Essay on Contemporary Anthropology), Paris: La Découverte, 2014.

49. 'Abd Allāh Nu'mān (Abdallah Naaman), *Al-Ittijāhāt al-'ilmāniyya fī'l-'ālam al-'arabī* (Secular Tendencies in the Arab World), Jounieh (Lebanon): n.p., 1990.

50.   Nazik Saba Yared, *Secularism and the Arab World*, London: Saqi Books, 2002.
51.   Hudā Naʿma (Hoda Nehme), *Abraz masālik al-fikr al-ʿilmānī wa'l-iṣlāḥī al-ʿarabī.*

CHAPTER 4

1.   See Polanyi, Karl, *The Great Transformation: The Political and Economic Origins of Our Time*, New York: Farrar & Rinehart, 1944.
2.   For more on the upheavals created by the petroleum era in the workings of European and American democracies, we refer to the fine work by Mitchell, Timothy, *Carbon Democracy. Political Power in the Age of Oil*, London: Verso, 2011. This book also effectively demonstrates the destabilising influence of the Anglo-Saxon oil cartel on the oil-producing countries of the Middle East.
3.   Ibrahim, Sonallah, *Zaat*, Cairo: The American University in Cairo Press, 2004.
4.   Béji, Hélé, *Désenchantement national. Essai sur la décolonisation* (National Disenchantment. An Essay on Decolonisation), Paris: Maspero, 1982.
5.   ʿĀmil, Mahdī (Mahdi Amil), *Naqd al-fikr al-yawmī* (Critique of Day-to-Day Thought), Beirut: Dār Al-Fārābī, 1988.
6.   See Corm, Georges, *Dette et développement* (Debt and Development), Paris: Publisud, 1981; *Le Nouveau désordre économique mondial. Aux sources des échecs du développement* (The New World Economic Disorder. The Sources of the Failures of Development), Paris: La Découverte, 1993; *Fī naqd al-iqtiṣād al-rayʿī* (Critique of the Rentier Economy), Beirut: Center for Arab Unity Studies, 2011.
7.   Nonetheless, I refer to the exhaustive work of Khaled Ziade, *The Development of Muslim Perspectives of Europe*, Beirut: Riyyāḍ al-Rayyis Books, 2010 (translated into Arabic by the same publisher: *Taṭawwur al-naẓra al-islāmiyya ilā ūrūbā*); as well as *Al-Muslimūn wa'l-ḥadāthat al-ūrūbiyya* (Muslims and European Modernity), Cairo: Ruʾyāt li'l-nashr wa'l-tawzīʿ, 2010. The thorough work on the same topic by Nazik Sābā Yārid (Nazik Saba Yared) should also be mentioned: *Al-Raḥḥālūn al-ʿarab wa ḥaḍārat al-gharb fi'l-nahḍat al-ʿarabiyyat al-ḥadītha* (Arab Travellers and Civilisation in the West during the Modern Arab Renaissance), Beirut: Muʾassasat Nawfal, 1979.
8.   A fine work that addresses this point is that of Usāma ʿĀnūtī (Usama Anuti), *Al-Ḥarakat al-adabiyya fī bilād al-Shām khilāl al-qarn al-thāmin ʿashar* (The Literary Movement in Syrian Districts in the Eighteenth Century), Beirut: Publications de l'Université Libanaise, 1971. The author recounts how the educated class, composed mainly of religious men, developed an interest in the sciences of the mind (*al-ʿulūm al-ʿaqliyya*) and the rules of rationality. Based on this, he challenges the assertion that the Arab renaissance began in the nineteenth century as a result of the shock caused by Napoleon's expedition to Egypt, and describes instead how its origins can be traced back to the eighteenth century literary movement.

9.   For a detailed analysis of the work undertaken by this commission, see Corm, Georges, *L'Europe et l'Orient. De la balkanisation à la libanisation. Histoire d'une modernité inaccomplie* (Europe and the Orient. From Balkanisation to Lebanisation. History of an Unfinished Modernity), Paris: La Découverte, 1989.

10. Thomas Edward Lawrence (1888–1935) is referred to here, not to be confused with his contemporary, the great British writer whose last name he shares, David H. Lawrence (1885–1930). In addition to the reputation he earned from the success of his autobiographical account of his adventures in the deserts of Arabia, Lawrence as a character was featured in a successful 1962 film by David Lean which received many awards.

11. See Thomas, Bertram, *Les Arabes*, Paris: Payot 1946, p. 215, n. 1, according to which the Arab contingent numbered as many as 10,000 men during the mobilisation of the tribes of the Arabian Peninsula, but on average it remained closer to 2,000 permanent troops (English original: Bertram Thomas, *The Arabs: The Life Story of a People who Have Left Their Deep Impress on the World*, New York: Doubleday, 1937).

12. See O'Zoux, Raymond, *Les États du Levant sous mandat français* (The States of the Levant under the French Mandate), Paris: Librairie Larose, 1931. An uncompromising description of the mistakes made by the mandate power in Syria and in Lebanon was provided by De Saint-Point, Valentine, *La Vérité sur la Syrie par un témoin* (The Truth about Syria from a Witness), Paris: Librairie du Luxembourg, 1929. This work goes against the current of a vast hagiographic literature boasting about the actions of the French in the Levant. For an equally critical perspective of the French mandate in Syria, see Poulleau, Alice, *À Damas sous les bombes. Journal d'une Française pendant la révolte syrienne de 1924–1926* (In Damascus During the Bombing. A Frenchwoman's Diary of the Syrian Revolt of 1924–1926), Yvetot, France: Bretteville Frères, 1925 (re-issued at the initiative of François Burgat who wrote its preface: L'Harmattan, Paris, 2012).

13. See Khoury, Gérard, *La France et l'Orient arabe. Naissance du Liban moderne, 1914–1920* (France and the Arab East. The Birth of Modern Lebanon, 1914–1920), Paris: Armand Colin, 1993; also, by the same author, *Une tutelle coloniale. Le mandat français en Syrie et au Liban* (A Colonial Tutelage. The French Mandate in Syria and Lebanon), Paris: Belin, 2006; Longrigg, Stephen H., *Syria and Lebanon under French Mandate*, Oxford: Oxford University Press, 1958; Corm, Georges, *Le Liban contemporain. Histoire et société* (Contemporary Lebanon. History and Society), Paris : La Découverte, Paris.

14. From which was born the Wafd ('delegation') Party, which he founded in 1919 and which quickly became the most important political party in Egypt (and which still exists today).

CHAPTER 5

1.　Furthermore, the emir made a commitment to grant substantial autonomy to the Lebanese province of Mount Lebanon where Christians made up a majority of the population.

2.　It should nonetheless be noted that the Centre for Arab Unity Studies – which will be discussed later – translated a remarkable book that explains anti-Zionist Jewish thought: Yakov M. Rabkin, *A Threat from Within: A Century of Jewish Opposition to Zionism*, London: Zed Books, 2006. This book was also published in Morocco by Éditions Tarik (Casablanca).

3.　On this subject, see the very well documented work of Jabbūr, George (George Jabbour), *Al-'Urūba wa'l-Islām fi'l-dasātīr al-'arabiyya* (Arabism and Islam in Arab Constitutions), Aleppo: Dār Al-Rāḥa, 1993.

4.　The excellent work by Calculli, Marina should be noted here: *Le Néopatrimonialisme des régimes et l'échec du système régional arabe* (Regime Neopatronialism and the Failure of the Arab Regional System), Master 2 in Political Studies, Institut de sciences politiques, Université Saint-Joseph de Beirut, 2012.

5.　See Beau, Nicolas, *Paris, capitale arabe* (Paris: an Arab Capital), Paris: Seuil, 1995; as well as Beau, Nicolas and Jacques-Marie Bourget, *Le Vilain Petit Qatar* (Ugly Little Qatar), Paris: Fayard, 2013.

6.　*Al-Hayat* was purchased in 1990 by the powerful Saudi Minister of Defence, Khalid bin Sultan, and made it into one of the top two largest daily pan-Arab newspapers. It was distributed simultaneously in all of the major Arab and European capitals, as well as in the United States.

7.　It became the Organisation of Islamic Cooperation in 2011 and in 2014 counted fifty-seven member states.

8.　It is important to remember that Iran was the first state in the region to nationalise its European petroleum interests, those of Great Britain. The decision was made in 1952 by a great Iranian bourgeois liberal and nationalist, Prime Minister Mohammed Mossadegh. This was followed by a very tense period in Iran during which the Shah, who disagreed with the Prime Minister, left the country. He returned a few months later as part of a coup planned by the army and supported by the CIA as well as a large part of the Shi'i clergy. Mossadegh was removed from power, and Iranian oil was denationalised.

9.　Nonetheless, considerable in-depth knowledge in European academic traditions still exists, which can be seen in some doctoral theses. Some of these focus on the smallest details, which unfortunately are not always relevant to understanding the general evolution of Arab societies.

10.　However, the work of the Egyptian economist Fawzī Manṣūr (Fawzi Mansur) should be noted: *Khurūj al-'arab min al-tārīkh* (The Arabs' Exit from History), Beirut: Dār al-Fārābī, 1991 and Cairo: Maktabat Madbūlī, 1993. This Marxist analysis, to which I will return, emphasises two main points. The first concerns disagreements of a tribal and religious nature between Arabs, which resumed after the death of the Prophet, as well as the revolts of slaves and the poor. What appears to have driven the Abbasid Caliphs to surround themselves with Turkish and Persian Praetorian guards whose regiments were composed of slaves was an attempt to better neutralise the rival ambitions of Arab factions, some of which were based on religious claims. The second point concerns the economic regime of the time, notably the land tax that weighed heavily on rural areas and which was not used to build a bourgeois capitalist system. This very interesting work also discusses the failures of modern industrialisation from the experiments of Muhammad Ali to those of Nasser and Sadat in Egypt as well as those of Boumediene in Algeria. It includes a useful commentary by Samir Amin, who clarifies his ideological and analytical disagreements with orthodox Marxism regarding underdeveloped countries, designated by the generic term 'capitalist formations of the periphery.' Admittedly, well-respected Orientalists focused broadly on 'Islamic' decline, most often attributing it to the fossilised practice of Islam. See notably, Brunschvig, Robert and Gustave E. von Grunebaum (eds.), *Classicisme et déclin culturel dans l'histoire de l'islam* (Classicism and Cultural Decline in the History of Islam), Paris: Maisonneuve et Larose, 1977. But hardly any work can be found on the disappearance of the Arabs from the management of what remained of the great Abbasid Empire.

CHAPTER 6

1.   This concerns two of the Sultan's main acts that characterised the period known as the *Tanzimat* (or 'organising principles'), including important reforms led by the Ottoman Empire in the nineteenth century (between 1839 and 1878) which culminated in the adoption of a constitution in 1876, but whose application was quickly suspended by Sultan Abdulhamid II after the first elections were held in 1877; see Mantran, Robert (ed.), *Histoire de l'Empire ottoman* (History of the Ottoman Empire), Paris: Fayard, 1979; as well as Lewis, Bernard, *The Emergence of Modern Turkey*, Oxford: Oxford University Press, 1961.

2.   Referred to here are *Umm al-Qurā* (The Mother of Cities), Aleppo: n.p., 1902–1903; and *Ṭabāʾiʿ al-Istibdād* (The Nature of Despotism), Aleppo: n.p., 1900.

3.   al-Zayn, Zayn Nūr al-Dīn (Zayn Nur al-Din al-Zayn), *Nushʾ al-qawmiyyat al-ʿarabiyya maʿa dirāsāt tārīkhiyya fiʾl-ʿilāqāt al-turkiyyat al-ʿarabiyya* (The Birth of Arab Nationalism and Historical Studies of Turkish-Arab Relations), Beirut: Dār Al-Nahār, 1968. The same opinion can be found in another Arab thinker, Wajīh Kawtharānī (Wajih Kawtharani), *Wathāʾiq al-muʾtamar al-ʿarabī al-awwal 1913* (Documents from the First Arab Congress of Paris in 1913), Beirut: Dār al-Ḥadātha liʾl-ṭibāʿa waʾl-nashr waʾl-tawzīʿ, 1980.

4. See Ṣāyigh, Anīs (Anis Sayigh), *Al-Hāshimiyyūn wa qaḍiyat Filasṭīn* (The Hashemites and the Palestinian Question), Sidon/Beirut: Manshūrāt jarīdat al-muḥarrir wa'l-maktaba al-miṣriyya, 1966. The centre, directed by Sayegh and established in Beirut, was the target of a bombing during the 1982 Israeli invasion during which Sayegh was seriously injured causing him to lose an eye.

5. See Ali Allawi, *Feisal I of Iraq*, New Haven and London: Yale University Press, 2014; as well as the beautifully written biography by Khalid Ziyāda (Khaled Ziade), *Ḥikāyat Fayṣal* (The Story of Faysal), Beirut: Dār Al-Nahār, 1999.

6. See Fakkar, Rouchdi, *Reflets de la sociologie prémarxiste dans le monde arabe* (Reflections of Pre-Marxist Sociology in the Arab World), Paris: Geuthner, 1974.

CHAPTER 7

1. al-Tahtawi, Rifa'a, *L'Or de Paris: Relations de voyage (1826–1831)* (The Gold of Paris: Notes from a Voyage), translated from the Arabic, presented and annotated by Anwar Luqa, Paris: Sindbad, 1988.

2. On this point see the remarkable thesis written by Hamdi Abdelkader, 'L'Egypte dans "Le Voyage en Orient" de Gerard de Nerval et la France dans "L'Or de Paris" de Rifa'at Al-Tahtawi' (Egypt in Gerard de Nerval's *Journey to the East* and France in Rifa'at al-Tahtawi's *Gold of Paris*), Montreal: University of Quebec, 2008.

3. See Jomier, Jacques, *Le Commentaire coranique du Manar. Tendances modernes de l'exégèse coranique en Egypte* (The al-Manar – Qur'anic commentary: Modern Trends in Qur'anic Exegesis in Egypt), Paris : G.-P. Maisonneuve & Cie, 1954.

4. Ḥusayn, Ṭāhā (Taha Husayn), *Mudhakkirāt Ṭāhā Ḥusayn* (Taha Husayn's Memoirs), Beirut: Dār al-Adab, 1967 (in English: *A Passage to France*, transl. by Kenneth Cragg, Leiden: Brill, 1976).

5. Amīn, Aḥmad (Ahmad Amin), *Ḥayātī* (My Life), Cairo: Maktabat al-Nahḍa al-Miṣriyya, 1961 (4th edition) (in English: *My Life: The Autobiography of an Egyptian Scholar, Writer, and Cultural Leader*, Leiden: Brill, 1978).

6. See Amīn, Aḥmad (Ahmad Amin), *Zuʿamāʾ al-iṣlāḥ fī'l-ʿaṣr al-ḥadīth* (The Leaders of Reform in the Modern Era), Cairo: Maktabat al-Nahḍa al-Miṣriyya, 1965. This work begins with a very short biography of Muhammad ibn 'Abd al-Wahhab (fifteen pages), which clearly shows the shortcomings of this preacher's thought since it only concerned ridding Muslim religious practice of the worship of saints, and denounces the violence with which he and his followers attempted to impose their views. This contrasts with the remarkably detailed portraits of the other reformist figures, especially those of Jamal al-Din al-Afghani (60 pages), 'Abd Allah Nadim (46 pages), and Muhammad 'Abduh (57 pages).

7. For further information, see Perrin, Emmanuelle, 'Le creuset et l'orfèvre: le parcours d'Ahmad Amin (1886–1954)' (The Crucible and the Goldsmith: the Career of Ahmad Amin), *Revue des mondes musulmans de la Méditerranée*, no. 95-98, 2002, http://remmm.revues.org/238, accessed 1 March 2019.

8. Amin, Hussein Ahmad, *The Sorrowful Muslim's Guide*, transl. Nesrin Amin and Yasmin Amin, Edinburgh: Edinburgh University Press/Aga Khan University Institute for the Study of Muslim Civilisations, 2018.

9. Abdel Razek, Ali ('Alī 'Abd al-Rāziq), *Islam and the Foundations of Political Power*, ed. Abdou Filali-Ansary, transl. Maryam Loutfi, Edinburgh: Edinburgh University Press/Aga Khan University Institute for the Study of Muslim Civilisations, 2012.

10. Ṭāhā Ḥusayn (Taha Husayn), *Mudhakkirāt Ṭāhā Ḥusayn*. These memoirs provide a great deal of information on the French university curriculum at the time the author was studying in Paris. He earned his *licence,* followed by his DEA (Diplôme d'études approfondies) and his doctoral degree, in an era when Latin was still a requirement. He also writes of the difficulties experienced as a blind student with exceptional auditory abilities as he struggled to adjust to reading Braille texts. This involved touch as opposed to hearing, which up until that point had been his only means to accessing knowledge as he had learned to memorise what he heard through the spoken voice.

11. See Suzanne Taha Hussein, *Avec toi. De la France à l'Egypte* (With You. From France to Egypt), Paris: Cerf, 2011.

12. This title was appropriated by Frantz Fanon for one of his major works, *Les Damnés de la terre*, Paris: Maspero, 1961 (in English: *The Wretched of the Earth*, transl. Richard Philcox, New York: Grove Press, 1963).

13. Taha Hussein, *Le Livre des jours* (The Book of Days), Paris: Gallimard, 1984 (published in English as *An Egyptian Childhood*, London: George Routledge & Sons, 1932; and *The Stream of Days*, transl. Hilary Wayment, London: Longmans, Green and Co., 1948).

14. Taha Hussein, *Le Voyage intérieur* (The Journey Within), Paris: Gallimard, 1992 (in English: *A Passage to France*, transl. by Kenneth Cragg, Leiden: Brill, 1976).

15. Galal, Abdel Fattah, 'Taha Hussein (1889–1973)', *Prospects. The Quarterly Review of Comparative Education*, UNESCO, vol. 23, no. 3-4, 1993.

16. Both works have been translated into English: Amin, Qasim, *The Liberation of Women* and *The New Women. Two Documents in the History of Egyptian Feminism,* Cairo: American University of Cairo, 2000.

17. Fahmy, Mansour, *La condition de la femme dans la tradition et l'évolution de l'Islamisme*, Paris: Félix Alcan, 1913 (New edition, *La condition de la femme dans l'islam* (The Condition of Women in Islam), Paris: Alia, 1990). For more on this subject, see Al-Ahnaf, Mustapha 'Sur quelques durkheimiens arabes' (Concerning a Few Arab Durkheimians), *Peuples méditerranéens*, 54-55, January-June 1991. This article describes how Fahmy was strongly attacked in Egypt for his doctoral thesis which criticised the marital behaviour of the Prophet, who took several wives (beyond the maximum number of four as stipulated in the Qur'an). The author had to maintain a low profile for a number of years before he was able to

find a university position. Qasim Amin, in contrast, never faced any problems of this kind.

18. Abdallah el-Yafi, *La Condition privée de la femme dans le droit de l'islam* (The Deprived Condition of Women in the Law of Islam), Paris: IMP Graphique, 1929. During legislative elections in Lebanon in 1964, one of El-Yafi's opponents attacked him based on the content of this thesis, which in his view did not comply with traditional Islamic law.

19. For more on this feminist activist who passed away prematurely at the age of thirty-six, leaving as her legacy only her poetry along with numerous articles on the subject of women, see Jadʿān, Fahmī (Fahmy Gedaan), *Usus al-taqaddum ʿinda muffakirī al-islām fīʾl-ʿālam al-ʿarabī al-hadīth* (The Foundations of Progress in Muslim Thinkers in the Contemporary Arab world), Beirut: Al-Muʾassasa al-ʿarabiyya liʾl-dirāsāt waʾl-nashr, pp. 479-485.

20. See Zayn al-Dīn, Naẓīra (Nazira Zayn al-Din), *Al-Sufūr waʾl-ḥijāb* (Unveiling and Veiling), Beirut: Maṭbaʿat Kozma, 1928; as well as *al-fatāt waʾl-shuyūkh. Naẓarāt wa munāẓarāt fīʾl-sufūr waʾl-ḥijāb wa taḥrīr al-ʿaql waʾl marʾa waʾl tajaddud al-ijtimāʿi fīʾl-ʿālam al-islāmī* (The Young Woman and the Shaykhs. Opinions and Controversies on Unveiling and Veiling, the Liberation of Reason and Women, and Social Renewal in the Muslim World), Beirut: Imprimerie américaine, 1929. For more on this feminist activist who has been forgotten today and who was very inappropriately described in her biography as a pioneer of 'Islamic feminism,' (which illustrates the impact of the Islamist focus in the academic world), see Cooke, Miriam, *Nazira Zeineddine, A Pioneer of Islamic Feminism*, Princeton, NJ: One World, 2010.

21. See Carmen Boustani, 'May Ziadé: vie et écriture' (May Ziade: Her Life and Writing), Les Cahiers du GRIF, no. 143, 1990, pp. 163-169.

22. For more on this subject see Belton, Brian and Clare Dowding, 'Nawal El-Saadawi, a Creative and Dissident Life', March 2000, http://infed.org/mobi/nawal-el-saadawi-a-creative-and-dissident-life/, last accessed 1 Mar 2019.

23. Fatema Mernissi, *Sheherazade Goes West*, New York: Washington Square Press, 2001.

24. Fatema Mernissi, *The Veil and The Male Elite: A Feminist Interpretation Of Women's Rights In Islam*, Boston: Addison-Wesley, 1991; *Islam and Democracy: The Fear of the Modern World*, New York: Perseus Books, 1992; as well as *Beyond the Veil*, Cambridge, MA: Schenkmann, 1975.

25. Fatema Mernissi, *The Forgotten Queens of Islam*, Cambridge: Polity Press, 1993.

26. Fatema Mernissi, *Doing Daily Battle: Interviews with Moroccan Women*, Toronto: Women's Press, 1988.

27. Fatema Mernissi, *L'Amour dans les pays musulmans: A travers le miroir des textes anciens* (Love in Muslim Countries through the Mirror of Old Texts), Casablanca: Éditions Le Fennec, 2007.

28. See Philipp, Thomas, *Jurji Zaidan and the Foundations of Arab Nationalism*, Syracuse, NY: Syracuse University Press, 2014; as well as Zaidan, George C. and Thomas Philipp (eds.), *Jurji Zaidan's Contributions to Modern Arab Thought and Literature*, Washington, DC: The Zaidan Foundation, 2014.

29. Émir Abdelkader, *Lettre aux Français* (Letter to the French People), Algiers: ANEP, 2005.

30. See Haddad, Mouloud, 'Sur les pas d'Abdelkader: la hijra des Algériens en Syrie au XIXe siècle' (Following in the Footsteps of Abdelkader: The Hijra of the Algerians in Syria in the Nineteenth Century), in Ahmed Bouyerdene, Éric Geoffrey and Setty G. Simon-Khedis (eds.), *Abdelkader, un spirituel dans la modernité* (Abdelkader, a Spiritual Man in the Midst of Modernity), Beirut: Presses de l'Institut français du Proche-Orient, 2012.

31. Tahir Al-Jazairi (1852–1920) should also be mentioned here, the son of another Algerian emigré to Syria, as well as his nephew Salim (1879–1916), who founded a secret association (Al Jamʿiyyāt al-Qaḥṭāniyya) together with other Arab figures from the Mashriq, to defend the rights of Arabs in the face of Ottoman power (see Choueiri, Youssef, *Arab Nationalism. A History of Nation and State in the Arab World*, Oxford: Blackwell, 2000, pp. 117-150).

32. Jadʿān, Fahmī (Fahmy Gedaan), *Usus al-taqaddum ʿinda muffakirī al-jslām*.

33. Ibid., p. 549. This excerpt was translated from Arabic into French in the original French version of this book. The English translation here was translated from the French by the translators.

34. Ibid., p. 551.

35. Edward Said, *Orientalism*; for more on the lasting influence of Said's thought, see the very interesting volume edited by Ridha Boulaâbi (ed.), *Les Orientaux face aux orientalismes*.

36. Berberova, Nina, *The Italics are Mine*, transl. Philippe Radley, New York: Alfred A. Knopf, 1992, pp. 171-172. In a later passage, the author adds, 'But in the Russian intelligentsia the elements of revolution and reaction never counterbalanced anything, there was no common 'shu', perhaps because Russians are not often capable of compromise – and the very word, in the Western world full of great moderating and creative significance, has the imprint in Russian of petty dishonesty.' (p. 172). The same applies to the Arab world.

37. The Boxer Rebellion was started by a series of attacks against the dominant European presence in China that culminated in the assassination of a German diplomat and the siege of the Legations in Beijing. European powers responded with military force by sending more than 100,000 troops. China was humiliated again when it was forced to sign another unequal treaty in 1901, to pay compensation, and to accept the military occupation of several of its regions. The levels of violence reached during this war were intolerable.

38. Mervin, Sabrina, *Un réformisme chiite. Oulémas et lettrés du Gabal ʿAmil (actuel Liban-Sud) de la fin de l'Empire ottoman à l'indépendance du Liban* (A Shiʿi

Reformism. Ulama and Scholars of Jabal 'Amil (present-day Southern Lebanon) from the End of the Ottoman Empire to the Independence of Lebanon), Paris: Karthala/CERMOC/IFEADF, 2000.

39.　For a good description of this system, see Al-Seif, Tawfiq, *Islam, Democracy and its Limits. The Iranian Experience since 1979*, London: Saqi Books, 2007.

40.　It is important to mention here a very courageous work by two young Saudi Shi'i scholars who uncompromisingly denounced the politicisation of the Shi'i community in Saudi Arabia. The authors show how the religious leaders of the Shi'i community, facing pressure and even persecution by the Saudi authorities, play the sectarian card rather than building a unifying national consciousness. See al-Ibrāhīm, Badr (Badr al-Ibrahim) and al-Ṣādiq, Muḥammad (Muhammad al-Sadiq) *Al-Ḥirāk al-shī'ī fī'l-sa'ūdiyya. Tasyīs al-madhab wa madhabat al-siyāsa* (The Shi'i Movement in Saudi Arabia. Politicisation of the Community and Communitarisation of Politics), Beirut: Al-Shabaka al-'arabiyya li'l-abḥāth wa'l-nashr, 2013.

CHAPTER 8

1.　Choueiri, Youssef, *Arab Nationalism*. This exhaustive work also connects the Arab nationalist struggle at this time with the circumstances facing the Ottoman Empire, which was increasingly being weakened by European colonial powers. It paints a very vivid portrait of numerous nationalist thinkers and activists, mainly from Syria, Lebanon, and Palestine. The Arabic edition of this book bears the very eloquent title of *Masārat al 'Urūba. Naẓra tārīkhiyya* (The Paths of Arab Identity. A Historical Perspective). Beirut: Centre for Arab Unity Studies, 2002 and 2012 (updated and expanded version). From the same author see *Arab History and the Nation-State. A Study in the Modern Arab Historiography, 1820– 1980*, New York: Routledge, 1989. See also Khalidi, Rashid (ed.), *The Origins of Arab Nationalism*, New York: Columbia University Press, 1991.

2.　See especially Khālid, Khālid Muḥammad (Khalid Muhammad Khalid), *Min hunā nabda'* (This is Where We Should Start), Cairo: Dār al-Nīl li'l-Ṭibā'a, 1950. This work was condemned by Al-Azhar. They attempted to have all copies confiscated, but the courts refused. This book, a true manifesto for a secular state, went through several editions. It was followed by another book on the heritage of the world's great humanist ideas: *Afkār fī'l-qimma. Ilaina...yā man at'abakum al-ẓalām* (Thoughts at the Summit. Come to us... Those Made Weary by Obscurity), Cairo: Maktabat Wahba, 1962. The remainder of the large body of work by this author is devoted to an open-minded rereading of Islamic religious heritage.

3.　See Corm, Georges, *Orient-Occident. La fracture imaginaire* (Orient-West. The Imaginary Fracture), Paris: La Découverte, 2002; and *L'Europe et le mythe de l'Occident. La construction d'une histoire* (Europe and the Myth of the West), Paris: La Découverte, 2009.

4. See Jabbūr, George (George Jabbour), *Al-ʿUrūba waʾl-Islām fiʾl dasātīr al-ʿarabiyya.*

5. al-Rīḥānī, Amīn (Amin Al-Rihani), *Al-Qawmiyyāt* (Nationalisms), Beirut: Dār Rīḥānī liʾl-ṭibāʿa waʾl-nashr, 1956.

6. Al-Rihani, Amin, *Kings of Arabia*, Princeton, NJ: Spencer Trask Foundation/ Princeton University, 1930 (see the website dedicated to this author listing all of his publications: www.ameenrihani.org).

7. Abdel-Malek, Anouar, *La Pensée politique arabe contemporaine.*

8. Al-Azmeh, Aziz, *Constantine Zurayk ʿArabī liʾl-qarn al-ʿashrīn* (Constantine Zurayk, an Arab for the Twentieth Century), Beirut: Institut des études palestiniennes, 2003.

9. ʿAbd Allāh ʿAbd al-Dāʾim (Abdallah Abd al-Daim), *Al-qawmiyya al-ʿarabiyya waʾl niẓām al-ʿālamī al-jadīd* (Arab Nationalism and the New World Order), Beirut: Dār al-Adab, 1994. This work is a collection of lectures and articles that address the issues and controversies related to Arab nationalism.

10. Ibid., p. 29.

11. Ibid., p. 33.

12. See Dandashlī, Muṣṭafā (Mustafa Dandachli), *Ḥizb al-Baʿath al-ʿarab al-ishtirākī 1940–1963, Idiyūlūjiya wa tārīkh siyāsī* (The Socialist and Arab Baath Party 1940–1963. Ideology and Political History), Beirut: n.p., 1979. This remarkable work on the history of the party thoroughly exposes the reasons for its divisions and its failures. For a work in French, see Audo, Antoine, *Zaki Al-Arsouzi. Un Arabe face à la modernité* (Zaki al-Arsuzi. An Arab Facing Modernity), Beirut: Dar El-Machrek, 1988, which relies heavily on Arsouzi's Alawite background to explain the content of his thought.

13. Dandashlī, Muṣṭafa, *Ḥizb al-Baʿath al-ʿarab al-ishtirākī*, pp. 15-20.

14. In 1961, when a military coup was staged by a group of Syrian officers who were rebelling against the union with Egypt established in 1958, Nasser refused to use force against them despite the request by Syrian authorities and the large protests in Syria in support of Nasser. The Egyptian President subsequently gave the order to Egyptian soldiers stationed in Syria to withdraw.

15. It was in this context that Michel Aflaq, a Christian, gave a magnificent lecture on April 5, 1943 at the University of Damascus on the occasion of the birthday of the Prophet Muhammad. The text of this lecture has been published in many complete works under the title 'Remembering the Arab prophet' (*dhikrā al-rasūl al-ʿarabī*). The main writings and transcripts of lectures by Michel Aflaq until the end of the 1950s were collected in Michel Aflaq, *Fī sabīl al-Baʿath* (On the Path of the Baath), Beirut: Dār al-Ṭalīʿa, 1959. Dār al-Ṭalīʿa, a publisher known for its progressive and Baathist leanings, also published several volumes of official party documents during the 1960s under the title *Niḍāl al-Baʿath fī sabīl al-waḥda waʾl-ḥurriya waʾl-ishtirākiya* (The Baath Struggle for Unity, Liberty, and Socialism).

16. al-Razzāz, Munīf (Munif al-Razzaz), *Al-tajruba al-murra* (The Bitter Experience), Beirut: Dār Ghandūr, 1967.

17. See Corm, Georges, *Le Proche-Orient éclaté*.

18. Balta, Paul, and Rulleau, Claudine (eds.), *La Vision nassérienne* (The Nasserist Vision), Paris: Sindbad, 1982.

19. For further details, see Corm, Georges, *Le Proche-Orient éclaté*.

20. See Naṣr, Mārlīn (Marlène Nasr), *Al-taṣṣawur al-qawmī al-ʿarabī fī fikr Jamāl ʿAbd al-Nāṣir (1952–1970). Dirāsa fī ʿilm al-mufradāt waʾl-dalāla* (The Arab Nationalist Vision in the Thought of Gamal Abdel Nasser (1952–1970). A Study of Semantics and the Meaning of Concepts), Beirut: Markaz dirasāt al-waḥda al-ʿarabiyya, 1981.

21. There are two important works in French that need to be mentioned, one by Lacouture, Jean, *Nasser*, Paris: Seuil, 1971; and another by the same author written with Simone Lacouture, *L'Egypte en mouvement* (Egypt on the Move), Paris: Seuil, 1956. Finally, it would be unthinkable not to mention the excellent book by Berque, Jacques, *L'Egypte. Impérialisme et révolution* (Egypt. Imperialism and Revolution), Paris: Gallimard, 1967, which stops at the Nasserist period but provides in broad brush strokes a rather interesting sociological and cultural timeline of all of the revolutionary events that took place in Egypt to undermine British domination.

22. FLOSY eliminated the Yemeni National Liberation Front under the influence of Nasser to the extent that, as soon as South Yemen became independent and British troops were evacuated in 1967, and the country was named the People's Republic of South Yemen (later to become the People's Democratic Republic of Yemen in 1970), FLOSY became the sole political party. The unification of both parts of Yemen, the north and the south, did not take place until 1990. It is important to mention here the excellent and moving biography of a Lebanese doctor who studied in France in the 1960s, where he was involved in Arab student associations. He subsequently left as a physician to join the resistance against the British occupation in the province of Dhofar, on the border between the Sultanate of Oman and occupied South Yemen. Afterwards, he returned to Lebanon to devote himself to humanitarian medical action where he almost lost his life during combat between various Lebanese (and Palestinian) factions. See Mehanna, Kamel, *Un médecin libanais engagé dans la tourmente des peuples. Les choix difficiles* (A Lebanese Doctor Engaged in the Struggles of Peoples. Difficult Choices), Paris: L'Harmattan, 2013.

CHAPTER 9

1. Khalil Saadeh, a physician, was a political activist in favour of independence for the entire Syro-Lebanese region from the time of the First World War. He wrote extensively in the Arabic-language press read by immigrants in Latin America

and elsewhere and gave many speeches to Lebanese and Syrian immigrant associations. A collection of his letters was published in two volumes: Saʿāda, Khalīl (Khalil Saadeh), *Sūriyya. Min al-ḥarb waʾl-majaʿa ilā muʾtamar al-ṣulḥ* (Syria from War and Famine to the Congress of Peace); and *Sūriyya waʾl-intidāb al-faransī* (Syria and the French Mandate 1920–1923), Beirut: Muʾassasat Saʿāda liʾl-thaqāfa (Saadeh Cultural Foundation), 2014, texts collected and presented by Badr al-Hajj and Salim Mujais.

2. This expression became very fashionable during the 1975–90 war in Lebanon, which pitted the coalition of the so-called 'Christian' parties against the coalition formed by the alliance between Palestinian revolutionary movements and so-called Lebanese 'progressive' parties. The Christian coalition was qualified by the latter as 'isolationist.'

3. Riad El-Sohl (1894–1951) had promoted the country's independence in 1943 and established a national pact between Christians and Muslims, together with the first president of the independent Lebanese Republic, Bechara el-Khoury (1890–1964). He was assassinated in 1951.

4. During the inter-war period, sympathy for fascism was strong in both Europe and the Middle East. In the Arab world, the idea of a strong leader who is respected and the notion of a highly structured party were very prevalent. In addition, Italy, Spain, and Germany were all opposed to the two colonial powers that dominated the Arab world. The Phalangist Party in Lebanon, created in the 1930s, initially brought together many intellectuals and respectable figures (who quickly left the party soon afterwards).

5. The Saadeh Cultural Foundation published the first two volumes of a very detailed biography of Antoun Saadeh: Mujais, Salim, *Antoun Saadé: A Biography (Vol. 1, The Youth Years)*, Beirut: Kutub, 2004; *Vol. 2, Years of the French Mandate*, Beirut: Kutub, 2009. Saadeh's widow left behind a very interesting memoir that provides a great deal of information about her husband's difficult relationship with the Syrian authorities (see Saʿāda, Juliette al-Mīr (Juliette al-Mir Saadeh), *Ḥawliyyāt. Mudhakkirāt al-amīna al-ūlā* (Chronicles. The Memoirs of Juliette al-Mir Saadeh, First Party Secretary), Beirut: Dār Saʿāda liʾl-nashr, 2004).

6. See Faligot, Roger, *Tricontinentale, Quand Che Guevara, Ben Barka, Cabral, Castro et Hô Chi Minh préparaient la révolution mondiale (1964–1968)* (Tricontinental Conference. When Che Guevara, Ben Barka, Cabral, Castro and Hô Chi Minh Prepared World Revolution), Paris: La Découverte, 2013.

7. Ben Barka, Mehdi, *Écrits Politiques (1957–1965)* (Political writings (1957–1965)), Paris: Syllepse, 1999.

8. Mauritania had previously been involved, but renounced its part of the former Spanish-occupied territory.

9. Suleiman, Yasir, *The Arabic Language and National Identity. A Study in Ideology*, Washington, DC: Georgetown University Press, 2003.

10. Khalidi, Walid, 'Thinking the Unthinkable,' *Foreign Affairs*, 56(4), July 1978: 695–713.

11. Khalidi, Walid (ed.), *From Haven to Conquest. Readings in Zionism and the Palestine Problem until 1948*, Beirut: Publications of the Institute for Palestine Studies, 1971.

12. Kassir, Samir, and Farouk Mardam-Bey, *Itinéraires de Paris à Jérusalem. La France et le conflit israélo-arabe* (Paris-Jerusalem Itineraries. France and the Arab-Israeli Conflict), Paris: Les livres de la Revue d'études palestiniennes, 1993.

13. These include, for example, 'The Israeli Security Industry, Strategic and Economic Functions,' 'The Iranian Nuclear Project. The Israeli View of its Consequences and Ways to Address It,' and even 'Shedding Light on the Impasse of Palestinian Political Elites' (essays published in Arabic).

CHAPTER 10

1. al-Ḥāfiẓ, Yāsīn (Yasin al-Hafiz), *Al-hazīma wa'l-īdīyūlūjiyyā al-mahzūma* (The Defeat and Defeatist Ideology), Beirut: Dār al-Ṭalīʿa, 1979.

2. al-Ḥāfiẓ, Yāsīn (Yasin al-Hafiz), *Al-lā ʿaqlāniyya fī'l-siyāsat al-ʿarabiyya* (Irrationality in Arab Politics), Beirut: Dār al-kunūz al-adabiyya, 1975.

3. al-Ḥāfiẓ, Yāsīn (Yasin al-Hafiz), *Al-tajribat al-tarīkhiyyat al-fitnāmiyya* (The Vietnamese Historical Experience: A Comparative Critical Evaluation with Arab Historical Experience), Beirut: Dār al-Ḥaṣṣad li'l-Nashr wa'l-Tawzīʿ, 1976.

4. al-Ḥāfiẓ, Yāsīn (Yasin al-Hafiz), *Ḥawl baʿaḍ qaḍāyā al-thawrat al-ʿarabiyya* (On Some of the Problems of the Arab Revolution), Damascus: Dār al-Ḥasad, 1997 (second edition).

5. Frantz Fanon (1925–1961) was a psychiatrist of Caribbean origin who in 1955 joined the ranks of the Algerian FLN as a doctor and treated the serious psychological disorders of the militant fighters that resulted from the war. Fanon's works had a strong influence in developing countries, and include *Black Skin, White Masks* (trans. Richard Philcox, New York: Grove Press, 2008), and especially *The Wretched of the Earth* (trans. Richard Philcox, New York: Grove Press, 2005), his most famous work, the preface of which was written by Jean-Paul Sartre. In the latter, Fanon specifically warned against the temptation of the elites in newly independent states to allow themselves to be corrupted by the former colonial powers. He also called for avoiding the pitfall of 'folklorisation' and exploitation of national cultural heritage, especially religious heritage, and instead to continue the fight for the wellbeing of the underclasses.

6. al-Ḥāfiẓ, Yāsīn, *Ḥawl baʿaḍ qaḍāyā al-thawrat al-ʿarabiyya*, pp. 42-43.

7. Ibid., p. 44.

8. Ibid., p. 45.

9. Ibid., p. 51.

10. al-ʿAẓm, Ṣādiq Jalāl (Sadiq Jalal al-Azm), *Naqd al-fikr al-dīnī*, Beirut: Dār al-Ṭaliʾa, 1967.

11. Issued on February 14, 1989, this fatwa by Khomeini paved the way for similar fatwas to be issued subsequently against Muslims or non-Muslims accused of damaging the reputation of the Prophet.

12. One of his major works was published in English and Arabic in 1992. It was entitled, 'The Mental Taboo, Salman Rushdie and the Truth within Literature,' (London: Riyāḍ el-Rayyis Books, 1992). Beyond his defense of Rushdie, in this book al-Azm specifically returns to his critical analysis of Edward Said's work as well as the that of the poet Adonis (Ali Ahmad Said) and some of his studies of the politico-cultural issues tearing the Arab world apart: the relationship with the United States, missteps regarding the Palestinian question, and the defense of philosophy as an element of progress, etc.

13. The same quirk even affected someone as learned as Kamal Joumblatt of Lebanon, a political figure and recipient of the International Lenin Peace Prize and head of the Lebanese Palestinian-Progressive Coalition from 1975–1990, a period of violent instability in Lebanon. In his memoirs, he writes that the Maronite community had oppressed Lebanese Muslims in the same way that white South Africans had oppressed the African majority, which he felt was the main factor explaining the 'civil' war (see Joumblatt, Kamal, *Pour le Liban* (For Lebanon), interviews conducted by Philippe Lapousterle, Paris: Stock, 1978).

14. Adūnis (Adonis), *Al-thābit wa al-mutaḥawwil: baḥth fī al-ibdāʿ wa al-ittibāʿ ʿind al-ʿarab* (The Constant and the Changing: A Study in Creativity and Imitation among Arabs), 7ᵗʰ ed., Beirut: Dār al-Sāqī, 1994 (first published 1973).

15. Laroui, Abdallah, *L'Idéologie arabe contemporaine* (Contemporary Arab Ideology), Paris: Maspero, Paris, p. 17.

16. Ibid., p. 27.

17. Ibid., p. 28.

18. Ibid., p. 145.

19. Ibid., p. 153.

20. Ibid., p. 163-164.

21. Laroui, Abdallah, *The Crisis of the Arab Intellectual. Traditionalism or Historicism?*, trans. Diarmid Cammell, Berkeley: University of California Press, 1977.

22. Laroui, Abdallah, *Islam et modernité* (Islam and Modernity), Paris: La Découverte, 1983.

23. Ibid., p. 93.

24. Ibid., p. 96.

25. al-ʿArwī, ʿAbd Allāh (Abdallah Laroui), *Mafhūm al-dawla* (The Concept of the State), Casablanca: Al-Markaz al-thaqāfī al-ʿarabī, 1981; *Mafhūm al-idīyūlūjiya. Al-adluja* (The Concept of Ideology. Ideologisation), Casablanca/Beirut: Al-Markaz al-thaqāfī al-ʿarabī/Dār al-Farabī, 1980; and

finally, *Mafhūm al-Ḥurriya* (The Concept of Liberty), Al-Markaz al-thaqāfī Casablanca: al-ʿarabī, 1981.

26.　al-ʿArwī, ʿAbd Allāh (Abdallah Laroui), *Al-ʿArab waʾl-fikr al-tārīkhī* (The Arabs and Historical Thought), Beirut: Dār al-Ḥaqīqa, 1973.

27.　Anwar Abdel-Malek became well known for his works on Egypt (especially *L'Égypte société militaire* (Egypt, a Military Society) and *L'Égypte moderne. Idéologie et renaissance nationale* (Modern Egypt. Ideology and National Renaissance) and his Marxist-inspired works on the sociology of Arab countries. Other writings focused on the 'nationalitarian' phenomenon, the 'dialectics of civilisations' in the light of Marxism, and the sociology of imperialism and military institutions in the developing world. These writings were published in a collected volume, Abdel-Malek, Anouar, *La Dialectique sociale* (Social Dialectics), Paris: Seuil, 1972.

28.　See Riad, Hassan, *L'Égypte nassérienne* (Nasserist Egypt), Paris: Minuit, 1964. Samir Amin wrote this book under a borrowed name out of fear of being imprisoned whilst he was still living in Cairo and Nasser's regime was persecuting Communists as well as the Muslim Brotherhood.

29.　See Amīn, Samīr (Samir Amin), *Azmat al-mujtamaʿ al-ʿarabī* (The Crisis of Arab Society), Cairo: Dār al-Mustaqbal al-ʿarabī, 1985. The publisher was careful to note in the preface that they disagreed with the author's framework of analysis, particularly regarding the Soviet and Chinese experiences.

30.　Ibid., p. 147 and subsequent pages of sub-chapter entitled, 'L'impasse du salafisme et de l'occidentalisation' (The Impasse of Salafism and Westernisation).

31.　Ibid., p. 150.

32.　Ibid., pp. 208-209.

33.　ʿĀmil, Mahdī (Mahdi Amil), *Azmat al-ḥaḍārat al-ʿarabiyya am azmat al-burjwāziyāt al-ʿarabiyya* (The Crisis of Arab Civilisation or the Crisis of Arab Bourgeoisies), Beirut: Dār al-Fārābī, 1974.

34.　Ibid., p. 130.

35.　Ibid., pp. 124-125.

36.　Mahdi Amil, *Naqd al-fikr al-yawmī* (Critique of Day-to-Day Thought), Beirut: Dār al-Fārābī, 1988.

37.　Adūnis (Adonis), *Al-thābit wa al-mutahawwil: baḥth fi al-ibdāʿ wa al-ittibāʿ ʿind al-ʿarab* (The Constant and the Changing: A Study in Creativity and Imitation among Arabs), 7th ed., Beirut: Dār al-Sāqī, 1994 (first published 1973).

38.　Ibid., p. 128.

39.　Ibid., pp. 147-150.

40.　Ibid., pp. 157.

41.　Jacques Berque, *Les Arabes d'hier à demain* (The Arabs from Yesterday to Tomorrow), Paris: Éditions du Seuil, 1960.

42.　Frantz Fanon, *The Wretched of the Earth*, transl. Richard Philcox, New York: Grove Press, 1963.

43.   Ibid.

44.   Ibid., n. 156.

45.   Ibid.

46.   Muruwwa, Ḥusayn (Husayn Mroué), *Al-nizāʿāt al-mādiyya fī'l-falsafat al-ʿarabiyya* (Materialist Conflicts in Arab and Islamic Philosophy), Beirut: Dar al-Fārābī, 1978.

47.   See Diyāb, Samīr (Samir Diyab), *Shajarat al-maʿarifa al-muthmira fī fikr shaykh al-maʿarifa al-mādiya. Al-mufakkir Ḥusayn Muruwwa* (The Fruitful Tree of Knowledge in the Thought of the Shaykh of Materialist Knowledge. The Thinker Husayn Mroué), www.lakome.com.

48.   See Abuzaid, Samir 'Professor Tayyeb Tizini', *Philosophers of the Arabs*, ur1.ca/jehkr.

49.   Khūrī, Ra'īf (Raif Khoury), *Ḥuqūq al-insān. Min ayna wa ilā ayna al-masir?* (Human Rights, Origins and Future), Beirut: Manshūrāt majallat al-Ṭalīʿa,1937. This text was written at a time when the havoc wrought by Stalin's reign in the Soviet Union was not yet widely known, at least not in the Middle East.

CHAPTER 11

1.   See Corm, Georges, *L'Europe et l'Orient. De la balkanisation à la libanisation. Histoire d'une modernité inaccomplie* (Europe and the Orient. From Balkanisation to Lebanisation. History of an Unfinished Modernity), Paris: La Découverte, 1989.

2.   See Laoust, Henri, *Les Schismes en islam. Introduction à une étude de la religion musulmane* (Schisms in Islam. Introduction to a Study of the Muslim Religion), Paris: Payot, 1965. The author, a remarkable scholar of Islamic theology and all of its schools, had no qualms about including Wahhabism among the heretical movements. He correctly showed that even within Sunnism, the dominant dogma of Islam, Ibn 'Abd al-Wahhab was in conflict with all of the major theologians of classical Islam. Wahhab's only model was Ibn Taymiyyah, a figure from the fourteenth century who had often been imprisoned for his extremist religious opinions in repudiating the philosophical and mystical openness of classical Islam, especially his incitements to kill non-Sunni members of Muslim religious minorities. It should be noted that the Ottoman Empire declared Wahhabism to be a dangerous, heretical movement and sent an expedition led by Muhammad 'Ali in the early nineteenth century to attempt to eradicate it and put an end to its conquests.

3.   Thus Jacques Pirenne, nonetheless a historian of great renown, described within the same historical periodisation the emergence of Wahhabism in the eighteenth century and that of the great liberal reform of Arab thought from the beginning of the nineteenth century to the mid-twentieth century. He categorised these phenomena together as the expression of Muslim nationalist reform in response

to the expansion of Western imperialism, with very little awareness of the distortion this creates. (See Pirenne, Jacques, *Les Grands Courants de l'histoire universelle* (The Major Currents of Universal History), Neuchâtel: La Baconnière, 1959, volume 5, pp. 460-463; see also, as a kind of counterclaim, in Chapter 7 above, the great reformist thinker Ahmad Amin's critique of the narrow-mindedness of the Wahhabi doctrine and its penchant for violence.

4.   For more details on this question see Corm, Georges, *L'Europe et l'Orient,* pp. 174-192.

5.   This was pointed out in a timely way by Badr al-Ibrahim, a very learned young Saudi physician, whose book on the politicisation of the Shi'i community in Saudi Arabia has been previously cited here, in an excellent article in which he compared the new war-like Islamic movement, Daesh, to Wahhabism: al-Ibrāhīm, Badr (Badr al-Ibrahim), 'Dā'ish wa'l-wahhābiyya wa'l-takfiriyya: al-ikhtilāf wa'l-tashabbuh' (Daesh, Wahhabism and Takfirism: Differences and Similarities), *al-Akhbār,* Beirut, 3 September 2014.

6.   Elshobaki, Amr, *Les Frères musulmans des origines à nos jours* (The Muslim Brotherhood from its Origins to the Present Day), Paris: Karthala, 2009.

7.   However, the unity of Pakistan, founded in 1947, was ended by a bloody independence war with the Bengalis who made up East Pakistan and were subjected to domination by West Pakistan. The war led to the creation of the independent state of Bangladesh in 1971. This proves once again, if proof were still needed, that religion alone is not enough to constitute a nation.

8.   Qutb, Sayyid, *La Justice sociale en Islam* (Social Justice in Islam), transl. Diah Saba Jazzar, Beirut: Dār Al-Bīrūnī, 2003 (the original edition was published in Cairo in 1948).

9.   Qutb, Sayyid, *Social Justice in Islam*, transl. John B. Hardie, Oneonta, NY: Islamic Publications International, 2002.

10. Ibid., p. 9.

11. An aspect of Qutb's work that was critiqued in a very realistic way by Samir Amin (see *supra*, Chapter 10).

12. These itineraries are parallel to those of European intellectuals, particularly French intellectuals, who went from a Marxist-type progressivism to a conservative neoliberalism (Bernard-Henri Lévy, Alain Finkielkraut, Annie Kriegel, Alexandre Adler, Stéphane Courtois, among others).

13. See Burgat, François, *L'Islamisme en face,* pp. 60-68 (English translation: *Face to Face with Political Islam,* London: IB Tauris, 1999), which focuses on the narrative of Adel Hussein's 'conversion' (the quote is taken from page 67). Moreover, Burgat describes it at length as something analogous to that of Tariq al-Bishri. I actually got to know Hussein very well, as he lived in Lebanon in the 1960s. When the two of us were having lunch in Cairo in the early 1990s, I asked him about this surprising conversion. He denied the fact that it was only driven by his desire to remain relevant within the Egyptian political scene

in which progressive ideology had been disparaged and Islamist ideology was on the rise!

14. See Aṭwī, Thanā' (Sana Atwi), *Ḥiwārāt fī'l-masārāt al-muta'akisa. Taḥawwulāt al-muthaqqaf al-lubnānī mundh sittīniyyāt al-qarn al-'ashrīn* (Dialogues on Contradictory Pathways. The Transformations of the Lebanese Intellectual since the 1960s), Beirut: Bīsān, 2013. One of these intellectuals of Christian faith converted to Shi'ism, another went from belonging to Palestinian revolutionary movements (Popular Front for the Liberation of Palestine) to belonging to the Lebanese Forces, a Christian militia that carried out gruesome massacres during the war in Lebanon from 1975 to 1990, and still another from Marxism and Arab nationalism to working for the Saudi-Lebanese multi-billionaire Rafiq Hariri, etc.

15. See Laurens, Henri, *Le Royaume impossible. La France et la genèse du monde arabe* (The Impossible Kingdom. France and the Genesis of the Arab World), Paris: Armand Colin 1990; as well as Rey-Goldzeiguer, Annie, *Le Royaume arabe. La politique arabe de Napoléon III (1861–1870)* (The Arab Kingdom. The Arab Policy of Napoleon III (1861–1870)), Algiers: SNED, 1977.

16. One of the books that attests to this was written by a former CIA agent, Eveland, Wilbur Crane, *The Ropes of Sand. America's Failure in the Middle East*, New York: Norton, 1980.

17. See Baer, Robert, *Sleeping with the Devil: How Washington Sold Our Soul for Saudi Crude*, New York: Three Rivers Press, 2003; as well as Beau, Nicolas and Jacques-Marie Bourget, *Le Vilain Petit Qatar.*

18. This is very well conveyed in a book by the former president of the Islamic Republic of Iran, Bani Sadr, Abolhassan, *Le Complot des ayatollahs* (The Conspiracy of the Ayatollahs), Paris: La Découverte, 1989.

19. Note that these two words are the same in both Arabic and Persian.

20. See Corm, Georges, *Pour une approche profane des conflits* (Towards a Secular Approach to Conflicts), pp. 204-246.

CHAPTER 12

1. Muḥammad 'Ābid al-Jābirī's (Mohammed Abed al-Jabri) main works include, most notably, *Naḥnu wa'l-turāth* (Heritage and Us), Casablanca: Al-Markaz al-thaqāfī al-'arabī, 1980; *Takwīn al-'aql al-'arabī* (The Formation of the Arab Mind), Beirut: Dār al-Ṭalī'a, 1984; *Buniat al-'aql al-'arabī* (The Structure of the Arab Mind), Casablanca: Al-Markaz al-thaqāfī al-'arabī, 1986; and other works, including one on 'The Arab Political Mind' (*al-'aql al-siyāsī al-'arabī*). Almost all of al-Jabri's works have been reprinted by the Centre for Arab Unity Studies in Beirut. Two of his works were translated into French: *Introduction à la critique de la raison arabe* (Introduction to the Critique of Arab Reason), Paris: La Découverte/Institut du monde arabe, 1994; and *La Raison politique en islam* (Political Reason in Islam), Paris: La Découverte, 2007.

As for the works by Georges Tarabachi regarding the 'critique of the Arab mind,' there are four volumes that focus on the 'deconstruction' of al-Jabri's work: *Naẓariyat al-ʿaql* (Theory of the Mind), 1996; *Ishkāliyyāt al-ʿaql al-ʿarabī* (Problematics of the Arab Mind), 1998; *Waḥdat al-ʿaql al-ʿarabī* (The Unity of the Arab Mind), 2002; *al-ʿAql al-Mustaqīl* (The Resigning Mind), 2004. All of these works were published in Beirut by Dār al-Sāqī. In addition, other works by this author include: *Madhbaḥat al-turāth fiʾl-thaqāfat al-ʿarabiyya* (The Massacre of Heritage in Arab Culture), 1998; *Hartaqatān: al-ʿilmāniyya ka-ishkāliyyat islāmiyya-islāmiyya* (Two Heresies in terms of Islamo-Islamic Problematics), 2 vols., 2008 and 2011; *Min Islām al-Qurʾān ilāʾl-Islām al-ḥadīth* (From the Islam of the Qurʾan to Modern Islam), 2010; and *Al-muʿjiza aw subāt al-ʿaql fiʾl-Islām* (The Miracle or the Slumber of Reason in Islam), 2008; all works published by Dār al-Sāqī, Beirut.

2.   Wright, Katharine Louise, 'The Incoherence of the Intellectuals. Ibn Rushd, al-Ghazali, al-Jabri, and Tarabichi in Eight Centuries of Dialogue without Dialogue,' Austin, TX: Graduate School of the University of Texas, Austin, 2012.

3.   Abdennur, Alexander, *The Arab Mind. An Ontology of Abstraction and Concreteness*, Ottawa: Kogna Publishing, 2008.

4.   On the techniques of historical stylisation in the service of an ideologically motivated thesis, see Corm, Georges, *L'Europe et le mythe de l'Occident. La construction d'une histoire* (Europe and the Myth of the West. The Construction of a History), Paris: La Découverte, 2010.

5.   Corm, Georges, *Histoire du pluralisme religieux dans le bassin méditerranéen* (The History of Religious Pluralism in the Mediterranean Basin), Paris: Geuthner, 1998.

6.   See Mehdi, Falih, *Fondements et mécanismes de l'état en islam: l'Irak* (Foundations and Mechanisms of the State in Islam, the Case of Iraq), Paris: L'Harmattan, Paris, which very clearly highlights the sources of Islamic political institutions in the Mesopotamian tradition of imperial and absolute power.

7.   Tarabichi, Georges, *Maṣāʾir al-falsafa bayn al-masīḥiyya waʾl-Islām* (The Destiny of Philosophy in Christianity and Islam), Beirut: Dār al-Sāqī, 1998. Unfortunately this valuable scholarly work has not been translated.

8.   I analysed this phenomenon from the point of view of the freedom of interpretation of sacred texts, for which an inverse historical trajectory characterises both the evolution of Christianity and Islam. The latter, after experiencing a flourishing of schools of Qurʾanic interpretation, 'closed' the doors to exegesis and allowed religious heritage to petrify. In Christianity, however, the diversity of interpretation of the sacred texts (the Gospels and the Epistles) was only accepted very gradually and was the result of long and vicious religious wars (see Corm, George, *Pour une lecture profane des conflits* (Towards a Secular Reading of Conflicts), pp. 204-246.

9.   I must add here that for Renan, even though Christianity was a Semitic religion at the outset, it was quickly taken over by Aryan Europe, which made it a central element in the history of Europe (see Corm, Georges, *Le Proche-Orient éclaté*, pp. 125-130).

10. Mohammed Abed al-Jabri, *Naḥnu wa'l-turāth*.

11. In an article published in the pan-Arab daily newspaper *Al-Hayat* on 9 June 2010, Tarabichi described the episodes of his relationship with al-Jabri. He described how initially al-Jabri's first book, which he had published in Beirut, strongly appealed to him. Then, subsequently, as had been the case with other great philosophers that he had idolised (Hegel, Marx, Lenin, Freud, but also Michel Aflaq, founder of the Baath party), he felt the need to 'kill the father' he had so admired. He described how he also realised that al-Jabri's epistemology was being transformed more and more into an anti-modernist ideological instrument in the service of stifling traditionalism. He added at the same time that it was thanks to al-Jabri that he delved into the issues of heritage and tradition, which he came to understand and also to criticise. 'For it is this heritage that is the structural field of all of our battles today', Tarabichi concluded. 'Our attitude with respect to heritage, and to critique and reconstruction of it, to the extent that we are a nation strongly attached to its tradition, is what will decide our place in human history and geography. We will either move forward towards modernity or turn inwards towards a new Middle Ages.'

12. The verbal violence of certain fundamentalists can go as far as denouncing partisans of secularism in the Arab world as traitors. Thus, a work published in Egypt was entitled, 'Secular and Traitor', with a secondary title 'Who are the Secularists? The Duty of Muslims towards Secularism. Secularism: Troubled Birth and Perverse Effects' (see Mūrū, Muḥammad, *'Ilmāniyyūn wa khawana*, Cairo: Dār al-Rawḍa, n.d.).

13. On this topic, see 'Abd al-Salām, Rafiq (Rafiq Abd al-Salam), *Fī'l- 'ilmāniyya wa'l-dīn wa'l-dimuqrāṭiyya. Al-mafāhīm wa'l-siyāqāt* (On Secularism, Religion, and Democracy. Concepts and Processes), Beirut: Al-Jazeera Centre for Studies, Arab Scientific Publishers, 2008.

14. Kepel, Gilles, *The Prophet and Pharaoh*, London: Saqi Books, 1985.

15. Abū Zayd, Naṣr Ḥāmid (Nasr Hamid Abu Zayd), *Al-tafkīr fī zamān al-takfīr. Ḍid al-jahl wa'l-zayf wa'l-khurāfa* (Thought in a Time of Religious Excommunication. Against Ignorance, Falsehood, and Falsification), Cairo: Sinā li'l-nashr, 1995.

16. Ibid., p. 37.

17. Ibid., p. 37.

18. Ibid., pp. 38-39.

19. Ibid., pp. 38-39.

20. Ibid., p. 40.

21. See Hafez, Ziad, *La Pensée religieuse en islam contemporain. Débats et critiques* (Religious Thought in Contemporary Islam. Debates and Critiques), Paris: Geuthner, 2012.

22. These include, among others, the attempted assassination of the Egyptian Minister of the Interior in 1990 during which the President of the Parliament was killed, the attempted assassination of the great novelist Naguib Mahfouz in 1994, and the massacre of European tourists in Luxor in 1997.

23. Most of Farag Foda's works are still available. They were all published by Dār wa maṭābiʿat al-mustaqbil publishers or by Al-hayāt al-miṣriyya al-ʿāmma liʾl kitāb in Cairo and can be purchased via the Nīl wa furāt website (nwf.com), last accessed 8 Mar 2019.

24. See also, Zakariya, Fouad, *Laïcité ou islamisme. Les Arabes à l'heure du choix* (Secularism or Islamism. For Arabs it is Time to Decide), Paris/Cairo: La Découverte/Al-Fikr, 1991.

25. Al-Ashmawy, Muhammad Said, *L'Islamisme contre l'islam* (Islamism against Islam), Paris/Cairo: La Découverte/Al-Fikr, 1990.

26. See al-Nayhūm, al-Ṣādiq (al-Sadiq al-Nayhum), *Islām ḍid al-Islām. Sharīʿa min waraq* (Islam versus Islam. A Paper Shariʿa), London: Riyāḍ el-Rayyis Books, 1994).

27. al-Masīrī, ʿAbd al-Wahhāb (Abdel Wahhab al-Messiri) and ʿAzīz al-ʿAẓma (Aziz al-Azmeh), *al-ʿilmāniyya taḥt al-majhar* (Secularism under the Microscope), Damascus: Dār al-Fikr al-Muʿāṣir, 2000.

28. Ibid., p. 22.

29. Ibid., p. 26.

30. Ibid., p. 143.

31. Ibid., p. 134.

32. Ibid., p. 159.

33. Ibid., p. 160.

34. Ibid., p. 162.

35. See the reproduction of the texts exchanged between these two authors entitled *al-Munāẓara al-dīniyya bayn al-shaykh Muḥammad ʿAbduh wa Faraḥ Anṭūn* (The Religious Confrontation between Shaykh Muhammad ʿAbduh and Farah Antun), presentation by Michel Geha, Beirut: Bīsān, 2014. See also the objections of Muhammad ʿAbduh to the views expressed by Gabriel Hanotaux about Islam in Abdou, Mohammed, *L'Islam: religion, science et civilisation* (Islam: Religion, Science and Civilization), Beirut: Dār Al-Bīrūnī, 2003.

36. See al-ʿAẓma, ʿAzīz (Aziz al-Azmeh), *al-ʿIlmāniyya min manẓūr mukhtalif*, Beirut: Dār al-Ṭalīʿa, 1993 (English translation: *Secularism in the Arab World: Contexts, Ideas and Consequences*, transl. David Bond, Edinburgh: Edinburgh University Press/Aga Khan University Institute for the Study of Muslim Civilisations, 2019); as well as *Dunyā al-dīn fī ḥāḍir al-ʿarab* (The World of Religion in the Arab Present), Beirut: Dār al-Ṭalīʿa, 1996.

CHAPTER 13

1. See especially, Ajami, Fouad, *The Arab Predicament. Arab Political Thought and Practice since 1967*, Cambridge: Cambridge University Press, 1992; *Dream Palace of the Arabs. A Generation's Odyssey*, New York: Vintage Books, 1999; *The Vanished Imam. Musa el-Sadr and the Shia of Lebanon*, Ithaca, NY: Cornell University Press, 1987.

2. See Corm, Georges, *Le Nouveau Gouvernement du monde. Idéologies, structures et contrepouvoirs* (The New Government of the World. Ideologies, Structures, and Counter-Powers), Paris: La Découverte, 2010.

3. Blin, Louis and Fargues, Philippe (eds.), *L'Économie de la paix au Proche-Orient*, 2 volumes (The Economy of Peace in the Middle East): Volume 1, *Stratégies* (Strategies); Volume 2, *La Palestine. Entrepreneurs et entreprises* (Palestine. Entrepreneurs and Enterprises), Paris: Maisonneuve et Larose/CEDEJ, 1995. These two volumes are the proceedings of a conference organised by CEDEJ in Strasbourg, France in June 1994.

4. Ibid., vol. 1, p. 36.

5. Leveau, Rémy, 'Les entrepreneurs au Proche-Orient: mise en perspective politique' (Entrepreneurs in the Middle East: A Political Perspective), *ibid.*, vol. 2, p. 245.

6. My contribution to this work therefore went somewhat in the opposite direction. My article entitled 'L'ajustement du secteur privé dans le monde arabe: taxation, justice sociale et efficacité économique' (The Adjustment of the Private Sector in the Arab World: Taxation, Social Justice, and Economic Efficiency), demonstrates the urgent need for structural economic reforms that aim to standardise and provide an institutional framework for the rich oligopolistic private sector, in order to lead it towards a virtuous circle of productivity and extension of employment opportunities, especially through reform of the tax code as well as by strengthening the role of the state in ensuring social justice. This sector emerged as a result of the benefits of the widespread rentier economy.

7. Sadiki, Larbi, *The Search for Arab Democracy. Discourses and Counter-Discourses*, New York: Columbia University Press, 2004.

8. See especially: Binder, Leonard, *Islamic Liberalism. A Critique of Development Ideologies*, Chicago: University of Chicago Press, 1988; Esposito, John (ed.), *Islam and Development. Religion and Socio-Political Change*, Syracuse, NY: Syracuse University Press, 1980; and, by the same author, *The Islamic Threat. Myth or Reality?*, Oxford: Oxford University Press, 1992; as well as, Voll, John O., *Islam and Democracy*, Oxford: Oxford University Press, 1996.

9. See especially the works of François Burgat previously cited.

10. Sadiki, Larbi, *The Search for Arab Democracy*, p. 54.

11. Ibid., pp. 70-71.

12. Ibid., p. 322-323.

13.   Ibid., p. 74.

14.   Ibid., p. 399-400.

15.   This has been described very well by Blanc, Pierre in *Proche-Orient. Le pouvoir, la terre et l'eau* (The Middle East. Power, Land and Water), Paris: Presses de Sciences Po, Paris, 2012. This author describes the agrarian and social counterrevolutions that arose as soon as Sadat became president of Egypt in the 1970s, and which subsequently expanded with the rise of neoliberalism and extended to other republics that had been socialist-leaning at the outset. This work is unfortunately an isolated exception.

16.   Portraits of some of these journalists appear in the collection of interviews conducted by Aṭwī, Thanā' (Sana Atoui), *Ḥiwārāt fī'l-masārāt al-muta'akisa.*

17.   The great Syrian novelist Ghāda al-Sammān (Ghada al-Samman) wrote a brutal description of the submission of intellectuals to these new billionaires in a novel which takes place in Geneva, in the palace of one of these characters who has managed to gather around him a coterie of admirers from Arab cultural circles. The title of the novel is very direct: 'The Night of the Billion' (*Laylat al-miliyār*, Beirut: Ghāda al-Sammān Publishing, 1986).

18.   Hafez, Ziad, *La Pensée religieuse en islam contemporain. Débats et critiques* (Religious Thought in Contemporary Islam. Debates and Criticisms), Paris: Geuthner, 2012.

19.   See Shaḥrūr, Muḥammad (Muhammad Shahrour), *al-Kitāb wa'l-Qur'ān. Qirā'a mu'āṣira* (The Book and the Qur'an. A Contemporary Reading), Damascus: al-Ahālī li'l-ṭibā'a wa'l-nashr wa'l-tawzī', 1990. The author also has a very rich website where his lectures and written correspondence with his readers are posted, www.shahrour.org, last accessed 8 Mar 2019. This work contains an introductory section devoted to Arabic linguistics written by a specialist in this area.

20.   See Hafez, Ziad, *La Pensée religieuse en islam contemporain*, which provides a very detailed analysis of Shahrour's thought (pp. 227-282).

21.   Nevertheless, al-Qimny quickly returned to writing, as demonstrated by his interesting blog (www.quemny.blog.com), which addresses the Egyptian situation in particular. A very interesting profile of al-Qimny, written by Tarik Salam, also appears there, 'Sayyid al-Quemny. Egyptian Muslim Thinker and Historian.'

22.   For more on this topic see Corm, Georges, *Pour une approche profane des conflits*, especially Chapters 9 and 10.

23.   Hani Ramadan was born in Geneva in 1959. He succeeded his father as Imam of the Mosque of Geneva and as director of the city's Islamic Centre. He became known for an extended opinion piece published in the French daily newspaper *Le Monde*, on 10 September 2002, entitled 'Sharia is misunderstood', in which he suggested that AIDS could be divine punishment for the dissolute morals of Western societies.

24. The French publication of a collection of texts written by Gamal al-Banna is very welcome. They are presented and translated by Dominique Avon and Amin Elias, with the collaboration of Abdellatif Idrissi: Al-Banna, Gamal, *L'Islam, la liberté, la laïcité et le crime de la tribu des 'Il nous a été rapporté'* (Islam, Freedom, Secularism and the Crime of the 'It Was Reported To Us' Tribe), Paris: L'Harmattan, 2013. (The expression the '"It was reported to us" tribe' refers to the many authors of the collections of the 'sayings and deeds of the Prophet' which constitute the central core of Islamic doctrine and jurisprudence. See also Akouri, Mouna A., *L'Enseignement de Gamal Al-Banna* (The Teachings of Gamal al-Banna), Cairo: Dar Al-Fikr al-Islami, 2005.

25. Ūzūn, Zakariyyā (Zakaria Ouzon), *Jināyat al-Bukhārī* (The Crime of al-Bukhari), Beirut: Riyāḍ el-Rayyis Books, 2002. Al-Bukhari (810–870) was one of the most famous scholars to have collected the sayings of the Prophet.

26. Belaïd, Sadok, *Islam et droit. Une nouvelle lecture des versets prescriptifs du Coran* (Islam and Law. A New Reading of the Prescriptive Verses of the Qur'an), Tunis: Centre de publications universitaires, 2000 (Original text in Arabic: *al-Qur'ān wa'l-tashrī'. Qirā'a jadīda fī āyāt al-aḥkām*, by the same publisher).

27. Filali-Ansari, Abdou, *Réformer l'islam. Une introduction aux débats contemporains* (Reforming Islam. An Introduction to Contemporary Debates), Paris: La Découverte, 2003; by the same author, *L'islam est-il hostile à la laïcité?* (Is Islam Hostile to Secularism?), Paris: Sindbad, 2001.

28. A large number of Belkeziz's works were published by the Centre for Arab Unity Studies in Beirut. One of the author's important works was published in English as *The State in Contemporary Islamic Thought: A Historical Survey of the Major Muslim Political Thinkers of the Modern Era*, London: I.B. Tauris, 2009.

29. Some of his most important works have been collected in Arkoun, Mohammed, *Pour une critique de la raison islamique* (Towards a Critique of Islamic Reason), Paris: Maisonneuve et Larose, 1984, with a substantial introduction entitled, 'Comment étudier la pensée islamique?' (How Can Islamic Thought Be Studied?), which clearly summarises his method and approach to religious heritage.

30. Kilani, Mondher (ed.), *Islam et changement social* (Islam and Social Change), Lausanne: Payot, 1998.

31. Barber, Benjamin R., *Jihad vs. McWorld: Terrorism's Challenge to Democracy*, New York: Times Books, 1995.

32. al-Anṣārī, Muḥammad Jābir (Mohammed Jaber al-Ansari), *Al-Fikr al-'arabī wa sirā' al-aḍdād* (Arab Thought and the Conflict of Contraries), Beirut: al-Mu'assasa al-'arabiyya li'l-dirāsāt wa'l-nashr, 1996.

33. Ibid., pp. 64-65.
34. Ibid., pp. 68-69.
35. Ibid., pp. 81-82. This is where the work of Mohammed Arkoun is extensively cited.

36. Ibid., pp. 84-85.

37. Ibid., p. 85.

38. This clearly disproves the thesis that all Arab Christians are proponents of secular and positivist thought, since in this case it is clear that they cling to their 'Orientalness'.

39. Muḥammad Jābir al-Anṣārī, *Al-Fikr al-'arabī wa sirā' al-aḍdād*, pp. 85-86.

40. Ibid., p. 90.

41. Ibid., pp. 598-600. Here the author's thought agrees with that of Mahdi Amil or Yasin al-Hafiz (see *supra*, Chapter 10), although he does not seem to be aware of their work.

42. Ibid., p. 641.

43. Ibid., p. 643.

44. Ibid., p. 644.

45. Ibid., p. 645. This conclusion recalls that of Paul Khoury on the same theme of the split between tradition and modernity discussed in Chapter 3.

46. Ḍāhir, Muḥammad (Muhammad Dahir), *Al-Ṣirā' bayn al-tayyārayn al-dīnī wa'l-'ilmānī fi'l-fikr al-'arabī al-ḥadīth* (The Struggle between the Religious and Secular Currents in Contemporary Arab Thought), Beirut: Dār al-Bīrūnī, 2009 (Second edition).

47. Ibid., p. 8.

48. Ibid., pp. 138-145.

49. Ibid., p. 145. This is why, the author adds, al-Afghani had many Christian and Jewish followers.

50. Ibid., p. 420 (see also Elshobaki, Amr, *Les Frères musulmans des origines à nos jours*).

51. Ibid.

52. Ibid., p. 426.

53. Ibid., p. 428.

54. Ibid., p. 440.

55. As the brother of King Hussein bin Talal of Jordan (1935–1999), Prince Hassan was for a very long time the designated heir to the throne. However, shortly before King Hussein's death, he replaced him with his son, the present King Abdullah, born in 1962.

56. Presentation and discussion of texts: *Al-wasaṭiyya bayn al-tanzir wal taṭbīq* (The Middle Way between Theory and Practice), Amman: Muntadā al-fikr al-'Arabī and Dār jarīr li'l-nashr wa'l-tawzī', 2005.

57. This was also inaugurated by Prince Hassan: *Al-wasaṭiyya. Ab'ād fi'l-turāth wa'l mu'āṣara* (*Wasatiyya*. Its Implications for Heritage and Modernity), Amman: Muntadā al-fikr al-'Arabī and Dār jarīr li'l-nashr wa'l-tawzī', 2007.

58. Alongside Michel Chiha, the thought of Charles Corm (1894–1963) should also be mentioned, since it inspired Chiha's thought. Charles Corm was one of the best known Francophone Lebanese writers and the author of a long poem

with Barresian echoes entitled *La Montagne inspirée* (translated into English as *The Sacred Mountain*, Louaize, Lebanon: Notre Dame University Press, 2004), in which he defends the idea of building a Lebanese nation on the basis of ancient Phoenician roots which alone are capable, in his view, of overcoming the community divide between Christians and Muslims. In the early days of the French mandate, he created a very informative journal entitled *La Revue phénicienne* (The Phoenician Review). The complete works of Charles Corm were recently published in a 10-volume set by Éditions de La Revue Phénicienne (1919). He also wrote an impressive play in 1928, *La Terre assassinée ou les Ciliciennes* (The Assassinated Land or the Cilicians), in which he describes the horror of the Armenian genocide and denounces the inability of the French army to protect the victims, people who had been encouraged by the French to claim their independence. The play was first published by Éditions de La Revue Phénicienne in 2005.

59. His collected works were published in several volumes by the Michel Chiha Foundation and by Éditions du Trident in Beirut.

60. In 1939, the French Mandate in Syria handed over the city of Antioch and its outskirts, including the port of Alexandretta, to Turkey as a reward for its neutrality in the new European war that was taking shape at that time. This is how Arab Christianity lost one of its most important sites of memory, a symbolic event that was followed in 1967 by the loss of the holy sites of Jerusalem due to the city's annexation and subsequent occupation by the State of Israel.

61. A synopsis of these three theses written by their author was published in Beirut in 1977 by Publications de l'Université Libanaise (Section Études Historiques, XXII) as *Recherches sur la pensée chrétienne et l'islam dans les temps modernes et à l'époque contemporaine* (Research on Christian Thought and Islam in Modern Times and in the Contemporary Period). It focused specifically on Islamo-Christian relationships since Napoleon Bonaparte's expedition to Egypt, and included a clear overview of medieval Christian knowledge of Islam.

62. To better understand the thought of Youakim Moubarac, see *Youakim Moubarac, un homme d'exception. Textes choisis et présentés par Georges Corm* (Youakim Moubarac, an Exceptional Individual. Texts Selected and Presented by Georges Corm). Beirut: La Librairie Orientale, 2004; as well as Stassinet, Jean (ed.), *Youakim Moubarac*, Lausanne: L'Âge d'Homme, 2005.

63. Fleyfel, Antoine, *La Théologie contextuelle arabe. Modèle libanais* (Contextual Arab Theology. The Lebanese model), Paris: L'Harmattan, 2011, and *Géopolitique des chrétiens d'Orient. Défis et avenir des chrétiens arabes* (The Geopolitics of the Christians of the East. Challenges and the Future of Arab Christians), Paris: L'Harmattan, 2013.

64. See especially, ʿAwn, Mushīr B. (Mouchir Aoun), *Al-Fikr al-ʿarabī al-dīnī al-masīḥī. Muqtaḍayyāt al-nuhūḍ waʾl-tajdīd waʾl-muʿāṣara* (Arab Christian

Thought. The Demand for Renaissance, Renewal, and Modernity), Beirut: Dār al-Ṭalīʿa, 2007.

65. Aoun, Mouchir B., *Heidegger et la pensée arabe* (Heidegger and Arab Thought), Paris: L'Harmattan, 2011. Given the importance of this author's work, his thought is the focus of a separate chapter in Antoine Fleyfel's, *La Théologie contextuelle arabe*.

CHAPTER 14

1. Special mention should be made here of an interesting special issue of the journal *Peuples méditerranéens* entitled 'Sciences sociales, sociétés arabes' (Social Sciences, Arab Societies), nos. 55-56, January-June 1991.

2. Nassar, Nassif, *La Pensée réaliste d'Ibn Khaldoun* (The Realist Thought of Ibn Khaldun), Paris: PUF, 1979.

3. Nassif Nassar, *Naḥw mujtamaʿjadīd. Muqaddimāt asāsiyya fī naqd al-mujtamaʿ al-ṭāʾifī*, Beirut: Dār al-Ṭalīʿa, 1970. Mahdi Amil's work, published a few years later, supported these views. See, Amel, Mehdi, *L'État confessionnel. Le cas libanais* (The Confessional State. The Lebanese Case), Montreuil: La Brèche, 1996 (original published in Arabic by Dar El-Farabi, Beirut, 1986). In my 1971 doctoral thesis on the way in which religious pluralism functions in the Middle East, I severely criticised the notion of maintaining a communitarian regime in the Arab world. This was a structure inherited from the *millets* of the Ottoman Empire and which needed to be developed into a secular system or risk seeing Lebanon erupt. Corm, Georges, *Contribution à l'étude des sociétés multiconfessionnelles. Effets sociojuridiques et politiques du pluralisme religieux* (Contribution to the Study of Multiconfessional Societies. Socio-legal and Political Effects of Religious Pluralism), Paris: Librairie générale de droit et de jurisprudence, 1971 (several successive editions of the Arabic translation have been published); new edition entitled, *Histoire du pluralisme religieux dans le bassin méditerranéen* (The History of Religious Pluralism in the Mediterranean Basin), Paris: Geuthner, 1998.

4. Nassar, Nassif, *Mafhūm al-umma bayn al-dīn wa'l-tārīkh* (The Concept of the 'Umma' between Religion and History), Beirut: Dār al-Ṭalīʿa, 1978.

5. Nassar, Nassif, *Taṣawwurāt al-umma al-muʿāṣira* (Modern Concepts of the Nation), Beirut: Dār Amwāj-Maktabat Bīsān, n.d.

6. Naṣṣār, Nāṣīf (Nasif Nassar), *Bāb al-ḥurriya. Inbithāq al-wujūd bi'l-fiʿl* (The Gate of Freedom. The Blossoming of Existence through Action), Beirut: Dār al-Ṭalīʿa, 2003.

7. Ibid., p. 53.

8. Naṣṣār, Nāṣīf (Nasif Nassar), *Al-Dhāt wa'l-ḥuḍūr. Baḥth fī mabaādiʾ al-wujūd al-tārīkhī* (The Self and Presence. Study of the Principles of Historical Existence), Beirut: Dār al-Ṭalīʿa, 2008.

9. Naṣṣār, Nāṣīf (Nasif Nassar), *Manṭiq al-sulṭa. Madkhal ilā'l-amr* (The Logic of Power. An Introduction to the Command), Beirut: Dār Amwāj, 1995.

10. Naṣṣār, Nāṣīf (Nasif Nassar), *Muṭāraḥāt li'l-ʿaql al-multazim. Fī ba ʿḍ mushkilāt al-siyāsa wa'l-dīn wa'l-idiyūlūjiya* (Theses for the Engaged Mind. On Some Problems Concerning Politics, Religion, and Ideology), Beirut: Dār al-Ṭalīʿa, 1986.

11. Naṣṣār, Nāṣīf (Nasif Nassar), *Fī'l-tarbiyya wa'l-siyāsa. Matā yasīr al-fard fī'l-duwal al-ʿarabiyya muwāṭinan?* (On Education and Politics. When Will the Individual in Arab Countries Ever Be Able To Become a Citizen?), Beirut: Dār al-Ṭalīʿa, 2000.

12. Naṣṣār, Nāṣīf (Nasif Nassar), *Al-ishārāt wa'l masālik. Min iwān Ibn Rushd ilā raḥāb al-ʿilmāniyya* (The Signs and the Pathways. From the Palace of Ibn Rushd to the Open Space of Secularism), Beirut: Dār al-Ṭalīʿa, 2011

13. Balqazīz, ʿAbd al-Ilāh (Abdellilah Belkeziz) (ed.), *Nāṣīf Naṣṣār. Min al-istiqlāl al-falsafī ilā falsafat al-ḥuḍūr* (Nassif Nassar. From Philosophical Independence to the Philosophy of Presence), Conference proceedings, Beirut/Casablanca: Centre for Arab Unity Studies/University Hassan II, 2014.

14. See Khoury, Paul, *Le Fait et le Sens. Esquisse d'une philosophie de la déception* (Fact and Meaning. Outline of a Philosophy of Disappointment), Paris: L'Harmattan, 2007 (originally published in Lebanon in 1996, distributed by Librairie Saint-Paul, Jounieh).

15. For more on the philosophy of Paul Khoury, see Aoun, Mouchir B., *Une pensée arabe humaniste contemporaine. Paul Khoury et les promesses de l'incomplétude humaine* (A Humanist Contemporary Arab thought. Paul Khoury and the Promises of Human Incompleteness), Paris: L'Harmattan, 2012.

16. Khoury, Paul, *Islam et christianisme. Dialogue religieux et défi de la modernité* (Islam and Christianity. Religious Dialogue and the Challenge of Modernity), Paris: L'Harmattan, 2011 (originally published in Lebanon in 1997, distributed by Librairie Saint-Paul, Jounieh).

17. al-Maḥmaṣānī, Ṣubḥī (Soubhi al-Mahmassani), Beirut: *Falsafat al-tashrīʿ fī'l-islām*, Maktabat al-kashshāf, 1946 (translated by Farhat J. Ziadeh as *The Philosophy of Jurisprudence in Islam*, Leiden: E.J. Brill, 1961).

18. al-Maḥmaṣānī, Ṣubḥī, *Al-dustūr wa'l dimuqrāṭiya* (The Constitution and Democracy), Beirut: n.p., 1952; an expanded edition was later published under the title, *Al-dimuqrāṭiya bayn al-dustūr wa'l-wāqiʿ* (Democracy between the Constitution and Reality).

19. al-Maḥmaṣānī, Ṣubḥī, *Arkān ḥuqūq al-insān. Baḥth muqāran fī'l-sharīʿat al-islāmiyya wa'l qawānīn al-ḥadītha* (The Foundations of Human Rights. Comparative Study of Islamic Legislation and Modern Laws), Beirut: Dār al-ʿilm li'l-malāyīn, 1979.

20. Mahmassani, Maher S., *Islam in Retrospect. Recovering the Message*, Northampton: Olive Branch Press, 2014.

21. Ṣaʿab, Ḥasan (Hassan Saab), *Islām al-ḥurriya wa lā Islām al-ʿubūdiyya* (The Islam of Liberty and not the Islam of Slavery), Beirut: Dār al-ʿilm li'l-ṭibāʿa, 1974, preceded by a work entitled *Al-Islām tijāh taḥadiyyāt al-ḥayāt al-ʿaṣriyya* (Islam Confronting the Challenges of Contemporary Life), Beirut: Manshūrāt Dār al-Adab, 1965.

22. Ṣaʿab, Ḥasan, *Al-Insān al-ʿarabī wa taḥaddī al-thawrat al-ʿilmiyya al-tiknūlūjiyya* (Arab Man and the Challenge of the Technoscientific Revolution), Beirut: Dār al-ʿilm li'l-malāyīn, 1973.

23. Bennabi, Malek, *Vocation de l'islam*, Paris: Éditions du Seuil, 1954; *Les conditions de la renaissance*, Algiers: Éditions En-Nahdha, 1949.

24. Bennabi, Malek, *Le problème des idées dans le monde musulman*, Paris: Éditions Albouraq, 2006 (originally published in Arabic in 1970).

25. Bennabi, Malek, *L'idée du Commonwealth islamique*, Algiers: Éditions Benmerabet, 2017 (originally published in 1959).

26. Bennabi, Malek, *Le musulman dans le monde de l'économie*, Algiers: El Borhane, 1996 (originally published in Arabic in 1972).

27. Originally published in Arabic by an unknown publisher in Beirut in 1972.

28. Triki, Fathi, *Philosopher le vivre-ensemble* (Philosophising Living Together), Tunis: L'Or du temps, 1998.

29. Triki, Fathi, *La Stratégie de l'identité*, Paris: Arcantère, 1998.

30. Khatibi, Abdelkebir, *La mémoire tatouée. Autobiographie d'un décolonisé*, Paris: UGE, 1971 (translated as *Tattooed Memory* by Peter Thompson, Paris: Éditions L'Harmattan, 2016).

31. Khatibi, Abdelkebir, *Amour bilingue*, Paris: Fata Morgana, 1983 (translated as *Love in Two Languages* by Richard Howard, Minneapolis: University of Minnesota Press, 1990)

32. Khatibi, Abdelkebir, *Maghreb pluriel*, Paris: Denoël, 1983.

33. Khatibi, Abdelkebir, *Figures de l'étranger dans la littérature française* (Figures of the Foreigner in French Literature), Paris: Denoël, 1987.

34. Abdelkebir Khatibi, *Imaginaire de l'autre* (The Imaginary of the Other), Paris: L'Harmattan, 1987; See also Alfonso de Toro's excellent contribution to the analysis of Abdelkebir Khatibi's thought, 'Abdelkebir Khatibi, fondateur des stratégies "planétaires" culturelles, littéraires et politiques. Représentation de la pensée hybride khatibienne dans le Maghreb', in de Toro, Alfonso (ed.), *Epistémologies. "Le Maghreb"*, Paris: L'Harmattan, 2009.

35. See Kilani, Mondher, *Pour un universalisme critique. Essai d'anthropologie du contemporain* (Towards a Critical Universalism. An Essay on Contemporary Anthropology), Paris: La Découverte, 2014.

36. Batatu, Hanna, *The Old Social Classes and the Revolutionary Movements in Iraq. A Study of Iraq's Old Landed and Commercial Classes and of its Communists, Ba'thists and Free Officers*, Princeton, NJ: Princeton University Press, 1978.

37. Batatu, Hanna, *Syria's Peasantry. The Descendants of its Lesser Rural Notables and their Politics*, Princeton, NJ: Princeton University Press, 1999.

38. Khālid, Manṣūr (Mansour Khalid), *Al-Sūdān. Aḥwāl al-ḥarb... wa ṭumūḥāt al-salām. Qiṣṣa baladayn*, London: Dār Turāth li'l-nashr, 2003, another monumental work of 1,080 pages (English translation, *War and Peace in Sudan. A Tale of Two Countries*, New York: Kegan Paul International, 2002; and London: Routledge, 2010). See also by the same author, *Janūb al-Sūdān fi'l-mukhayyilat al-ʿarabiyya. Al-ṣūra al-zāʾifa wa'l-qamʿ al-tārīkhī* (South Sudan in the Arab Imaginary. False Image and Historical Oppression), London: Dār Turāth li'l-nashr, 2000. This complex figure was the subject of a feature article in *Ahram Weekly*, no. 635, 24-30 April 2003.

39. See the highly informative article by Faleh Abdul-Jabbar, 'Sectarianism in Iraq, a critique by Ali Al-Wardi', *Contemporary Arab Affairs*, 7 (4), October 2014. In the same edition of this journal, and by the same author, there is another excellent article that provides an overview of the sociological thought of the Arab world: 'Reflections on Arabs and Sociology: Insights into Sociological Schools of Thought in the Arab World, Challenges and Issues.'

40. al-Ruṣāfi, Maʿrūf (Maruf al-Rusafi), *Kitāb al-shakhṣiyyat al-Muḥammadiyya aw ḥall al-lughz al-muqaddas* (The Book of the Muhammadan Personality or the Solution to the Problem of the Sacred), Cologne: Manshūrāt al-jamāl, Al-Kamel Verlag, 2002.

41. al-Dūrī, ʿAbd al-ʿAzīz (Abd al-Aziz al-Duri), *Al-takwīn al-tārīkhī li'l-ummat al-ʿarabiyya. Dirāsa fi'l-hawiyya wal waʿī* (The Historical Constitution of the Arab Nation. Study of Identity and Consciousness), Beirut: Markaz dirāsāt al-waḥda al-ʿarabiyya, 1984.

42. al-Dūrī, ʿAbd al-ʿAzīz (Abd al-Aziz al-Duri), *Muqaddima fi'l-tarīkh al-iqtiṣādī al-ʿarabī* (Introduction to Arab Economic History), Beirut: Dār al-Ṭaliʿa, 1969.

43. Laroui, Abdallah, *The History of the Maghrib: An Interpretive Essay*. Princeton, NJ: Princeton University Press, 1977. See also by the same author, *Les origines sociales et culturelles du nationalisme marocain,* Paris: Maspero, 1976.

44. Lacheraf, Mostefa, *L'Algérie. Nation et société* (Algeria. Nation and Society), Paris: Maspero, 1965.

45. Harbi, Mohammed, *Aux origines du FLN. Le populisme révolutionnaire en Algérie* (The Origins of the FLN. Revolutionary Populism in Algeria), Paris: Christian Bourgois, 1975.

46. Pierre Chaulet was a professor of medicine and one of the first activists to join the FLN. He was given a state funeral in Algiers when he died in 2013.

47. Chaulet, Claudine, *La Terre, les Frères et l'Argent. Stratégie familiale et production agricole en Algérie depuis 1962* (Land, Brothers, and Money. Family Strategies and Agricultural Production in Algeria since 1962), 3 volumes, Algiers: Office des publications universitaires, 1987; *La Mitidja autogérée: enquête sur les exploitations autogérées agricoles d'une région d'Algérie, 1968–1970* (The Self-

managed *Mitidja*: Study of Agricultural Operations in an Algerian Region 1968–1970), Algiers: SNED, 1971.

48. An example is the pioneering novel by the Egyptian writer ʿAbd al-Raḥmān Sharqāwī (Abd al-Rahman al-Sharqawi), *Al-Arḍ* (The Land), Cairo: Dār al-kātib al-ʿArabī li'l-ṭibāʿa wa'l-nashr, 1954 (English translation: *Egyptian Earth* by Desmond Stewart, Austin, TX: University of Texas Press, 1990); or the novel by ʿAbd al-Raḥmān Munīf, born in Jordan (1933–2004), *Al-Ashjār wa qatl Marzūq* (The Trees and the Killing of Marzuq), Beirut: Al-Muʾassasat al-ʿarabiyya li'l-dirāsa wa'l-nashr, 1973.

49. Blanc, Pierre in *Proche-Orient. Le pouvoir, la terre et l'eau* (The Middle East. Power, Land and Water), Paris: Presses de Sciences Po, Paris, 2012.

50. See, however, Corm, Georges, *Le Nouveau désordre économique mondial* (The New World Economic Disorder), Paris: La Découverte, 1993; as well as *Al-iqtiṣād al-ʿarabī am al-taḥaddī* (The Challenge of the Arab Economy), Beirut: Dār al-Ṭalīʿa, 1977, and *Al-tanmiyyat al mafqūda. Dirāsa fī'l-azmat al-ḥaḍāriyya wa'l-tanmawiyyat al-ʿarabiyya* (Unobtainable Development. Study of the Crisis of Arab Civilisation and Development), Beirut: Dār al-Ṭalīʿa, 1981.

51. Amin, Galal A., *The Modernization of Poverty. A Study in the Political Economy of Growth in Nine Arab Countries*, Leiden: E. J. Brill, 1974.

52. Amin, Galal A., *The Illusion of Progress in the Arab World. A Critique of Western Misconstruction*, Cairo: American University in Cairo Press, 2006.

53. Amīn, Jalāl A. (Galal A. Amin), *Falsafat ʿilm al-iqtiṣād. Baḥth fī taḥayyuzāt al-iqtiṣādiyyīn wa fī'l-usus ghayr al-ʿilmiyya li-ʿilm al-iqtiṣād* (The Philosophy of Economics. Study of the Biases of Economists and the Unscientific Basis of Economic Science), Cairo: Dār al-Shurūq, 2008.

54. See Amīn, Jalāl A. (Galal A. Amin), *Al-mashriq al-ʿarabī wa'l-gharb. Baḥth fī'l-dawr al-muʾaththirāt al-khārijiyya fī taṭawwur al-niẓām al-iqtiṣādī al-ʿarabī* (The Arab Mashriq and the West. Study of the Role of External Factors in the Evolution of the Arab Economic System), Beirut: Markaz dirāsāt al-waḥda al-ʿarabiyya, 1979.

55. Sayegh, Youssef A., *The Arab Economies* (volume 1) and *The Determinants of Arab Economic Development* (volume 2), London: Croom Helm, 1978.

56. Sayegh, Youssef A., *The Determinants of Arab Economic Development*, pp. 50-51.

57. Ṣāyigh, Yūsuf A. (Youssef A. Sayegh), *Al-Khubz maʿa 'l-karāma: al-muḥtawā al-iqtiṣādī al-ijtimāʿi li'l-mafhūm al-qawmī al-ʿarabī* (Bread with Dignity: The Economic and Social Content of the Arab National Concept), Beirut: Dār al-Ṭalīʿa, 1961.

58. Sayegh, Youssef A., *Elusive Development. From Dependence to Self-Reliance in the Arab Region*, London: Routledge and Kegan Paul, 1991.

59. He is one of the few Arab economists to have written an entire book (based on his doctoral thesis) on the private sector. Sayegh, Youssef A., *Entrepreneurs of Lebanon. The Role of the Business Leader in a Developing Economy*, Cambridge, MA: Harvard University Press, 1962.

60. A biography of the author's younger days was written based on the recorded memories of his wife and children: *Yūsuf Ṣāyigh: Sīra ghayr muktamala* (Youssef A. Sayegh: Unfinished Biography), Beirut: Dār Riyāḍ al-Rayyis, 2009. It contains a lot of useful information on Lebanon, Syria, and Palestine, where the author lived before the creation of Israel, at a time when people could cross borders without any difficulty. It also clearly shows the homogeneity of the social environments of these three countries and their economic, educational, and family ties. There is also another collective work that provides an exhaustive overview of Sayegh's life and work. See Sayigh, Rosemary (ed.), *Yusif Sayigh, Arab Economist and Palestinian Patriot. A Fractured Life Story*, Cairo: The American University in Cairo Press, 2015.

61. Dajānī, Burhān (Burhan Dajani), *Kitabāt fi'l-iqtiṣād* (Articles on Economics), Beirut: Institute for Palestine Studies, 2004; two other volumes bring together his political articles, most of which focus on the spoliation of Palestinian rights.

62. Sid-Ahmed, Abdelkader, *L'Économie arabe à l'heure des surplus pétroliers* (The Arab Economy at a Time of Oil Surpluses), Paris: ISMEA, 1975; *Développement sans croissance. L'expérience des économies pétrolières du tiers monde* (Development without Growth. The Experience of Oil-producing Economies in the Third World), Paris: Publisud, 1983.

63. Henni, Ahmed, *Le Cheikh et le Patron* (The Shaykh and the Boss), Algiers: OPU, 1993; *Le Syndrome islamiste et les mutations du capitalisme* (The Islamist Syndrome and the Mutations of Capitalism), Paris: Éditions Non Lieu, 2008; *Le Capitalisme de rente. De la société industrielle à la société des rentiers* (Rentier Capitalism. From an Industrial Society to a Rentier Society), Paris: L'Harmattan, 2012.

64. ʿAbd al-Fāḍil, Maḥmūd (Mahmoud Abdel-Fadil), *Al-fikr al-iqtiṣādī al-ʿarabī wa qaḍāyā al-taḥarrur wa'l-tanmiya wa'l-waḥda* (Arab Economic Thought and the Issues Related to Deregulation, Development and Unity), Beirut: Centre for Arab Unity Studies, 1982.

65. ʿAbd al-Fāḍil, Maḥmūd (Mahmoud Abdel-Fadil), *Al-ʿArab wa'l-tajruba al-āsiyāwiyya. Al-durūs al-mustafādā* (The Arabs and the Asian Experience. Useful Lessons.), Beirut: Centre for Arab Unity Studies, 2000.

66. Ḍahir, Masʿūd (Massoud Daher), *Al-nahḍat al-ʿarabiyya wa'l-nahḍat al-yabāniyya. Tashabbuh al-muqaddimāt wa ikhtilāf al-natāʾij* (The Arab Renaissance and the Japanese Renaissance. Similarities of Origins, Differences of Outcomes), Kuwait: ʿĀlam al-maʿārifa, 1999.

67. See in particular Issawi, Charles, *Economic History of the Middle East and North Africa*, London: Methuen, 1982; Issawi, Charles (ed.), *The Economic History of the Middle East, 1800–1914*, Chicago: University of Chicago Press, 1966.

68. Zahlan, Antoine B., *Acquiring Technological Capacity. A Study of Arab Consulting and Contracting Companies*, London: MacMillan Academic and Professional, 1991. See also *Ṣināʿat al-inshāʾāt al-ʿarabiyya* (A Study of the Arab Building and Public Works Sector), Beirut: Centre for Arab Unity Studies, 1985.

69. Zahlan, Antoine B, *Science and Science Policy in the Arab World*, London: Croom Helm, 1980.

70. Zaḥlān, Anṭwān B. (Antoine B. Zahlan), *Al-'Arab wa taḥadiyyāt al-'ilm wa'l-taqāna. Taqaddum min dūn taghyīr* (Arabs Faced with the Challenge of Science and Technology. Progress without Change), Beirut: Centre for Arab Unity Studies, 1999.

71. Zahlan, Antoine B, *Science, Development and Sovereignty in the Arab World*, New York: Palgrave MacMillan, 2012; see also, *Al-bu'd al-taknūlūjī li'l-waḥdat al-'arabiyya* (The Technological Dimension of Arab Unity), Beirut: Centre for Arab Unity Studies, 1981.

CONCLUSION

1. See Corm, Georges, *Le Nouveau Gouvernement du monde. Idéologies, structures et contrepouvoirs* (The New Government of the World. Ideologies, Structures, and Counter-Powers), Paris: La Découverte, 2010

2. For a discussion of the socio-economic causes of the Arab revolts, see Corm, Georges, 'The socio-economic factors behind Arab revolutions', *Contemporary Arab Affairs*, 5, (3), July-September 2012.

3. See *Géopolitique et crise de la postmodernité* (The Religious Question in the 21st Century. Geopolitics and the Crisis of Postmodernity), Paris: La Découverte, 2006.

4. Not to mention the 'Islamic' finance channels that have continued to expand since the 1980s, particularly through the development of a network of Islamic banks in the oil-producing monarchies and emirates, and the establishment of Islamic financing schemes within large international banks. Again, one cannot but be surprised at the number of books and doctoral theses on what amounts to legal window dressing which does nothing to change the reality of the rentier capitalism that I have often denounced in this work.

5. See Corm, Georges, 'The Political Economy of Democratic Transition in the Arab Situation', *Contemporary Arab Affairs*, 87 (1), 2015 (in Arabic: 'Al iqtiṣād al-siyasī li'l-intiqāl al-dimuqrāṭī fī'l-waṭan al-'arabī', *Al-Mustaqbal al-'arabī*, 426, August 2014); this text is based on a lecture presented at Carthage Palace in Tunis on 14 June 2014.

6. The policies of President George W. Bush aimed at remaking the Middle East in order to introduce democracy. This is not unlike those of European colonial powers that sought to reform the Ottoman Empire and, afterwards, to further its dismantling based on ethnic and religious identities. The military and political interventions by the United States and some European nations following the 2011 popular revolts can also be interpreted as the continuation of these policies. If the Ottoman Empire was Europe's sick man in the nineteenth century, today the Arab world has taken over this role.

BIBLIOGRAPHY*

Abdelkader, Hamdi, *L'Egypte dans voyage en orient de Gérard de Nerval et la France dans L'Or de Paris de Rifa'at Al-Tahtawi*, Unpublished doctoral thesis, Montreal: Université du Québec, 2008.

Abdelkader, *Lettre aux Français*, Algiers: ANEP, 2005.

Abdel-Malek, Anouar, *La Pensée politique arabe contemporaine*, Paris: Seuil, 1970.

———, *La Dialectique sociale*, Paris: Seuil, 1972.

Abdel-Malek, Anouar, Abdel Aziz Belal and Hassan Hanafi (eds.), *Renaissance du monde arabe*, Louvain: Duculot, 1972.

Abdel Razek, Ali, *Islam and the Foundations of Political Power*, ed. Abdou Filali-Ansary, tr. Maryam Loutfi, Edinburgh: Edinburgh University Press/Aga Khan University Institute for the Study of Muslim Civilisations, 2012.

Abdennur, Alexander, *The Arab Mind. An Ontology of Abstraction and Concreteness*, Ottawa: Kogna Publishing, 2008.

Abdou, Mohammed, *L'Islam. Religion, science et civilisation*, Beirut: Dār Al-Bīrūnī, 2003.

Ajami, Fouad, *The Vanished Imam. Musa al Sadr and the Shia of Lebanon*, Ithaca, NY: Cornell University Press, 1987.

———, *The Arab Predicament. Arab Political Thought and Practice since 1967*, Cambridge: Cambridge University Press, 1992.

———, *The Dream Palace of the Arabs. A Generation's Odyssey*, New York: Vintage Books, 1999.

Akouri, Mouna A., *L'Enseignement de Gamal Al-Banna*, Cairo: Dar Al-Fikr al-Islami, 2005.

* This bibliography only contains works that were written in French or translated into French, or written in or translated into English. The titles, publishers, and publication dates of works published in Arabic and cited throughout the book can be found by referring to the author's name in the index.

Al-Ashmaway, Muhammad Saʿid, *L'Islamisme contre l'islam*, Paris/Cairo: La Découverte/Al-Fikr, 1989.

Al-Azm, Sadiq Jalal, *The Mental Taboo. Salman Rushdie and the Truth within Literature*, London: Riyāḍ el-Rayyis Books, 1992.

Al-Banna, Gamal, *L'Islam, la liberté, la laïcité et le crime de la tribu des 'Il nous a été rapporté'*, Paris: L'Harmattan, 2013.

Allawi, Ali, *Faisal I of Iraq*, New Haven, CT: Yale University Press, 2014.

Al-Seif, Tawfiq, *Islamic Democracy and its Limits. The Iranian Experience since 1979*, London: Saqi Books, 2007.

Al-Tahtawi, Rifaʾat *L'Or de Paris. Relation de voyage (1826–1831)*, translated, presented and annotated by Anouar Louca, Paris: Sindbad, 1988.

Amil, Mahdi, *L'État confessionnel. Le cas libanais*, Montreuil: La Brèche, 1996.

Amin, Galal A., *The Modernization of Poverty. A Study in the Political Economy of Growth in Nine Arab Countries*, Leiden: E. J. Brill, 1974.

———, *The Illusion of Progress in the Arab World. A Critique of Western Misconstruction*, Cairo: American University in Cairo Press, 2006.

Amin, Hussein, *Le Livre du musulman désemparé. Pour entrer dans le troisième millénaire*, Paris: La Découverte, 1992.

Amin, Qasim, *The Liberation of Women and the New Women. Two Documents in the History of Egyptian Feminism*, Cairo: American University in Cairo Press, 2000.

Aoun, Mouchir B., *Heidegger et la pensee arabe*, Paris: L'Harmattan, Paris, 2011.

———, *Une pensée arabe humaniste contemporaine. Paul Khoury et les promesses de l'incomplétude humaine*, Paris: L'Harmattan, 2012.

Arkoun, Mohammed, *La Pensée arabe*, Paris: Presses universitaires de France, 1975.

———, *Pour une critique de la raison islamique*, Paris: Maisonneuve et Larose, 1984.

Audo, Antoine, Zaki Al-Arsouzi, *Un Arabe face à la modernité*, Beirut: Dar El-Machrek, 1988.

Ayubi, Nazih N., *Over-Stating the Arab State. Politics and Society in the Middle East*, London: I. B. Tauris, 1995.

Baer, Robert, *Or noir et Maison-Blanche. Comment l'Amérique a vendu son âme pour le pétrole saoudien*, Paris: J.-C. Lattès, 2003.

Balta, Paul and Claudine Rulleau (eds.), *La Vision nassérienne*, Paris: Sindbad, 1982.

Bani Sadr, Abolhassan, *Le Complot des ayatollahs*, Paris: La Découverte, 1989.

Barber, Benjamin R., *Jihad vs. McWorld: Terrorism's challenge to democracy*. New York: Times Books, 1995.

Batatu, Hanna, *The Old Social Classes and the Revolutionary Movements in Iraq. A Study of Iraq's Old Landed and Commercial Classes and of its Communists, Baʿthists and Free Officers*, Princeton, NJ: Princeton University Press, 1978.

———, *Syria's Peasantry. The Descendants of its Lesser Rural Notables and their Politics*, Princeton, NJ: Princeton University Press, 1999.

Beau, Nicolas, *Paris, capitale arabe*, Paris: Seuil, 1995.

Beau, Nicolas and Jacques-Marie Bourget, *Le Vilain Petit Qatar. Cet ami qui nous veut du mal*, Paris: Fayard, 2013.

Béji, Hélé, *Le Désenchantement national. Essai sur la décolonisation*, Paris: Maspéro, 1982

———, *Islam Pride. Derrière le voile*, Paris: Gallimard, 2012.

Belaïd, Sadok, *Islam et droit. Une nouvelle lecture des versets prescriptifs du Coran*, Tunis: Centre de publications universitaires, 2000.

Ben Barka, Mehdi, *Ecrits politiques (1957–1965)*, Paris: Syllèpse, 1999.

Bennabi, Malek, *Les conditions de la renaissance*, Algiers: Éditions En-Nahdha, 1949.

———, *Vocation de l'islam*, Paris: Éditions du Seuil, 1954.

———, *L'idée du Commonwealth islamique*, Algiers: Éditions Benmerabet, 2017.

———, *Le problème des idées dans le monde musulman*, Paris: Éditions Albouraq, 2006.

———, *Le musulman dans le monde de l'économie*, Algiers: El Borhane, 1996.

———, *Le Rôle des musulmans dans le dernier tiers du XXème siècle*, Beirut: n.p., 1972.

Berberova, Nina, *C'est moi qui souligne*, Arles: Actes Sud, 1989.

Berque, Jacques, *L'Egypte. Impérialisme et révolution*, Paris: Gallimard, 1967.

———, *Les Arabes*, Paris: Sindbad, 1973.

Binder, Leonard, *Islamic Liberalism. A Critique of Development Ideologies*, Chicago: University of Chicago Press, 1988.

Blanc, Pierre, *Proche-Orient. Le pouvoir, la terre et l'eau*, Paris: Presses de Sciences Po, 2012.

Blin, Louis and Philippe Fargues (eds.), *L'Economie de la paix au Proche-Orient*, Paris: Maisonneuve et Larose, 1995.

Boulaâbi, Ridha (ed.), *Les Orientaux face aux orientalismes*, Paris: Geuthner, 2013.

Boullata, Issa J., *Trends and Issues in Contemporary Arab Thought*, Albany, NY: State University of New York Press, 1990.

Bouyerdene, Ahmed, Eric Geoffroy and Setty G. Simon-Khedis (eds.), *Abdelkader, un spirituel dans la modernite*, Damascus: Presses de l'Institut français du Proche-Orient, 2012.

Brunschvig, Robert et Grünebaum, Gustave E. von (eds.), *Classicisme et declin culturel dans l'histoire de l'islam*, Paris: Maisonneuve et Larose, 1977.

Burgat, François, *L'Islamisme au Maghreb: la voix du Sud*, Paris: Karthala, 1988.

———, *L'Islamisme en face*, Paris:La Découverte, Paris, 1995.

———, *L'Islamisme à l'heure d'Al-Qaida. Réislamisation, modernisation, radicalisations*, Paris: La Découverte, 2005.

Calculli, Marina, *Le Néopatrimonialisme des régimes et l'échec du système régional arabe*, mémoire de Master 2 en études politiques, Beirut: Institut de sciences politiques, Saint Joseph University, 2012.

Carré, Olivier and Seurat, Michel, *Les Frères musulmans (1928–1982)*, Paris: Gallimard, 1983.

Carré, Olivier, *Mystique et politique. Lecture révolutionnaire du Coran par Sayyid Qotb, Frère musulman radical*, Paris: Le Cerf/Fondation nationale des sciences politiques, 1984.

————, *Le Nationalisme arabe*, Paris: Fayard, 1993.

Ceu Pinto, Maria do, *Political Islam and the United States. A Study of U.S. Policy towards Islamist Movements in the Middle East*, Reading: Garnet Publishing, 1999.

Chaulet, Claudine, *La Mitidja autogérée. Enquête 1968–1970*, Algiers: SNED, 1971.

————, *La Terre, les Freres et l'Argent. Stratégie familiale et production agricole en Algerie depuis 1962*, Algiers: Office des publications universitaires, 1987.

Chevallier, Dominique (ed.), *Renouvellements du monde arabe. 1952–1982*, Paris: Armand Colin, 1987.

Chiha, Michel, *Palestine*, Beirut: Editions du Trident, 1969.

Choueiri, Youssef, *Arab History and the Nation-State. A Study in Modern Arab Historiography, 1820–1980*, New York: Routledge, 1989.

————, *Arab Nationalism. A History of Nation and State in the Arab World*, Oxford: Blackwell, 2000.

Cooke, Miriam, *Nazira Zeineddine. A Pioneer of Islamic Feminism*, Princeton, NJ: One World, 2010.

Corm, Charles, *La Terre assassinée ou les Ciliciennes*, Beirut: Éditions de La Revue Phénicienne, 1928.

————, *La Montagne inspirée*, Beirut: Éditions de La Revue Phénicienne, Beirut, 1934.

Corm, Georges, *Le proche orient éclaté. 1956–2012*, Paris: Gallimard, 1983.

————, *Youakim Moubarac, un homme d'exception. Textes choisis et presentes par Georges Corm*, Beirut: Librairie orientale, 2004.

Dakhli, Leyla, *Une génération d'intellectuels arabes. Syrie et Liban (1908–1940)*, Paris: IISMM-Karthala, 2009.

Djaït, Hichem, *La Personnalité et le Devenir arabo-islamiques*, Paris: Seuil, 1974.

————, *La Grande discorde. Religion et politique dans l'islam des origines*, Paris: Gallimard, 1989.

Elshobaki, Amr, *Les Frères musulmans des origines à nos jours*, Paris: Karthala, 2009.

El-Yafi, Abdallah, *La Condition privée de la femme dans le droit de l'islam*, Paris: IMP Graphique, 1929.

Esposito, John, *The Islamic Threat. Myth or Reality?*, New York: Oxford University Press, 1992.

————, (ed.), *Islam and Development. Religion and Sociopolitical Change*, Syracuse, NY: Syracuse University Press, 1988.

Esposito, John L. and Voll, John, *Islam and Democracy*, New York: Oxford University Press, 1996.

Étienne, Bruno, *L'Islamisme radical*, Paris: Hachette, 1987.

Eveland, Wilbur Crane, *The Ropes of Sand. America's Failure in the Middle East*, New York: Norton, 1980.

Fahmy, Mansour, *La Condition de la femme dans la tradition et l'évolution de l'islamisme*, Paris: Felix Alcan, 1913 (new edition: *La Condition de la femme dans l'islam*, Paris: Allia, 1990).

Fakkar, Rouchdi, *Reflets de la sociologie prémarxiste dans le monde arabe. Idées progressistes et pratiques industrielles des saint-simoniens en Algérie et en Egypte*, Paris: Geuthner, 1974.

Faligot, Roger, *Tricontinentale. Quand Che Guevara, Ben Barka, Cabral, Castro et Ho Chi Minh preparaient la revolution mondiale (1964–1968)*, Paris: La Découverte, 2013.

Fanon, Frantz, *Peau noire, masques blancs*, Paris: Seuil, 1952.

———, *Les Damnés de la terre*, Maspero, Paris, 1961.

Filali-Ansary, Abdou, *L'islam est-il hostile à la laicité?*, Paris: Sindbad, 2001.

———, *Réformer l'islam? Une introduction aux débats contemporains*, Paris: La Découverte, 2003.

Fleyfel, Antoine, *La Théologie contextuelle arabe. Modèle libanais*, Paris: L'Harmattan, 2011.

———, *Géopolitique des chrétiens d'Orient. Défis et avenir des chrétiens arabes*, Paris: L'Harmattan, 2013.

Foulquier, Jean-Michel, *Arabie saoudite. La dictature protegée*, Paris: Albin Michel, 1995.

Ghandour, Abdel-Rahmane, *Jihad humanitaire. Enquête sur les ONG islamiques*, Paris: Flammarion, 2002.

Hafez, Ziad, *La Pensée religieuse en islam contemporain. Débats et critiques*, Paris: Geuthner, 2012.

Hallaq, Boutros and Toelle, Heidi (ed.), *Histoire de la littérature arabe moderne. 1800–1945*, Arles: Actes Sud, 1987.

Harbi, Mohammed, *Aux origines du FLN. Le populisme révolutionnaire en Algérie*, Paris: Christian Bourgois, 1975.

Henni, Ahmed, *Le Cheikh et le Patron*, Algiers: Office des publications universitaires, 1993.

———, *Le Syndrome islamiste et les mutations du capitalisme*, Paris: Non Lieu, 2008.

———, *Le Capitalisme de rente. De la société du travail industriel à la société des rentiers*, Paris: L'Harmattan, 2012.

Hervé-Montel, Caroline, *Renaissance littéraire et conscience nationale. Les premiers romans en français au Liban et en Egypte. 1908–1933*, Paris: Geuthner, 2012.

Hourani, Albert, *Arabic Thought in the Liberal Age, 1798–1939*, London: Oxford University Press, 1967.

———, *A History of the Arab Peoples*, London: Faber and Faber, 1991.

Howard, Richard, *Love in Two Languages*, Minneapolis: University of Minnesota Press, 1990.

Hudson, Michael, *Arab Politics. The Search for Legitimacy*, New Haven, CT: Yale University Press, 1977.

Hussein, Taha, *Le Livre des jours*, Paris: Gallimard, 1984.

————, *Le Voyage intérieur*, Paris: Gallimard, 1992.

Ibn Khaldoun, *Le Livre des exemples*, Paris: Gallimard, 2002.

Issawi, Charles, *The Economic History of the Middle East, 1800–1914*, Chicago: University of Chicago Press, 1966.

————, *Economic History of the Middle East and North Africa*, London: Methuen, 1982.

Jomier, Jacques, *Le Commentaire coranique du Manar. Tendances modernes de l'exégèse coranique en Egypte*, Paris: G. P. Maisonneuve & Cie, 1954.

Joumblatt, Kamal, *Pour le Liban (propos recueillis par Philippe Lapousterle)*, Paris: Stock, 1978.

Kassab, Elizabeth Suzanne, *Contemporary Arab Thought. Cultural Critique in Comparative Perspective*, New York: Columbia University Press, 2010.

Kassir, Samir et Mardam-Bey, Farouk, *Itinéraires de Paris à Jerusalem. La France et le conflit israélo-arabe,* Paris: Les livres de La Revue d'études palestiniennes, 1993.

Kepel, Gilles, *Le Prophète et Pharaon. Les mouvements islamistes dans l'Egypte contemporaine*, Paris: La Découverte, 1983.

Khalid, Mansour, *War and Peace in Sudan. A Tale of Two Countries*, New York: Kegan Paul International, 2002.

Khalidi, Rashid, *The Origins of Arab Nationalism*, New York: Columbia University Press, 1991.

Khalidi, Walid (ed.), *From Haven to Conquest. Readings in Zionism and the Palestine Problem until 1948,* Beirut: Institute for Palestine Studies, 1971.

Khatibi, Abdelkebir, *La mémoire tatouée. Autobiographie d'un décolonisé*, Paris: Les Lettres nouvelles, 1971.

Khoury, Gérard, *La France et l'Orient arabe. Naissance du Liban moderne, 1914–1920*, Paris: Armand Colin, 1993.

————, *Une tutelle coloniale. Le mandat français en Syrie et au Liban*, Paris: Belin, 2006.

Khoury Paul, *Tradition et modernité. Instruments d'enquête*, Munster, n.p., 1981.

————, *Une lecture de la pensée arabe actuelle. Trois études*, n.p., Munster, 1981.

————, *Tradition et modernité. Thèmes et tendances de la pensée arabe actuelle*, Beirut: P. Khoury, 1983.

————, *Tradition et modernité. Matériaux pour servir à l'étude actuelle de la pensée arabe. Inventaire sélectif de la production littéraire arabe. Bibliographie partiellement annotée*, Beirut: P. Khoury, 1984.

————, *Tradition et modernite. Matériaux pour servir à l'étude actuelle de la pensée arabe. Analyse descriptive d'ouvrages arabes typiques*, Beirut: P. Khoury, 1985.

————, *Le Fait et le Sens. Esquisse d'une philosophie de la déception*, Paris: L'Harmattan, 2007.

————, *Islam et christianisme. Dialogue religieux et défi de la modernité*, Paris: L'Harmattan, 2011.

————, *Amour bilingue*, Montpellier: Fata Morgana, 1983.

————, *Maghreb pluriel*, Paris: Éditions Denoël, 1983.

————, *Le Figure de l'étranger dans la littérature française*, Paris: Éditions Denoël, 1987.

————, *Imaginaire de l'autre*, Paris: L'Harmattan, 1987.

Kilani, Mondher (ed.), *Islam et changement social*, Lausanne: Payot, 1998.

————, *Pour un universalisme critique. Essai d'anthropologie du contemporain*, Paris: La Découverte, 2014.

Lacheraf, Mostefa, *L'Algérie. Nation et société*, Paris: Maspéro, 1965.

Lacouture, Jean, *Nasser*, Paris: Seuil, 1971.

Lacouture, Jean and Simone Lacouture, *L'Egypte en mouvement*, Paris: Seuil, 1956.

Laoust, Henri, *Les Schismes en islam. Introduction à une étude de la religion musulmane*, Paris: Payot, 1965.

Laroui, Abdallah, *L'Idéologie arabe contemporaine*, Paris: Maspero, 1967.

————, *L'Histoire du Maghreb. Un essai de synthèse*, Paris: Maspéro, 1970.

————, *La Crise des intellectuels arabes. Traditionalisme ou historicisme*, Paris: Maspéro, 1974.

————, *Islam et modernité*, Paris: La Découverte, 1983.

Laurens, Henri, *Le Royaume impossible. La France et la genèse du monde arabe*, Paris: Armand Colin, 1990.

Lewis, Bernard, *Islam et laïcité. La naissance de la Turquie moderne*, Paris: Fayard, 1977.

Libera, Alain de, *Penser au Moyen Age*, Paris: Seuil, 1991.

Longrigg, Stephen H., *Syria and Lebanon under French Mandate*, London: Oxford University Press, 1958.

Mahmassani, Maher S., *Islam in Retrospect. Recovering the Message*, Northampton: Olive Branch Press, 2014.

al-Mahmassani, Soubhi, *The Philosophy of Jurisprudence in Islam*, Leiden: E.J. Brill, 1961.

Mantran, Robert (ed.), *Histoire de l'Empire ottoman*, Paris: Fayard, 1979.

Mehanna, Kamel, *Un médecin libanais engagé dans la tourmente des peuples. Les choix difficiles*, Paris: L'Harmattan, 2013.

Mehdi, Falih, *Fondements et mécanismes de l'Etat en islam: l'Irak*, Paris: L'Harmattan, 1991.

Mervin, Sabrina, *Un réformisme chiite. Oulemas et lettres du Gabal 'Amil (actuel Liban-Sud) de la fin de l'Empire ottoman à l'indépendance du Liban*, Paris: Karthala/ CERMOC/IFEADF, 2000.

Miquel, André and Henri Laurens, *L'Islam et sa civilisation, VIIe-XXe siècle*, Paris: Armand Colin, 1990.

Mitchell, Timothy, *Carbon Democracy. Le pouvoir politique à l'ère du pétrole*, tr. Christophe Jaquet, Paris: La Découverte, 2013.

Monteil, Vincent, *Clefs pour la pensée arabe*, Paris: Seghers, 1974.

Naba, René, *Guerre des ondes... guerre des religions. La bataille hertzienne dans le ciel méditerranéen*, Paris: L'Harmattan, 1998.

Nassar, Nassif, *La Pensée realiste d'Ibn Khaldoun*, Paris: Presses universitaires de France, 1979.

O'Zoux, Raymond, *Les États du Levant sous mandat français*, Paris: Librairie Larose, 1931.

Pappé, Ilan, *Le Nettoyage ethnique de la Palestine*, Paris: Fayard, 2008.

Philipp, Thomas, *Jurji Zaydan and the Foundations of Arab Nationalism*, Syracuse, NY: Syracuse University Press, 2014.

Pirenne, Jacques, *Les Grands Courants de l'histoire universelle*, Neuchâtel: La Baconnière, 1959.

Polanyi, Karl, *La Grande Transformation. Aux origines politiques et économiques de notre temps*, Paris: Gallimard, 1983.

Poulleau, Alice, *À Damas sous les bombes. Journal d'une Française pendant la révolte syrienne de 1924–1926*, Yvetot: Bretteville Frères, 1925 (republished Paris: L'Harmattan, 2012).

Qotb, Sayyed, *La Justice sociale en islam*, Beirut: Dar El-Biruni, 2003.

Quadri, Goffredo, *La Philosophie arabe dans l'Europe médiévale. Des origines a Averroès*, Paris: Payot, 1947.

Rabkin, Yakov M., *Au nom de la Torah. Une histoire de l'opposition juive au sionisme*, Laval, Quebec: Presses de l'université de Laval, 2004.

Reinhart, Tanya, *Détruire la Palestine ou comment terminer la guerre de 1948*, Paris: La Fabrique, 2002.

———, *L'Héritage de Sharon. Détruire la Palestine suite*, Paris: La Fabrique, 2006.

Rey-Goldzeiguer, Annie, *Le Royaume arabe. La politique arabe de Napoléon III, 1861–1870*, Algiers: SNED, 1977.

Riad, Hassan, *L'Egypte nassérienne*, Paris: Minuit, 1964.

Rodinson, Maxime, *La Fascination de l'islam*, Paris: Maspéro, 1980.

Roy, Olivier, *Afghanistan, islam et modernité politique*, Paris: Seuil, 1985.

Saba Yared, Nazik, *Secularism and the Arab World*, London: Saqi Books, 2002.

Sadiki, Larbi, *The Search for Arab Democracy. Discourses and Counter-Discourses*, New York: Columbia University Press, 2004.

Said, Edward, *L'Orientalisme. L'Orient créé par l'Occident*, Paris: Seuil, 1981.

Saint-Point, Valentine de, *La Vérité sur la Syrie par un témoin*, Paris: Cahiers de France, 1929.

Sand, Shlomo, *Comment le peuple juif fut inventé*, Paris: Flammarion, 2010.

———, *Comment j'ai cessé d'être juif*, Flammarion, Paris, 2013.

———, *Comment la terre d'Israel fut inventée. De la Terre sainte à la mère patrie*, Paris: Flammarion, 2014.

Sayegh, Youssef A., *Entrepreneurs of Lebanon. The Role of the Business Leader in a Developing Economy*, Cambridge, MA: Harvard University Press, 1962.

———, *The Arab Economies*, London: Croom Helm, 1978.

———, *The Determinants of Arab Economic Development*, London: Croom Helm, 1978.

————, *Elusive Development. From Dependence to Self-Reliance in the Arab Region*, London: Routledge, 1991.

Sayigh, Rosemary (ed.), *Yusif Sayigh. Arab Economist and Palestinian Patriot. A Fractured Life Story*, Cairo: American University in Cairo Press, 2015.

Serouya, Henry, *La Pensée arabe*, Paris: Presses universitaires de France, 1960.

Seurat, Michel, *L'État de barbarie*, Paris: Seuil, 1989.

Sharabi, Hisham, *Arab Intellectuals and the West. The Formative Years. 1875–1920*, Baltimore: Johns Hopkins University Press, 1970.

Sid-Ahmed, Abdelkader, *L'Économie arabe à l'heure des surplus pétroliers*, Paris: ISMEA, 1975.

————, *Développement sans croissance. L'expérience des économies pétrolières du tiers monde*, Paris: Publisud, 1983.

Stassinet, Jean (ed.), *Youakim Moubarac,* Lausanne: L'Age d'Homme, 2005.

Suleiman, Yasir, *The Arabic Language and National Identity. A Study in Ideology*, Washington, DC: Georgetown University Press, 2003.

Taha Hussein, Suzanne, *Avec toi. De la France à l'Egypte*, Paris: Cerf, 2011.

Thomas, Bertram, *Les Arabes*, Paris: Payot, 1946.

Thompson, Peter, *Tattooed Memory*, Paris: Éditions L'Harmattan, 2016.

Toro, Alfonso de, *Epistémologies*, Paris: L'Harmattan, 2009.

Triki, Fathi, *La Stratégie de l'identité*: Paris: Arcantère, 1998.

————, *Philosopher le vivre-ensemble*, Tunis: L'Or du temps, 1998.

Wright, Katharine Louise, *The Incoherence of the Intellectuals. Ibn Rush, al-Ghazali, al-Jabri, and Tarabichi in Eight Centuries of Dialogue without Dialogue*, unpublished MA thesis, Austin: Graduate School of the University of Texas, 2012.

Zahlan, Antoine B., *Science and Science Policy in the Arab World*, London: Croom Helm, 1980.

————, *Acquiring Technological Capacity. A Study of Arab Consulting and Contracting Companies*, London: MacMillan Academic and Professional, 1991.

————, *Science, Development and Sovereignty in the Arab World*, New York: Palgrave MacMillan, 2012.

Zaydan, George C. and Thomas Philipp (eds.), *Jurji Zaydan's Contributions to Modern Arab Thought and Literature*, Washington, DC: The Zaydan Foundation, 2014.

Ziadé, Khaled, *The Development of Muslim Perspectives of Europe*, Beirut: Riyāḍ el-Rayyis Books, 2010.

INDEX